Unveiling Your Sacred Truth

*The innermost essence of all of the Buddha's teachings,
together with a supplementary explanation of the methods for entering
into the profound path of the Kalachakra Six Vajra Yogas.*

བདེ་ག་ཤེགས་སྙིང་པོའི་འཇུག་རིམ་རྟོགས་ལྡན་གསར་པའི་ཁྲུ་ཆོར་

ༀ།།རབ་ལམ་རྗེའི་རྣལ་འབྱོར་དྲུག་ལ་འཇུག་ཚུལ་འཕྲོས་དོན་དང་བཅས་པ་ཀུན་འདུས་རྣལ་བསྡུན་ཡང་སྙིང་།།

— BOOK ONE —

The External Reality

by Shar Khentrul Jamphel Lodrö

ཤར་མཁན་སྤྲུལ་རིན་པོ་ཆེ་འཇམ་དཔལ་བློ་གྲོས

Dzokden

Author: Shar Khentrul Jamphel Lodrö

First Edition

ISBN (Paperback): 978-1-958229-57-6
ISBN (ePub): 978-1-958229-58-3

Published by:
Dzokden

This work was produced by Dzokden, a non-profit institution operated entirely by volunteers. This organization is dedicated to propagating a non-sectarian view of all the world's spiritual traditions and to teaching Buddhism in a way that is both completely authentic and at the same time practical and accessible to Western culture. It is especially dedicated to spreading the Jonang tradition, a rare gem from a remote part of Tibet that preserves the precious teachings of the Kalachakra.

For more information about scheduled activities or available materials, or if you would like to make a donation, please contact:

Dzokden
3436 Divisadero Street
San Francisco, CA 94123
USA
www.dzokden.org
office@dzokden.org

Contents

Shar Khentrul Jamphel Lodrö Rinpoché

Acknowledgments

On behalf of the Tibetan Buddhist Rimé Institute, I would like to thank everyone who has been involved in making this book a reality. First and foremost is of course our kind teacher Khentrul Rinpoché, whose profound teachings and patient guidance has made the Kalachakra System accessible to us all. We are eternally grateful for having the opportunity to meet such an incredible path and for being involved in preparing this book series.

We would specifically like to thank the members of the editorial team who have worked diligently throughout the last year to prepare this latest edition. We sincerely appreciate the efforts of Vanessa Mason, Holly Reilly and Val Mason. We are very grateful for all the kind support and feedback we have received from the TBRI community as a whole, but in particular that of Julie O'Donnell whose tireless efforts behind the scenes keeps the conditions present for us to do our work. We would also like to thank Edward Henning for his generosity in sharing many of his resources on Kalachakra.

We have done our best to reproduce the intent of Rinpoche's teachings to the best of our ability. That being said, I apologise for any errors that we may have inadvertently introduced as a result of our own limitations. We would appreciate any feedback that you may be inclined to offer.

It is our sincere aspiration that this book provide you with an authentic doorway to enter into the Kalachakra Path. May it bring benefit to your life and may it become the cause for you and all sentient beings to achieve lasting genuine happiness and freedom from suffering.

May it become a cause for Rinpoché to have a long and healthy life, may his vast vision for the flourishing of the Jonang Dharma be realised and may the golden age of Shambhala be manifested.

Joe Flumerfelt
Belgrave, Australia
October 2015

Shakyamuni Buddha

Introduction

Unveiling Your Sacred Truth was written to expound the spiritual path as taught by Buddha Shakyamuni. Throughout this text, I have attempted to present the core tenets of Buddhism in an approachable way without losing the essence of the Buddha's ancient wisdom. It is my hope that Unveiling Your Sacred Truth will enable you to live purposefully and compassionately.

When you pick up a Dharma book such as this one, you are not simply reading the words of the author. Through Unveiling Your Sacred Truth you connect with the unparalleled wisdom of the Buddha and come to know the great practitioners of the past and present who realised Buddha Dharma for themselves. This Buddhist ancestry, known as a lineage, is critical for spiritual development as it is their stories, commentaries and realisations that we rely upon for guidance and inspiration.

The Buddha's teachings were taught for an extensive variety of people, each experiencing dissatisfaction and suffering in different ways. As a result, there are different levels of benefit from studying these teachings that we can all aspire to achieve. On the most basic level, we can each find practical tools to help us lessen our day-to-day stresses and to live a more meaningful life. On a deeper level, we can realise our incredible potential and cultivate the causes for long lasting, genuine happiness, both for ourselves and others.

Of all the Buddha's teachings, the system that I personally feel most connected with is that of the Kalachakra Tantra. In my opinion, it is the most skilful system for realising this extraordinary potential and for actualising enlightenment within a single lifetime. While most people relate these teachings to advanced esoteric practices, the Kalachakra Path is in fact a complete system which is suitable for practitioners at all stages of their spiritual development.

OVERVIEW OF THE KALACHAKRA PATH

Kalachakra literally means *wheel* (chakra) of *time* (kala). It is the name given to a system of practices that originated with the Buddha Shakyamuni and have been passed down through the ages in an unbroken lineage to this day. The Kalachakra system is focused on helping people to make sense of their experiences in such a way that allows them to cultivate greater peace and harmony in their personal lives and their relationships with others.

The Kalachakra is unique in that it provides teachings on a comprehensive scope of topics that support a wide variety of practitioners at different stages in their spiritual development. Within one unified framework, we find a wealth of profound wisdom that is both immediately relevant and direct in its approach.

The main subject matter of Unveiling Your Sacred Truth is the presentation of the complete Kalachakra Path. The path is progressive in nature, providing clear step-by-step instructions for guiding you through the many layers of your lived experience. I have broken this path up into three separate books, where each book focuses on one specific layer of reality, moving in a linear fashion from gross to subtle. As such, it is recommended that the material be studied in sequence so that the necessary foundations can be developed for each subsequent practice.

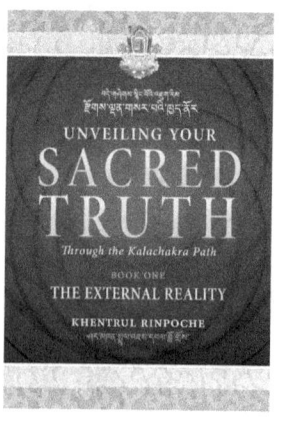

Book One:
The External Reality

We begin our journey by first studying the characteristics of our immediate experience. Specifically, we are looking at the ordinary world that we encounter each and every day, with the aim to develop the wisdom that will allow us to live more meaningful and balanced lives. At this stage, the focus is on pragmatic strategies, firmly rooted in an experiential approach to understanding reality.

This book introduces many potentially new ideas that will challenge you to think more broadly about the nature of our shared universe. These ideas form the basis for understanding a Buddhist worldview which in turn is the foundation for a profound system of contemplative practice.

Please remember that at this stage of study, it is not necessary to personally adopt a Buddhist worldview in order to receive benefit from the techniques that it inspires. If you encounter an idea you simply cannot accept, then that's ok. Instead of rejecting the idea completely, simply let it be and focus on developing more experience through the various exercises. In time you may find that your understanding shifts and you gain a new perspective on things. In this way, your own personal view can evolve in a natural and organic manner.

This book has been divided into three parts, each representing a different phase of your spiritual journey. There are different ways you can study this material, but I would suggest you work through sequentially in cycles. Begin by focusing on part one, reading through from beginning to end. Then go back and read it through again but during this round, spend more time familiarising yourself with the exercises. Continue in this way until you feel you have a relatively stable grasp of the material and feel ready to move on to the next part of the book.

Part One—Creating Space for Reflection

For the vast majority of people, the main reason for picking up a book like this one is a basic desire to overcome the many problems and obstacles that we face in our everyday lives. In the West, while we may have developed some degree of material affluence, we are often lacking in our ability to cope with the many challenges that this lifestyle generates. At times, it can feel like we are drowning in an ocean, struggling to keep our heads above water.

As long as we find ourselves in such a situation, we have very little chance to actually transform our experience in any meaningful way. Therefore, the very first step must be to find some degree of stability in our life and to create a space in which we can make choices that are conducive to greater happiness, peace and harmony.

We can do this through the use of two primary methods: *Buddhist Psychology* and the practice of *Meditation*. Together, these methods provide a wealth of tools we can use to observe our experience, identify problems and develop viable strategies for how to respond in the most constructive way.

When our minds become more stable, we are more capable of dealing with life's many ups and downs. It is as if we have pulled ourselves out of the water onto a life raft and we can finally rest, and catch our breath. With less preoccupation on treading water and keeping our head above the waves, we find we have more time to reflect on what is truly important to us.

Part Two—Reflecting on Your Present Situation

The next step in our journey is to use our new vantage point to take a long and hard look at the nature of the reality in which we live. All too often we neglect to stop and see what's really going on and as a consequence, our perception of what is important and what is not can become distorted. We become confused, spending all of our precious time obsessing about things that ultimately are not capable of bringing us lasting genuine happiness.

Through the systematic analysis of four topics known as the *Four Convictions of Renunciation*, we learn how our individual actions play a direct role in the perpetuation of unsatisfactory situations. By further expanding the scope of our understanding we also begin to see that the choices we make in the present are constantly shaping our future. On the basis of this understanding we develop a sense of responsibility for how we live our lives and the determination to take full advantage of the conditions that are presented to us.

On the basis of these contemplations, we may find that our priorities begin to shift. We start to see that what we once thought of as true sources of happiness, are in fact the causes of suffering. Recognising this, we focus our attention on finding the methods that are actually capable of generating the results we seek. It is at this point that we may develop the desire to engage more fully in the practice of a spiritual path. We can liken this process to scanning the horizon, seeing an island in the distance and making the choice to paddle our life raft towards the safety of dry land.

Part Three—Developing Faith in a Path

With a strong desire for change, the next challenge is to identify the most skillful way to bring that change about. We are each unique individuals with unique conditions with which to work. Therefore, we need to find a set of methods that are particularly suited to our personal needs. Like someone who is sick, we must find a medicine that is capable of curing our specific illness.

Over the many thousands of years of human history, many wisdom traditions have arisen, each providing a wide range of teachings and methods that can be used for bringing greater meaning and purpose into one's life. At this stage in our spiritual development, it is important to establish a broad awareness of these different traditions so that we can develop faith in the path that we choose to follow.

The Kalachakra Path that is presented in these books is derived from the Jonang Tradition of Tibetan Buddhism. To understand how this tradition relates to other forms of Buddhism, we will be looking more closely at the *core teachings of the Buddha and the various interpretations that arose from those teachings*. This will provide us with a general theoretical context for understanding the practices that are described in the subsequent books.

By the end of this book, you should have all the information you need to know whether you wish to continue on this path. As we move into the next phase of our development, challenges will arise as you work to build up constructive habits. For this reason you will need to have faith in what you are doing. For some, that faith will arise very quickly, while for others, it may take some time to clear away doubts. Whichever the case, as long as you are sincere with yourself and with others, then you can be confident you are going in the right direction.

Book Two:
The Internal Reality

By focusing outward, we are able to develop strategies for coping with whatever comes up in our lives. We can find ways to apply our wisdom in order to act constructively in the face of adversity. But no matter how effective our strategies may be, they are unable to generate a long lasting transformation that is capable of breaking the cycle of our suffering and opening the door to genuine happiness. For that, we must turn inward. We must look directly at our own mind and begin to experience its natural potential.

In the second book, we explore the phenomenological world of appearances and how those appearances actually exist. While we continue to work with concepts on a theoretical level, we increasingly shift our emphasis towards direct experience. It is not enough simply to understand what is happening, we must develop first-hand experience of what those concepts are describing. It is through converting understanding into experience that we are truly able to integrate these ideas into our way of being. This process of transformation is facilitated through various practices known as the *Kalachakra Preliminary Practices* (ngöndro).

Book Three: The Enlightened Reality

Through working with our internal reality we are slowly refining our ability to distinguish between the impure appearances of the external reality and the pure appearances of the enlightened reality. Like cleaning the lens on a telescope, when we have cleared away the gross obscurations from our mind, we are able to catch a glimpse of our true nature. While this nature is not yet fully manifested, that first glimpse provides us with a basis with which to work; a foundation upon which to expand.

In the previous two books, we worked with teachings that are common to all of the Tibetan Buddhist traditions. In this final book we focus on the unique practices that are specifically presented in the *Kalachakra Tantra*. For the practitioner who is ready to dedicate herself to the path, these profound methods provide everything that is needed in order to achieve enlightenment within a single lifetime.

GETTING THE MOST OUT OF THIS BOOK

As you read through the material, it can be helpful to keep a few key points in mind. The following is some general advice that applies to any form of dharma study, whether reading a book or listening to a teaching.

The Right Attitude for Studying Dharma

When we encounter the Buddhist teachings, it is important to generate an attitude of great enthusiasm. If we are able to recognise that through these teachings we are being introduced to ideas that can ultimately lead us to greater peace and happiness, this should be a relatively easy task. That being said, cultivating a bright and alert mind is a skill that takes time to develop and you will need to make a prolonged effort to overcome the different obstacles that may arise. One teaching that highlights these difficulties is known as the *Three Defects of a Pot*:

1. We should not be like an **upside-down pot** on which liquid is being poured, being distracted or so closed minded that the teachings cannot penetrate. Listen with an open mind, a ready mind.

2. Nor should we be like a **pot with a hole in it**. No matter how much liquid is poured in, it drips away and we retain nothing of what is learnt.

3. Finally, do not be a **pot containing poison**. Avoid falling prey to preconceptions and fixed ideas. This will cause you to misconstrue what you hear and manipulate Dharma into something it is not, like nectar poured into poison.

As you read through each chapter, try to maintain an open, receptive attitude that is fully engaged in the material and free from any preconceptions or judgemental attitudes. Every now and again check up to see the quality of attention that you are bringing to your reading. Remind yourself of this simple teaching whenever you need the inspiration to improve your method of study.

Stopping to Reflect

Throughout this text I have inserted different exercises that you can use as an opportunity to reflect upon the material that you are studying. It is important that we don't allow ourselves to become overwhelmed by the theory. Breaking up your reading with short periods of personal reflection can provide you with valuable insights into how the material relates to your personal experience.

Even if a section does not follow with a particular exercise, it is still a good habit to select passages of the text, read through them a few times and make sure you are really understanding what is being said. Then put the book down and consider how these teachings relate to your life. Think of examples from your own experience that illustrate the various principles.

Another good habit to develop is to write out questions that arise while reading. Keep a notepad nearby and when a question comes up, simply jot it down. When you are finished reading a section, look back at the questions and see if they have been answered. If the question persists, then consider discussing the topic with a teacher or another spiritual friend when the opportunity arises.

Taking Joy in the Journey

Finally, no matter what your motivation, I am confident that the timeless wisdom of the Buddha-dharma has the capacity to bring you some degree of benefit if you can maintain an open heart and an open mind.

Remember that this is a journey of discovery; a process of transformation. It will take time for the concepts and practices to develop in your mind and therefore it is important to be patient with yourself. Work through the ideas at your own pace, taking as much time as you need. After reading through a few chapters, go through them again and see if your understanding has shifted. Often you may find that later teachings shed new light on earlier ones, peeling back layers and uncovering a deeper meaning.

Above all, cultivate a sense of joy in having this precious opportunity. It shouldn't be dry, nor tedious. Instead think of it as an adventure and revel in the challenges that it presents. In Buddhism we talk about planting the seeds for future realisation; this simply means that any confusion we face here and now is the basis for future understanding to arise.

> *"In the beginner's mind there are many possibilities,*
> *but in the expert's mind there are few"*
> — *Shunryu Suzuki* —

PART ONE

Creating Space for Reflection

CHAPTER ONE

Understanding the Mind

Think back to the start of your day, to the very first moment you can remember. Here you are sleeping, perhaps in the middle of a dream, and then suddenly you're awake. Sometimes it's very clear, with no doubt in your mind, you definitely know you're awake. The sun is shining through your window and the dream world you were in just a few moments ago is no longer there. At other times though it can be a little confusing and you may not be sure of things, maybe you are still dreaming, maybe you're awake; it's not completely clear.

Either way, eventually the waking world wins out and you get out of bed and so your day begins. Most of us have some sort of morning routine, a series of actions that we do day in and day out. A habit we have formed over many years, it can sometimes feel like we're on autopilot and we're often not even consciously aware of what we are doing. There is an experience of having a shower. The sound of the taps turning, the water flowing, the pitter patter feeling of water droplets on the skin and the sight of steam fogging up the panes of glass. In each moment we are receiving a constant stream of information; sights, sounds, tastes, smells, and sensations all combining into a rich sensory experience.

But it's not just the senses is it? While you lather the shampoo into your hair, thoughts of the day start popping up. Perhaps today is a particularly important day, like the start of a new job. You may be a little anxious, unsure about your new co-workers or your new boss. Maybe it's excitement. You may think back to all the hard work that brought you to this point. All of these thoughts, feelings and memories form another level of how you experience your world.

In Buddhism, this constant flow of experience is known as "mind". Like a mirror, the mind reflects whatever is presented to it. The mind is not the H_2O

molecules of the water droplets, it is your subjective experience of those water droplets as they hit your skin. Likewise, it is not the waves of light travelling into your eyes, nor is it the energy pulses that travel down the optic nerve. It's not even the network of neurons which activate in your visual cortex. What it is, is the experience of a hot, soapy shower, with the sun streaming in through the window.

Between the body and the mind, which do we tend to emphasise more in our lives? Which is more important: the objective physical world of things "out there" or the subjective experiential world of things "in here"? Just turn on the TV and look at what the ads focus on. For the most part, there seems to be an overwhelming belief in western society that the physical world is clearly the most important. There is this notion that all of our problems can be fixed if we just learn how to manipulate our physical world in just the right way.

If we stop and seriously analyse this idea we will discover many inconsistencies. There are many beautiful people out there who have everything they could ever want and yet they are completely miserable. They could be living in the most extravagant of homes and yet their experience is one of boredom and dissatisfaction. On the other hand, someone could be living in the most destitute of conditions and still be content and happy. They may not even own a single possession other than the clothes on their back, but they are still satisfied and filled with joy.

Given the choice, which would you prefer: a life filled with happiness or one filled with sorrow? I think we can all agree that we naturally prefer the former. No matter what the external conditions may be, if we can experience happiness, then that will always win out. By recognising that happiness occurs within the mind, then it should be clear that the mind is the most important phenomenon for us to understand.

It is therefore rather surprising how little our western culture actually knows about it. Fortunately, ancient wisdom traditions such as Buddhism have invested considerable time in developing a robust *science of the mind*. In this first chapter, we will look into the various characteristics of the mind as understood in *Buddhist Psychology* and how we can work with it in order to overcome the many problems that we face in our lives.

THE MIND—WHAT IS IT?

We will begin by first developing some sense of what the mind is. To do this, we will need to clear away a few common misconceptions that are very prevalent in our society. The biggest misconception is that the mind *is* the brain. There is this belief that the mind is essentially a physical entity and that our experiences are emergent properties of that entity. Based on this assumption, scientists sift through the various neurons and synapses of the brain, trying to understand how it is that our experiences arise from them. So far they have been unsuccessful.

What they have been able to identify is that there is a very close *correlation* between the electrical activity within the brain and corresponding experiences in the mind. This would suggest that there are two distinct types of phenomena that are capable of influencing each other. Different, and yet related.

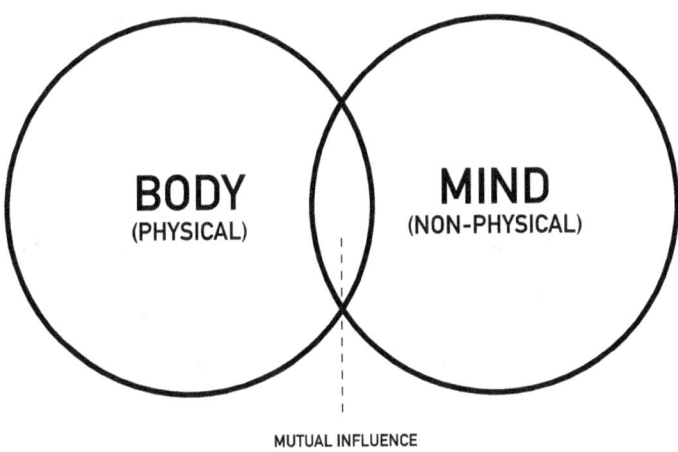

Figure 1-1: *The relationship between body and mind.*

According to Buddhist psychology, the mind is non-physical in nature. This means that it is not made up of particles, nor does it exist within a specific location in space and time. Instead, it is characterised as being clear and knowing. The clarity here refers to the basic capacity for the mind to give rise to appearances, while the knowing is the mind's capacity to be aware of those appearances.

While the activity within the brain does influence the appearances which arise in the mind, it cannot be said that the brain is the same as the mind. Likewise, the thoughts and ideas which arise in the mind, are able to influence electrical activity in the brain which can lead to the formation of new neural pathways or can trigger particular physical behaviours. It is a two-way street of mutual influence. To see this in action, let's conduct a very simple experiment: stop reading this book for a second, raise your right arm and lower it again.

Let's look at what was going on in this seemingly simple activity. Different wavelengths of light bouncing off the page of this book enter into your eyes and are converted into electrical pulses. These pulses travel into the brain activating various neurons and this brain activity causes the appearance of letters to arise in the mind. The awareness of these letters causes the appearance of their meaning to then take place. This awareness of meaning in turn causes a pattern of neurons to fire and the electrical pulse travels through the nervous system into the arm, causing the muscles to contract. The arm then rises. Then after a period of time passes, the memory of the meaning of what was read, triggers another chain reaction that results in the arm lowering. All of these little interactions between the body and mind are happening in an unbelievably short span of time, so fast that we perceive them to be happening almost instantaneously.

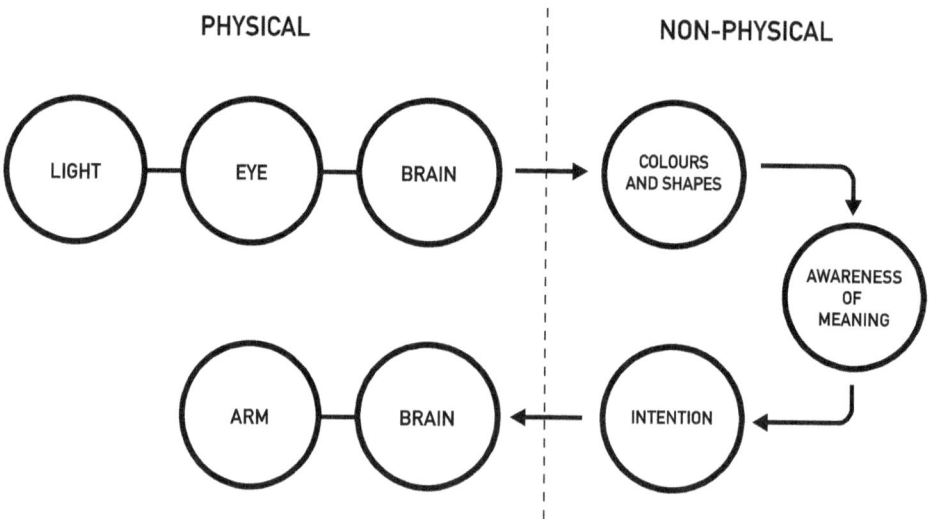

Figure 1-2: A simple illustration for how the body and mind influence each other.

Buddhists argue that while there is undoubtedly a strong relationship between the brain and the mind, that relationship represents only a small portion of the mind's overall capacity. We can think of the mind like the entirety of space and the brain as a single solar system within that space. Contemplation of the solar system alone can lead us to feel astounded by its sheer size and form, we may even become curious about its origins. But in the greater scheme of things, it is, however, just one system, within one galaxy, within one universe. Whereas space on the other hand is ubiquitous in nature, defying any attempt to comprehend its sheer enormity. No matter what arises within this space, the space is never changed and yet, without the space, nothing could ever arise.

If we accept that the mind is non-physical, then we must accept that physical phenomena are unable to detect the mind. There is a common belief that everything which exists must be detectable through physical measurements. Until it is measured, it is believed that it does not exist. This however is a misconception. While our machines can detect fluctuations of subtle energy or shifts in quantum fields, they will never be able to detect the corresponding appearances that arise in the mind. What they can detect are the correlated influences that those non-physical phenomena have on the physical world. In the end, this leads us to the conclusion that the only thing that is capable of detecting a non-physical phenomenon is another non-physical phenomenon—in this case the mind itself.

Realising this, the great yogic meditators and philosophers such as Siddhartha Gautama (Buddha Shakyamuni) have made great efforts to develop a range of mental techniques for directly observing the mind with the mind. Through prolonged engagement with these techniques they learned that the mind could be trained and conditioned to manifest specific desirable qualities. In fact, through working with the mind, they were able to completely transform the way in which they related with their world.

If we consider scientific and technological advancement over the last century, it is easy to see that our knowledge of the world has experienced significant growth. This did not come about overnight. It required countless people dedicating their time and effort, to uncover the secrets of the physical universe. Likewise, the great meditators of the past devoted their lives to discovering the true nature of the mind. They gave up all worldly comforts and pleasures, as well as concern for name and fame, to discover this hidden nature and to understand all of the phenomena related to the mind. The following sections will now explore some of the discoveries these masters have made.

THE CONTINUITY OF MIND

One of the first observations made by these masters is that something does not arise from nothing. Nor can something all of a sudden turn into nothing. Just like physical energy, there is a principle of conservation at work. Energy is never created nor is it destroyed, it is merely transformed and reconfigured. Likewise, the mind is a continuity, where each moment gives rise to the next, which gives rise to the next and so on and so forth.

In any given moment, there must have been a moment directly preceding it which acted as the basis for the next moment to arise. This means that we cannot find a beginning of mind. There was never any moment where nothing became something.

The fact that there is one moment presently arising is also the basis for the next moment to arise. Which experience arises will depend on the conditions in the present. While the next moment will not be exactly the same as the previous, it will still be mind and therefore we can never posit an end to mind either. There will never be a moment where something becomes nothing. In this way, we can say that the mind is a beginningless and endless process of transformation.

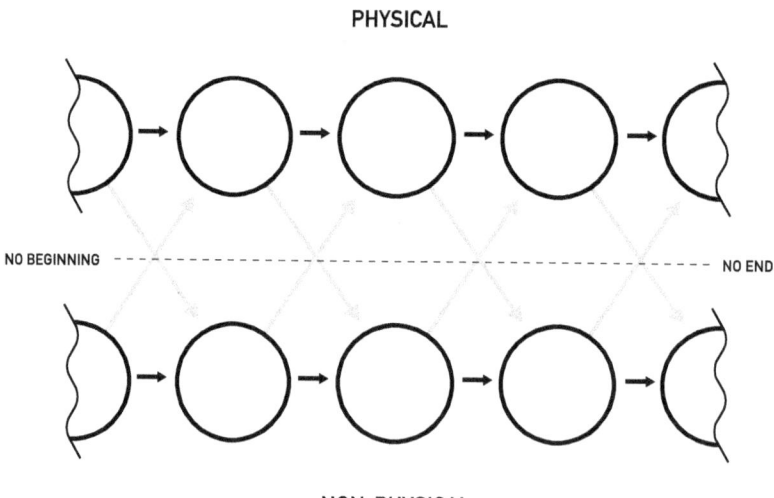

Figure 1-3: *The endless continuum of momentary changes.*

This process can be called the *External Wheel of Time* (Kalachakra). In this context, "wheel" refers to the endless process of moment to moment awareness; a cycle with no beginning, no middle and no end. While "time" refers to continual movement and change; the constantly shifting appearances in the mind, arising from the mutual influence between physical and non-physical phenomena.

Why is any of this important to us? It is important because this understanding can help us recognise the causal connection between our past, present and future experiences. We can easily see that some experiences are more preferable to us than others. The ones we like, we call happiness, while the ones that we do not like, can be called suffering. By analysing which conditions give rise to happiness and which give rise to suffering, we are able to modify our behaviour accordingly. What we call training the mind is simply the process of intentionally shaping how our mental continuum develops.

Exercise 1.1—Stepping Back Through Time

- *Sit quietly with your back straight, adopting a relaxed state of mind.*

- *Consider where you are right now. How did you get here? What events led up to this moment? As you identify different actions, consider the thoughts which motivated those actions. Step back slowly, reconstructing the causal chain of events from this moment all the way back to the moment that you woke up in the morning.*

- *Now consider the last week. Select a few moments that made a particular impression on you. Think of both the mental experiences and the physical actions that you engaged in. Keep going back, as though you were following a trail of breadcrumbs.*

- *Look back even further, considering the major events that have occurred over the course of the last year. Consider how each of these events has contributed to this present moment that you are now experiencing.*

- *Now look back through your life and identify different moments that you feel were significant to who you are as a person. Consider how these turning points influenced your subsequent decisions.*

- *Go into as much detail as you can within the time that you would like to spend. When you are tired of thinking, just rest for a moment.*

THE SUBTLETY OF MIND

Another major discovery by the great contemplatives of the past, was that the mind has many layers of subtlety. Each layer builds on top of the layers beneath it, forming a more elaborate and specific configuration. When the mind is sufficiently trained, it is able to distinguish these different levels.

This idea is very similar to the notion of subtlety in the physical world. At a very gross level, we can think of solids, liquids and gases. These are things that everyone can experience. Through our understanding of the basic laws of physics, we can learn how these different types of matter interact.

On a more subtle level, we can think of atoms with their various atomic components (electrons, neutrons, protons, etc). Again, by understanding the various laws that function here, we are able to effect even greater changes on the grosser level. Just think of the way that we manipulate electricity to power so much of our technology.

Even more subtle is the level of quantum particles. At this level the laws of classical physics break down and everything functions in a very different way. So different in fact, that the scientific community is still working through how this layer affects the others. In time I am sure we will see some truly extraordinary discoveries coming from this research.

Just as with the physical world, within the mind we can identify three main levels of subtlety:

1. **Gross Mind:** At a gross level, all of the physical and mental aspects of our experience are closely tied to the brain. It is the very obvious level of experience that is immediately presented to us through our different

senses. It is also at this level that we identify with an "ego", which is specific to an individual person and only lasts for a single lifetime. Rational thinking and intuition are progressively finer degrees of the gross mind.

2. **Subtle Mind:** We then have the subtle level of the mind, which can be likened to a sort of mental stem cell. It is completely unconfigured allowing it to arise in any number of different configurations. Although we cannot necessarily call it a human mind at this stage, it can be identified as an individual mindstream. It is this subtle mind that is capable of giving rise to an endless sequence of lives, where each life is one configuration of mind, such as a human or animal. We can think of it like water, alternating between being liquid and being frozen solid. The type of mind that is developed through meditative training is generally focused on the unconfigured state of this subtle level of mind.

3. **Very Subtle Mind:** The very subtle mind is the mind of clear light, also known as our Buddha-nature or ground luminosity. It has no physical basis at all and is neither human nor an individual continuum as it transcends all of these categories. The very subtle mind can only be completely discovered by the mind itself, through supreme concentration and meditation practice. The advanced practices presented in Buddhist tantra are specifically designed to allow a contemplative to experience this level of mind.

Level	Physical	Non-Physical
Gross	Atoms and Molecules: Solids, Liquids and Gases	Six Senses: sights, sounds, smells, tastes, tactile sensations and mental events (thoughts, memories, emotions)
Subtle	Sub-Atomic Particles: Protons, Neutrons, Electrons	Unconfigured Mindstream
Very-Subtle	Quantum Particles: Leptons, Quarks, Bosons	Mind of Clear-light (pristine awareness or buddha-nature)

Table 1-1: Levels of subtlety in the body and mind.

When we combine this understanding of the different levels of mind with the fact that the mind is an endless continuity, we arrive at the understanding that the mind has existed before this life and will continue after this life. From the moment we are born, to the moment we die, we are generally experiencing one particular configuration of a gross mind. After we die, this gross mind dissolves and all that is left is the subtle mind. From this subtle mind a new gross mind emerges. We call this process *reincarnation*.

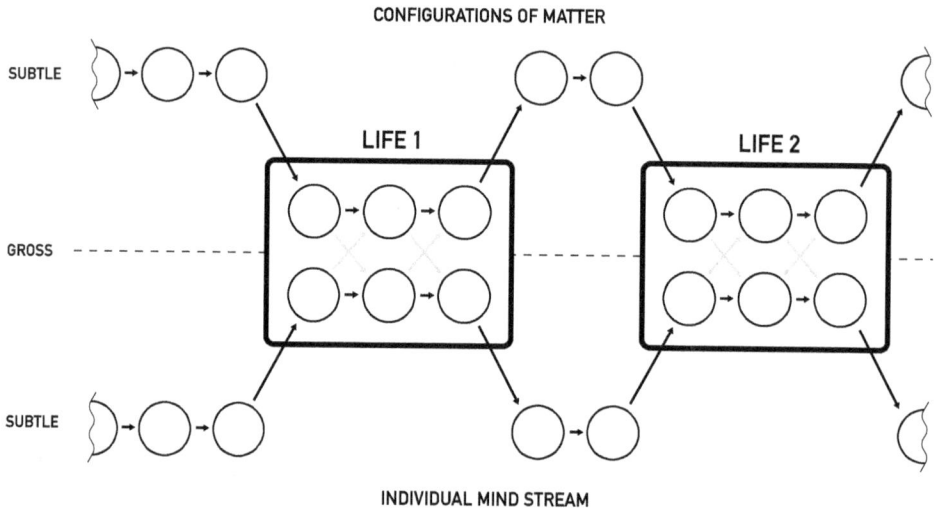

Figure 1-4: The formation and dissolution of lives over time.

A highly realised meditation practitioner is able to control their subtle mind in such a way, that they can effectively choose the shape their next gross mind will take. This degree of control allows them to maintain a continuity of practice across lives and thereby facilitate their ongoing mastery of the mind. Because they do not forget all of their "research", they are able to access increasingly more subtle levels of mental experience.

A closer examination by scientists and scholars regarding the notion that mind exists as something separate from physical existence, could encourage the application of contemplative research within other scientific disciplines. It is interesting to speculate what discoveries science could make if the notion that mind can only be investigated by the mind itself was embraced.

A MODEL OF THE MIND

Slowly, slowly we are building up a model for how the mind works. The more detail we give this model, the more information we have available for making decisions. Remember that we are not studying the subject of the mind so we can simply have a nice model of some intangible thing. Our aim instead, is to use this model to help us make constructive decisions in our lives. Through such examination of the mind, we are attempting to identify the source of our suffering and develop practical strategies for overcoming that suffering.

Within Buddhism, there are many different ways to classify the mind. We can work with it as a single entity, as we did above, or we can divide it up into different component parts. Each system of classification highlights different aspects of how the mind works. When used together, these classifications provide us with a more complete picture of what is going on.

In the following sections we will look at a number of classifications that relate to the gross and subtle levels of mind. Since the very subtle level is only accessible to advanced yogic practitioners, we will leave that for future discussions.

Primary and Secondary Minds

The most generic classification of the mind is to simply divide it in two:

1. **Primary Minds:** A primary mind is our experience of basic perception. It is *what* we are aware of. There are different types of primary minds, each identified by the types of objects that they perceive. For example, a visual consciousness which perceives shapes and forms is considered a primary mind. While the grosser levels of consciousness are mostly objective in nature, there are also more subtle levels which are focused on the subjective experience of an agent or observer.

2. **Secondary Minds:** A secondary mind is a particular way of relating with an object. It is more about *how* we are aware of something. The various types of secondary minds are each defined by the type of relationship that is created between a perceived subject and a perceived object. An example would be the secondary mind of "attention" whose function is to engage the mind with a particular aspect of the object that is appearing.

The use of the terms "primary" and "secondary" should not be understood in relation to time. Instead, they are both co-emergent properties of the mind, happening simultaneously. The word primary here refers more to the fundamental nature of these minds. It is the recognition that without the perception of the subject and object then there would be no basis upon which to create relationships.

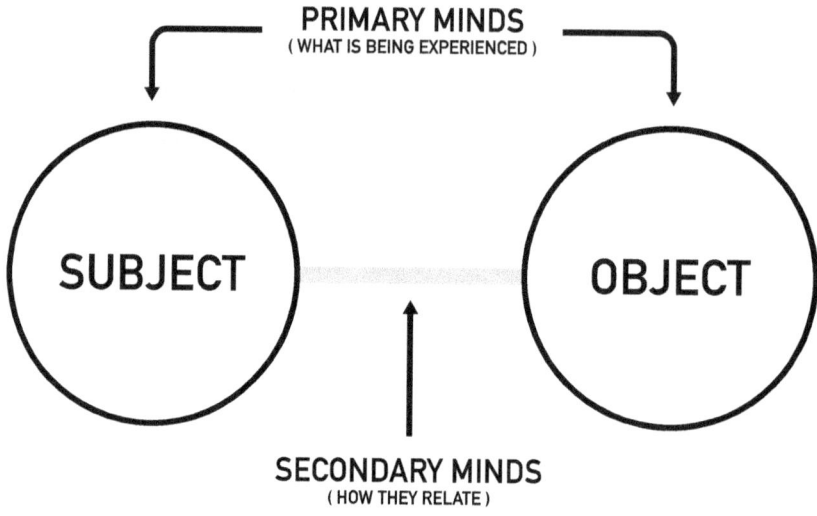

Figure 1-5: How primary and secondary minds establish a dualistic view.

Both of these categories provide us with an opportunity for different types of analysis. Through studying the primary minds, we are able to get a sense for the basic components that make up mind. Then by studying the secondary minds, we are able to understand the different ways that these components can relate to each other. In particular, we are able to identify patterns of relationships that are conducive to harmonious experience and those which lead to problems.

The Eight Forms of Consciousness

We will now look at the different types of primary minds that we can experience at the gross and subtle levels. Remember that what we generally refer to as mind is actually a composite phenomenon built up from many different types of mind working at different levels. In this case, the type of mind that we will be focusing on is known as *consciousness*. Consciousness refers to any awareness that is conditioned by the dualistic relationship between subjects and objects. We can call the continuity of such a consciousness, a *mindstream*. Since every person has a unique perspective, then their mindstream will be equally unique. If we look at our own personal mindstream, we can identify two main categories of consciousness:

Sensory Consciousness

A sensory consciousness is any consciousness that is directly tied to a physical sense organ. For example, our visual consciousness is produced when light bounces off an object and comes into contact with the sense organ of the eye. The information is transmitted into a particular pattern of electrical activity which in turn gives rise to the experience of colours and shapes.

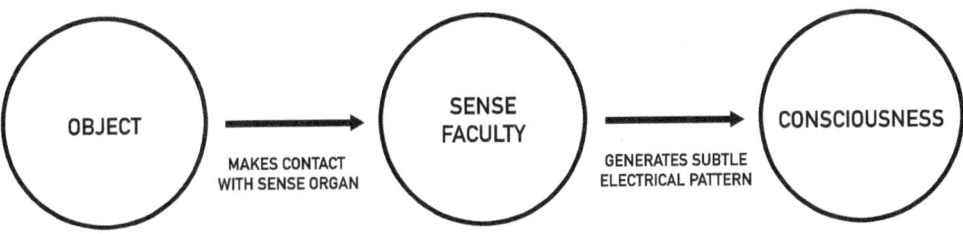

Figure 1-6: Components of a sensory consciousness.

When we expand this basic pattern to each of the other sense organs we can identify five forms of sensory consciousness:

Object	Faculty	Consciousness	Experience
Light waves	Eye	Visual	Colours and shapes
Vibrations	Ears	Auditory	Rhythms and tones
Chemical compounds	Nose	Olfactory	Smells
Chemical compounds	Tongue	Gustatory	Flavours
Configurations of matter	Body	Tactile	Sensations of solidity, fluidity, heat and movement

Table 1-2: The five types of sensory consciousness.

All of these forms of consciousness are perceived directly in the mind, which means when the conditions come together, the experience will arise. They are non-conceptual in nature. They are also extremely gross forms of mind as they rely heavily on the physical presence of the sense organs. Take away the sense organ and the corresponding consciousness ceases to arise in the mind.

Similarly, we can see that over time, as our sense organs deteriorate, the corresponding qualities of our sensory consciousness also deteriorate. Vision becomes blurry, sounds are muffled, tastes become bland. Some of these things can be adjusted through technology (glasses or hearing aids), or through surgery to fix the sense organ (removing cataracts for instance). All of this points to the fact that sensory consciousness is not always clearly representing the reality that is being presented to it. Sometimes we are only getting a partial or distorted aspect of it.

Mental Consciousness

When the mind is not conditioned by a sense organ, we can refer to it as mental consciousness. Unlike the five types of sensory consciousness, the mental consciousness has the capacity to be aware of what is perceived. For instance, if we perceive a flower, the visual consciousness is like a mirror that reflects the details such as the color and shape, but it has no understanding of what it is reflecting. The visual consciousness sees the object, but the mental consciousness *knows* the object. It is this basis of awareness that is able to generate conceptual models which represent phenomena that may or may not be perceived by a sensory consciousness. When we look at the mental consciousness, we are able to identify three distinct categories of mind:

3. **Gross Mental Consciousness:** This is the rational mind. It is made up of thoughts, mental imagery and subjective feelings (like emotions). This is the type of experience that most of us associate with the word "mind". It is very much dependent on the condition of the brain as a support. If the brain is damaged, our capacity for this gross mental consciousness to manifest fully is somewhat limited. The experience that we label "memory" occurs when the gross mental consciousness generates mental images that recreate past experiences.

4. **Deluded Consciousness:** This type of consciousness is used to refer to any mistaken perception of reality. In particular though it generally refers to the mistaken perceptions that we have in relation to our sense of self. This type of consciousness provides the basis for the development of all manner of distorted states of mind that we call "afflictions". Some afflictions are gross, while others are more subtle. What they all have in common though, is that they distort our understanding of reality and create the conditions for us to experience suffering.

The deluded consciousness can be very difficult to detect because it causes a proliferation of concepts to arise in the gross mental consciousness. With so many thoughts swirling around, it is often hard to identify the misconceptions that fuel it. Through meditative practice, it is possible to calm the mind sufficiently to be able to identify these deluded minds. There are four basic misconceptions that form the root of this consciousness.

The first is the belief in a substantially existent self. This is the conviction that the ego exists as some sort of separate entity that we label as "self". The second is the belief that this ego has attributes of existing in a particular way, providing the conditioning for "how" the self exists. Thirdly is our conviction that this self is more important than anyone else which can be referred to as self-cherishing. Finally there is ignorance, the belief that this self inherently exists, independent of our labelling it as such. Until we eliminate the deluded mind consciousness, our perception will always be influenced by these four misconceptions and the mental afflictions which arise from them. Like a glass of dirty water, the pure nature of our mental consciousness is obscured by the presence of these deluded concepts.

5. **Foundation Consciousness:** The most subtle form of mental consciousness is known as the foundation consciousness (also known as the alayavijñana or substrate consciousness). It is the basis of all consciousness —how we think about and experience the world, our environment, all sensed or perceived objects and even how our body appears to us. It is

the foundation of the mind and the storehouse which conditions the other types of consciousness. All of our habitual tendencies are stored in this consciousness and it is this consciousness which is believed to continue across lifetimes. It is considered to be neutral in that there is no concept of good nor bad at this level. There is merely an awareness of being aware. It is this consciousness which the deluded consciousness mistakenly conceives of as a "me". This basic sense of self is then further elaborated with various characteristics by the gross mental consciousness.

Foundation consciousness can be likened to the deepest ocean depths. Our emotions and thoughts are the turbulent waves on the surface and although they are part of the ocean they do not disturb the water deep below. When we are unconscious or faint, or find ourselves in a deep state of meditative absorption, all other consciousnesses dissolve back into this foundation consciousness. Everything absorbs into this never-ending continuum. When the deluded mind has been eliminated, the foundation consciousness arises in a pure form.

Exercise 1.2—Identifying the Gross Mind

- *Sit quietly for a few moments in order to calm the mind.*

- *With your eyes open, look around slowly. Become aware of the many colours and shapes you can see through your eyes. Close your eyes for a moment and see how these colours and shapes change. Open them and observe how the appearances arise once again. This is your visual consciousness.*

- *With your eyes closed, become aware of whatever sounds are presently manifesting. Get a sense for the qualities of the sounds and how they shift over time. Observe how the sounds layer on top of each other, each contributing to an overall experience. This is the auditory consciousness.*

- *Spend some time smelling different aromas. Perhaps select some food and become aware of the variations of smells as they waft through your nostrils. This is the olfactory consciousness.*

- *Likewise, try tasting different foods. See if you can distinguish the different components of what you are tasting. Observe how the taste arises when the food touches your tongue, how it lingers after the food is swallowed and then finally how it dissolves over time. This is the gustatory consciousness.*

- *With your hand, press down on something that is hard. Feel the solidity of the object, the firmness. Then take a drink of water and hold it in your mouth. Feel the sensation of the liquid sloshing about. Now scan through your body and observe any areas of heat or cold. Notice how some areas feel more active than others. Become aware of the movement of your breath as it flows in and out. Feel the contraction and expansion of your chest or abdomen. Finally, look for any areas in your body where no particular sensation is arising. Try to get a sense for the empty spaces. This is the tactile consciousness.*

- *Now, sitting quietly for a moment, imagine that you are sitting in a beautiful meadow in the middle of spring time. At the edge of the meadow is a forest of tall trees, casting their shadows along the ground. The sky is clear and the sun is shining. You can feel its warmth on your skin. Just in the distance is a small pond. You can see the ripples of fish swimming just below the surface. Try to really feel as though you are present in this scene. This is the gross mental consciousness.*

In total we can identify eight different forms of consciousness. Of these eight, six are considered to be gross in nature: the five types of sensory consciousness and the gross mental consciousness. The deluded consciousness is a mixture of both gross and subtle minds, while the foundation consciousness is considered to be subtle.

Subtlety	Type	Consciousness
Gross	Sensory	1. Visual Consciousness
		2. Auditory Consciousness
		3. Olfactory Consciousness
		4. Gustatory Consciousness
		5. Tactile Consciousness
	Mental	6. Gross Mental Consciousness
Gross and Subtle		7. Deluded Consciousness
Subtle		8. Foundation Consciousness

Table 1-3: Summary of the "Eight Forms of Consciousness".

How a Mental Consciousness Arises

To begin to understand the dynamics between these different forms of consciousness, we can use a simple five part model known as the *Five Aggregates.* Each step illustrates the sequential process in which a mental consciousness is generated. This process is defined as follows:

6. **Form:** We begin with appearances arising within a sensory or mental consciousness. We can call these appearances *forms.* Assuming that all of our faculties are functioning properly, we are normally receiving six distinct streams of information corresponding to the six senses (five physical and one mental). These forms, create the objective focus of our mind. Since this process is instantaneous in nature, when we refer to the appearance of the mind as an object to the mental consciousness, we are referring to the present consciousness becoming aware of a previous moment of mental consciousness.

7. **Perception:** The present mental consciousness can only ever be aware of one stream of information at any given time. While we may perceive the sensation of things like sight and sound happening at the same time, this is actually an illusion created by our mental consciousness jumping back and forth between these two at a very rapid rate. When the mental consciousness becomes aware of a particular stream of appearances, it leaves a mental impression on the mind. This impression is known as *perception.* The main function of perception is to create a mental image

with which the mental consciousness is able to establish a connection.

8. **Feeling:** On the basis of the characteristics of this mental image, the mind will experience an initial reaction. This reaction is the most basic relationship that is drawn between the perceived object (the mental image) and the perceiving subject (the awareness of that image). It is produced when the mental image triggers the various habitual propensities that are stored within the foundational consciousness and manifests as a compulsion to either engage or disengage from the object.

9. **Mental Formations:** Once the initial connection has been made between subject and object, then a whole range of related cognitive patterns will arise. We can think of the foundational consciousness as being like a big interconnected network. When one propensity is activated, then that causes other propensities to activate, like the ripples produced by dropping a rock in a pond. These propensities manifest as a wide range of conceptual designations that shape or condition the type of relationship that you are developing with the object. In a way, the mind is building up a story around the initial feeling, fleshing out the details with conceptual overlays.

10. **Consciousness:** The resulting moment of mental consciousness that arises from this process will be dependent on the type of story that was projected by the mental formations. If the story was based on deluded misconceptions, then the interpretation of the experience will be in discord with reality. This distortion will serve as the basis for suffering to arise in the form of unpleasant feelings. Likewise, if the interpretation is in accordance with reality, then that will serve as a basis for happiness to arise.

To understand this process, we can use a simple example:

Imagine that you are sitting in a restaurant. You have just finished your meal and are waiting for dessert, a nice big slice of chocolate cake. The waiter approaches the table and sets down the dessert. To your horror, there is a slice of lemon pie. You look up at the waiter indignantly and say, "Where is my chocolate cake?"

Let's look at what is going on in the mind. First, let's start with the form. Your visual consciousness experiences the appearance of a white circle, with a light brown triangle, filled with what looks like a yellowish blob. Your mental consciousness picks up on these colours and shapes and builds up a mental image in the mind. You happen to hate lemon pie and your initial reaction to seeing this form is one of disgust. And now the mental formations start in. This is not a chocolate cake. This is a lemon pie. I hate lemon pie. I want chocolate, not lemon. Why is this lemon pie here? Why did this person bring this terrible thing to me? Why do such bad things always happen to me? And so on and so forth.

As we build up concepts around the experience, we create a feedback loop. Our feeling of aversion grows stronger the more we fan the flames. Eventually it gets so strong that we feel compelled to do something about it. In this case, your face contorts into what is commonly identified as anger, and you lash out verbally at the poor waiter.

Things are not always as exaggerated as I am making them out to be here. Sometimes our reactions are very subtle and the conceptual overlays equally as subtle. At other times, they can be much worse. Think of an episode of extreme road-rage for example. Through this simple model, we can start to see how the way we conceive of a situation, plays a significant role in our overall experience of that situation.

REVIEW OF KEY POINTS

- The mind is the source of all our happiness and is therefore the most important phenomenon that we need to understand.

- The mind is not the same as the brain. It is a non-physical phenomenon which has gross aspects that are closely linked to the brain and subtle aspects which are not.

- The mind is an eternal continuity of experience with no beginning nor end.

- The present moment of mind is a result of previous moments of mind, while the future moments are the results of the present. This means that by training the mind in the present, we can give shape to the experiences which will arise in the future.

- The mind operates at different levels of subtlety: gross, subtle and very subtle.

- The mind can be divided into primary minds and secondary minds, where primary minds are used to describe what is appearing to the mind and secondary minds are used to describe how we relate to those appearances.

- There are eight forms of primary minds: five types of sensory consciousness and three types of mental consciousness.

- We can understand the nature of how a mental consciousness arises through the use of five categories: form, perception, feeling, mental formations and consciousness.

Manjushri, Bodhisattva of Wisdom

CHAPTER TWO

Working with Destructive States of Mind

In the previous chapter, we suggested that the mind is the primary cause for whether we experience happiness or suffering. Our external conditions, the people and circumstances that surround our lives every day, can only act as conditions which catalyse our experiences. In order to achieve a more positive and constructive life, we therefore need to understand how the mind works.

Every one of us can recall times in our lives when we have felt anxiety, anger or sadness. Through our study of the various primary minds, we are able to gain a general understanding of how consciousness arises, but we are not able to accurately determine what causes these undesirable states of mind. To accurately diagnose their causes (and thereby understand how to remedy them), we need a more detailed model from which to work. The following is just such a model.

THE FIFTY-ONE MENTAL FACTORS

A mental factor is a specific way of relating the mind to an object. These different types of relationships influence how a moment of mental consciousness is experienced. They can be understood to be like the different ingredients that go into making a cup of tea. Depending on the relative amounts of the ingredients, the resultant experience of the tea will be different.

In this next section we will be presenting a general overview of the six categories of mental factors that are identified in Buddhist psychology. For the sake of brevity I will not go into detail of all of the mental factors. If you would like a more complete presentation, please refer to the appendix in this book.

1. Omnipresent Mental Factors

This first set of mental factors are the most fundamental ingredients for a moment of cognition. Since they arise in every single moment of sensory and mental consciousness, they are referred to as being *omnipresent*. These factors are mostly tied to the mechanics of direct perception, providing a basis for the conceptual mind to arise. There are five *Omnipresent Mental Factors*:

1. **Sensation:** Sensation provides the basic connection that is absolutely necessary for the mind to experience an object with the six senses. When a sense consciousness perceives an object through a sense organ, then a sensation arises. It is not only the gross feeling which everyone recognises but includes the more subtle sensation which pervades every perception. This quality of sensation is inherent in every mental state and comprises all immediate associations with the object, whether they are pleasant, unpleasant or neutral, taking place within a nanosecond. The main point to understand is that any type of consciousness that is arising, in every instant of experience, contains an element of sensation.

2. **Discrimination (or Distinguishing):** Discrimination is when our sense field takes an uncommon characteristic of an object or an outstanding feature of an object and ascribes conventional significance to it. It doesn't label or name the object but discriminates it as one thing rather than another. For example, distinguishing light from dark, or distinguishing a table from the background; no words are required. This is all happening immediately, simultaneously and constantly with everything we are experiencing. Without distinguishing, the mind could not link the object with further mental processes.

3. **Intention (or Volition):** This is the conscious and spontaneous urge that causes the mind to engage with and experience objects, or a conscious aim that guides action. Without intention, mind could not direct its attention towards an object. All mental activity has intention.

4. **Contact:** Contact is how we connect with an object. It occurs with the meeting of three factors: the preceding moment of consciousness (which could be any of the types of consciousness), the object, and

the sense faculty. Without contact, mind could not encounter the object and establish a relationship or feeling with it. It differentiates that an object of cognition is pleasant, unpleasant, or neutral, providing the foundation for experiencing it with a feeling of happiness, unhappiness, or indifference.

5. **Attention (and Mental Engagement):** Mental engagement is the penetration of consciousness onto an object through paying some level of attention to it. Any type of consciousness, no matter how briefly it arises, is always engaged with a particular object. Attention is present in every split second for all beings, and without it, the mind could not remain fixed on an object experienced by any of the six senses resulting in a complete loss of stability.

If any of these mental factors are missing, a relationship between subject and object cannot be established. As long as all five are active (no matter how strongly), you at the very least have the basis for a connection that can then support other mental factors to arise. By strengthening these omnipresent mental factors, you can strengthen the connection they create. The stronger the connection, the more information your mind will have to work with and therefore the more accurate its perception of reality will be.

Exercise 2.1—Establishing a Connection

- *Sit quietly for a few moments in order to calm the mind.*

- *Choose a particular form of consciousness to focus on. This can be one of the five senses or the mental consciousness. Try to identify a specific experience to use as your subject of analysis.*

- *Consider the subject that you have chosen. Maybe it's the visual appearance of a flower, or a cup. Whatever the phenomenon, establish in your mind the scenario in which the subject appeared to your mind. Note what is actually appearing. This appearance is the sensation.*

- *What are the details of this sensation? What are its characteristics? Get a sense of how the mind isolates and separates the sensation from the background. How clearly is this sensation appearing to you. This separation of the object is discrimination.*

- *Where is your mind focused? Is it locked onto the sensation or is the sensation more in the periphery? This directionality of the mind is intention.*

- *Now consider, how is this sensation arising in my mind? Through which sense faculty am I perceiving it? Bring to mind the three conditions: object, sense faculty and consciousness. Identify each of these. For example, the light waves could be the object, the eye the faculty, and when they meet, a visual consciousness of a flower arises. This coming together of conditions is contact.*

- *Finally, how strong is your engagement with this sensation? Are you completely absorbed in the sensation or does it occupy only one portion of your mind? This strength of focus is attention.*

2. Object-Determining Factors

Through the omnipresent mental factors, the mind is able to establish a connection with the appearances arising in the six senses. The next set of mental factors allows the mind to actually know what is appearing to it. This knowledge manifests in the form of a particular degree of certainty that the object is this and not that. In total, there are five *Object-Determining Mental Factors*:

- **Aspiration:** Aspiration is concerned with the desire or the intent to achieve or obtain something, whether it is worthwhile or not. It is the mind which takes interest in an object and wishes to know it more completely. Aspiration acts as the basis for effort and produces diligence.

- **Belief (Firm Conviction):** Belief is the stable holding of a specific object or subject to be as it is; to have a firm conviction that it is this and not that. Perhaps there is an obvious proof that what is believed is actually true, or there may be much evidence that it is so, either through direct experience, logical reasoning or scriptural reference. One may also assume or believe "blindly" without any evidence. In each of these cases, the belief arises in direct relationship to the object or subject.

- **Mindfulness:** Mindfulness can be referred to as a type of "mental glue" which holds an object in focus, keeping it clear in the mind, as if one is conjuring up an image through referring to it in conversation. This can be over a long or short period of time, and the object may include the present moment. Mindfulness is achieved by cultivating awareness of one's thoughts, actions and motivations.

- **Concentration:** Concentration means that one focuses the mind single-pointedly in one direction on a single object or a topic of investigation, without any distraction. This is a state of undistracted focus, just like twisting a thread to a fine point in order to put it through the eye of a needle.

- **Wisdom:** Wisdom is the antidote to doubt. It is a discriminating awareness that adds a level of decisiveness to distinguishing an object of cognition, knowing the reality of an object regardless of what it is. Comprehending that all of conventional existence is impermanent on a subtle level is an example of wisdom. Real wisdom always leads to peace and tranquillity, as it teaches us that everything is interdependent and naturally gives us insight into what is best for oneself and others. This is very different to some kinds of knowledge which can be harmful and can lead to great suffering, such as knowing how to design weapons. Of course the knowledge itself is not harmful, but it is not grounded in true wisdom.

When these mental factors are strong, the certainty that one has in what is being perceived is also strong. With greater certainty, you will be able to act more effectively in accordance with the situation. If these factors are weak, then there will be a great deal of uncertainty regarding what is actually happening, which will increase the possibility of making mistakes.

Exercise 2.2—Knowing What an Object Is

- *Sit quietly for a few moments in order to calm the mind.*

- *Choose a particular form of consciousness to focus on. This can be one of the five senses or the mental consciousness. Try to identify a specific experience to use as your object of analysis.*

- *How interesting do you find the object? Get a sense for how much the object attracts your attention. This desire to engage with the object is aspiration.*

- *How firm is your mind holding the object? Do you have conviction that you are indeed experiencing the object in a realistic way or is there doubt? Could what you are experiencing be an illusion? The strength of certainty that the object is as it appears is belief.*

- *How stable is your apprehension of the object? Are you getting just a momentary engagement, or is the mind able to sit with the object for some degree of time? This stability of mind that holds the object continually is mindfulness.*

- *How focused is your mind? Is it holding the object single-pointedly or is it distracted by many different objects? Are you completely absorbed in the object or is your attention divided? The ability to focus single-pointedly is concentration.*

- *Do you know what you are perceiving? Is it a table, a chair, a sound, a thought? What is it? The ability to discriminate various characteristics and to actually know what they are is wisdom.*

3. Root Mental Afflictions

While the Omnipresent and Object-Determining Mental Factors may not necessarily be easy for us to observe, they are nonetheless the foundation upon which all other conceptual minds are built. The remaining sets of mental factors are all more obvious examples of the different types of concepts that influence how we relate with an object.

Any mental factor which causes the mind to become agitated is known as an affliction. They are also referred to as defilements and afflictive obscurations, they are disturbing, negative emotions which can cause us to lose our composure, self control and provoke us to make unskilled decisions. Bringing suffering to ourselves and others, afflictions are like mud that sticks to us like glue, obscuring the good qualities we have inside.

An affliction is a specific way of relating with objects that is not in accord with reality. They all involve some degree of distortion. For this reason they are considered part of the *Deluded Consciousness*. As we will see, there are a wide variety of derivative mental afflictions, but they can all be condensed down into six *Root Mental Afflictions*.

1. **Attachment:** Clinging to the positive qualities of a perceived object.

2. **Aversion:** Clinging to the negative qualities of a perceived object.

3. **Ignorance:** Not knowing a particular aspect of reality.

4. **Wrong View:** Actively believing in a misconception.

5. **Pride:** Believing that one's own qualities are superior to those of others.

6. **Afflicted Doubt:** Having no confidence in something which is true.

As these afflictions play a major role in our experience of suffering, I will be covering them in greater detail later in this chapter.

4. Derivative Mental Afflictions

Of the six root afflictions, three are particularly powerful: attachment, aversion and ignorance. These three are often referred to as the Three Poisons as they are responsible for a wide range of destructive states of mind. In total, there are twenty derivative mental afflictions, each grouped by the root affliction/s that they are most related to

Root Affliction/s	Mental Factor
Aversion	1. Fury
	2. Resentment
	3. Hostility
	4. Harmfulness
Attachment	5. Miserliness
	6. Excitement
	7. Self-infatuation
Aversion and Attachment	8. Jealousy
Ignorance	9. Concealment
	10. Laziness
	11. Lethargy
	12. Lack of Faith
	13. Forgetfulness
	14. Heedlessness
Attachment and Ignorance	15. Deceit
	16. Hypocrisy
Attachment, Aversion and Ignorance	17. Lack of Conscience
	18. Shamelessness
	19. Non-introspection
	20. Distraction

Table 2-1: The Twenty Derivative Afflictions.

5. Virtuous Mental Factors

Unlike the afflictions, virtuous mental factors are considered to be derived from an accurate understanding of reality. Because they are free from distortions, they are able to act as antidotes to the afflictive states of mind. When they are present, they tend to have a pacifying or harmonious effect on the mind.

These eleven *Virtuous Mental Factors* are:

1. Faith

2. Moral shame

3. Fear of Unwholesomeness

4. Non-attachment

5. Non-hatred

6. Non-ignorance

7. Diligence

8. Pliancy of Mind

9. Conscientiousness

10. Equanimity

11. Non-harmfulness

6. Variable Mental Factors

The last set of mental factors have the potential to be either virtuous or afflictive states of mind. Because they are neutral in nature, they will take on the general "flavour" of the other mental factors which are present. These four *Variable Mental Factors* are:

1. Sleep

2. Regret

3. Gross Detection

4. Discernment

Of these six categories, the first two contribute to the quality of the information that you are able to perceive. The third and fourth categories are distorted interpretations of reality and therefore need to be abandoned, while the fifth should be cultivated. The sixth should be developed skillfully in connection with the virtuous states of mind.

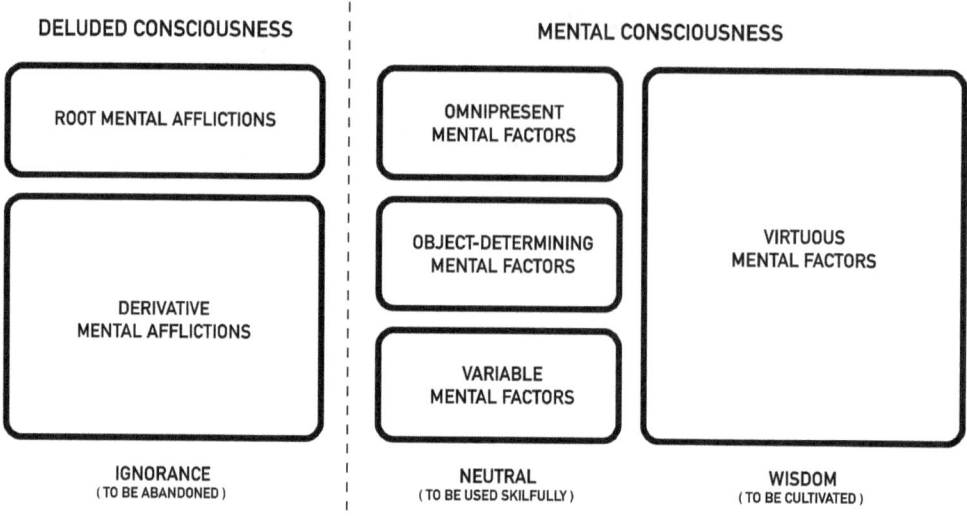

Figure 2-1: Overview of the "Fifty-One Mental Factors".

ESTABLISHING VALID PERCEPTION

With our considerably more detailed model of the mind, we can now begin to see how what we are experiencing is not always in accordance with reality. Distortions can be introduced through the physical sense organs, through the warped concepts of the deluded consciousness or through a combination of both. Simply put, how our mind perceives things is often not the way things really are. For this reason, it is increasingly important to consider how we can know whether our experiences are valid representations of reality or not.

To answer this question, we must first identify the different types of phenomena that we are capable of experiencing. In general, there are three types:

1. **Obvious:** Obvious phenomena can easily be perceived by our five physical sense consciousnesses as well as the mental consciousness. Examples include things like a chair, an emotion, a memory or an elephant. These are phenomena that anyone should be able to experience.

2. **Hidden:** A hidden phenomenon is any phenomenon that is obscured from being perceived directly. An example of such a phenomenon is the subtle impermanent nature of our bodies. Although they are changing many thousands of times every second, as the cells continually divide

and regenerate, this constant transformation is hidden from our sight. In order to detect this movement, we need to use technology to augment our sight or meditative practices to improve the quality of our minds. In this way, we can see that a hidden phenomenon is not inherently hidden, it is only hidden whilst the necessary conditions are not present for it to become obvious.

3. **Very Hidden:** A very hidden phenomenon is a phenomenon that is so complex that we cannot experience it with either the gross or subtle minds. An example of such a phenomenon is an understanding of all of the causes and conditions that came together to form the specific patterns of a peacock's feather. Or similarly, understanding all of the causes that determine an individual's momentary experience of happiness or suffering.

We can define a valid perception as any experience which accurately knows a given aspect of a phenomenon. In order to develop valid knowledge about each of the above types of phenomena, we must rely on the following forms of perception:

Direct Perception

A direct perception is anything appearing to the mind on the basis of an undistorted sensory or mental consciousness. An example would be our ability to know a flower by way of its smell. For the most part, the untrained mind can only directly perceive obvious phenomena by way of the physical senses or the gross mental consciousness. More subtle forms of direct mental perception are possible, but unless we have trained our mind through the practice of meditation, they occur so rapidly that we are unaware of them.

Just as meditation can improve our capacity to perceive phenomena more directly, so too can physical technologies help extend our sensory capacity. In science we use all manner of devices to sense phenomena that are beyond the range of our normal human capacity. Just think how a giant telescope allows us to observe galaxies that are billions of light years away, or how a simple sequence of time lapse photography can show us the movement of plants or glaciers.

Of all the forms of valid perception, direct perception carries with it the greatest certainty. For if it is direct, there are very few distortions or overlays between your mind and the phenomenon that is being observed. Fortunately, all phenomena have the potential to be known directly, even the hidden and the very hidden phenomena. When the mind is properly trained and all of the distortions are removed, there are no longer any barriers to what we can know.

Logical Reasoning

When you are unable to observe a phenomenon directly, then you must settle for knowing it indirectly. We do this by way of building up a conceptual model that represents the given phenomena. On the basis of this model, we are able to make logical inferences which help us to extend our knowledge.

Take for instance the example of fire. A fire is an obvious phenomenon, and therefore we can know it through direct experience. From that experience we can attribute various characteristics to it, such as when it burns, it produces smoke. On the basis of this very simple model, we can infer that whenever we see smoke, there must be a corresponding fire. In this way, even if we are unable to directly perceive the fire, we can indirectly know it through the direct perception of a sign, like smoke rising into the sky.

Science uses logical reasoning to know indirectly a wide variety of phenomena. Consider how we have come to know the origins of our universe. No one has ever travelled back in time to witness the big bang. Instead, scientists have developed mathematical models which allow them to reverse engineer the causal sequence based on observations they are currently able to make.

For logical reasoning to have any strength in our minds, we must have faith in the model on which the reasoning is dependant. Faith is developed in a given model when direct observations can be made to corroborate it; take any well designed scientific experiment. For example, first the scientist establishes a hypothesis—a prediction for a certain outcome based on a given model. Then an experiment is conducted which produces a number of direct observations. These observations are compared to the hypothesis and they either support the model or they don't. With each supporting observation, our conviction that a model accurately represent reality grows.

In Buddhism the same holds true. The model of the mind we have been studying so far is the result of considerable research carried out by advanced contemplative practitioners. As they engaged intensively with training their minds, they were able to make more and more direct observations and many phenomena which were hidden to others, became obvious to them. They then used their observations to create a model which makes it possible for people without the same training, to know the hidden aspects of the mind indirectly. This model can be tested by anyone who is willing to conduct the contemplative experiments that are presented in their teachings.

Faith in Authority

How many people have actually seen a quark? I think for the vast majority of us, quantum particles are a very hidden phenomenon. We simply do not have any sense of what they are or how they exist. While we know there are models to describe how quantum reality functions, the models themselves are presented by extremely complex mathematics that are indecipherable to the untrained mind. Therefore, the only way we can know them is through the testimony of people who understand the models and on the basis of those models, have run experiments.

We call these people "authorities". An authority is someone that we believe to have valid knowledge regarding a particular phenomenon. We develop faith in these people for a number of reasons:

1. **Experience:** When we know the training that a person has gone through, we gain confidence in their status as an expert in a given field. Here we are placing our faith in both the body of knowledge that has been passed on to that person and in the experience they have developed through putting that knowledge into practice. Consider the confidence you derive from going to a doctor who has been practising for twenty years, versus going to a doctor who has just graduated from medical school.

2. **Consistency:** When we have witnessed an authority to be correct regarding subjects we can understand, we have greater confidence that they may also be right about things we cannot understand. An example

would be the faith we place in the scientific community. Since science has produced many tangible benefits in our day-to-day lives, most people have no problem in trusting "scientific facts". This is despite having minimal or even no understanding of the science behind those facts.

3. **Motivation:** The degree of trust we place in someone will also depend significantly on the perceived motivation behind why this person is sharing a given piece of information. If the person has proven themselves to be trustworthy and we see they genuinely want to help us, it is much easier to accept what they say to be true. At the very least we recognise their sincerity regarding their knowledge and so we don't feel they are attempting to deceive us. It's then up to us to choose whether or not we put our faith in their idea. Consider the example of two people recommending a particular drug for you to take. On the one side there is a representative of a pharmaceutical company who wants to sell you his latest product. On the other, you have a friend who is a biochemist and believes this drug can help you. Which one would you trust more?

As we will discover in our study of Buddhism, there are many ideas of phenomena that we cannot directly perceive at this time. Some of these ideas can be proven indirectly through reasoning but only if you develop faith in the models that are being presented.

If we consider the qualities of the historical Buddha (the source of these models), we can begin to see why he is considered a valid source of information. Firstly, we can see that all of his insights arose out of his direct experience during intensive training as a contemplative practitioner. He developed the conditions for these experiences to arise during more than six years of dedicated research, followed by another four decades of putting those insights into practice. Since then, his teachings have been practised by millions of people over the span of more than two thousand years, proving them to be efficient and capable of producing the claimed results. Finally, the Buddha's motivation is ultimately one of supreme compassion, where every word he taught was specifically designed to alleviate suffering. It is for these reasons that the Buddha is considered to be a genuine and trustworthy authority.

Fortunately though, the Buddha himself did not believe in blind faith. Instead, he encouraged his students to put his teachings into practice and to see for themselves the benefits they could produce. In general it is then preferable to keep an open mind to new ideas; taking them as "working hypotheses" of sorts. Then over time, we can test them with our own experience and develop greater confidence in their truth.

Phenomena	Type of Perception	Relationship	Certainty
Obvious	Direct Perception	Direct	Strongest
Hidden	Logical Reasoning	Indirect (through conceptual model)	Middling
Very Hidden	Faith in Authority	Indirect (through faith)	Weakest

Table 2-2: Ways of knowing reality.

MANAGING DESTRUCTIVE EMOTIONAL STATES

Through our study of Buddhist psychology we have been able to identify the core mechanisms for how our experience arises. We have established a theoretical understanding of the different types of experiences that we have and the different ways in which we relate to those experiences. Now it's time to put all of this theory into practice. We need to learn how to bring these ideas into our lives so they can help us improve the quality of our lived experiences. To do this, we will look more closely at the six root afflictions in order to identify specific strategies for reducing their destructive influence.

The general approach here is to become familiar with specific wholesome states of mind which act as antidotes to the afflictions. The training is fairly straightforward:

1. Identify which afflictions arise in your experience.

2. Cultivate the antidotes to those afflictions in formal training.

Through this process we are effectively applying a counterforce to the afflictive minds. With persistence, we will weaken the affliction so much that it no longer has the capacity to overwhelm us. This will bring greater confidence in the face of adversity and help us to ultimately experience greater stability and calmness in life.

The Six Root Afflictions and Their Antidotes

In the beginning of your training, the focus should be on developing clarity regarding what each of the afflictions are and which antidotes can be used to counteract their influence.

Attachment

Attachment arises when we hold onto or cling to an object too dearly. The object could be a person, a feeling, a particular material possession or even an idea. Whatever it is, attachment causes us to lock onto and exaggerate the desirable qualities of that object. This creates a strong sense of craving to possess the object or to never let it go. The nature of attachment narrows our field of focus and blinds us to the effects it has on ourselves and those around us.

The problem which arises from attachment is that it builds up a fantasy that cannot be fulfilled by the object. We start to see the object as being a true source of happiness and we suffer when inevitably this belief is proven to be false. Take for instance what we often refer to as "romantic love". When a person first falls in love, they can see only the positive qualities in their partner. They see their partner as perfect and believe the way they feel is a direct result of being around them. Initially they are inseparable but as time passes, the person starts to notice tiny imperfections. At first they are insignificant because the attachment is still very strong. Eventually however, the imperfections start getting larger and the fantasy world this person has built up comes crashing down. If the person can develop a more realistic perspective of their partner, there is the chance of a longer lasting relationship. But if the person clings to the fantasy, expectations are unlikely to be met and a break-up is almost certain.

The antidote to attachment is to build up a more realistic view of the object that you are attached to, rather than fuelling the fantasy. Don't wait for the bubble to burst; instead consider the impermanent nature of the object and how it will change over time. Imagine the object in different situations and how it will not always be like it is now. Continuing with the romantic love example, in order to build up a healthier and more balanced relationship with your partner, reflect on their negative qualities while reminding yourself that they are not perfect and that their imperfections are just as much a part of them as the qualities that you love so much. In general, try to develop a broader understanding of the object of attachment that takes in more of its characteristics, not just those that you are attached to.

Exercise 2.3—Grounding Ourselves in Reality

- *Sit quietly for a few moments in order to calm the mind.*

- *Identify a physical object that you feel very attached to. It should be something that you would find very difficult to be separated from.*

- *Now bring to mind the various qualities of this object. Start with everything that you love about it. This causes your attachment to manifest. Identify how it feels.*

- *Now consider those qualities of the object that you think are not so great. Think about the different imperfections that it has, or the different ways that it could be better. After spending some time thinking about the faults of this object, note how you now feel towards it.*

- *Take some time to get a sense for the balance between those qualities that attract you and those qualities which you feel are unsatisfactory. Consider the totality of the object, not just one aspect. Look at how this object has changed over time.*

- *Release all thoughts and simply rest for a few moments.*

Aversion

Anger, fear, resentment and hatred are all manifestations of aversion. You can think of aversion as the opposite of attachment. Instead of grasping onto the desirable qualities of an object, we instead grasp onto the undesirable ones. Just as with attachment, we build up a fantasy, only this time we try to convince ourselves just how terrible the object is. The nature of aversion is to reject the object and want to get away from it.

We can see this at play when someone does something to offend us, perhaps saying something that hurts our feelings. Our mind reacts to the pain it is feeling by telling itself a story about that person, "Why was he so mean to me? What did I ever do to him? He is such a selfish and uncaring person. I wish someone would hurt him like he hurt me. He doesn't deserve to be happy." Very quickly, anger and hatred build up in the mind until we have completely demonised the other person. Sometimes it can get so out of hand, we can hold onto a grudge for years on end and all the while we are miserable.

And this is the truly sad thing about hatred. The only person it harms is the person who has it in their mind. As long as we allow aversion to dominate our life, we cannot experience any sense of peace. The antidote to aversion is to cultivate a sense of greater connection or closeness with the object of our aversion. If this is a person, we can think about how they are just like us, wanting to be happy and to be free from suffering. The reason they lash out is because they are confused and dominated by mental afflictions. On this basis we can develop a sense of compassion towards them. Instead of rejecting them, we cultivate the desire that they can experience genuine happiness and wellbeing so they then can stop hurting others.

There will of course be some people that we find it very difficult to feel compassion for. Maybe we feel that their behaviour is so horrendous (such as a serial killer) that they don't deserve our compassion. Having compassion for someone does not mean that you condone their behaviour. It means that you recognise that they are sick and suffering. You try to develop a sincere desire that they may be free from this sickness, because only then will they stop doing these terrible things. When working with difficult people, we need to start small and build up our capacity. As we learn to work with minor annoyances, we can eventually build up our compassion and learn to live with those who we perceive as having deeply harmed ourselves or others.

Exercise 2.4—Compassion for Those Who Harm You

- *Sit quietly for a few moments in order to calm the mind.*

- *Bring to mind a situation where you feel that someone has annoyed or upset you. Re-create the scenario in your mind, adding as much detail as you can so the experience is vivid in your mind. Without getting overwhelmed, allow the aversion to arise and observe how it feels.*

- *Now bring your focus to this person. Why do you think they did what they did? What did they believe was happening? What did you believe was happening?*

- *Try to get a sense for the state of mind that this person possessed. Can you identify the presence of any afflictions? If so, which ones? How did those afflictions motivate the actions that triggered your feelings?*

- *Now imagine the same scenario if this person was free from those afflictions. Do you think they would have acted in the same way? How could this scenario have played out differently?*

- *Recognising the distorted influence that the afflictions have on this person, nurture the desire for this person to be free from those destructive states of mind.*

- *Rest your mind for few moments.*

Ignorance (of Truth)

There are two types of ignorance that we need to consider; the ignorance of truth and wrong view. The ignorance of truth refers to a mere "not knowing" of how reality actually exists. Because we do not have knowledge of certain phenomena, we cannot understand what is going on in our experience and therefore we make unwise choices.

A good example of this is our ignorance of the law of cause and effect. For most of us, we are not aware of which sorts of actions lead to which sorts of results, and therefore we mistakenly engage in all manner of activities that bring us the exact opposite of what we are seeking.

The antidote to this sort of ignorance is to familiarise yourself with the teachings through study and reflection. Right now, you are doing just that. In this chapter alone, you have been learning about the nature of the mind. Hopefully, the knowledge you have gained will help you to work with your experience in a more constructive way.

Exercise 2.5—Identifying Opportunities to Learn

- *Sit quietly for a few moments in order to calm the mind.*

- *Consider your present situation. In what sort of environment are you currently living? What sorts of activities are you engaging with? What sorts of people are you encountering?*

- *Within this context, what sorts of problems do you face? Identify a number of examples of things in your life you think could be improved. Consider all of your hopes and dreams, and what you feel you need to be able to make them happen.*

- *What knowledge are you missing that limits your capacity to overcome those obstacles or to achieve your goals? Identify a few topics you think would be helpful to know more about.*

- *Consider how you could learn more about these topics. Could you take a class or buy a book? Do you know anyone you could talk to about these topics? Think of the different sources of information that you have access to, and develop the resolve to investigate further.*

Wrong View

The second form of ignorance is the ignorance of holding a wrong view. With this type of ignorance, not only do we fail to know reality as it is (ignorance of the truth) but we actually believe it to exist in a way that is false. It is an active misconception of reality. We can develop wrong views through our culture or through our misinterpretation of our experience.

Two very common forms of wrong view are to assert too much existence to things (known as eternalism) or too little (known as nihilism). Both of these views set up a distorted understanding of reality. When we use distorted assumptions, all of the concepts we build up on top of them also carry the same distortion. This leads us to drastically misinterpret our experience and prevents us from reaching the truth. It is this pervasive influence that makes wrong view the root for so many other afflictions to arise.

The antidote for working with a wrong view is to challenge that view with logical reasoning or direct experience. Because a wrong view is a mere fabrication of the mind, then it does not have the support of reality behind it. When we actually investigate how things exist, the wrong view will break apart as it cannot withstand the analysis.

Exercise 2.6—Challenging Non-Existence

- *Sit quietly for a few moments in order to calm the mind.*

- *Bring to mind an idea you are certain does not exist or at least one you're fairly sure does not exist. Imagine someone were to approach you and begin talking about this idea. Maybe it's the idea that our mind is an eternal continuity which reincarnates life after life. Maybe it's the idea that all phenomena are inherently physical in nature. Try to identify your initial reaction to whether you believe or don't believe in the idea you have chosen.*

- *Now consider the reasons for why you don't believe in this idea. Identify all of the arguments why this phenomenon just simply can or cannot exist.*

- *Then shift positions and try to imagine that you are defending the idea. How would you respond to each of the arguments? What reasons can you think of for why someone should believe in this idea?*

- *Of the two sides (the challenger and the defender), which points do you think have greater strength? Has the process of analysis strengthened your belief or weakened it? If you were so certain that something didn't exist, can you now entertain the thought that it might be possible? Try to get a sense for the direction in which your mind is moving.*

- *Rest your mind for a few moments.*

Pride (Arrogance)

This mental affliction manifests as a way of protecting the ego. We each have certain qualities that we identify with. Over time, we come to hold tightly to those qualities, viewing them as better than those of others. The nature of pride is to isolate, separating itself from those around it.

When it leads to developing greater self-confidence, some degree of pride in one's capacity can be beneficial. The problem is when you establish an attitude of disdain or disrespect towards others which can then lead to all manner of conceit and overconfidence. When we get to this extreme, we stop learning from others. We close ourselves off and we atrophy.

The antidote to pride is to develop greater humility. We can do this by considering very complex subjects that we know nothing about. The goal here is to recognise your own limitations. By cultivating the desire to learn from others, you directly oppose the attitude that thinks it knows everything.

Another useful technique is to contemplate the many ways in which you rely on others. Through recognising the benefit you receive from other people, you learn to appreciate their presence in your life. This reinforces your sense of interconnection and helps to bring everyone to the same level.

Exercise 2.7—Gratitude for Those Who Help You

- *Sit quietly for a few moments in order to calm the mind.*

- *Bring to mind all of your best qualities as a person. Think of everything that makes you really special and unique. In what ways are you better than others? Allow a sense of pride to arise. How does it feel?*

- *Now consider all of your weaknesses. Consider the areas of your life where you are not particularly skilfull. Think of examples of people who are very good at the things that you are not. Nurture an appreciation for their qualities. How does it feel?*

- *Looking back, think of how you acquired the qualities that you are so proud of. Did these qualities just naturally manifest or did they develop over time? Who did you rely on to help you develop them? Think of the role your parents and teachers have played in supporting you in your journey. Think of all the people who have made it possible for you to gain the experiences that you required to learn. Imagine what your life would have been like if they hadn't helped you when you needed it? Allow the feeling of gratitude towards these people to arise.*

- *As your focus shifts off of yourself and towards others, notice whether that sense of pride is still strong.*

- *Rest your mind for a few moments.*

Afflicted Doubt

People don't often consider doubt as a serious affliction, but in fact, it is a very negative state of mind. To achieve anything we must have conviction that we can accomplish our goal. Performing actions with hesitation or misgivings can render them weak and lead us to give up halfway through. If we never fully engage with activities then we can never fully reap the benefits that those activities have to offer. It is this type of doubt that we have to be aware of.

Let's say that you'd like to learn how to meditate. You start going to a meditation class where you learn different techniques. You like how you feel when you do them, but you are unsure about dedicating any time to the practice. There's just so much that needs to be done and you don't feel like you are capable of making the time. Because you lack the confidence to commit yourself to what you are doing, you only practice every now and again. The result is that the practice never really gathers any momentum. You end up losing interest and you move on to try something else.

This is how doubt works. It sucks the power out of your actions and causes you to constantly bounce around from this to that. Without conviction you cannot stay on course. You veer off all the time and never get anything done. The antidote to this problematic attitude is to spend the time to develop faith in whatever action you are doing. You can consider the various benefits that an action will bring you. Imagining everything you will be able to do when you complete the activity, adds energy to your determination and gives you the strength to not falter in the face of doubts. Instead of abandoning a worthwhile course of action, you learn to persevere in the face of difficulties and to finish what you start.

Exercise 2.8—Strengthening Your Conviction

- *Sit quietly for a few moments in order to calm the mind.*

- *Choose a personal aspiration you have for yourself; something you always wanted to do, but have never really gotten around to doing. Perhaps you'd like to develop a regular meditation practice or you'd like to reduce your tendency to get angry. Preferably it is something you will take some time to complete; something that will require considerable effort on your part.*

- *Bring to mind all of the benefits you will receive by fulfilling this aspiration. Identify the reasons why this activity would be a good thing for you to do. How will it help you in your life?*

- *Now consider all of the drawbacks from not pursuing your aspiration. What problems will you face? How will doing nothing change your present situation?*

- *Imagine your life after having completed this aspiration. Imagine the knowledge that you will have gained. Imagine the capacity that you will have developed. Breath life into this vision as much as you can and nurture the longing to see this potential future become a reality.*

- *Rest your mind for a few moments.*

Working with each of these meditations in regular sessions can help weaken afflictive states of mind so that they do not arise so strongly during your day-to-day experience. Remember that we are highly habituated to these mental factors and therefore, expect this process to take some time. If you are both patient and consistent, you can be sure you will see results.

Affliction	Antidote
Attachment	Contemplate the faults of the object or its impermanent nature
Aversion	Contemplate loving kindness and compassion
Ignorance	Study and reflect on the teachings
Wrong view	Challenge your views through logical reasoning and meditation on the nature of reality
Pride	Cultivate humility and an awareness of interdependence
Afflicted Doubt	Develop faith and devotion

Table 2-3: Summary of the root afflictions and their antidotes.

REVIEW OF KEY POINTS

- Mental factors are secondary minds which describe the relationship between a given subject and object pairing.

- There are five categories of mental factors: omnipresent mental factors, object-determining mental factors, root mental afflictions, derivative mental afflictions, virtuous mental factors and variable mental factors.

- We need to rely on valid perceptions so that we can make the most constructive decisions in relation to the situations that arise in our experience.

- There are three types of phenomena that we have the potential to experience: obvious, hidden and very hidden.

- There are three corresponding forms of valid perception: direct perception, logical reasoning and faith in authority. We can know obvious phenomena through direct perception. We can know hidden phenomena indirectly through logical reasoning. We can know very hidden phenomena indirectly through our faith in authoritative sources.

- To work with the afflictions you must first be able to identify when an affliction has arisen. You can also review your experience in order to identify patterns and draw insights. Once you've identified some problem areas, you can spend time contemplating the antidotes to those afflictions. The more familiar you are with these antidotes, the less powerful the affliction will become.

- There are six root afflictions: attachment, aversion, ignorance, wrong view, pride and afflicted doubt.

CHAPTER THREE

How to Meditate

Buddhist psychology is wonderful for helping to bring greater awareness into how we relate with our mind. It is, however, limited in that the insights we are able to access are directly related to the quality of mind that we have. If our mind is overwhelmed by dullness, distraction or any manner of uncontrolled emotions, then the quality of information we are likely to glean will be superficial at best. To access a deeper level of understanding, we need to learn new methods to help make our mind a more effective tool for analysis.

Meditation can be used to purify and refine our mind. On one level, it can contribute to a more balanced, calm and peaceful life, while on a deeper level, it can help us to develop an incredibly strong and focused mind. From a Buddhist perspective, when these two aspects are brought together, along with the development of greater compassion and a release of attachment to worldly interests, they have the potential to lead us to the discovery of our own enlightened nature.

This is possible because meditation works directly with the mental consciousness which is non-physical in nature. Since the mental consciousness is not limited by the physical body like the different types of sensory consciousness, it has the potential to be refined to an infinite degree of subtlety. For this reason, the practice of meditation is capable of leading to truly extraordinary results.

WHAT IS MEDITATION?

Over the last few decades, meditation has slowly been gaining in popularity around the world and many people have heard about its many benefits for health and the management of stress. Unfortunately the meaning of meditation is generally misunderstood, remaining limited and frequently oversimplified.

Meditation is much more than merely sitting down to relax. Meditation is like a vast ocean, encompassing an amazing treasury of different skills and methods.

From the Buddhist viewpoint, meditation is best described as the technological foundation for its *science of the mind*. It is the electron microscope that allows contemplative practitioners to look deep within their own experience and to gather valuable insights into the nature of their reality. Just as a scientist can observe their world through different technologies, so too can a contemplative make observations using different styles of meditation. No matter what form the meditation practice takes, its purpose is always to use the direct observation of experiences in order to facilitate a process of personal self discovery.

The Tibetan word for meditation is *gom*, meaning both "familiarity" and the process of "becoming familiar". It means learning to recognise and become habituated with the true nature of your experience. To put it more simply, it is to understand ourselves through working with our minds. As you practise meditation, you become more accustomed to a truer sense of who you are, making this view more solid and stable. Rather than just being something intellectual, this view can then become part of your living reality, enabling the development of deeper wisdom and compassion.

On a basic level, we can think of meditation as a tool for cultivating mental wellbeing and for achieving greater balance in our lives. Take for instance the tension that we are habituated to carrying around with us in our bodies. This tension arises from a combination of specific cultural influences and a compulsive flow of unhealthy thought patterns. Our mental states essentially cause energy to be locked away in different parts of the body, generating discomfort and a general lack of ease. Through meditation it is possible to calm these discursive thoughts and to discover a balanced perspective from which we can relate to the world. This balance brings greater ease to our bodies that in turn releases the pent up energy, allowing us to be more effective and clear-minded in all of our actions.

While relieving stress can be very beneficial, it is important to remember that it is not the main purpose of meditation. From the Buddhist perspective, our aim must always be to go beyond the superficial experiences of bliss and to use meditation to completely transform the way in which we relate with our daily experiences. In this way, meditation is not an escape from the harshness of reality, but instead a way of engaging more fully with everything that is happening in your life.

CATEGORIES OF MEDITATION

When we look at the broad range of meditation techniques, it is possible to identify two general categories of practice:

1. **Placement Meditation (shamatha):** This first category refers to a collection of techniques which are designed to develop a particularly focused and flexible mind known as single-pointed concentration. The essential nature of these practices is to train the mind to bring its full attention to a chosen object for as long as the meditator desires. The object that is used can vary significantly across different meditation techniques. This form of meditation can be likened to developing a laser-like mind that can be used to make extremely precise observations about the mind.

   The name Shamatha (which literally means 'calm abiding') is also used to describe the resultant state that is produced by these techniques. As the meditator progresses in this practice, their gross mind becomes dormant, revealing increasingly subtle levels of mind. Like a diver descending past the turbulent waves of the surface, he is able rest in the calm, unmoving depths of the ocean. What we call "achieving Shamatha", is the same as the meditator resting his awareness in the foundational consciousness. This state is characterised as being blissful, still and extremely vivid.

2. **Insight Meditation (vipashyana):** The second form of meditation is used to refer to any meditative technique which actively seeks to develop insight into the nature of a given phenomenon. We can think of placement meditation as a very powerful microscope and insight meditation as the experiments that you run with that microscope. The essential nature of this form of meditation is that it analyses the characteristics of a phenomenon through direct observation of that phenomenon. We

can extend this to include the indirect observation of a phenomenon through conceptual reasoning. It is for this reason that we can also refer to insight meditation as "analytical meditation".

If we think of a candle, shamatha is like the stability of the flame, while vipashyana is like the brightness. To see a picture clearly you need a flame that is both steady and bright. Similarly, to discover the true nature of your experience you need a mind that is also stable and bright. This does not mean that shamatha and vipashyana are completely separate. Many teachers liken these two methods to two ends of a stick, or two sides of a hand. The more calm and single-pointed your mind, the more likely you are to develop insight. The more insight you develop, the easier it is for your mind to be focused and calm. In order to completely eradicate negative emotions and unproductive mental states, it is necessary for both to be present. This is known as the *union of shamatha and vipashyana*.

THE BASIC STRUCTURE OF MEDITATION PRACTICE

No matter which technique you are currently emphasising, all formal meditation practice uses a similar structure:

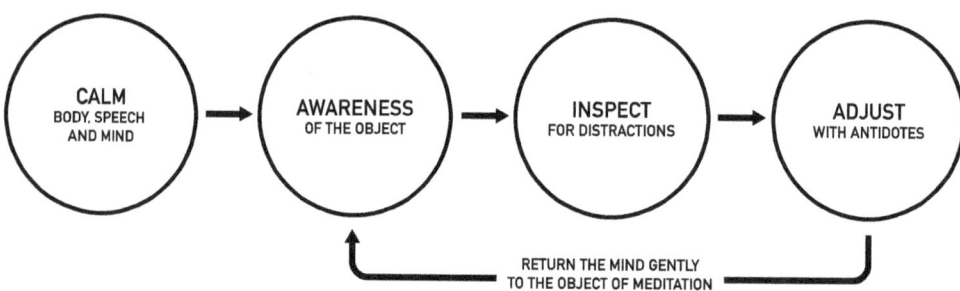

Figure 3-1 Structure for a typical meditation session.

This basic procedure can be used to observe a fairly simple object like the flow of the breath, or it can be used to observe a more complex object such as an elaborate mental image. Whichever object we choose, we use two basic faculties to train the quality of our mind:

1. **Mindfulness:** This is our capacity to remember what it is that we are intending to do. When we are mindful, we are fully engaged with our object. It is the opposite of being distracted. We can think of it like the glue which keeps us connected with an object.

2. **Introspection:** This is our capacity to be aware of what is presently happening in the mind. It is like a security guard that is able to "check up" and make sure that we aren't carried away in some form of excitation or sinking into laxity. Introspection allows us to control the quality of mind. It is a trigger for engaging mindfulness and bringing our attention back to the object.

As these two faculties grow in strength, the mind becomes increasingly more refined. The specific qualities which characterise this state of mind are:

1. **Relaxation:** Through the process of meditation the body learns to let go of all its habitual tensions, resulting in a blissful feeling of spaciousness and ease. This quality is the foundation which allows our attention to sustain itself for as long as we desire.

2. **Stability:** Through the repeated application of mindfulness, the mind becomes absorbed in the chosen object. This is likened to achieving a state of "flow", in which you are totally focused on what you are doing with no distractions.

3. **Vividness:** Through the cultivation of introspection, we are able to achieve a heightened awareness of what is happening within the mind. This awareness allows us to pick up more and more aspects of the object, like watching high-definition television.

These three qualities are like the roots, trunk and foliage of a tree. As our practice grows, the roots of relaxation go deeper, the trunk of stability gets stronger and the foliage of vividness reaches higher.

THE BENEFITS OF MEDITATION

The key to meditation is to develop a continuity of practice that allows you to build up these qualities over time. One of the biggest challenges for a beginning meditator is to maintain the discipline needed to develop this continuity. When we lose our inspiration to practise or find ourselves procrastinating, it can be helpful to reflect upon the different benefits that a healthy meditation practice can bring to our lives:

1. **Increased Awareness:** Meditation practice increases our awareness of what is going on in our lives. With greater awareness, we can learn to approach life in a more calm and clear manner. This can help you to feel present and grounded with a greater sense of connection to all of your experiences. Instead of being dominated by your emotions and thoughts, you can learn to engage more fully with life without losing your perspective.

2. **Creates Space for Choice:** Meditation practice provides you with space to make constructive decisions. As you become less reactionary to external events, you become more capable of understanding how different situations arise. This insight gives you the opportunity to choose how best to respond. In this way you are able to bring greater wisdom, patience and kindness into your relationships.

3. **Improves Health:** The mind and body are inextricably linked. Destructive mental states can contribute to a wide variety of illnesses. Through meditation, you can develop improved coping skills, memory recollection, greater efficiency of brain functions, better sleeping patterns, increased relaxation responses, less anxiety and depression and in some cases a decrease in chronic pain. While meditation is not a magic bullet, it has been proven to have a significant effect on the overall health of those who practise it. It has been documented to reduce blood pressure and heart rate, improve immune functions and benefit a wide range of physical conditions such as heart disease, diabetes and even cancer. As the scientific community continues its research into the correlations of meditation and health, we will likely see more benefits emerge.

4. **Makes Enlightenment Possible:** Ultimately though, for a Buddhist practitioner, the greatest benefit of authentic meditation practice is that

it is the key to opening the door to enlightenment. It does this by providing us with the mental acuity that is needed in order to observe the very nature of reality. Through meditation, we can explore the very subtle level of our minds and unlock our greatest potential.

Regardless of your personal intention, if you set out on this journey with sincerity you will undoubtedly receive many benefits from the transformative process that meditation practice has to offer.

BEGINNING A MEDITATION PRACTICE

Now that we have been introduced to the general aspects of what meditation is, we can begin to look at what is needed in order to develop a personal meditation practice. When we are just starting, it is important not to over complicate things. Meditation is actually a very simple process. The key is to give yourself the chance to experience the benefits of this process.

For that, we need to first create a space in our busy schedules where we can begin to familiarise ourselves with these techniques. We have the tendency to think we don't have any time, and yet this is not really true. We make time for all manner of activities that bring us no significant benefit. In fact, many of the activities we engage in directly contribute to our personal suffering. So before we start making excuses for why we can't meditate, we need to take a really sincere look at our daily habits.

Exercise 3.1—Finding Time

- *Sit quietly for a few moments in order to calm your mind.*

- *Consider your daily routine. Start from when you get up, through to when you go to sleep. Get a sense for where you are spending your time. What are your priorities?*

- *Now consider the benefits that you derive from those activities. For instance, what is the result of watching TV for two hours? We do not have to be judgemental about these activities, simply identify what you get out of it.*

- *Can you see any opportunities in your schedule for ten, fifteen or thirty minutes of time, that you could use to be alone and dedicate to developing your mind? If not, are there any habits that you have that you could reduce in order to make space in your schedule? For example, what would happen if you woke up fifteen minutes earlier than normal? Would you be willing to lose fifteen minutes of dreaming in order to develop greater balance in your life? Consider other changes that you could make in your routine that would provide you with more opportunities to practise.*

Choosing a Meditation Object

Once we have created a time for our meditation practice, we can begin by choosing an appropriate object of focus. We can choose to work exclusively with one type of meditation object or we can choose from a variety of methods. There are in fact an infinite number of meditation objects to suit people with different temperaments and personality types.

Your choice can be based on your experience or preference, or a teacher can recommend one to you. A particular object is usually chosen to help you overcome a particular weakness, or because it builds on your strengths. For example, if you have a short temper, loving kindness may be a suitable object as it can serve as an antidote to your anger. If your personality is more oriented towards feelings, you may be drawn to a devotional practice, using the mental image of a Buddha as an object. Similarly, for those who like to think a lot, you may be suited to certain forms of analytical meditation.

If your aim is to achieve single-pointed concentration, then as your concentration begins to improve, you may choose to shift your focus to objects which are increasingly more subtle. In the beginning a moving object such as slow walking or breathing may be most suitable, but at a certain point it is better to concentrate on a stable, non-moving object such as a holy image or a mental visualisation. Always remember that to reach the subtle states of our mind we will eventually need to work with the mental consciousness directly.

Traditionally, meditation objects can be divided into eight categories or types:

1. **Breathing Meditations:** If your mind is afflicted predominantly with excessive thoughts (which is quite common with our busy and tense lifestyles) focusing on the natural flow of the breath can be an effective way to relax the body and mind. It includes spontaneous breathing and controlled breathing. The use of the breath as a meditation object is described at great length later in the next chapter.

2. **Mental Visualisations:** For those with a background in Christianity or other faith-based religions and are drawn to prayer or devotional practices, you might find visualising a deity such as Jesus, the Virgin Mary or Buddha most effective. A visualisation could also be something as simple as imagining a candle or flower.

3. **Mantra Meditations:** Especially suited to those with an intuitive personality-type, this is where a sound or group of syllables is repeated. You may be attracted to a particular form depending on your personal temperament. Some examples from Buddhism are provided in the table below:

Buddha Figure	Mantra	Attributes to Develop
Manjushri	OM AH RA PA TSA NA DHI	Wisdom
Chenrezig	OM MANI PADME HUNG	Compassion
Vajrapani	HUNG VAJRA PHET	Compassionate power and strength
Medicine Buddha	TAYATA OM BEKANZE BEKANZE MAHA BEKANZE RADZA SAMUDGATE SVAHA	Healing
Green Tara	OM TARE TUTARE TURE SVAHA	Strength to overcome obstacles and achieve all activities

Table 3-1: Common Buddhist mantras.

4. **Movement Meditations:** Mindfulness of body movement such as in slow walking or yoga is another effective focus for relaxing and concentrating the mind. For walking meditation, you can focus intently on each

movement of each foot, synchronising them with the breath; breathing in, aware of the left foot, breathing out, aware of the right foot. You can also combine slow walking with a mantra such as *"bud-dho"* which is commonly used in the Thai tradition. With each step you quietly recite one syllable.

5. **Meditation on Energy Centres (chakras):** Energy centres are another type of meditation object, although in Tibetan Buddhism they are generally used in advanced practices. Performing these practices as a beginner is like building a house without a solid foundation, and is unlikely to lead to much benefit. Several non-Buddhist yogic schools offer powerful methods to activate the chakras and can be very effective for certain types of people.

6. **Jhana Meditations:** Once a meditator has achieved the state of Shamatha, then they are able to continue through a process of progressively more subtle states of absorption known as Jñanas. You can learn more about these techniques in my book *"An Authentic Guide to Meditation"*.

7. **Analytical Meditations:** It is possible to use the process of thinking as a meditative object. In this practice the meditator chooses a topic to reflect upon such as impermanence, loving kindness or karma. The practice is to maintain a train of thought without getting lost in distractions. We will be examining this form of meditation in greater detail during subsequent chapters.

8. **Awareness Meditations:** This type of meditation focuses on taking the mind itself as the object of meditation. It can be practised objectively by focusing on the space of the mind and the various contents of that mind (such as thoughts, feeling, etc), or it can be focused subjectively on the awareness itself. In both these approaches you are developing a mind that is undistracted and free from grasping.

The first five categories explicitly emphasise the development of single-pointed concentration, while the final three categories are more focused on developing insight. That being said, each category does have the potential to develop both concentration and insight.

Main Emphasis	Object	Personality Type
Concentration	Breathing	Prone to excessive thoughts
	Mental Visualisation	Devotional
	Mantra Recitation	Intuitive
	Movement	Restless
	Energy Centres	Focused Mind
Insight	Mental Absorption	Advanced Practitioner
	Analysis	Thinker
	Awareness	Relaxed

Table 3-2: Types of meditation objects.

Creating the Right Environment for Meditation

For a seed to grow into a tree, certain conditions are required, such as fertile soil, sunlight and rain. Similarly, in order to train the mind in meditation, we need various outer and inner conditions. The following are the primary conditions that you will need to maximise the benefit that you derive from your practice.

The Right Location

It is helpful to prepare a location that is conducive to meditation practice. Ideally, it should be quiet, clean, free from clutter and free from interruptions or distractions. Certain locations suit different types of practice. For example, a peaceful forest environment can help with the development of calm and concentration, while a vast open view can be an effective place to cultivate insight. An environment which is noisy or contains many distractions may be a hindrance for beginners, however if you can develop a good meditation practice in spite of such challenges this may actually lead to greater accomplishment.

The Right Posture

As we have seen, our mind can have significant effects on our physical body. Likewise the body has an important effect on our state of mind. It is therefore very important that we establish a physical posture that is conducive to developing a stable mind. As long as we are embodied beings, we need to be skilful in the way we make use of our body. If the meditator is likened to a passenger that wishes to cross a great ocean, then the body can be thought of like a boat to carry us across. Once we get to the other side though, the boat is no longer needed.

During meditation it is important that our posture allows us to be relaxed and comfortable while maintaining a state that is both alert and aware. The posture we choose will have a direct influence on our ability to remain still over potentially long periods of time. Therefore, it is worthwhile taking the time to get it right. The following postures can be used for both formal or informal sessions of meditation:

1. **Sitting:** When sitting, you should use a comfortable, straight-backed padded chair, a meditation stool or a cushion on the floor. The hands rest together either in the lap or on the thighs, while the back is straight like an arrow and the chin is slightly tucked in.

2. **Lying down:** If your mind is agitated you can also lie on your back with your arms by your side and hands open, although this posture should be avoided if your mind is dull. To support a greater clarity of mind, you can lie on the right side with your right hand underneath your face, legs together with the knees slightly bent and your left arm down the left side of your body.

3. **Walking and standing:** Be sure to have an upright but relaxed posture with your arms hanging naturally in front of your body. You should hold your right hand in your left, or you can interlace your fingers if you find this difficult.

The Seven-Point Posture of Vairochana

For Buddhist meditation, one particular posture has been proven to be particularly effective. Each aspect of this posture helps the meditator to control the flow of energy in his body, which in turn assists him to achieve higher states of concentration.

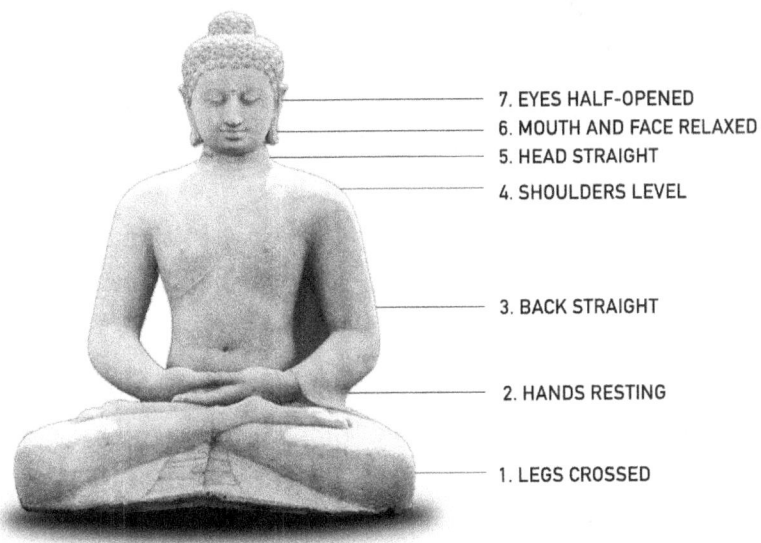

7. EYES HALF-OPENED
6. MOUTH AND FACE RELAXED
5. HEAD STRAIGHT
4. SHOULDERS LEVEL

3. BACK STRAIGHT

2. HANDS RESTING

1. LEGS CROSSED

Figure 3-2: Seven main points for a stable meditation posture.

The posture consists of the following features:

1. **Legs (crossed):** Ideally the legs should be crossed in what is known as the vajra posture, which has the left foot resting on the right thigh and the right foot on the left thigh. If this position is too difficult, any comfortable cross-legged posture will do, although it should be noted that more stability is achieved if the buttocks are raised so that the hips tilt forward. As our bodies are very sensitive to our environment, sitting on the ground can connect you to the immense earth beneath, giving you a sense of its great energy. A good cross-legged position provides excellent physical balance and also represents a union of method and wisdom.

   Equally important to sitting in the appropriate position is to be comfortable. The optimal sitting posture contributes to the development of your meditation, but sitting comfortably means that you will be less distracted in your meditation and you will find it much easier to relax your body. You may therefore choose to sit on a chair with your legs relaxed, knees at right angles and buttocks firmly supported by the chair, remembering to keep your back straight.

2. **Hands (in the lap):** Hands should rest gently in the lap, with the right hand placed on top of the left hand, palms facing up. For female meditators placing the left hand on top of the right may be more effective. The tips of the thumbs should touch slightly a little below the navel. The position of the hands expresses the unification of method and wisdom during your practice. You should feel a sense of relaxation from your shoulders to your wrists and down to your hands, allowing any tension in your upper body to be released.

3. **Back (spine straight):** The body should be held upright like an arrow or a pile of golden coins placed one on top of the other. Care should be taken not to lean sideways, backward or forward. A straight back helps your mind stay alert and attentive and also has an enormous effect on the inner winds, which are the subtle movements of energy that circulate within the body and mind. These winds are closely related to the breath and in certain advanced practices, can be used with great effect. Once you have settled into position, take a moment to imagine your body from the top of your head to your base. You can make slight adjustments throughout the meditation to ensure your posture is balanced and straight. The goal is to remain still, relaxed and alert; being stiff and immobile is a hindrance to awareness.

4. **Shoulders and elbows (drawn back and slightly away from the body):** The shoulders and arms should be drawn back a little and slightly curved so they are evenly placed on either side of the body. This helps the lungs to expand correctly and aids breathing during meditation. The elbows should remain a little away from the body.

5. **Head and neck (chin slightly lowered):** The head should be straight and centred; not too high or bent down too low. Keep the chin slightly tucked in and the nose held in line with the navel. Try not to bend the neck sideways or backwards.

6. **Mouth (face relaxed and tip of the tongue touching the upper palate):** The teeth and lips should be held in a natural position with the

teeth barely touching. Keeping the face and jaw relaxed will help prevent excessive swallowing, while placing the tip of the tongue gently behind the upper teeth helps to sharpen the mind and avoid dryness and dribbling. If your mind is quite agitated and you find it difficult to achieve a calm state, placing the tongue behind the bottom teeth can aid in loosening and calming the mind.

7. **Eyes (gazing past the tip of the nose):** The eyes should not be opened too wide, nor should they be completely closed. If they are too widely opened you may become easily distracted, and if completely closed your mind may become foggy or dull. When beginning, however, keeping the eyes softly closed may help your body enter into a deeper state of relaxation. After meditating like this for a little while, you will naturally become more balanced and may want to open the eyes slightly. If you are using a visualised object as your focus for meditation, or if you find your mind is too agitated, you are likely to benefit from closing your eyes.

    There are different methods of directing your gaze. The first is to gaze directly in front of you at any colour that is not too bright, or at a pleasant or holy object such as a flower or an image of the Buddha. The second more common method is to direct the eyes downwards; gently and serenely gazing into the space a little in front of the tip of your nose. Keep your eyes still without focusing too strongly and allow natural blinking to occur. Both these methods are suitable for beginners. Other specific meditation methods involve gazing upward into an expansive space with eyes wide open. This may actually happen quite naturally when the mind has reached a certain level of calm and clear insight begins to arise.

Anyone who perseveres with practising the *Seven-point Posture of Vairochana*, regardless of how hard or painful it may initially seem, will eventually find it extremely comfortable and beneficial for health. The main benefit, however, is that it will assist your meditation practice and mental development in the long-term. If you are not really concerned about practising intensively and attaining shamatha, it is just as effective to practise in any position that you find comfortable and easy to relax in.

The Right Attitude

For Buddhist practitioners the right attitude refers to many important inner conditions, such as possessing the correct motivation and intention. These aspects are necessary for successful progress on the spiritual path. For those just beginning with a meditation practice however, having the right attitude can be viewed in a more practical sense. As you enter into your practice, you should let go of your personal story, abandoning whatever concerns you may have about the past or future. Try to bring your mind into this present moment, free from distractions and expectations. In particular, you should abandon thoughts of discouragement if your practice is not going well, and avoid being carried away by pride and excitement if you encounter "good" experiences during meditation.

Preliminary Practices

In order to begin meditation with a mind that is calm and receptive, it is useful to carry out a few preliminary practices:

1. **Exhaling the foul air:** The first of these is a brief practice from the Tibetan tradition which involves visualising all your impurities as smoke and forcefully blowing them out through your nostrils over three deep breaths. This helps to remove from the subtle body the counterproductive currents of energy which are associated with attachment, aversion and ignorance. As the breath and mind are intimately connected, this practice is an excellent starting point for any meditation. Science has also discovered that three deep breaths switches on the parasympathetic nervous system, bringing on the relaxation response in the body.

2. **Rocking the body:** The second preliminary practice is to rock your body from side to side until it comes to its natural resting place. Check that your spine is straight without being tight, and relax into the position. The purpose of this is to create a stable base for the meditation practice.

3. **Becoming aware of all outside phenomena:** Become aware now of your sensory experience by taking in the sounds, tastes, smells and sights that are occurring around you. The aim is to bring the mind completely into the present moment without creating a storyline. Just be present.

Exercise 3.2—A Simple Practice of Mindfulness of Breathing

Preliminary Practices:

- *Take a moment to review your posture, ensuring that you are seated in a relaxed and yet vigilant way.*

- *Take three long deep breaths, and with each exhalation, imagine releasing all of your worries and concerns.*

- *Rocking your body gently from side to side, allow your body to settle into position.*

- *Now consciously release all memories of the past and all plans for the future. Bring your awareness into this present moment. This is your time and for the length of this session, nothing else matters.*

Main Practice:

- *Allow your awareness to completely fill your body, like a nebulous cloud that spans from the top of your head to the point where your body meets with the ground. At this point, simply become aware of the various tactile sensations within your body.*

- *Of these sensations, identify those sensations that you relate to the steady rhythm of your in and out breaths. You don't need to do anything to create these sensations, simply observe what sensations naturally arise.*

- *See if you can maintain your awareness of one full cycle of breath. Observe how it feels when the air flows in. Observe how it feels when the inhalation stops and the air begins to flow out. Observe how it feels when all of the air is released. Observe how it feels as you wait for the next breath to arise.*

- *Spend some time becoming familiar with this process.*

- *Now use each out breath as an opportunity to further release all tensions in your body and mind. As you breathe out, allow yourself to become more and more relaxed, while at the same time remaining clear and present.*

- *Using your faculty of introspection, checkup every now and again to ensure that you are not slipping into a stupor or falling asleep. If you do find that you are getting dull, then brighten your mind by paying greater attention to the in breath. When you are once again present and engaged, return to focusing on the out breath.*

- *Continue in this way for the remainder of the session.*

OBSTACLES TO MEDITATION PRACTICE

Learning to meditate is not easy. For most people it can be the first time they make a conscious effort to look at their mind and are therefore quite surprised to discover how noisy it actually is. Focusing the mind on a single object may sound relatively simple, but in actuality, it is a significantly challenging task and just as with learning any other skill, it takes practise.

Being aware of the obstacles that are commonly faced when practising meditation is therefore an important step in making progress in your practice. This knowledge allows you to understand the current state of your mind, which then enables you to apply the appropriate methods to overcome obstacles. The hindrances that emerge during meditation are often the same as the hindrances that emerge in daily life, so by learning to deal with them in formal sessions, you are developing a very useful skill. Being aware of the obstacles can also help you to make a more realistic assessment of your present capacity and thereby avoid unrealistic expectations about your practice. This will make it easier to develop constructive habits over the course of time. At a more advanced level, it can also help you identify precisely what stage of the meditation path you have reached and how to proceed even further.

The Five Faults and the Eight Antidotes

The five faults and eight antidotes provide us with an effective framework to recognise and overcome the hindrances which interfere with our ability to meditate. They describe the different obstacles to successful meditation that emerge as you progress through the different attentional states leading to Shamatha. Knowledge of these faults and their antidotes can help you deal with them as quickly and effectively as possible, not only during meditation but in daily life as well. The five faults, along with their corresponding antidotes, are as follows:

1. Laziness

(Antidotes: aspiration, faith, diligence and mental pliancy)

Laziness is a stagnant state of mind that can prevent us from even sitting on the cushion to begin with. It can therefore be a major obstacle to our practise of meditation. Coming in different guises, it is more than just hanging around and doing nothing. We can in fact identify three types of laziness:

1. **Complacency:** This is when we have a disinterest or are uninspired to meditate. Complacency occurs when we would rather lie on the couch and watch television.

2. **Lack of self-confidence:** This refers to lack of self-confidence in our ability to meditate, creating the feeling that we could not possibly attain any realisations such as Shamatha or any other achievements.

3. **Being habitually busy:** Also known as active laziness, this type can be quite deceptive as it occurs when we occupy ourselves with many worldly tasks. We can find the energy to catch up with friends or go to the movies, but the thought of meditating makes us feel suddenly tired.

Laziness can be overcome by developing *faith* in the excellent qualities that meditation can produce, both within our practice and within our daily lives; only then will we value meditation enough to make it a priority in our life. The more we realise the benefits, the more *aspiration* we will have to practise, which in turn encourages the development of *diligence* and joyful effort. Through the power of familiarity we can achieve *physical and mental pliancy*—a unique and blissful flexibility of body and mind.

If you become discouraged because you do not feel you are making progress, it can be helpful to recognise the incredible effort we put into other areas of our lives, such as bringing up children or learning a trade. If we really consider the benefits of meditation, we may come to the conclusion that it is worth devoting time and effort to the task of developing our mind.

2. Not Knowing or Forgetting the Instructions
(Antidote: mindfulness)

This fault refers to a lack of mindfulness on how to meditate properly. It occurs when the object of meditation is forgotten or the instructions have not been learnt adequately so the mind frequently wanders off to other objects. Changing the meditation focus too often, especially within a single session, is also a sign of this fault.

The remedy for this is to cultivate a level of *mindfulness* that allows you to retain the object of meditation and prevents you from forgetting the instructions. Mindfulness refers both to remembering the instructions and engaging the mind so it becomes "full" of the object. Once you have established some mindfulness, you can begin to develop *vigilance*. This means observing the meditating mind itself and detecting when the mind has wandered off the object, even in a subtle way. You will then be able to apply the appropriate remedy. It is like a non-participating commentator reporting on what is happening but not actually joining in.

3. Mental Dullness and Agitation
(Antidote: vigilance)

Coarse Agitation

During the beginning stages of meditation the mind can appear quite agitated. It frequently moves toward external stimuli such as the sounds of activity going on around us. It also constantly wanders off, thinking other thoughts. It could be a song, a scenario from earlier in the day, or an idea about what to cook for dinner; anything other than the meditation object. This agitation occurs when concentration is held too tightly or you have not sufficiently relaxed, causing you to hold tension in your body. When the distracted mind veers off its object of focus completely, it can be quite easy to detect. In the beginning however, it may take several minutes for the untrained mind to actually notice that the object has been lost. Coarse agitation is likened to the movement of a cloud, which is easy to recognise when it occurs.

Applying the remedy is generally not too difficult at this stage and there are several things that can be attempted. You can lower the object, imagining that it is quite heavy. Relaxing your body by concentrating on bodily sensations or placing your tongue against your bottom teeth with your eyes closed for awhile can be helpful. Another technique to subdue the mind is to visualise a black dot by your seat. If you are very fidgety, physical exercise will tire you and cause the mind to wander less. Initially wandering thoughts may take some time to detect, but with time and practise such awareness becomes natural.

Coarse Dullness

This arises when the mind lacks clarity and becomes excessively withdrawn. We feel cloudy and on the verge of falling asleep. Here, clarity refers to a clear, fresh and bright state of mind, rather than to clarity of the meditation object.

You can brighten or elevate the object of meditation by slightly raising your eyes or paying closer attention to its details, as if you would fall off the edge of a cliff should you lose the object. Recollecting something wholesome or inspiring or imagining a white light at your forehead between your eyes can brighten the mind as well. Another technique is to meditate at an elevated location with a vast view, or to find a place which is cool and breezy. Splashing your face with water, exercising outdoors and adhering to a light diet can also help.

You must take great care however, to distinguish tiredness due to laziness, from tiredness because you genuinely need rest. It is worth noting that ill will towards oneself, such as having unrealistic expectations of one's practise, can manifest as tiredness. If you are genuinely weary, you will continue to feel fatigued despite applying the above remedies. In this case it is important to rest, as pushing too hard can be counterproductive.

Subtle Agitation

Subtle agitation is harder to recognise and occurs when part of the mind is comfortably resting on the object of meditation while another part has wandered off without you noticing. Much more difficult to detect, it is likened to a quickly moving monkey.

To remedy subtle agitation you must develop a particularly strong and powerful *vigilance*. This cannot be obtained through intellectual means; only via your own experience and practice. Through the momentum gained with repeated practice, your mind will eventually be able to identify subtle agitation as soon as it arises and return quickly to the object.

Subtle Dullness (sinking)

The fault of subtle dullness, or sinking, is not usually a problem for beginners as they are generally too agitated. It is only recognised when a meditator is more advanced and has the ability to focus on the object with some degree of stability. Subtle dullness occurs when there is fixation and some clarity but no intensity. This means there is little vitality or strength with which the object is being held. This is much harder to detect and eliminate. Many meditators in fact become stuck here, feeling as though their meditation is going very well. This is a common trap.

The remedy for subtle sinking is to develop a particularly strong, powerful and vivid intensity, which can only be cultivated with incredible discipline. This is not something that can be described intellectually but only experienced by skilled practitioners. It can also help to refresh the mind by reflecting on a topic that inspires you, such as gratitude towards your teacher, and the incredible benefits of training the mind. These thoughts exalt and uplift the mind.

4. Under-Application
(Antidote: application of remedies)

This means not taking enough action to correct dullness, agitation or laziness when they arise. You fail to apply the remedy, often because you are too lethargic or complacent.

The remedy here is to take action and *apply the relevant antidote*. Sometimes it can help to interrupt the meditation by walking around for a while, stretching the body, splashing your face with cool water or getting some fresh air. On returning to your seat you may find it easier to resume your meditation. Again it can also help to bring to mind the many benefits of meditation practice.

5. Over-Application
(Antidote: equanimity)

This is the mistake of applying remedies when they are not necessary, or applying them excessively. An example might be when sinking and agitation have been recognised and corrected, you still continue to apply more corrective action.

The antidote to this problem is to apply *equanimity*. In other words, leave it alone.

If you memorise these five faults and eight antidotes, your meditations will no longer be a "hit and miss" affair, but rather a dynamic process from which you are sure to benefit.

Fault	Antidote
1. Laziness	1. Aspiration
	2. Faith
	3. Diligence
	4. Mental pliancy
2. Not Knowing or Forgetting the Instructions	5. Mindfulness
3. Mental Dullness and Agitation	6. Vigilance
4. Under-Application	7. Application of Remedies
5. Over-Application	8. Equanimity

Table 3-3: The Five Faults and Eight Antidotes.

The Five Hindrances

Like the five faults, the five hindrances can completely dominate your practise. As you progress along the meditation path however, they will gradually weaken and subside, allowing you to discover a mind which is naturally calm and clear.

1. Sensory Desire

Sensory desire refers to an attachment to objects of the five senses—attractive sights, sounds, smells, tastes and tactile sensations. When we meditate, we are attempting to transcend our senses by letting go of our concern for our body. This hindrance therefore manifests when our mind "goes to" distractions such as the pain in our back, the smell of the neighbor's BBQ or music coming from the room next door.

The key to overcoming this hindrance is to abandon it little by little. First you can learn to be mindful and receptive of sense objects without reacting to them, and gradually you will be less inclined to be distracted or "pulled away" by them in meditation.

2. Ill Will

Ill will in meditation appears as a dislike toward the object of focus or the meditation itself, causing the mind to wander elsewhere. It can also be directed toward oneself through feelings of guilt or unreasonable expectations.

The remedy for this hindrance is to generate love and kindness toward the object of ill will. Meditation can sometimes seem like a chore, so it can be helpful to view it as a dear friend, whom you have come to love and appreciate. Being kind toward yourself is also very important as learning to understand your faults and having the courage to forgive them, allows you to let them go and move on.

3. Dullness and Drowsiness

This hindrance refers to a heaviness of body and dullness of mind which causes intermittent mindfulness. It can actually lead to falling asleep whilst meditating without even realising it.

The key to overcoming dullness is to first make peace with it and stop fighting it; otherwise the mind tends to swing wildly between dullness and agitation. If you are in a relaxed state and begin to slip into dullness, it is important to tighten the mind slightly, perking up your alertness as if you were walking on the edge of a cliff face. You can also reflect on the precious opportunity you have to develop your mind with meditation practice or other inspirational topics. If you still feel tired however, it is best to just rest rather than force the meditation. Sometimes dullness may not be the problem but rather ill will, as we tend to escape into dullness if we don't enjoy what we are doing.

4. Restlessness

Restlessness occurs when our mind moves from one thought to the next and then on to the next thought and then on to another; like a monkey continually swinging from branch to branch.

Restlessness is overcome by cultivating an inner sense of contentment, free from expectations and happy to be still and silent. It can also help to loosen up the meditation and ensure the body is relaxed.

5. Uncertainty or Doubt

This hindrance arises when we ask ourselves inner questions while trying to still the mind and focus on the meditation object. We may ask ourselves "Can I do this?" "Why am I bothering with this, what's the point?" Doubt can also take the form of constant assessing; "I wonder what attentional state I have reached?", or "How is my practice going?" Such questions are obstacles as they are posed at the wrong time, and so only serve to distract.

This can be overcome by understanding why we take the time to meditate, possessing clear instructions before beginning, and having a good teacher to guide you. Self-doubt can be overcome with determination and experience, while reviewing your meditation at the end of the session is far more skilful than during the practice.

Hindrance	Antidote
1. Sensory Desire	Reduce sensory pull through mindfulness.
2. Ill Will	Direct loving-kindness to oneself
3. Dullness and Drowsiness	Recognise it, don't fight it.
4. Restlessness	Cultivate contentment
5. Uncertainty or Doubt	Understand the benefits of meditation and know what you are doing.

Table 3-4: The Five Hindrances.

REVIEW OF KEY POINTS

- Meditation is a collection of techniques that help us to familiarise our minds with positive qualities.

- There are two main forms of meditation: placement meditation and insight meditation. Placement meditation is also known as shamatha and involves improving the quality of our mind. Insight meditation is also known as vipashyana and helps us to develop wisdom about the nature of different mental phenomena.

- There are two faculties that we use during a typical meditation session: mindfulness and introspection. Mindfulness keeps our mind engaged with the object of meditation, while introspection helps us to recognise when our mind has become distracted.

- Meditation helps us to develop three positive qualities of the mind: relaxation, stability and vividness. Relaxation allows us to sustain our attention over time. Stability allows us to keep our mind focused on an object. Vividness allows us to observe increasingly subtler characteristics of the object that we are meditating on.

- Meditation has many benefits such as increasing our general awareness, creating space for us to make wise decisions, improving our physical health, and making it possible to develop our spiritual potential.

- In order to experience the benefits of meditation you must make time for regular practise.

- There are different meditation objects that you can choose, depending on your personality type and specific needs.

- Part of setting up a successful meditation practice is to have the right location, right posture and right attitude.

- There are many obstacles which can arise in meditative practice. By understanding the five faults and the five hindrances, you can develop the capacity to apply antidotes and thereby improve the quality of your sessions.

CHAPTER FOUR

Stages of Meditation

Meditation is a process that develops over an extended period of time. It is a process that is specifically designed to tame the mind and make it flexible enough so we can use it in a constructive way. We can think of our mind like a mischievous sheep who keeps escaping from the herd. While the shepherd is busy tending to the other sheep, this one sheep keeps wandering off into the mountains. The shepherd goes looking for this sheep, eventually finding her and bring her home to safety. But the sheep is persistent and keeps running away, so the shepherd keeps an eye on this particular sheep and is able to catch her before she gets too far. Each time, he calmly collects the sheep and brings her back to the shelter of the herd. The shepherd becomes so aware of this little sheep that soon he is able to catch her the moment she steps a hoof in the direction of the mountains. Eventually, the sheep learns to stay with the herd and the shepherd no longer needs to chase after her.

In a similar fashion, through the use of the two faculties of mindfulness and introspection, the meditator learns how to monitor and direct the mind in a consistent way. The more that we use these qualities, the stronger they become. Over time they allow us to condition the mind in such a way, that it no longer gets lost among all its distractions, becoming capable of being used more effectively for whatever task we intend to do.

Through years of contemplative research, the great meditators of the past have identified a consistent sequence of stages that a practitioner will pass through as she engages with these practices. These experiences form a clear map we can all follow, helping us to recognise our own position within this process. As we will see, being able to accurately evaluate one's own development can be useful to draw our attention to the different obstacles we are likely to face at any given stage.

USING THE BREATH AS AN OBJECT

In order to illustrate this process, we will walk through each of the stages of meditation using the tactile sensations of the breath as our object of meditation. For those with a very busy, stimulating environment, prone to excessive thinking and anxiety, *mindfulness of breathing* is a particularly effective method for overcoming the nervous energy that drives these problems. Of all of the methods taught by the Buddha, this one was by far the most popular.

The exercises in this chapter are drawn specifically from the *Satipatthana Sutta* in the Theravada tradition. The Buddha gave this teaching in order to demonstrate how mindfulness of breathing could be used as a basis for generating the union of shamatha and vipashyana. The first portion of this teaching gives instructions for sixteen ways of focusing on the breath (anapanasati), each designed to effectively calm the mind down while at the same time, developing a clear awareness of one's present experience. Together, these practices represent a gradual progression that can be summarised in five stages:

1. Mindfulness of the present

2. Placing the mind on the object

3. Keeping the mind on the object

4. Fine-tuning the mind

5. Unifying the mind

I will be describing these stages in greater detail below so for now, it is sufficient to know that the first two of these stages emphasise the development of relaxation. The third emphasises the cultivation of mindfulness which results in increased stability of concentration. While the fourth and fifth stages emphasise the cultivation of greater clarity or vividness of attention, based on the foundation of relaxation and stability previously developed.

Progression through these phases is not black and white. During one session you may reach different levels at different times. On some days you may experience stage one, while other days you may experience stage three. We can therefore more accurately gauge our present capacity, based on the average experience taken from multiple sessions over a given period of time. When you are consistently experiencing a given stage, then you can be considered to have "attained" that stage. Bare in mind though, that grasping onto these stages as things to achieve can introduce a number of obstacles into your practice. It is much better to maintain a relaxed and patient approach, free from any unnecessary expectations.

Within the Tibetan tradition, these five stages of meditation are understood on the basis of nine attentional states. This teaching was first presented by the great Indian scholar Kamalashila during his commentary on the teachings of Buddha Maitreya. These nine attentional states are defined as:

1. Placing the mind on an object

2. Continuous placement

3. Patched placement

4. Close placement

5. Disciplining the mind

6. Pacifying the mind

7. Fully pacifying the mind

8. One-pointedness

9. Equanimity

The main difference between these two approaches is that the five stages focus more on the quality of mind being developed, while the nine attentional states focus more on the types of obstacles that arise.

THE FIVE STAGES AND NINE ATTENTIONAL STATES

In order to gain a more detailed understanding of this process, we will merge the two systems into a single presentation. The relationship of each stage, relative to each attentional state is illustrated in the following table:

Stage of Meditation	Attentional State	Emphasis
1. Mindfulness of the present moment		Relaxation
2. Placing the mind on the object	1. Placing the mind	
	2. Continuous placement	
3. Keeping the mind on the object	3. Patched Placement	Mindfulness
	4. Close Placement	
	5. Disciplining	
4. Fine tuning the mind	6. Pacifying	Vigilance
	7. Fully Pacifying	
5. Unifying the mind	8. One-pointedness	
	9. Equanimity	

Table 4-1: The Five Stages and the Nine Attentional States.

Stage 1—Mindfulness of the Present Moment

For many of us, life is a constant bombardment of sensory stimulation and frantically juggling a seemingly endless stream of things that need to be done. Not surprisingly then, when we first sit down to meditate, it can be quite difficult to remain mindful of the meditation object. Therefore the aim of this first stage, is to create a receptive frame of mind that is able to actually engage with the object.

The sad reality is that no matter how carefully we select our location to practice, there will always be something to distract us. At first it might be the sound of a dog barking in the distance. This sound might trigger a train of thoughts like, "I need to buy some food for my dog. I hope my dog is alright. I miss my dog. I can't wait to see my dog." Before we know it, we are lost in a cascade of mental chit chat.

In order to reduce our environment's capacity to trigger such distractions, we need to train ourselves to accept the conditions around us. Rather than reacting to the external stimuli, we simply notice it and accept it, without being carried away by it. Use the breath to consciously relax the body and anchor your awareness to be present within the moment and present within your body.

Exercise 4.1—Relaxing into the Present Moment

- *Adopt a comfortable meditation posture and engage in the preliminary practices. Take three long deep breaths, releasing all tension. Gently rock the body to settle the posture. Release all memories of the past and thoughts of the future, bringing your mind into this present moment.*

- *Bring your awareness to the very top of your head. As you breath out, imagine releasing all of the energy into that area of your body. Relaxing it fully.*

- *Now shift your awareness downwards, bringing it into the region of your face. Become aware of the tactile sensations in this area. Breathing out, release all tensions and relax fully.*

- *Slowly make your way down through the body, stopping for a moment at each point. Make the conscious effort to observe the sensations in that area, then release all the tension with the out breath.*

- *Throughout this process maintain a calm, yet alert mind, engaged in the activity and working with whatever presents itself to you.*

- *When you have finished scanning through your body, rest for a few moments in the sensations produced. Just observe how you are feeling.*

Stage 2—Placing the Mind on the Meditation Object

"...like a waterfall cascading over rocks"

By first cultivating mindfulness of the present moment, you will discover how an alert mind can co-exist with a relaxed body. However, in order to develop a more direct type of concentration, it can be helpful to narrow your focus onto a single object; in this case your breath. If you were to skip straight to stage two, without relaxing the body into the present moment, you would very likely constrict both your mind and body, aggravating any pre-existing tension and preventing you from engaging with the practice.

According to the first line of the Satipatthana Sutta, the most effective way to begin this practice is to simply observe how you experience the breath:

Breathing in aware of the short breath, breathing out aware of the short breath. Breathing in aware of the long breath, breathing out aware of the long breath.

The key to meditation at this stage is to maintain a relaxed state of mind, and the biggest obstacle you will face is the tendency for your mind to control the breath. This instruction therefore allows you to maintain close awareness of the natural flow of the breath, while at the same time resisting the urge to control it. Letting go of the tendency to control your breath by simply noticing when it stops of its own accord, helps you to relax. While directing your attention to the length of the breath heightens your alertness.

To achieve greater relaxation it is beneficial to be aware of the breath throughout the whole body, yet you may find it more natural to focus on a specific area such as the chest, belly or nostrils. As you become aware of the whole body "breathing", your breath will naturally become more subtle and smooth. This feeling is known as the inner wind, which can sometimes feel like energy currents travelling through the body. You can visualise this subtle breath circulating around, going through each part in turn, or you can imagine your whole body is exhaling and inhaling, like a wave. Placing your tongue behind the bottom teeth and slowing down the out-breath can also help your body to relax.

Exercise 4.2—Mindfulness of Breathing for Relaxation

- *Adopt a comfortable meditation posture and engage in the preliminary practices.*

- *Perform a brief scan through your body from top to bottom, relaxing all tensions through the out breath.*

- *Allow your awareness to fill the entire body; relaxed and loose.*

- *Become aware of the tactile sensations that correspond to your in and out breath. These may include the rise and fall of the chest or abdomen or the feeling of air moving through the nostrils. It doesn't matter, simply identify the sensations which indicate that you are breathing.*

- *Adopt a mental posture of an impartial observer. Now watch how these sensations develop over time. Particularly pay attention to the relative duration of each phase of the in and out breath. Make a mental note when they are long, or when they are short.*

- *If you find that your mind is filled with many thoughts, then you can generate a very specific thought by counting the breaths. At the very end of the in breath, mentally count "one". Then release all effort on the out breath. Again, watching the breath flow in, count "two" and again release on the out breath. Repeat this process, counting up to ten and then back to one.*

- *When the mind has calmed down, stop counting and simply return to observing the relative duration of each breath.*

- *As you approach the end of the session, release all efforts and rest in the present moment.*

This stage of breath meditation roughly equates to the first two of the nine progressive attentional states as laid out in the Tibetan System. The focus here is on understanding the meditation instructions and achieving a relaxed state of body and mind. These first two attentional states are:

1. **Placing the Mind on an Object:** In the beginning, keeping the mind fixed on the object requires a lot of effort. Your ability to maintain focus initially will be quite limited and there may only be brief moments when you can do so. It might even seem that your mind is more disturbed than before you started and you may get the sense that your discursive

thoughts are increasing. This however is likely to mean that only now are you becoming aware of the usual state of your mind. This realisation is an excellent first achievement.

This first state is attained through the power of hearing or listening to the teacher's instructions on the method of meditation and which object to choose. It is achieved when you can place the mind on the desired object of meditation for at least a second or two. If your object is the breath this may be achieved on your first attempt, though if your object is a complex visualisation this may take several weeks to accomplish.

2. **Continuous Placement:** During this stage the periods of distraction are still longer than the periods of concentration, but the periods during which you are able to stay fixed on the object become more frequent. The mind is becoming more stable and you can occasionally maintain an uninterrupted focus for about one to five minutes. There is also the sense that discursive thoughts are decreasing. This stage is achieved through the power of reflection. You are able to fix the mind on the object but still need to recall the instructions over and over again with understanding.

These first two attentional states are aimed at connecting the mind to an object and this requires a focused engagement. The main faults to overcome at this point are *laziness* and *forgetting the meditation object*.

At this stage the movement of thoughts through the mind is likened to a waterfall cascading over rocks. This does not mean the quantity of our thoughts is increasing, but rather, we are becoming aware of them for the first time.

Attentional State	Main Fault	Power	Movement
1. Placing the mind	Laziness	Hearing	Like a cascading waterfall
2. Continuous placement	Forgetting the Object	Reflection	

Table 4-2 Placing the Mind on an Object.

Stage 3—Keeping the mind on the meditation object

"Becoming like a river flowing through a gorge."

In the previous stage you began to experience a continuous focus on the breath, directing your attention to an awareness of its length, or counting the breath while the body becomes more and more relaxed. Once you develop some stability with this method, you can simply let your attention flow with the breath following it through its entire length. Your mind becomes more absorbed in the breath from the first moment of the inhalation to the last moment, noticing the gap in between and then following the exhalation from beginning to end. In this way, with your body already quite relaxed, you begin to develop continuous mindfulness followed by vigilance. According to the sutta, you should simply know that:

Breathing in aware of the whole body (of the breath),
Breathing out aware of the whole body (of the breath).

This instruction is usually taken to refer to the length of the breath, though some interpret it to mean that you should be aware of the breath moving through your entire body. As in the previous stage, you should focus on the breath wherever it comes naturally, moving your focus lower if you need to relax more (for example at the belly) and moving it higher if you need to enhance your vigilance (for example at the tip of the nose). At the same time however, you should maintain a peripheral awareness of the whole body while you are breathing.

The goal of this stage is to become so absorbed in the breath that you will not be distracted by sounds, sights or even uncomfortable sensations in the body. This is especially useful if your body is tired. Instead of allowing your mind to become cloudy, use vigilant efforts to tighten up your focus and clearly capture every instant of the breath.

Exercise 4.3—Mindfulness of Breathing for Stability

- *Adopt a comfortable meditation posture and engage in the preliminary practices. Perform a brief body scan, adopting a relaxed yet alert state of mind.*

- *Direct your attention to the region of your lower abdomen, becoming aware of the tactile sensations that correspond with the breath.*

- *For the length of a single breath, try to observe how the cycle of that breath develops. First note the beginning of the breath. How does it feel when the breath first starts to flow into the body?*

- *Then note the middle. How does it feel when the in breath stops and the flow reverses outward?*

- *Finally note the end. How does it feel when the breath is released naturally, without making any effort?*

- *Once you are familiar with each phase of the cycle, then observe how it feels when one breath finishes and the next begins.*

- *Become aware of this constant flow in and out. Observing the full cycle with a relaxed yet engaged mind.*

- *As you approach the end of the session, release all efforts and simply rest in the present moment.*

The corresponding attentional states, which aim at establishing mindfulness and then vigilance, are as follows:

3. **Patched Placement:** At this stage you become aware of any distractions to your concentration and have developed the ability, through the power of mindfulness, to bring the mind back to the object of meditation as soon as it wanders, just as if you were placing a patch over a hole in a

cloth. In this way you reset your concentration and are able to remain uninterruptedly focused, generally for about five to ten minutes. You begin to become more mindful and therefore progress towards real meditation, where your attention is fixed on the object most of the time in virtually all of your meditation sessions. Arriving even at this third state is a big achievement and can make a big difference to your ability to control the mind in everyday life.

4. **Close Placement:** Your focus is so strong at this point that the mind never completely loses fixation upon the object, and coarse agitation is no longer an obstacle. The mind therefore withdraws from a broad range of things and your focus narrows further. Although you are able to hold the object continuously, there is still the need to develop increasing levels of clarity or intensity and to also deal with subtle agitation. This is when part of your mind strays from the object of concentration but you do not lose it completely. During this fourth state, the power of mindfulness is achieved as you are now able to hold the object with such stability that you easily return to it whenever you are distracted. However, you still need to make sure that this stability does not come at the expense of relaxation. You may need to apply techniques to relax the mind in order to deal with subtle agitation, such as keeping the tongue behind the bottom teeth.

5. **Disciplining the Mind:** We have now developed the capacity to overcome coarse dullness and agitation, and we have increased the watchfulness or vigilance of our mind. The main obstacle at this state is subtle dullness or sinking, which arises when withdrawal of the mind from extraneous objects has proceeded too far. Masquerading as a stable and peaceful state of mind, there is a significant danger of failing to recognise subtle dullness. It therefore requires much discipline and effort to overcome. Removal of this obstacle requires a tightening of your awareness with increasing levels of vigilance. This can be challenging to achieve, without undermining stability and can sometimes be quite a delicate balancing act. At this level we need to generate an uplifted mind through inspiration, for instance by recollecting the good qualities of

shamatha or the Buddha's teachings. This helps to lift the meditation object and make it smaller or sharper. Here we must ensure that the tongue now rests behind the top teeth.

At this stage involuntary thoughts continue to arise, although now instead of a waterfall, they flow like a river moving smoothly through a gorge. While there is still a little resistance to practising, the results of our efforts are becoming quite apparent.

Attentional State	Main Fault	Power	Movement
3. Patched Placement	Coarse Agitation	Mindfulness	Like a river rapidly flowing through a gorge.
4. Close Placement	Coarse Dullness	Mindfulness	
5. Disciplining	Subtle Dullness	Vigilance	

Table 4-3 Keeping the mind on the meditation object.

Stage 4—Fine Tuning the Mind

"Like a river flowing slowly through a valley."

Having achieved continuous mindfulness of the breath with a high level of discipline, you then need to calm the breath down. If you jump to this step too soon you may fall prey to dullness and drowsiness. You must therefore ensure that you complete the previous stages, capturing the whole breath before you can try calming it down, just as you must first capture a wild horse before you can tame it.

The Sutta continues, giving the instruction:

Breathing in calming the body (of the breath),
Breathing out calming the body (of the breath).

Difficulty may arise here as we have used substantial willpower to accomplish the previous stages. What is now required is a gentle and persistent letting go. This can be a fine balancing act and it may help to lower the breath and place more emphasis again on relaxing the body.

The Sutta continues:

Breathing in aware of joy, breathing out aware of joy.
Breathing in aware of happiness, breathing out aware of happiness.

This refers to the emergence of joy and happiness (piti and sukha in Pali) as the breath calms down—like the golden light of dawn emerging on the eastern horizon. You now develop fully sustained attention of the "beautiful breath" and only traces of discursive thought remain. When you can easily remain with the object for a long time, experiencing a great amount of joy and happiness, the mind becomes very concentrated.

Exercise 4.4—Mindfulness of Breathing for Vividness

- *Adopt a comfortable meditation posture and engage in the preliminary practices. Perform a brief body scan, adopting a relaxed yet alert state of mind.*

- *Bring your awareness to the upper lip, just at the entrance to the nostrils. Become aware of the subtle sensations there, as the breath flows in and out. Allow all other sensations and experiences to fade into the background. Allow your full interest to rest in this small region.*

- *On each in breath, carefully distinguish the flow of sensations. Recognise that the sensations arise without the need to do anything. Adopt a mental attitude of being a passive observer, like an old man sitting on a park bench, watching the birds.*

- *Relax into this mode of observation, free from trying to control the breath in any way and undistracted from your object of meditation.*

- *As the breath becomes more subtle, the sensations will become more difficult to detect. Be content that you do not need to do anything to "create" any sensations. Simple still your mind further, and look more intensely at the object. Allow yourself to absorb completely into the flow of the breath.*

- *As you approach the end of the session, release all efforts and simply rest in the present moment.*

You are now able to move on to the next step which according to the Sutta, is:

Breathing in aware of the mind, breathing out aware of the mind

At this stage your attention is so refined that the breath seems to completely disappear and is replaced by a more subtle *acquired sign* (nimitta). The physical sensation of the breath and your sense of touch are shut down as you now experience the breath as a purely mental object, perceived by some as a white light, a blue pearl or perhaps a sensation of rapture. Like a full moon emerging from behind the clouds, the world of the five senses has dissolved and the mind can be clearly seen. This subtle object now becomes the focus of your meditation and carries you through to the higher attentional states.

The acquired sign is like a shy animal which will only come close to you if you are absolutely still. It is also like a dark room, in which you can eventually see shapes as your eyes become accustomed to the darkness. In the same way, the acquired sign gradually emerges from the mind's formless stillness.

The next two lines of the Sutta tell us what to do if subtle forms of dullness or excitement arise while you are focused on the acquired sign:

Breathing in gladdening the mind, breathing out gladdening the mind
Breathing in concentrating the mind, breathing out concentrating the mind

It may be that your experience of the acquired sign is dull or stained, perhaps because your mental energy is low. The antidote for this is to bring more joy into the meditation and experience this subtle mental object more fully. You can focus more intently on the centre of the sign, sharpen your attention or perhaps return to the previous stage, focusing on the beautiful breath. You can also heighten your joy by recollecting the benefits of virtues such as loving kindness.

If, on the other hand, the appearance of the sign is unstable, you must ensure that your mind is perfectly still and concentrated. This not only means keeping the image still, but keeping the "knower" still as well; the aspect of mind which "sees" the image. When the acquired sign first arises you may encounter fear or excitement, just as when you meet a stranger for the first time. In the same way that you learn to relax in this stranger's company as you get to know them, you can learn to loosen the mind a little and stay present with the beautiful sign.

There are two attentional states which correspond to these stages of breathing meditation:

6. **Pacifying the Mind:** Subtle dullness has been overcome during the previous stage by the power of inspired vigilance, however some traces still remain. There is now a danger of overly invigorating the mind, causing subtle agitation or excitement to arise which needs to be pacified. During this sixth state, mindfulness becomes more intense, having been refined through uninterrupted attention. A stronger faculty known as complete vigilance is also developing. This enables subtle excitement to be confronted, although it is not yet completely eliminated. The quality of attention thus becomes like a clear radio channel, without any extraneous noise or static. At this level you no longer experience resistance to meditation practice and your sessions may last an hour or more.

7. **Fully Pacifying the Mind:** With inspiration and perseverance, complete vigilance is further developed, and so the remaining traces of subtle dullness and excitement are eliminated, vanishing completely. You are thus able to abandon both these subtle obstacles, as soon as they are produced, through the power of enthusiastic diligence. In this way as soon as sinking sets in you arouse your attention, and when agitation occurs you loosen up slightly. These attention imbalances are thus swiftly recognised and are easily remedied with quite delicate adjustments.

Attentional State	Main Fault	Power	Movement
6. Pacifying	Subtle Agitation	Vigilance	Like a river flowing slowly through a valley.
7. Fully Pacifying	Under Application	Effort	

Table 4-4: Fine Tuning the Mind.

Stage 5—Unifying the Mind

"Like an ocean unmoved by waves."

The practice of breath awareness has now fully shifted to awareness of a beautiful and stable mental sign. Having overcome almost every trace of dullness and excitement, the meditation is now proceeding smoothly and effortlessly. You learn to trust your experience completely and remain absorbed in the object, trying to relinquish all control as the intense beauty of the sign holds your attention without your assistance. You simply enjoy the ride as your attention is either drawn to the centre, or the light expands and envelops you.

To continue with the example of the shy animal that only comes close to you when you are still, you will notice that more animals materialise as your stillness increases. At first only ordinary animals appear, but now strange and wonderful animals start to emerge. Similarly, further signs come out, which carry you to even deeper levels of meditation. In particular, an even more subtle mental sign known as the *counterpart sign* (patibhaga nimitta) appears, as if breaking out from the subtle acquired sign. It is far more purified and has neither colour nor shape. The appearance of this sign corresponds to the attainment of shamatha.

This description is equivalent to the final two attentional states which lead directly to Shamatha:

8. **One-Pointedness:** At this state you develop a special spontaneous ability to fix one-pointedly on the object for as long as you wish. A little exertion is required at the beginning of the meditation but then you flow with the momentum of the practice without interruption or further exertion. Subtle sinking and excitement are therefore eliminated with a small degree of effort through the power of enthusiastic diligence. In this eighth state you attain uninterrupted engagement, which means the mind can focus with continuous absorption on the object of concentration. This is in contrast with the previous stages which are all achieved with interrupted engagement. At this level you can sustain

highly focused attention for about three hours or so, and your mind is still "like an ocean unmoved by waves"; ruffled only by the occasional ripple.

9. **Equanimity:** At the ninth state there is an effortless entering into, and abiding within deep meditation. The mind places itself on the object of its own accord, effortlessly and spontaneously. This is achieved through the power of complete familiarity and spontaneous engagement. The mind is now perfectly pacified and the arising of subtle dullness and excitement is no longer possible during your meditation session. You are now able to maintain flawless concentration for at least four hours. If however, you discontinue your practise then dullness and excitement can still return as they have not been completely eliminated.

Attentional State	Main Fault	Power	Movement
8. One-pointedness	Over Application	Effort	Like an ocean unmoved by waves.
9. Equanimity	None	Familiarity	

Table 4-5: Unifying the Mind.

THE ATTAINMENT OF SHAMATHA

When Shamatha is actually achieved, there is a radical shift in your body and mind, like a butterfly emerging from its cocoon. Your mind at this stage has gone beyond the desire realm and you have now gained access to the form realm, a subtle dimension of consciousness that transcends the realm of the physical senses.

This shift is characterised by specific experiences that take place in a short period of time. Firstly, a powerful wind enters through your crown and dissolves throughout your body, feeling as though you have been filled with the power of a blissful dynamic energy. Your body and mind are now imbued with a special kind of pliancy, as the body feels buoyant and freed from physical dysfunction, filling the mind with an overwhelming sensation of joy. You have a sense of complete freshness and increased mental capacity, as your mind is like an oil lamp unmoved by the wind, resting bright and clear.

Once you have attained Shamatha you can enter this state at will and meditate for as long as you wish without interruption. You can even survive without basic requirements such as food, drink or sleep. During meditation your attention is completely withdrawn from the physical senses, discursive thoughts and mental images, though you can cue yourself to emerge from meditation after a specified period. Afflictive tendencies however are not completely eradicated and strong emotions may still surface under certain conditions. If on the other hand you are following a Buddhist path, at this level of realisation, Shamatha can be used as a tool to gain direct insight into our true nature. This can lead to the complete elimination of all afflictive emotions and mental states, and to the attainment of enlightenment.

THE FOUR APPLICATIONS OF MINDFULNESS

Having thoroughly trained in mindfulness of breathing, the meditator's mind is now a perfectly honed instrument for making introspective observations. The later portion of the Satipatthana Sutta, describes four practices which can be used to generate insight into the nature of one's experience. These four practices are known as the *Four Applications of Mindfulness* and represent the core teachings on vipashyana. These four are as follows:

1. **Mindfulness of the Body:** This includes mindfulness of breathing; knowing when you are experiencing a long or a short breath, being aware of its movement and the calmness this brings through the whole body. It also refers to mindfulness of body position; knowing when you are walking, standing, sitting or lying, where you are going and how you are moving. It is mindfulness of eating, drinking and defecating, when you are talking and when you are keeping silent. Finally, it is mindfulness of the elements which make up your body, its unattractive features and mindfulness of its impermanence and imminent death.

2. **Mindfulness of Feelings:** This is simply knowing when you are experiencing happiness, or a painful feeling or even the awareness of a neutral emotion. These can come about through contact with the five senses or through contact with mental objects, such as perceptions, memories, thoughts and mental images. More subtle feelings may also arise when your mind is calm, such as a sense of contentment or mild annoyance or irritation.

3. **Mindfulness of States of Mind:** This includes knowing that a mind with desire is a mind with desire, while a mind without desire is a mind without desire. Similarly, you know when anger, ignorance, distraction and concentration are present, and you know when these states are absent. You also know when the mind is liberated, and when it is not.

4. **Mindfulness of Phenomena:** This means you are mindful of all phenomena or contents of the mind. It can include awareness of sensory objects such as sounds, visual objects, tastes, smells and tactile sensations, as well as mental objects such as memories and thoughts. It also refers to knowing the nature of such phenomena is impermanent, suffering (which is to say, uncontrollable) and devoid of self-nature.

Each of these forms of mindfulness is distinguished by the object the meditator is focused on. Through close observation, the meditator is able to recognise how each of these different types of phenomena arise, how they abide and how they eventually pass away. With the realisation of the impermanence of these phenomena, the meditator also considers each set on the basis of how they appear internally, externally and both internally and externally. This method specifically highlights the types of relationships that we develop around these experiences.

A SUMMARY OF THE PATH OF SHAMATHA

It is customary for the nine progressive attentional states of the Tibetan tradition to be depicted by an illustration of an elephant, a monkey and a monk, as shown below. The key elements within this illustration are:

Symbol	Meaning
monk	the meditator
flame	effort
elephant	the mind
monkey	distractions
rabbit	subtle sinking / lethargy
black colour	a mind dominated by one of the five faults
white colour	a mind free from the five faults

Table 4-6 Symbolism used in the following illustration.

Figure 4-1 The Nine Progressive Stages of Shamatha.

At first, the black monkey has complete control of the elephant, demonstrating how we are naturally dominated by distractions. The monk initially works very hard to bring the mind under his control and the fire symbolises the great effort that is required. With persistence, the monk gradually starts to manage the elephant and so with great discipline we begin to overcome mental dullness. The elephant becomes whiter, symbolising the slow eradication of coarse dullness through the effort of meditation. At this point however, a small black hare appears on top of the elephant, signifying subtle dullness. Continuing meditation practise diligently, we arrive at the next stage, at which point the monkey no longer has control of the elephant. As we still have difficulties with less frequent levels of agitation and dullness, the monkey persists on the occasional interruption.

As the monkey gradually becomes less and less disruptive, the monk gains greater control of the elephant, which has slowly become completely white. Finally we reach the stage where the monkey has no influence over the elephant at all as our mind has been completely pacified. We are now in full control of our emotions rather than driven by them. This is shown by the monk meditating next to the mollified elephant. Beyond this stage, we see the monk meditating while sitting on top of the elephant. Still further on, two rainbows emerge from the monk's heart, symbolising the development of supernatural powers upon mastery of placement meditation. We have then gained the ability to focus the single-pointed mind on the development of insight meditation. Depending on which type of path is being followed, progress through the various stages of deepening insight is made, until enlightenment is finally reached.

According to the Theravada tradition, accomplishing Shamatha using the breath as an object places you at the threshold of experiencing the jhanas—states of concentration which are even more brilliant and powerful, leading directly to insight. The Buddha summarised this path by stating that mindfulness of breathing was "one thing which, when developed and cultivated, would fulfil four things"—the *Four Applications of Mindfulness*. These "four things which, when developed and cultivated, would fulfil seven things"—the *Seven Factors of Enlightenment*: mindfulness, investigation, energy, joy, tranquillity, concentration and equanimity. These "seven things which, when developed and cultivated, would fulfil two things"—true knowledge and liberation.

REVIEW OF KEY POINTS

- In the Theravada tradition there are five stages that represent the gradual progression towards achieving Shamatha: mindfulness of the present, placing the mind on the object, keeping the mind on the object, fine-tuning the mind and unifying the mind.

- In the Tibetan tradition there are nine attentional states that are used to describe the same progression: placing the mind on an object, continuous placement, patched placement, close placement, disciplining the mind, pacifying the mind, fully pacifying the mind, one-pointedness and equanimity.

- During the first and second stages the focus is on developing relaxation, then in the third it emphasises mindfulness and finally in the fourth and fifth the focus is on vigilance.

- Through mindfulness of breathing, you will eventually abandon the tactile sensations of the breath and switch to a very subtle mental object known as the acquired sign. This in turn will give way to an even more subtle object known as the counterpart sign.

- When you achieve Shamatha, your body and mind will experience a radical energetic shift. This produces an unprecedented degree of physical and mental pliancy that allows you to direct the mind effortlessly wherever you desire.

- On the basis of calming the mind, you then engage in the practice of the Four Applications of Mindfulness, in order to develop insight into the nature of your experience.

PART TWO

Reflecting on Your Present Situation

CHAPTER FIVE

How to Practice Dharma

With the psychological tools we learned in the first few chapters, we are now better equipped to cope with the many ups and downs that life throws at us. Then with the contemplative tools of meditation, we are provided with a basic methodology for the cultivation of positive qualities which further reduces the impact those ups and downs can have on our minds. Together, they provide us with a more stable platform upon which to really start probing into the nature of our experience.

You might ask, why would we want to do such a thing? What is motivating us to go deeper? The answer is that we all want to be happy and we don't want to suffer. It really is that simple. If we are sincere, we can see that underlying all of our actions is this basic motivation, constantly pulling us towards some types of phenomena and pushing us away from others.

Even though we are all seeking some form of happiness, very few of us are aware of what genuine happiness actually feels like. It is for this reason, we first need to get a sense of what is meant by this term. In Buddhism we speak of two types or levels of happiness:

1. **Worldly Happiness:** This form of happiness is the pleasure that we derive from our interaction with external stimuli. When we encounter a beautiful image, taste a delicious piece of food or smell an enchanting fragrance, the experience that arises in the mind as a response to these appearances is called "worldly" happiness. It is worldly, because it depends on the external world in order for it to manifest.

2. **Genuine Happiness:** This form of happiness is not reliant on anything outside of your mind. It arises naturally from the innate characteristics of the mind itself. It can be experienced when you are able to live your

life in accordance with that nature. While worldly happiness is something that you *receive from* the world, genuine happiness is something you *bring to* the world.

The confusion arises when we fail to recognise that we are all motivated by a desire to experience long lasting, genuine happiness and yet, we only ever search for worldly happiness. Since worldly happiness is dependent on external objects, it can only ever offer us momentary pleasure. The moment the object is gone or when we become accustomed to its presence, the corresponding pleasure also fades away. Sadly we are looking for genuine happiness in the wrong place. Like trying to get water out of a rock, worldly happiness simply doesn't have the capacity to give us what we want.

In the end, it's a question of satisfaction. Deep down there's a sort of gut wrenching feeling that "something is missing". No matter what situation we find ourselves in, there is always something lacking, something that's just not quite right, isn't there? On a fundamental level, it seems as though we are living in a perpetual mode of dissatisfaction. This begs the question, is there anything we can do about it? Do we just have to accept this reality? Or are there changes that we can make in our lives in order to bring about a more lasting form of satisfaction?

According to the Buddha's teachings, there are causes for our dissatisfaction and therefore it is possible to remove those causes. The way to do this is through the practice of Dharma. The word dharma is a sanskrit word which has many different connotations. In this case we are using it to refer to all types of phenomena. A dharma is something that creates the cause for a specific result to occur. So we can speak of *Worldly Dharmas* that produce worldly happiness, or we can speak of *Sacred Dharmas* which produce genuine happiness. When we refer to "practising Dharma", we are referring to the cultivation of the latter.

Sacred Dharma is like a mirror. It reflects our experience in such a way that allows us to develop insight into how that experience is arising. It challenges us to really take a long and hard look at our behaviour and to ask some tough questions. If we can answer these questions honestly, then it becomes possible to learn from our mistakes and to make changes in our lives; changes which ultimately will lead us to genuine happiness.

THE EIGHT WORLDLY DHARMAS

When we begin to talk about the difference between worldly and sacred dharmas, it is very easy to develop an attitude that anything worldly is "bad" and anything sacred is "good". This can lead us to develop a very pessimistic and depressed outlook on daily life. The fact of the matter is we live in this world—this is our reality. What we need to do is to understand our relationship to this reality in a healthy and productive way. Instead of living in a distorted fantasy, we want to strip away our misconceptions and arrive at a more realistic perspective.

To do this, we will analyse the worldly dharmas by way of four pairs of phenomena. These *Eight Worldly Dharmas*, represent four things that we strive to have and four things that we try to avoid at all costs. As we will see, the root affliction that drives these different polarities is attachment. We are either attached to having something or attached to not having something. The more attachment that is present, the more suffering we experience. By studying these four topics and reflecting on the implications, we can start to lessen that attachment.

Focus	Attachment	Aversion
1. Resources	Gain	Loss
2. Sensations	Pleasure	Pain
3. Influence (Power)	Recognition	Being Ignored
4. Self Worth	Praise	Criticism

Table 5-1: The Eight Worldly Dharmas

Gain and Loss

The first pair to look at is related to our relationship with external resources. Gain refers to the drive to acquire more wealth as a means of experiencing greater happiness. The general assumption here is that "more is better". The more money I have, the bigger my house, the better my car, the nicer my clothes, and somehow all of this will lead to increasing my happiness. Loss refers to the opposite; it is our deep seated fear of being without the resources we think we need. While gain manifests as an insatiable craving for things, loss is like an undercurrent of anxiety that prevents us from truly enjoying the things we do have.

When a person has a lot of attachment to wealth, their lives tend to revolve around making money and expanding their personal possessions. We can see this attitude very clearly in the emphasis our societies place on economics and the consumer culture.

Exercise 5.1—Material Possessions

- *In a relaxed posture, establish a neutral mind through the practice of mindfulness of breathing.*

- *Identify a few of your most prized possessions. Choose one, and think back to the moment when you acquired this object. How did you feel back then? Compare this feeling with how you feel now in relation to this object. Has the feeling changed at all? Do you still feel the same thrill, the same joy, the same sense of satisfaction?*

- *Now consider everything that went into acquiring that object. Think of the energy that you invested in it. Think what you've had to do to keep that object safe. Think of the insurance we take out, the repairs we make and the general effort we spend to keep our objects from changing.*

- *Now think of all of the different objects you have owned over the course of your lifetime. How long do they last before you feel you need to replace them? Those you have kept, imagine how it would feel if they broke or someone stole them.*

- *Get a sense for how your relationship to things has changed over time. Compare those moments when material possessions have been your main priority and those moments when they haven't. Is there any difference in the quality of your experience?*

- *As you think over these questions, different insights may arise in your mind. If they do, then pause your meditation and simply rest in your awareness of the certainty that this is how things are.*

Pleasure and Pain

The second pair looks at our relationship with sensory experiences. This is by far the most immediate of the four pairs. On the one side we seek out all manner of experiences that we label as pleasurable, while on the other side, we try to avoid the experiences of pain and discomfort. For every person, the types of objects that will trigger pleasure or pain will be different. This is important to remember as we tend to think the objects in themselves contain some built in capacity to produce the experience of either pleasure or pain. In reality though, these two exist only in the mind.

When attachment to experience is very strong, we will often see a heavy emphasis placed on different types of "thrill-seeking". This may come in the form of an obsession for certain types of foods or substances (like alcohol or drugs), the constant desire for sexual gratification or the need to always experience new and amazing situations. Because all of these experiences are momentary in nature, the most they can offer is momentary happiness.

Exercise 5.2—Sensory Experiences

- *In a relaxed posture, establish a neutral mind through the practice of mindfulness of breathing.*

- *Think of one of your favourite foods. Consider the qualities of the food that make it your favourite. Bring to mind the experience of eating this food. Is there any difference between actually tasting the food versus simply remembering the taste of it? Consider how long the experience of tasting the food lasts before it turns into a mere memory.*

- *Now consider the time it takes to prepare your food. How important is it that the food tastes good? How much effort do you invest in making this happen? Don't think of just the immediate preparation. Also consider the energy that was spent in acquiring the right ingredients and learning how to make the food.*

- *Now bring to mind all of the little things that we do during our day to avoid the experience of discomfort. Consider how we surround ourselves with beautiful things to avoid seeing ugliness, or how we spray fragrances everywhere in order to avoid certain smells. Think of the different ways we protect ourselves from painful situations.*

- *No matter how much we try to protect ourselves, inevitably we encounter things which elicit unwanted feelings. Think of some examples of recent experiences that you have had. What was your reaction to these experiences? Did they have a large or small impact on your mind?*

- *Rest in any insights that arise.*

Recognition and Being Ignored

With this third pair, we are now focusing on the quality of influence that we have on others. What we are calling recognition is the desire for other people to respect you and think highly of you. It is a general concern for how your actions impact or change the behaviour of others. Someone who receives a great deal of recognition or fame from others will be able to influence those people more effectively. Likewise, if someone is completely ignored by others, their actions have no power to influence anyone.

The presence of power or the absence of power can also be an object of attachment. When this attachment is strong, it can lead to a constant need to be liked or to establishing a position where you are able to control or manipulate others. We can see this form of attachment very clearly in the world of celebrities, politics and business.

Exercise 5.3—Influence

- In a relaxed posture, establish a neutral mind through the practice of mindfulness of breathing.

- Consider the various people with whom you feel connected right now. How would you characterise the strength of your relationship to these people? Are you equally close to each of them, or are there some that you are closer to than others? Consider how this closeness affects the amount of influence you have over these people.

- Consider how this closeness developed. At what point did these people stop being strangers and became your friends or family? Think of the energy you have invested in developing these relationships.

- Now consider how important it is to you, to have these people in your life. What would you do if all of your friends abandoned you? How would this make you feel? Consider all of the actions you engage in to ensure that this doesn't happen.

- Look back over your life and reflect on the different people that have come into your life at different moments. Consider the influence you had on their lives then and compare that to the influence you have on their lives now. What effect do past relationships have on your present life?

- Rest in any insights that arise.

Praise and Criticism

The last pair is focused on the perceived value of who we are as individuals. It is intimately related to our conception of self and how others relate to that self. When people praise a quality that we possess or an action that we have performed, we feel a sense of great self-worth. Inversely, when someone criticises our qualities or actions, then we feel like our self is somehow lessened.

When people become attached to their self-worth, they tend to focus on pleasing others in order to elicit praise. It is not about whether they are able to exert any influence on others; it is an attachment to the momentary experience that arises when they do something that causes others to express their appreciation or respect. It is a craving for anything that reinforces the ego, and an equally strong insecurity with anything that is seen to attack that same ego.

Exercise 5.4—Self Worth

- *In a relaxed posture, establish a neutral mind through the practice of mindfulness of breathing.*

- *Consider the various qualities that you believe most define you as a person.*

- *Bring to mind a moment when someone complimented you or praised you in front of others. How did this make you feel?*

- *Now compare this with a moment when someone openly criticised you. How did that make you feel? How did you react to this criticism?*

- *Now think back through different phases of your life. Consider how you reacted to praise or criticism as a young child, then as a teenager, then as a young adult, and so on up to your present age. As your sense of self evolved over time, what relationship did it have to the way that you reacted to praise or criticism?*

- *Rest in any insights that arise.*

In summary, when our lives are primarily driven by concern for these worldly dharmas, we are constantly engaged in an endless process of rearranging our world in order to fulfill our hopes and avoid our fears. This sort of life can feel like a constant struggle with everyone around us, the environment itself and even our own sense of ourselves. It is a life spent in anxiety, worry and discontent, especially when we fail to meet our own expectations.

Understanding these worldly dharmas however is not to suggest that it is wrong to want to be admired for our skills, or enjoy the taste of good food. Nor are we mistaken in not wanting to feel the pain of rejection. Creating an awareness of how attached we are to these aspects, gives us the opportunity to change our perspective of how we approach them. Reducing our fixation upon their possession or avoidance can help us to "loosen up" and relax a little bit. To have an attitude that recognises that it's nice to have particular things but that they are not always needed or to accept that we don't always have to receive praise to know we have done a good job, can lead to a greater tolerance for the things we do have and help us to be less uptight about what we don't have. In other words, it teaches us to be more content with whatever is arising.

Sometimes our perception of the worldly dharmas can be quite limited and we often become too intently focused in the one direction. As a consequence we fail to see any other possibilities. For example, we may be so fixed on the idea that our family needs "the dream home" in order to be happy that we work extensive hours to earn the money required, but because we no longer have the time to spend with our loved ones the actual result is unhappiness. With gain can also comes loss, and we might find it useful to ask ourselves what is the cost of getting what we want? We might achieve recognition but the price we pay could be our freedom, or we might earn immense wealth but at the cost of great energy. We don't have to sacrifice the things we would like or fool ourselves into believing we don't care what other people think of us. If we can be more mindful about how these eight dharmas drive our life experience and examine them more deeply, we may be able to strike the right balance between each pair and thus experience a greater sense of equanimity.

DHARMA PRACTICE

Our default mode is to become attached to worldly dharmas. This is nothing more than a deeply ingrained habit. Unfortunately this particular habit happens to generate a wide range of problems in our lives. Therefore, in order to counteract this habit, we need to exert considerable effort. We call the process of exerting effort "practising Dharma".

The above analysis of the *Eight Worldly Dharmas* is an example of such practice. Through the process of working through each of the different topics, you are making an effort to develop insight into those topics. The result of this effort is that you are able to develop some degree of realisation that functions to lessen your attachment to these eight types of phenomena.

The practice occurs when we are able to take in knowledge with clear understanding and then integrate that knowledge into our life. When we fail to integrate the knowledge we receive then we do not develop any new habits. The information remains at an intellectual level and doesn't penetrate to our experience. This is fine as long as we are not experiencing any sort of problems. The moment they arise though, we slip right back into our habitual way of seeing things and we continue to make the same mistakes over and over again. Therefore, simply listening to the teachings without putting them into practice has no long-term benefit.

The primary purpose of Dharma practice is as a means of taming the mind—to ultimately make the mind more useable. This process is very similar to tanning a piece of leather. Right now, our minds are like a piece of hard, dry skin. They have been hardened by our culture's strong emphasis on the external world; an emphasis that solidifies how things actually exist, locking them into being just this or just that. What limited inner focus we do have is often dominated by ego, self-cherishing and all manner of biased attachments. All of these conditions dry out our mind, like a piece of skin left out in the sun. If we were to try to bend this skin, it would be stiff and possibly even break. Similarly, as long as our mind is rigid and fixed, it will resist any attempt to bend or adapt. By practicing Dharma, we are learning how to soften the mind, to make it more flexible and pliable.

Developing a mind with these characteristics enables us to be better prepared to cope and deal with the wide array of situations we find ourselves in everyday, such as a work mate being excessively critical of our performance. Instead of reacting with anger and harsh words, or internalising our hurt (both of which only create more difficulties), having a mind that is pliable may enable us to look at the situation differently. Our colleague could be having a bad day and is just blowing off steam, perhaps there is an element of truth in their words or maybe we just feel it's not worth getting into an argument about. Taming our mind through Dharma practice helps us learn to respond rather than react. It creates a space where we can be aware that our actions have consequences and although we may not be able to accurately predict the outcomes, we can choose our responses to act with greater wisdom. It also allows us to be more accepting of difficult circumstances, simply making life easier.

In general, we can distinguish between two types of practice:

1. **Formal Practice:** This refers to the many specific spiritual practices that you can engage in such as reciting prayers or mantras, performing prostrations or sitting on a cushion to meditate. These are most clearly identified as activities where the primary purpose is to cultivate spiritual qualities.

2. **Casual Practice:** Informal practice refers to all of the other activities that are not explicitly focused on spiritual goals. This can include all kinds of worldly activities that we engage with on a daily basis. These activities provide the context for integrating the insights generated in formal practice into one's experience.

Both of these forms of practice are important to the process of taming the mind. Ideally, you would want to have a dedicated time each day for engaging in formal practice and then use the rest of your time for casual practice. In this way, your entire day becomes an opportunity for taming the mind.

We mentioned earlier the taking in of knowledge and understanding. If we find ourselves caught up in a strong emotion and we are able to stop and examine how our mind is or we find ourselves checking our intention and analysing consequences before responding to a difficult situation, then we have taken in the understanding. We are applying Dharma knowledge and integrating it into our daily life, going beyond understanding the language to allow the meaning to penetrate. This is what spiritual practice is all about. If it is not relevant to your normal individual life then it is unlikely to be of benefit.

We can also view Dharma practice as a way of preparing our minds for the cultivation of greater wisdom and wonderful qualities such as love, compassion, joy and equanimity. Imagine a rocky and barren plot of land only capable of growing weeds. With hard work and discipline, a farmer can remove the stones, pull out the weeds and turn the soil with organic matter to transform it into a healthy field, capable of producing a rich, nutritional and bountiful harvest. Without spiritual practice, our minds resemble this unfruitful land.

It is overgrown with afflictions, such as attachment and self-cherishing. When we begin to practice Dharma, we are gradually working to remove the "weeds" and to transform our mind into a fertile base from which all positive qualities can develop and grow.

As we begin to tame and prepare our mind, initially it may seem a considerably difficult task, as when we first took up meditation. Turning the mind inward, we were able to see for the first time how chaotic and repetitive our thoughts actually were. In the same way, as we become more aware of the nature of the thoughts that propel our actions, we may start to realise the influence that the Eight Worldly Dharmas have on our lives. Noticing the extent of our attachments and aversions can sometimes feel frustrating and we may feel put off by the amount of "weeds" that we discover. For this reason, we need to be patient with ourselves, allowing the process to develop over time. If you don't give up, then you may look back in a few years time and be quite amazed at the changes that you have gone through.

DEVELOPING INSIGHT THROUGH ANALYTICAL MEDITATION

Previously we have encountered a number of exercises that asked you to contemplate or think about specific topics. As we learned in the chapter on meditation, this is a form of practice known as *analytical meditation*. The primary purpose of this technique is to cultivate greater wisdom. In general, we can identify three levels of wisdom:

1. **The Wisdom of Hearing:** This represents the insights which are generated through the process of studying the teachings regarding a particular topic. The result of this form of wisdom is that you develop a clear comprehension of what the teachings are saying. You are able to distinguish the different topics and know how they are presented.

2. **The Wisdom of Reflecting:** This next form of wisdom represents the insights that arise when you actively think about the teachings you have received and understand their meaning. Through the process of asking questions and clearing away doubts, you develop greater clarity and certainty in your understanding.

3. **The Wisdom of Meditation:** This last form of wisdom is related to the direct insights that arise when you convert your understanding into experience. Through repeatedly meditating on a particular subject, you develop greater and greater familiarity. This familiarity allows you to experience specific states of mind without the need for conceptual elaboration.

Of these three levels of wisdom, it is only the wisdom of meditation that is capable of directly counteracting a deep rooted misconception, for it is only at this level that we are able to actually establish an experience of the phenomena being observed. That being said, we must not disregard the other forms of wisdom as they provide the necessary conditions for the wisdom of meditation to arise. Without first studying, there is nothing to be reflected upon. Without first reflecting, then there is no understanding to be established. Without that understanding, there is no basis for experiencing the meaning.

For this reason, a big part of our Dharma practice is to spend time studying and reflecting upon different topics that can help us develop a perspective that is more conducive to genuine happiness. Our primary tool for doing this is analytical meditation. The following is a brief presentation of a basic process that we can use to get the most out of this powerful technique.

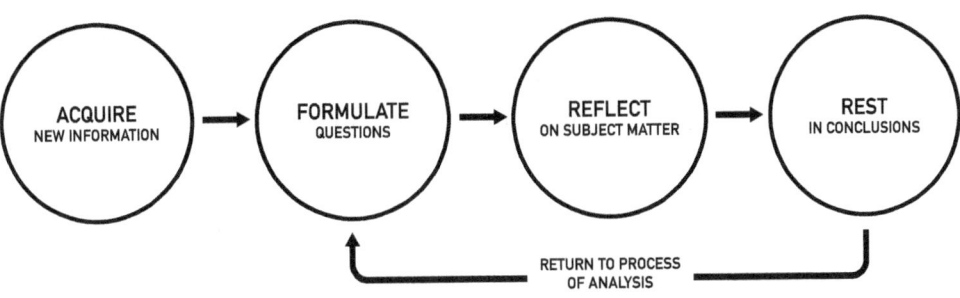

Figure 5-1: The Process of Analytical Meditation.

1. **Acquire information:** The first step before engaging in analytical meditation is to acquire some new information through the process of studying. This can be in the form of reading a book or listening to a teaching. The main thing is to give yourself some material to work with.

2. **Formulate questions:** The next step is to identify a number of questions that are raised in relation to the information you have just acquired. You can analyse the material to identify the various statements that are being made, then, formulate the statements as questions so that you can investigate them.

3. **Reflect on the subject matter:** After bringing your mind into a neutral state, direct your attention to one of the questions. Start to explore how this question relates to your life in light of the teachings you have received. As you think about the implications of your answers, you may find that more questions arise. Follow those lines of reasoning and see where they take you. Continue in this fashion, exploring the topic from as many angles as you can.

4. **Rest in the conclusion:** After spending some time thinking things over, you will start to develop a greater certainty regarding the answer to your original question. When that certainty is strong, you can stop the process of analysis and simply rest in the certainty that "this is how it is".

5. **Alternating analysis and resting:** When that feeling of certainty fades, return to the process of investigation, either repeating your analysis or selecting a different question to work with. When you experience the same sense of certainty and conviction you can rest again as before. In this way you alternate between analysis and resting meditation, gradually deepening and refining your understanding.

Jamgon Kongtrul gives some useful guidelines about how to alternate between analytical and resting meditation in his *Treasury of Knowledge*:

> *If due to intense analysis the ability to rest deteriorates,*
> *Do more resting meditation and replenish the stillness.*
> *If due to prolonged resting you no longer want to analyse,*
> *Do analytical meditation to strengthen the mind's clarity.*

Thus if you find the mind gets agitated by practising analytical meditation, you should allow it to settle by relaxing the body and practising placement meditation for a while. On the other hand, if your placement meditation leads to dullness, you can increase your mental clarity by resuming your analysis. Furthermore, when you become accustomed to the process of alternating between analysis and resting, you eventually reach a stage where less analysis is needed to give rise to certainty. In this way, when you are starting out, you may find more analytical meditation is needed, then in time, you will transition to more placement meditation.

THE FOUR CONVICTIONS OF RENUNCIATION

Over the course of the next four chapters, we will be exploring four specific topics which are used to generate the mental quality of *renunciation*. This quality is an essential foundation for the engagement in any sort of spiritual path. For this reason, it is worthwhile that we spend a little time trying to understand what we mean by this term.

In the most basic of ways, renunciation involves a "strong turning away". We recognise that something is a destructive force in our lives and we turn away from it. This implies that there is also a turning towards something else. So in a way, renunciation can be understood to be a shift in focus—a movement away from a destructive focus and towards a constructive one.

The four topics that we will be studying are known as the *Four Convictions of Renunciation*. They are specifically designed to facilitate the transition away from a life driven by attachment to the eight worldly dharmas, and towards a life focused on taming the mind through practising Dharma. They do this through either helping us to understand the nature of our present conditions or by highlighting the potential that those conditions have.

Focusing heavily on the eight worldly dharmas can have a narrowing effect on our minds. They habituate us to an extreme view which tells a very specific story about what is important and what isn't. The Four Convictions help us to open up our perspective and to take in a broader range of understanding. The story they tell is a story of possibilities, where change is genuinely achievable. This is very important to remember in the beginning when it is all too easy to get overwhelmed by apathy and fixed in a habitual way of thinking.

Renunciation can also be understood as a form of self-focused compassion—the desire to be free from suffering. It is this desire to be free which motivates us in the beginning, and it is this desire that we will eventually extend to encompass everyone else. If we are unable to sincerely wish ourselves to be free from suffering, then it is impossible for us to honestly wish this for others. When cultivated strongly, this mind of renunciation can become a powerful force behind all manner of spiritual practices.

Traditionally the four topics are presented in a particular order. They start with the *preciousness of this human life,* move on to *impermanence and death,* followed by the *suffering of cyclic existence* and finally the *karmic law of cause and effect.* I have found that many of these meditations assume a previous familiarity with the Buddhist worldview, which is understandable for audiences in ancient India and Tibet, but can cause some western students to experience many unnecessary obstacles. For this reason, when teaching these topics to westerners, I find it helpful to shift the order slightly in order to first lay the groundwork of the worldview and then to understand the implications of that view. The following is a general overview of this approach:

1. **The Karmic Law of Cause and Effect:** We start by first developing our understanding of the natural law of mental causality known as *Karma.* This fundamental principle is key to understanding how experience is shaped through actions of the body, speech and mind. When we understand this principle more clearly, we are able to develop the mind of renunciation that turns away from engaging in non-virtuous actions and focuses more on engaging with virtuous modes of conduct.

2. **The Suffering Nature of Cyclic Existence:** Through an understanding of karma we can develop a model for understanding how our actions produce a cycle of continual reincarnation. On the basis of this model, we then shift our attention to an analysis of the unsatisfactory nature of our experiences within this process. We look at the full spectrum of experience on gross, subtle and very subtle levels. This helps us to cultivate the mind of renunciation that turns away from cyclic existence and towards freedom from suffering.

3. **The Precious Human Life:** With the desire to be free from suffering, we now need to develop the conviction that we are capable of achieving our goal. To do this, we contemplate the amazing potential of the various conditions that are present in this specific human life. In this way,

we develop the mind of renunciation that turns away from working only for the benefit of this life, and instead moves towards working for the benefit of future lives.

4. **Death and Impermanence:** The last topic focuses on helping us to overcome the strong habituation we have to the eight worldly dharmas. Our existing habits act as a strong counterforce to any sort of worthwhile change. For this reason, we need to break our attachment to the worldly dharmas and develop a sense of urgency in our practice. We do this by meditating on the impermanent nature of cyclic existence, particularly on the impermanence of our own lives. This topic helps us to develop the mind of renunciation that turns away from laziness and procrastination and turns towards an attitude that is engaged with practising the Dharma.

For many people, these topics can be particularly challenging because they describe a worldview that is significantly different from the materialistic models used within the scientific community. For this reason, it is important to maintain an open mind about all of these ideas and to work through them in a methodical way. Remember that every model the Buddha presented in his teachings is coming from a wealth of contemplative research derived from the observation of phenomena through direct experience. This research has been replicated by thousands upon thousands of subsequent contemplatives who have corroborated his findings. This means that no matter how foreign a particular idea may sound, there is the potential for you to also know these phenomena personally if you are willing to put in the effort to replicate the research. Therefore, treat each idea as a working hypothesis and explore the implications of taking them as true. Then over time, if you feel that the model is compelling, you may naturally choose to explore it further.

Topic	Renunciation Of	Focuses On
1. The Karmic Law of Cause and Effect	Non-virtuous actions	Virtuous actions
2. The Suffering Nature of Cyclic Existence	Cyclic existence	Freedom from suffering
3. The Precious Human Life	Worldly Dharmas	Practicing Dharma
4. Death and Impermanence	Laziness and Procrastination	Active engagement

Table 5-2: The Four Convictions of Renunciation.

REVIEW OF KEY POINTS

- There are two forms of happiness: worldly happiness that is based on external stimuli and genuine happiness that is based on the intrinsic nature of our minds. We long for genuine happiness and yet focus on worldly happiness, leading to a general sense of dissatisfaction.

- A dharma is any phenomena which acts as a condition for producing a specific result. There are worldly dharmas that have the potential to produce worldly happiness and there are sacred dharmas that have the capacity to produce genuine happiness.

- The Eight Worldly Dharmas are: attachment to gain with aversion to loss, attachment to pleasure with aversion to pain, attachment to recognition with aversion to being ignored and attachment to praise with aversion to criticism.

- Dharma practice is the process of making the effort to remove the influence of mental afflictions on the mind. Through this process the mind is tamed and therefore becomes more useable.

- There are two types of practice: formal practice and casual practice. Both are necessary to help integrate the Dharma into your life.

- We can use analytical meditation to develop wisdom. There are three types of wisdom: the wisdom of hearing, the wisdom of reflection and the wisdom of meditation. You can alternate between analytical meditation and placement meditation as a way of sharpening your mind.

- Renunciation recognises the faults of a given way of thinking and desires to abandon those faults.

- The Four Convictions of Renunciation are four topics which we analyse in order to turn our minds away from destructive habits in favour of more constructive habits, such as practising Dharma. They are: the karmic law of cause and effect, the suffering nature of cyclic existence, the precious human life and reflecting on death and impermanence.

CHAPTER SIX

The Karmic Law of Cause and Effect

Take a look around you. We are surrounded by objects aren't we? All manner of things, some big, some small, some round, some flat. Some are naturally formed while others were made by people or machines. Where did all of these objects come from? How did they come to be here with you right now?

If we stop and actually think about it, we will see that each of these objects is the result of a whole sequence of events which led to a final result of the thing that you see before you. Take a wooden table for instance:

Somewhere there was a person who had the idea to build a table. He pulled out a piece of paper and started sketching how the table would look. When he was satisfied with his design, he went out and bought some wood and nails. He then took the wood to his workshop and began to cut it with a saw. He carved into the wood, shaping it to match the designs he had drawn. Once all the pieces were complete, he used his hammer and nails to join all the pieces together. After many hours of hard work, the table was complete.

According to Buddhism, all phenomena depend on causes and conditions. Something cannot come from nothing, and this means that everything must arise in dependence on something which has come before it—a cause. Each cause then leads to a certain result when the particular conditions are present. We call this principle the *Natural Law of Causality*. From this description we can identify two types of causes:

1. **Substantial Cause:** This is the actual substance from which the effect arose. It is what is transformed by the various conditions in order to produce the result. In our example of the table, the wood is the substantial cause of the table. For a flower, we could say the substantial cause was a seed.

2. **Supporting Conditions:** This refers to all of the different circumstances that needed to be present in order for a specific result to occur. With our table, the supporting conditions were the person who designed the table, the paper on which the design was drawn, the different tools that were used to shape it, and all of the other contributing factors that made the table possible.

While there is only ever one substantial cause, there can be an almost infinite number of supporting conditions. Just consider everything that went into creating the hammer that was used to build the table. Or where did the paper come from that was used to sketch the design? Not to mention everything that had to occur for the person to have the idea to actually create the table in the first place. It is this incredible diversity of conditions which makes causality a rather complex phenomenon to study.

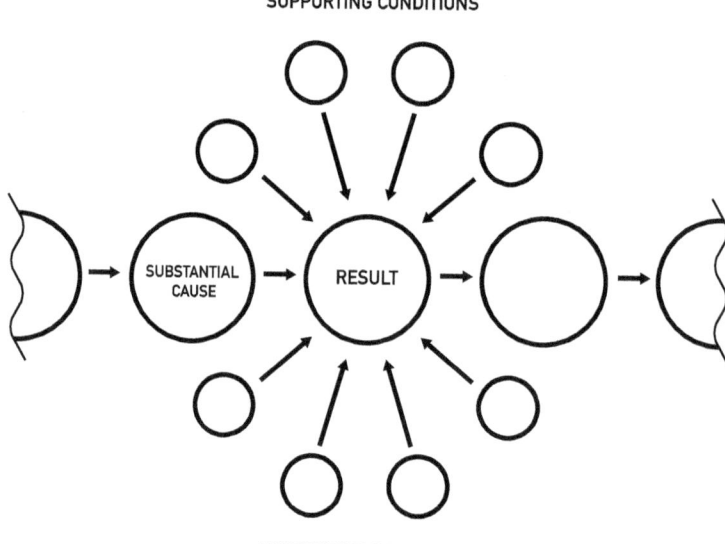

Figure 6-1: Substantial cause and supporting conditions.

Modern science has given us a great understanding of the causes and conditions which have led to the evolution of the physical world over the last few millions of years. But this is only one aspect of reality. As you will remember from our discussions in previous chapters, from the Buddhist perspective, the mind is not a physical phenomenon and yet it too is shaped by causes and conditions. The model which describes this relationship is known as the *Karmic Law of Cause and Effect*, or simply the *Law of Karma*.

Karma is a sanskrit word that literally means "action". The term is used to refer specifically to the effects that are generated by our actions of body, speech and mind. Here, an action is identified as any behaviour that is driven by intention. Since intention is a mental factor (see Chapter Two), then this means that all actions originate in the mind.

Let's use a simple example to illustrate this point:

You start to get the feeling of being thirsty. Slowly the desire builds up for something to quench your thirst. Eventually this desire becomes strong enough for you get up and go to the kitchen, grab a glass and fill it with water. You drink it down in a few gulps. The feeling of thirst is gone.

If we analyse the karmic causes and effects in this situation, we can see the feeling of thirst arises in the mind. This feeling then triggers an aversion to that thirst and over time, this aversion grows in strength. Eventually we reach a threshold where the aversion is too great, and we feel the need to do something. The idea to get a glass of water then arises. This idea triggers a sequence of neurons to fire which in turn trigger a number of physical actions, such as walking to the kitchen, getting the glass, filling it up and drinking it down. The water then hydrates our body, shifting its chemistry, causing more neurons to fire and in our mind, the feeling of thirst is reduced. As the feeling dissolves, the aversion to that feeling dissolves as well.

The effect we are looking at is the mind that is free from the suffering of feeling thirsty. The substantial cause for that state of mind is the continuity of the mindstream, for only mind can give rise to mind. All of the physical components in this scenario act as supporting conditions that are able to influence what the mind perceives. Likewise, the effect of hydration in the body is a result of introducing H_2O into the system. While the mind acts as a supporting condition to trigger that chemical reaction, the substantial cause is the physical molecules of the water. It is very important to remember to keep the physical and non-physical separate. While they are capable of influencing each other, there is never a situation where one transforms into the other.

To fully understand all of the karmic influences that go into any particular moment of experience is an example of a very hidden phenomenon. It is simply too complex for the mind of a sentient being to fathom. Fortunately, through the power of his meditative concentration, the Buddha was able to observe a wide variety of causal sequences and identify a number of basivc patterns which describe how karma works. In this chapter we will explore these patterns in order to understand the dynamics of how karma influences the quality of our lived experience.

KARMIC SEEDS AND THE MIND STREAM

While the above example can show us how intention drives transformation in the mind, it does not tell us much about the reasons why we felt thirsty, nor about why we experienced aversion to that thirst. To understand our reactions to different phenomena, we need to look at the process of how our mindstream becomes habituated.

Every time we engage in a particular action of body, speech or mind, we are reinforcing a particular habit. In our example, the gross habit is to quench thirst with water. On a more subtle level though, we could say the habit is to respond to the feeling of thirst with aversion. Every time we react in this way, we increase the probability that we will respond in the same way in the future. We call this habitual tendency a *karmic seed*.

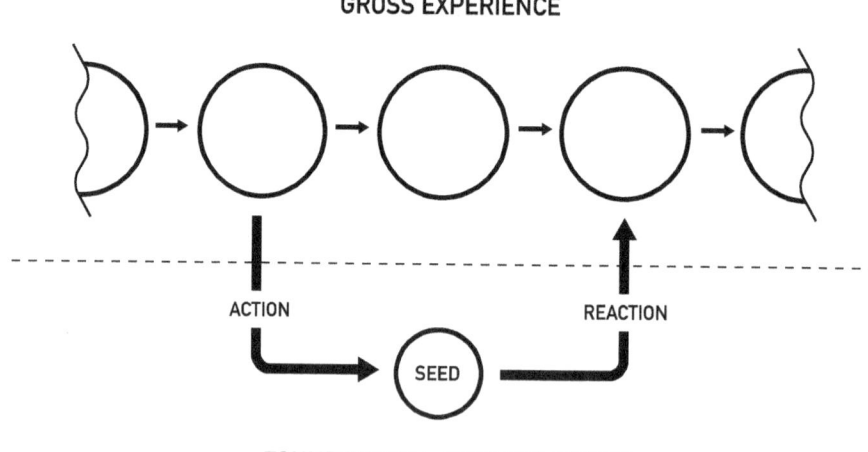

Figure 6-2: How actions form habitual patterns in the mind.

Through a single day, we are engaged in a constant process of action and reaction. Phenomena arise in the mind, we react to them and new seeds are sown. It is very much like the way neural pathways become strengthened as they are repeatedly used. The only difference is, as the mind is non-physical there is no process of natural atrophy. Once a seed has been sown, it will remain in the mind until such time as it "ripens" in the form of an experience, or it is weakened by the application of a counter-force. We will look at both of these transformations later on.

For now, the main thing to understand is that our mind is storing a vast number of habits which are being perpetuated in each and every moment. These habits are stored within the foundational consciousness (see Chapter One), and condition how our experience will arise.

Let's consider the following example:

Many people take on the challenge of starting a new business with the aspiration of gaining success and profit. At the same time, they are all hoping not to lose their investment money, nor their credibility. And yet, despite all of their care- ful business planning, market research and long hours of work, somehow their business fails. They did everything right and yet the result never manifested. At the same time, other people go into business with the exact same aspirations, but do only a fraction of the preparation and work. Despite this, for some reason they succeed and achieve great rewards. Two similar scenarios playing out, two totally different results.

If we ask why did one succeed and one fail, we can identify a wide range of different supporting conditions that might have affected the outcome. We can blame the economy, the product, or all sorts of external things. In Buddhism, we would suggest that these external factors are all secondary conditions. Yes, they definitely have an effect, but the primary cause is the ripening of karmic seeds.

To understand this, consider how both of these situations involved human beings. From a karmic perspective, one person experienced the joy of success, while the other experienced the suffering of failure. These are the karmic results of the two scenarios. Those experiences arose from a whole sequence of choices that were made by each individual. What choices they made were based on the steady stream of karma ripening in their respective mindstreams. How they reacted to things, set up the sequence of events, leading them to the present moment. So while the quality of the product may have been one of the reasons why the business failed, the Law of Karma teaches us to recognise the causes for why that particular product was created in that particular way. When we do this sort of analysis, we are inevitably led back to the mind.

Since the mind is an endless continuity, it then stands to reason that not all of our habits are related to experiences we have had in this lifetime. This can be very difficult for some people to accept, because it means that our experience is being shaped by things that we can't even remember. The fact that we cannot remember the past though, does not mean we cannot be influenced by it.

We can see the influence of karma from past lives in the natural qualities that different children exhibit. It is the ripening of their previous karma that shapes how they experience the world and the various decisions that they make. It is the same principle that is at play when an adult tries to ride a bike. Even though they may not have ridden a bike for many years, they are able to trigger the seeds that were planted previously and thereby quickly re-learn the ability. This phenomenon is commonly known as "intuition" or "instinct".

Similarly, if we possess any natural talents, special aptitudes or skills, then the karmic seeds for these may have been planted many lifetimes ago. These skills will be second nature to us compared with another person who may not have practised such skills in their previous lives. This is a simple explanation of the childhood prodigy—when a child shows exceptional talent in a particular area at a very early age. From a karmic perspective, they are simply remembering what they have already done without the need to be taught. This also explains why different people have vastly different capacities during any one lifetime.

Regarding Continuous Rebirth

Historically, many wisdom traditions such as Hinduism, Islam, Jainism and even some forms of Christianity have held the belief in continuous rebirth. For over 2,500 years many extraordinary Buddhist practitioners have examined this concept extensively, assisted by powerful meditation practices. They have discovered through first-hand experience that the mind is indeed a continuity that is perpetually conditioned by its karmic propensities. Based upon these direct experiences, many hundreds of Buddhist texts have been written, providing access to thousands of scriptural references and systems of logic.

Recounted in the Jataka Tales, are many stories of the Buddha's own past lives. He speaks openly in order to benefit those listening to his teachings, especially when children were present. To give an example:

The Buddha once recollected that prior to his present rebirth as an Indian prince, he was born into a family of Brahmans known for their pure conduct and became a great scholar and teacher. He then entered a forest retreat and began a life as an ascetic, renouncing all desire for wealth and gain. It was here that he encountered a starving tigress who was emaciated from giving birth and was about to eat her own new born cubs in order to survive. With no food in sight, he was moved by immeasurable compassion and offered his body as food to the tigress.

In the Tibetan Buddhist tradition we see evidence of past lives with the recognition of tulkus (the recognised reincarnation or emanation of a guru or enlightened being) such as His Holiness the 14th Dalai Lama. They are recognised by specific tests such as the recognition of objects which belonged to their predecessors as well as their innate and often extraordinary ability to understand certain Buddhist teachings. Many of them also have the ability to recollect key events of their past lives in the same way that we remember things that happened to us during our childhood. Some, such as the Dalai Lama and Karmapa line of reincarnations, are also able to give indications of the circumstances for their future births.

This phenomenon of remembering past lives is not only found in historical records but has also been observed today in modern society. There are thousands of people who claim to remember their past lives, recognising their previous family members and possessions, despite never having encountered them in their current life. There are accounts of such people rediscovering hidden assets, valuable objects belonging to their earlier identities, as well as recollecting certain incidents. In some cases it was possible to confirm their memories through those who were still living.

Although it may not be a mainstream field of research, several books have been written on this subject and the evidence gathered is certainly compelling. Dr. Ian Stevenson, for example, has described and substantiated over 2,000 cases of children recalling their previous lives, many of which are detailed in his book *Parapsychology Research on Exceptional Experiences.*

The famous Indian Buddhist master Bhavaviveka, was once asked the question, "How do we know that someone has experienced death before their current birth?" His answer was simple:

Because it is possible for some people to recall their previous lives.

As we move forward, it is important to try and wrap our heads around the implications of continuous rebirth as they will play a major role in our ability to develop a broader and more expansive understanding of reality. For some the idea will appear logical and easy to digest. While others may have a very strong habit of thinking in terms of only one life, and therefore this idea may be more challenging.

Remember that it's possible for anyone to develop the necessary skills to directly experience the memories of past lives. It's just a matter of whether or not we are willing to make the effort. In the meantime, this doesn't mean you need to accept things with blind faith. Simply keep an open mind, and use your reasoning to explore all possibilities. If you are able to do this, you may find there are a great number of benefits in holding this view.

THE FOUR NATURAL LAWS OF KARMA

If we were to summarise the observations made by the Buddha, we could identify four distinct patterns to help us get a sense of how karma manifests over time. While there are more subtle patterns we need to be aware of, these four points provide a basic framework we can use to integrate an understanding of karma into our day-to-day activities.

1. Results are definite.

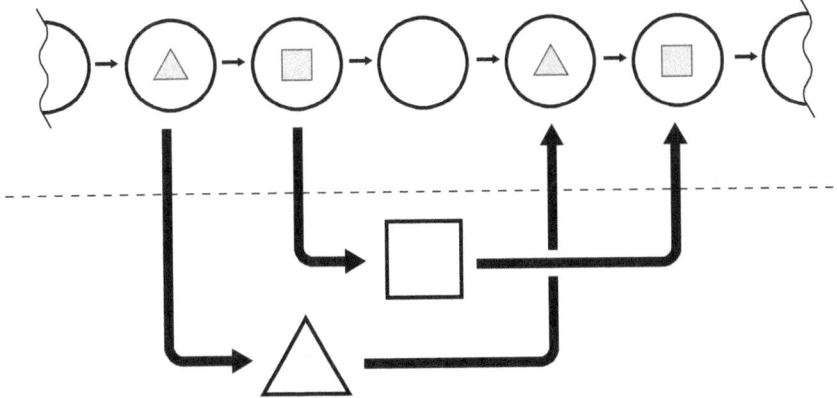

Figure 6-3 Every cause has a result of similar nature.

When you plant an apple seed, you will get an apple tree, not an orange tree. In the same way, specific karmic seeds will only give rise to specific karmic results. This means that if you engage in actions that are dominated by afflicted states of mind, then the karmic seeds created by those actions will definitely generate the experience of suffering. Whereas, the karmic seeds created by virtuous minds will definitely generate happiness.

2. If there is a result, there must be a cause.

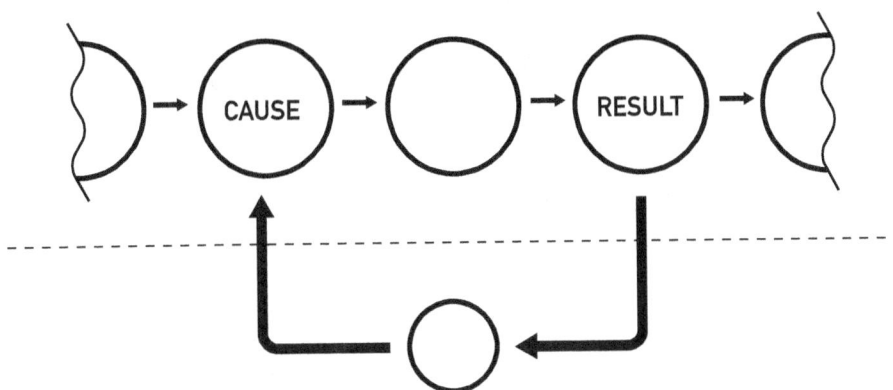

Figure 6-4 Every result has a corresponding cause.

Something cannot come from nothing, therefore it is impossible to experience a result if you have not first created the cause for that experience. We have to be careful not to think of karma like some sort of system of reward and punishment. In Buddhism, there is no higher being keeping tabs on your conduct, judging whether to give you happiness or suffering. Instead, the responsibility lies with you, as it is your actions which are creating the causes for the results that you experience. No matter what happens, if you experience it, then you must have created the cause for it.

In one extreme example of this, a man jumped out of the eighty-first story of the World Trade Centre in New York City, on the day of September 11th. He survived the fall with only a broken leg. From a Buddhist perspective, this seemingly impossible feat occurred because that person had not created the causes to die in that way.

3. If there is a cause, there must be a result.

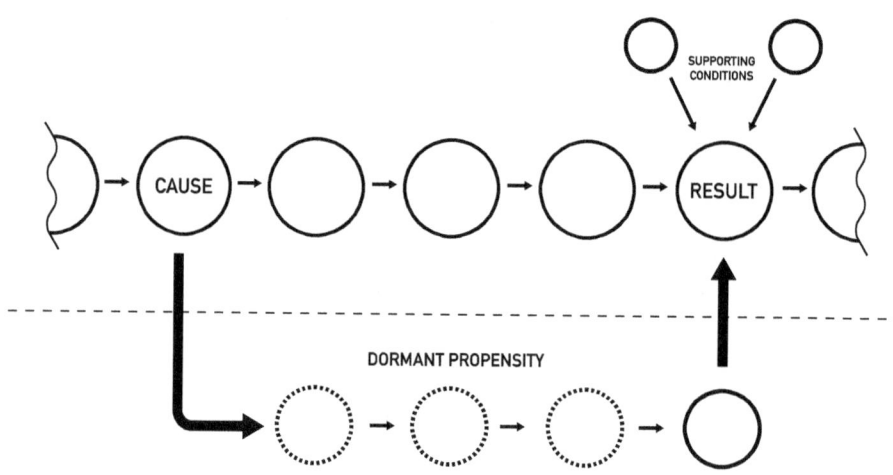

Figure 6-5 Every cause will eventually lead to a result.

Just as a result cannot come from nothing, a cause will not simply disappear over time. As non-physical phenomena, karmic propensities do not naturally deteriorate. This means that no matter how long it takes, when the conditions come together, that seed will ripen as a result. Until that moment, the propensity remains dormant as a potential in the mindstream.

The only way to avoid experiencing a particular result is to engage in actions which apply a counterforce to the undesirable habit. The process of weakening certain propensities is know as "purification". We will be discussing this further in Book Two of this series.

4. Karma expands.

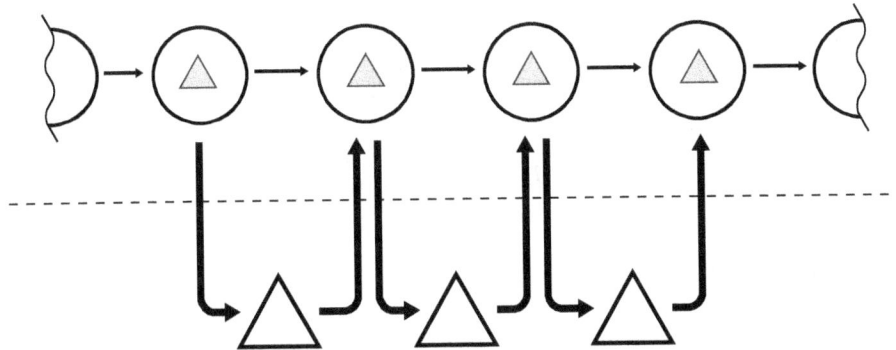

Figure 6-6 Habitual propensities are self perpetuating.

Every time we engage in actions of body, speech or mind, we are adding energy to existing habitual tendencies. The more energy we add, the stronger those habits become and the more they are capable of influencing our experience. This creates a type of feedback loop where more and more of our actions are being influenced by these dominant habits.

When we consider that no action is lost until it ripens, then it is possible for very small actions to grow over time. This leads us to the conclusion that every action matters. No matter how insignificant the action may seem, it is possible for it to give rise to a huge number of results. Like a tiny seed that grows into a majestic tree.

Exercise 6.1—The Dynamics of Karma

- *In a relaxed posture, establish a neutral mind through the practice of mindfulness of breathing.*

- *Review the events of your day, moving slowly through each action that you remember. Try to include everything you did, everything you said and everything you thought. Look at the state of mind behind each of* these actions. Would you characterise your mind as being afflicted, virtuous or neutral in these moments? Recognising that karma is definite, consider the general results your actions will generate. Did you create the causes for happiness? Or did you create the causes for suffering?

- Now think back to a time when you experienced some degree of happiness. Bring the details of the experience to mind, trying to make it as vivid as possible. Where did this experience come from? What were some of the conditions that help make that experience manifest? Consider your state of mind in that moment and how it contributed to the experience.

- Likewise, consider a difficult moment in your life, perhaps a moment of frustration or conflict. Without placing blame on one thing or another, consider the different causes and conditions that had to come together for that experience to arise. While other people and things may have triggered the experience, where did the suffering occur? How does being aware of the karmic influence in the event, change your way of viewing it?

- When you look back over your life, how frequently was your mind carried away by afflictions such as attachment or aversion? How much of a rollercoaster has it been? If every one of those moments generated karmic propensities in your mind, and those propensities will not dissolve naturally, then what are the implications?

- Now consider the way your actions influence others. Choose a few examples of actions you have engaged in during your life, and follow the chain of events those actions triggered. Consider how tiny actions accumulate over time. Can you identify examples from your life where a seemingly insignificant decision has lead you to a very significant experience?

- Rest in any insights that develop.

WAYS OF UNDERSTANDING KARMA

Due to the centrality that karma plays in conditioning our moment-to-moment experience, the vast range of effects that karma has on our lives is very difficult to comprehend. For this reason, it can be helpful to narrow our focus to some degree and work with specific aspects of the Law of Karma in isolation. For this reason, Buddhism provides a variety of different methods for classifying karma. Through studying these different classifications we are able to build a more detailed understanding of the various influences at play, while avoiding being overwhelmed by the complexity of the subject.

Karma Experienced by Oneself and Others

When we consider the types of actions that people engage in, we can see that some are internal to an individual's mind (such as thoughts and emotions), while others are externalised into the physical world (such as things we do or say). While actions of the mind are private, actions of the body and speech are shared and therefore they have the capacity to influence more than just a single person.

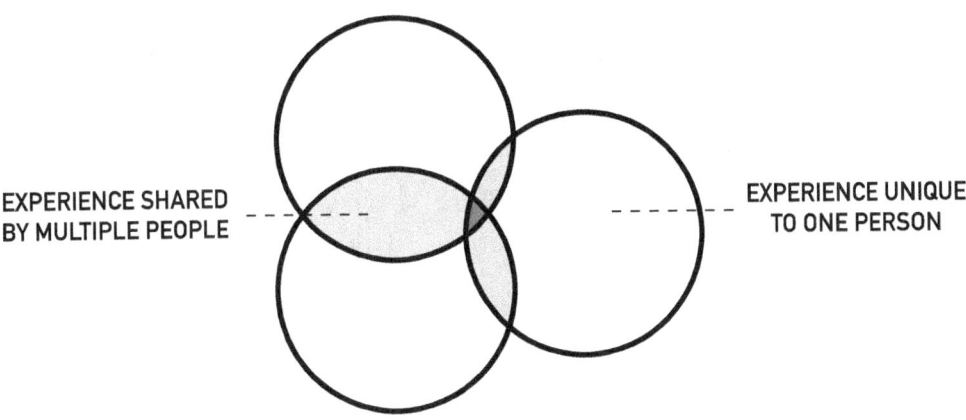

EXPERIENCE SHARED
BY MULTIPLE PEOPLE

EXPERIENCE UNIQUE
TO ONE PERSON

Figure 6-7: Overlap of experience across multiple individuals.

By looking at the scope of the influence of our actions, we can identify two types of karma:

1. Collective Karma

Karma that is shared across multiple individuals is considered to be collective karma. It essentially forms a bond or connection between people, generating some degree of similarity of experiences. For instance, we all share the collective karma to be born as human beings on the planet Earth. This means that we all have similar bodies, with similar sensory organs, which give rise to similar types of consciousness. It is this similarity that allows us to communicate our experiences to each other and be able to understand what is being said. Compare this with dolphins. While they share the collective karma to be born on Earth, they do not share the karma to be born as humans. This means their experience is significantly different from our own, making it difficult (but not impossible) to communicate clearly.

Collective karma can work at different magnitudes. It can be universal, global, or more localised. For instance, when we consider the formation of various tribes and countries around the world, we can say that those people have collective karma together. So even though we are all human, we are more connected with those of a particular country or region. Even within a single country we have more collective karma with those people who live in the same city or neighborhood as us.

The bonds which connect us are not just geographical, we can also be connected through our beliefs and concerns. Just consider all those who practice a particular type of wisdom tradition. There is a similarity in how they view and understand the world. This accounts for how it is possible that so many westerners have developed an interest in Buddhism even though they grew up in countries where Buddhism was generally unknown.

Collective karma is produced every time we interact with another person. Through our shared experience, we are both planting similar seeds in our mindstreams. The more we share our experience, the more similarity develops between the karmic propensities stored in our mindstreams. This then causes us to react in similar ways to different situations, leading to similar decisions being made, and therefore, to similar actions being engaged in.

2. Individual Karma

While our personal karma may have a great deal of similarities with the karma of others, it is never exactly the same. This is primarily due to the fact that our physical and verbal actions are only one part of our activities. The vast majority of our karma is created through the various conceptual patterns of our thoughts and subjective experiences. Since these reactions are private to a single individual, they produce a unique pattern of karmic propensities.

It is for this reason that identical twins growing up in the same environment can still exhibit distinct variations in their personalities or capabilities. It also explains why some people can experience an incredibly long and prosperous life, while others might encounter misfortune and find their lives ended prematurely. Just consider the vast diversity of physical features that arise out of the specific expression of our genes. All of this is considered an example of individual karma.

Exercise 6.2—Shared Experience

- *In a relaxed posture, establish a neutral mind through the practice of mindfulness of breathing.*

- *Select a specific event from your life that you can remember clearly. This event should involve multiple people. Spend some time establishing the details of the situation so that everything appears vividly to the mind.*

- *Now consider which aspects of your experience you believe would have been similar to the experience of those around you. Perhaps think of the different types of consciousness as one way of identifying different aspects of the experience. Consider how strong the similarities are between the different people in the event. Think not only of the general similarities, but also the more specific ones as well. Try to identify the different connections that exist between this particular group of people.*

- *Now consider what aspects of this experience are unique to you. Think about the variations in things like beliefs, personal histories, or emotional responses. Try to clearly differentiate between what aspects are collective, and which are individual.*

- *Rest your mind in any insights which arise.*

Karma Based on the Intensity of Intention

According to the discussion of karma in the text *"The Primary Ground"* by the great Indian scholar Asanga, intention plays a key role in the manner in which a karmic seed is formed. Depending on the intention involved, some actions create a stronger impression on the mind, while others are much weaker. We can call a strong impression "heavy" and a weak impression "light". Because of the relative intensity of a heavy karma, the results will be proportionately strong. Likewise, the more light the karma, the less impact the result will have.

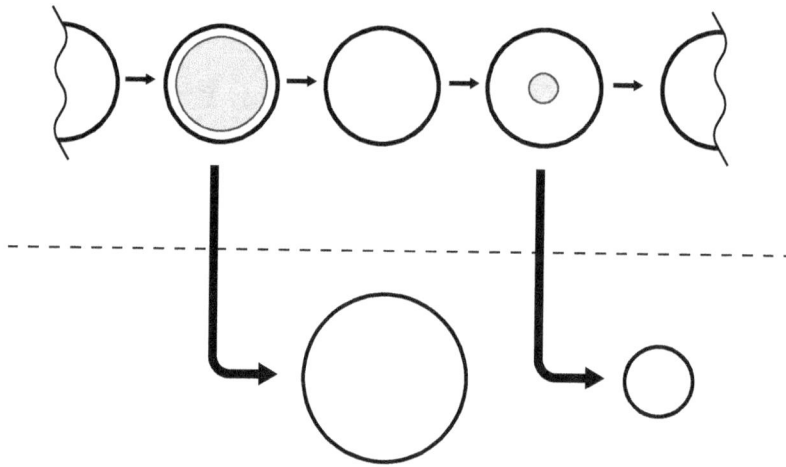

Figure 6-8: The strength of one's intention determines the strength of the karmic imprint.

Intention is a mental factor and as such it is possible to establish an intention without actually carrying out the action either physically or verbally. When this happens, we can say the action is incomplete. A completed action on the other hand is any action we actually carry out with our body or speech. When we combine these two characteristics, we are presented with four possibilities of how karma can be created:

1. Karma with weak intention and not completed.

A weak intention is something like a whim or impulsive reaction to something. It generally does not involve a lot of thought leading up to the action. An intention can also be weak when we have a lot of doubt regarding whether to do something or not. The doubt prevents the intention from having any real power. While such an intention will leave traces in the mind, it is simply too weak to cause any significant results on its own. Through the application of regret, the effects of such light karma can be removed relatively easily.

2. Karma with weak intention and completed.

When we engage in rash, unthinking actions, we will generally create a lighter karmic result. This is because the actions do not carry with them the strength of a clearly defined intention. Due to the immediacy of the physical or verbal action however, it will make a stronger impression than simply having a thought pop into the mind.

Examples of this sort of karma include actions performed in non-lucid dreams, actions performed accidentally or actions performed against one's will. Because the mind is not fully engaged with the action, the karmic result can generally be remedied through the application of an appropriate degree of regret.

3. Karma with strong intention but not completed.

If the intention to act is very strong, this will result in a heavier karmic propensity being generated in the mind. An example of this sort of intention would be if a person was thinking about killing someone. The more time they spent thinking about killing that person, the stronger their intention would grow and the heavier the imprint left on the mind. But no matter how much time they spent premeditating the act, they may never actually encounter the opportunity to act on that intention. Since the act was never completed, the karmic intensity would not be as heavy as it could have been.

4. Karma with strong intention and completion.

The heaviest form of karma is created through the combination of a strong intention that is carried out to completion. If we spend the time forming a very clear and strong intention, then any actions that we engage in based on that intention will be extremely powerful. This is true for all types of actions, whether they result in suffering or in happiness.

Exercise 6.3—Types of Intention

- *In a relaxed posture, establish a neutral mind through the practice of mindfulness of breathing.*

- *Take a moment to think about all of the random thoughts that pop into your mind during the course of a given day. Think about the types of scenarios that your mind considers. Can you identify any unwholesome attitudes connected with these thoughts? Get a sense for the general pattern of these thoughts. Recognising that even these thoughts are leaving traces in your mind, develop some degree of regret that these afflicted states of mind are arising and resolve to be more aware of what is going on in your mind.*

- *Now consider some events from your past where you acted rashly without thinking. Maybe you lost your temper and said something that hurt someone's feelings. Maybe you did something by accident that resulted in someone else getting hurt. Whatever it was, bring it to mind clearly. Recognise that it happened, regret that it happened and strengthen your resolve to be more aware of your actions in the future.*

- *Identify an occasion when you spent a lot of time thinking about doing something, but you never actually did it. Maybe you had wanted to speak with someone that you like, but were too shy. Perhaps you thought about telling someone off, but never did. If the action was constructive, then develop the aspiration to engage in this action in the future. If it was destructive, then recognise that it is harmful, regret having thought about doing it, and make a strong resolve to never do it.*

- *Finally, think about a time when you developed a really strong intention and carried through with that intention. Maybe you set yourself a challenge and through hard work and determination you were able to achieve your goal. Perhaps you plotted how to enact revenge on someone who harmed you and then carried through with your plans. Again, rejoice in any constructive intentions that you have developed and regret any negative actions that you have engaged in. Make a strong determination to not repeat these harmful behaviours in the future.*

- *Rest your mind in any insights which arise.*

Karma Based on the Magnitude of the Result

The magnitude of the result will always correspond to the intensity of the cause. So the more powerful the cause, the more powerful the experience of the result.

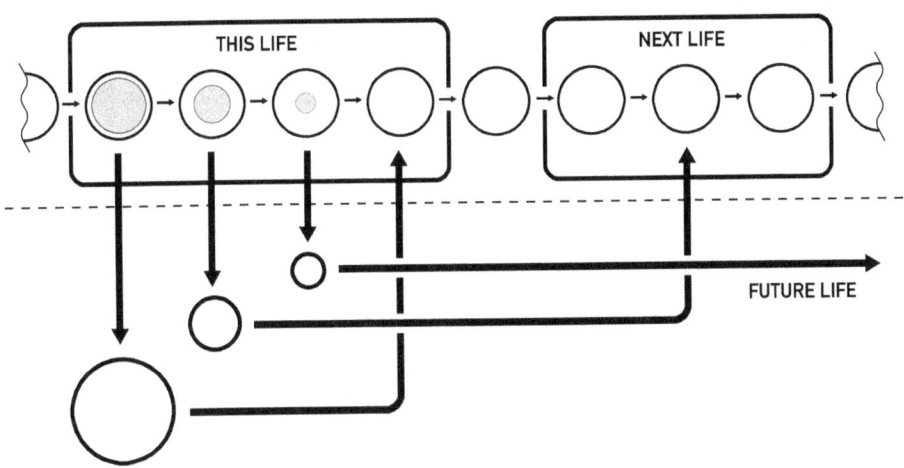

Figure 6-9: Heavier karma generally ripens faster.

When we look at the types of results that can arise from different intensities of karmas, we arrive at three points:

1. Result experienced in the current lifetime.

When a very strong intention is combined with an action directed towards a powerful object, then it is possible to experience the result of that karma within this same lifetime. A powerful object is considered any person who has greatly benefited you in this life such as a spiritual teacher or those who have loved you unconditionally such as your parents. Of all the people that you encounter, these people are the most influential to you. Therefore, any actions you do in relation to these people will carry a particularly strong influence on your mind. Those people who are experiencing great suffering can also be considered powerful objects as they can act as the basis for generating extremely powerful intentions of compassion and altruism.

2. Karmic result to be experienced in the next life.

Some actions are powerful enough to leave very deep imprints on the mind. So deep in fact, that when a person transitions between this life and the next, these imprints dominate their experience to such a degree, they guarantee to determine the shape that the next life will take. The strength of these actions is a combination of extremely powerful and destructive intentions being directed towards very powerful objects. In Buddhism, we refer to these actions as the *Five Heinous Crimes*:

1. Killing one's father

2. Killing one's mother

3. Killing a highly realised being

4. Drawing blood from an enlightened being

5. Creating a schism within a spiritual community

Engaging in any of these actions has serious karmic repercussions as they are all based on harming or separating oneself from those influences which are capable of guiding you towards genuine happiness. Instead of generating the happiness you seek, they generate the exact opposite—an extreme form of suffering.

3. *Karmic result to be experienced in subsequent lives.*

For the most part, the results of actions that we perform in this life will be experienced in future lives. Since karma does not decay, no matter how long it takes, eventually the conditions will come together for that karma to ripen. This is why we must not assume that all of our experiences in this life are a result of actions performed in this life. While the actions of this life help to create the conditions for our karma to ripen, the actual karmas that are ripening are usually coming from past lives.

This is why some people who are kind and have a very good heart may still have to experience a difficult life. They may be unsuccessful in their careers or suffer illnesses, but that doesn't mean their kindness and merit are not powerful. It may be that they are experiencing a few remaining negative karmic seeds ripening from previous lifetimes. The power of the person's merit often lets them experience and reduce this negative karma first, after which they begin to experience the results of the oceans of positive karma they have accumulated.

On the other hand, there are some people who have very little compassion and frequently harm others, yet still have a successful life and temporary happiness. In this case there are only a few meritorious karmas remaining from their previous lives, and upon their completion, due to their accumulated negative karmic seeds, they will surely experience suffering.

Exercise 6.4—*The Intensity of Actions*

- *In a relaxed posture, establish a neutral mind through the practice of mindfulness of breathing.*

- *Bring to mind those people you feel most connected with. Now consider the effect this person has on you. If such a person says something to you, does it carry more weight than if it were coming from someone else? Likewise, when you do something in relation to this person, would you remember it more than the same action with someone else? Try to get a sense for the importance that this person holds in your life.*

- *Now imagine what it would mean to you, to do something to benefit this person. How would it make you feel to know you brought this person some degree of happiness or satisfaction?*

- *Consider the opposite. How would you feel if you harmed this person? What would happen if you did something that made it impossible for them to remain in your life? Imagine the trauma you would feel if you had intentionally caused this person's life to end?*

- *Now look back over your life and compare the types of actions you have engaged in and the types of experiences you have had. Can you identify any situations where no matter how good your intentions, the only result was your own or other's suffering? Also think about times when your mind was filled with destructive intentions and yet everything seemed to work out for you. While it may have felt good at the time, what sort of result do you think these actions will produce?*

- *Rest your mind in any insights that arise.*

Karma at the Time of Death

During the course of one lifetime, we will experience a continual flow of karmic propensities ripening in accordance with the conditions that arise. At the same time, we will create new propensities on the basis of how we react to that flow of experience. Fortunately for us human beings, we have some degree of intelligence which allows us to shape our intentions through the choices we make.

When the conditions arise for this life to end, we will experience a dissolution of all our gross states of mind as the body is no longer capable of supporting our consciousness. This includes our capacity to influence how we react to things. At this time, we dissolve into the natural flow of our experience and are swept away by the countless habits we have formed in this and previous past lives. The question then arises "where will these habits take me?" What sort of life will be produced after this one? The answer will depend on which habits are activated at the moment of death.

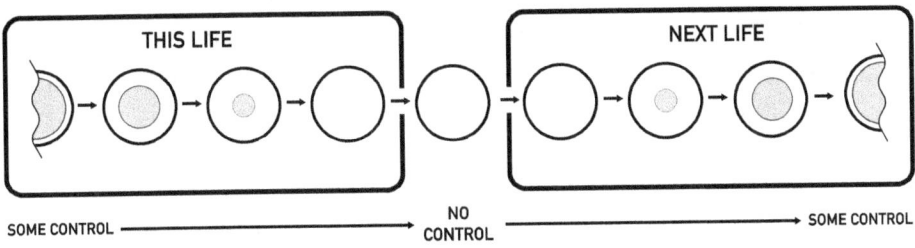

Figure 6-10: As we approach death, our consciousness dissolves and habits take over.

The Order that Karma Ripens

Up until the point where our gross conceptual minds dissolve, we are able to direct our consciousness towards particular types of objects. The more we focus on a particular object, the more we nurture its capacity to ripen related karmas. When these karmas ripen, they will determine the subsequent moments of consciousness, which in turn will determine the shape of our next rebirth. If we lack awareness during this important process, then our mind will naturally be drawn towards karmas in the following order:

1. No matter what state of mind we are in (whether virtuous or non-virtuous), if the mind is powered by a strong intention, then the karma to first ripen, will be the karma that corresponds most directly to that intention.

2. Failing that, if there are multiple karmic propensities that relate to our state of mind, then the karmic propensity that took the longest to produce or that we are most strongly habituated to, will ripen first.

3. Failing that, the heaviest karma (the one which carries the greatest effect) will be experienced first.

4. Failing that, the most recently created karma will be the first to ripen.

5. Failing that, the karma completed with the most powerful motivation will ripen first.

6. Failing that, the karma directed towards the most powerful object (as explained earlier) will be the one that is experienced first.

7. Failing that, the karma that was dedicated with the strongest virtuous intention will ripen first.

8. If all of the above factors are equal and if our state of mind at the time of our death is not very powerful, the karma that ripens first will depend on previous forms of karma which are most closely related to the state of mind at the moment of death.

As we can see, this process highlights the complex nature of karma while also demonstrating its fluid and dynamic aspects. Of particular note here is the importance that awareness and intention play in allowing us to influence which karma ripens first.

Projecting and Completing Karma

Generally speaking, when we think about karma in relation to how it shapes a future rebirth, we can speak of two main categories:

1. **Projecting Karma:** This is any karma that has been strengthened sufficiently to ripen at the moment of death with the power to propel the mind into a specific shape or form of experience. For instance, if our mind is dominated by hatred, anger or paranoia at the time of death, then this state of mind will cause certain karmas to ripen which will propel the mind to take on the experience of extreme suffering and torment. Likewise, a mind which is at peace and filled with an altruistic motivation to benefit others, will cause a very different karma to ripen, which in turn will produce an entirely different experience.

2. **Completing Karma:** While projecting karma determines the general shape that the experience will take, completing karmas fill out the specific details of that experience. Take the example of your present human body. The fact that you are human is considered to be the result of your projecting karma. The shape, size, colour and features of your human body is an example of the result of completing karma.

What is important to recognise here is that our past, present and future lives are all the result of *multiple* karmas ripening. While one karma may have been the primary influence on what form you take, countless other karmas are also contributing to your specific experience. This is why we see such a great diversity in the types of people in our world.

Exercise 6.5—When Life Flashes Before Your Eyes

- *In a relaxed posture, establish a neutral mind through the practice of mindfulness of breathing.*

- *Imagine that you are sitting in a hospital bed. You can feel your body getting weaker and you know you do not have long left to live.*

- *If you had the chance to choose, how would you like to spend your last moments? What attitude would you like to cultivate at that time? Which thoughts would bring the greatest peace to your mind?*

- *Now look back over your life and consider the states of mind you feel you are most habituated to. Think of how you act when you are not making any particular effort to control your behaviour. Are you usually anxious or high-strung? Are you often quick-tempered or grumpy? What are the traits that you most identify with?*

- *Then consider some of the major turning points in your life. The events which made a very large impact on who you are as a person. Think about the influence these events have had on you and how your life developed.*

- *Bring to mind the goals you have held in this life. Think about all of the energy you have invested in them. Think of the way these goals have shaped your decisions.*

- *Consider those people who have been particularly influential in your life (for instance parents or teachers). Consider your actions in relation to these people. How would you characterise the relationships?*

- *Identify the most meaningful virtuous actions you have engaged in during your life so far. How did these actions bring benefit to those around you?*

- *Rest in any insights that arise.*

Karma Based on the Type of Result

By the power of our projecting and completing karma, we each take on a particular form of existence. There is a coming together of body and mind, which forms the basis upon which a sentient being is able to experience a range of phenomena. When we look at the different types of experiences that our karma generates, we can identify the following patterns:

1. The Karmic Result Similar to the Cause

When we engage in an action, we can be sure that the result will be of a similar nature to the cause that was created. For instance, the nature of telling a lie is deception. Therefore, the karmic result of lying is to experience others trying to deceive you. Likewise, the nature of stealing is to deprive someone of experiencing something. This leads to the karmic result of not having what you need.

In addition to the experience which is similar to the cause, there is also the experience of being habituated to that particular action. This means that every karmic propensity is the cause for creating another karmic propensity of a similar nature. So if you were to steal, not only would you be deprived of things, but you would also have the habit to steal more. In this way, our karma not only shapes our experience but also perpetuates how the mind is conditioned.

2. The Karmic Effect on the Environment

From the Buddhist perspective, the physical and non-physical worlds are constantly influencing each other. While we are accustomed to thinking of the physical world as being separate from us, Buddhism challenges us to recognise the ways in which our minds shape the very environments in which we live. From our own perspective, the ripening of our karma changes how we perceive our surroundings.

For instance, someone who has killed a lot in the past, will tend to experience their environment as being without joy, dangerous and life-threatening. If they have stolen a lot, then they will tend to perceive their environment as being barren and devoid of the resources they desire. If you are constantly lying and cheating, you will experience an environment which is hostile and deceptive, filled with people who you can't trust.

3. The Uncertain Number of Karmic Results

Often people have a rather simplistic view of cause and effect, believing that one cause leads to one particular effect. This is not necessarily the case. To use an analogy, within one tree, there is the potential for many fruit to ripen. Likewise, some karmas are so strong they have the capacity to produce many results over the course of time. Eventually the energy of that propensity will dissipate, but until it does it can still influence how experiences arise.

This principle also holds for many weak karmas. Sometimes, a single karma does not have enough power to ripen in any significant way. However, if it is combined with other karmas of a similar nature, it can generate a result. This is why it is so important to pay attention to all actions, whether big or small. Every little thing adds up in the end and can turn out to make a huge difference.

Exercise 6.6—The Experience of Karma

- *In a relaxed posture, establish a neutral mind through the practice of mindfulness of breathing.*

- *Bring to mind some major events from your life. Think of both the highs and lows that you feel have marked the course of your experience. For each event, consider the karma that was ripening in that moment.*

- *First, start with looking at the subjective experience of the event. How did it feel to you? What was the nature of that feeling? For instance maybe its nature was loss, or conflict, or harmony. Try to identify some words to describe the general pattern of the experience.*

- *Now consider the types of actions that share that pattern. For instance, if you experienced great loss, then that correlates to causing great loss. What sort of actions can create these causes?*

- *When you have identified some original causes, consider if you are still engaging in those sorts of activities in this life. Identify the strength of habit that you have in relation to this type of action.*

- *Now consider how you relate to your environment based on this action. Let's say you identified a propensity for hurting others, what sort of state of mind does this promote? Will you be able to rest easy or will you always be anxious and defensive? How does your state of mind shift your experience of where you live?*

- *Rest in any insights that arise.*

ESTABLISHING AN ETHICAL FOUNDATION FOR LIFE

Through studying the Law of Karma, we are able to gain greater insight into the interdependent relationship between our actions and our experiences. By understanding the influence of different types of actions, we are able to identify which forms of behaviour are conducive to achieving our goals and which are not. This is the basis for the system of ethical conduct as understood from a Buddhist perspective.

If we consider all of the different types of actions that we do, we can speak of Three Doors:

1. **Body:** These are all physical actions performed with our body in interaction with the external world. This may include interacting with people or with inanimate objects.

2. **Speech:** All verbal actions performed as communication between two people. For it to be considered speech, there must be some degree of understanding related to the meaning of the sounds that are generated.

3. **Mind:** These are all the thoughts that arise in the mind on the basis of intention. That is to say that the person must willfully generate the thought for it to be considered an action.

Of these three, the mind is considered the most important as the mind is where the intention for an action is formulated. If an action is performed with an intention that is conditioned by an afflicted state of mind, then we can call that action *non-virtuous*. Likewise, if the action is performed with an intention conditioned by a virtuous state of mind, then it will be a *virtuous* action. In this context, virtue is not a moralistic description of some universal right or wrong. Instead, it is merely an indicator to the degree of distortion present in a state of mind. If the mind is at least partially in accordance with reality, we call it virtue, while if it is not, then we call it non-virtue. Everything is always in relation to how closely we are experiencing reality *as it is*. For more on this subject please refer to the discussion of mental factors in Chapter Two.

When identifying what actions of body, speech and mind correspond with particular karmic consequences, we create for ourselves the opportunity to proceed in life with awareness that we alone are the ones responsible for whether we experience happiness or suffering. Additionally, by understanding that the unfortunate circumstances occurring in our lives are the result of our past actions, we can become more accepting of them, comprehending that how we respond to the ripening of such negative karma will determine what habitual tendencies we create for ourselves. We can therefore change the patterns of our past to create a better future. The way we do this is through the accumulation of merit.

Merit from a Buddhist perspective is not the doing of good deeds; instead, the doing of good deeds produces merit. All virtuous actions create positive karmic propensities which have the capacity to produce the experience of happiness. Our habituation to these propensities is what we are referring to as "merit". It takes a lot of effort to build up positive habits. We are so habituated to creating negative karmas that they accumulate like dust on a bookshelf.

When we tame our minds through practising Dharma, we increase our mindfulness of how we act and respond to the vast array of circumstances in our lives. If we choose to act in a wholesome and virtuous way, we plant positive seeds and generate a great deal of merit in our mindstreams. As our merit grows, we engage with more virtuous acts which in turn plants more seeds and generate the positive reinforcement needed to strengthen our habituation to virtue. The more habituated we become, the more positive qualities can naturally and spontaneously arise in our minds.

Striving to practise wholesome actions has nothing to do with feeling guilty or being rigid in how we behave. The focus is more on gaining confidence in which actions are beneficial and which are not. Understanding the Karmic

Law of Cause and Effect can provide the basis for leading a more ethical and fulfilling life and help us realise that negative actions in both the long and short term, only lead to our own suffering. With time and experience, our trust in this natural law of karma will grow.

To help us in this process, the Buddha identified a very simple framework for developing mindfulness of our actions. Essentially there are ten actions of body, speech and mind that should be abandoned and ten that should be cultivated.

Abandoning the Ten Non-Virtuous Actions

This first set represents those actions which should be abandoned. While there are countless types of non-virtuous actions, most are derivatives of the following ten:

1. **Killing:** This means to take another sentient being's life. The essence of this act is to remove the conditions that support life. It is the forceful separation of a mind from the body that it is attached to. If you kill, then you are creating the causes for not having the conditions which support life, which means you will experience great sickness and suffering.

2. **Stealing:** This means to take something which does not belong to you. The essence of this act is to deprive someone of resources. The effect of stealing is that you create the causes for not having access to resources such as food, clothing, shelter, or wealth. You are creating the conditions to never have enough and to always be looking for more.

3. **Sexual Misconduct:** Sexual misconduct occurs when you use your sexuality as a method for inflicting harm on others. It is a violation of a very intimate act which has specific significance between two people. The essence of this act is some degree of betrayal, resulting in the destruction of a relationship. The effects will be that your relationships with others will be very difficult and your partners will be unfaithful.

4. **Lying:** This means to purposefully speak untruths with the intention to deceive another person. The essence of this action is deception

and creates the causes for you not to be able to trust anyone. The information you receive will often be distorted and confusing.

5. **Divisive Language:** This action occurs whenever you purposefully say something that creates divisions between people. The essence of this act is the creation of disharmony. The result of always trying to divide people is that you will find it very difficult to relate with others and will be surrounded by people who speak badly about you.

6. **Speaking Harshly:** This means to use verbal abuse as a method for hurting other people. This can include obvious abusive language or more subtle forms such as sarcasm and passive aggressive comments. The essence is to trigger mental suffering through communication. The effect is to hear many unpleasant words that cause you to experience suffering.

7. **Worthless Chatter:** This means to engage in speech with no purpose on the basis of afflicted states of mind such as attachment or aversion. This includes all forms of gossip and meaningless banter. The essence of this act is meaninglessness and results in you hearing many pointless words which bring no benefit to your life.

8. **Covetous Thoughts:** This is the act of thinking about acquiring an object on the basis of afflicted states of mind. It is an act of sustained desire, fueled generally by attachment. The essence is dissatisfaction and results in a mind which can never be content and is always envious of the things that other people have.

9. **Harbouring Ill-will:** This is the act of thinking about harming someone. It is the wish that a particular person would encounter the causes for suffering. Its essence is hatred and results in a mind that is always paranoid and suspicious about others, fearful of being harmed.

10. **Holding Incorrect Views:** This is the act of developing certainty in a thought that is not in accordance with reality. Its essence is confusion and results in a mind that is ignorant about truth and is therefore confused about everything.

When we relate these actions to the three doors, we can see that the first three are related to the body, the next four are related to speech, and the last three are related to the mind. The actions of body and speech are listed in descending order of their relative intensity. Whereas the actions of the mind are listed in ascending order of influence. By consciously avoiding any or all of these actions you will be preventing the creation of a significant number of negative karmas and will be generating a positive counterforce to your existing karmic habits.

Cultivating the Ten Virtuous Actions

Abandoning non-virtue is a great foundation for weakening negative habits, but that's only half of the story. In order to cultivate merit, we really need to start laying down positive karmic propensities through engaging in the cultivation of virtue. The following are ten actions which can help you to do that:

1. **Saving Lives:** This means to actively go out of your way to save the life of others. It is a mind which sees the value in life and creates the conditions for others to prolong their lives as much as possible. This includes helping sentient beings stay out of harm's way, such as a fly who is beating itself against a window trying to get out. The effect of this action is to experience a long and healthy life.

2. **Generosity:** By making your resources available to others you are creating the conditions to fulfill their needs. This creates the causes for you to also receive all the resources that you need.

3. **Ethical Discipline:** This is the act of making effort to avoid non-virtue and making effort to cultivate virtue. The result of doing this is that you will develop an appearance which is pleasing to others and your relationships will be peaceful.

4. **Speaking Truth:** By always speaking the truth, you are creating the causes for people to trust you. Your speech will be strong and filled with conviction and therefore people will listen to what you have to say and value your opinion.

5. **Reconciling Disputes:** When you make the effort to bring people

together by overcoming conflict, then you are creating the causes to experience harmony in your own relationships.

6. **Pleasant Speech:** If you are courteous to others and speak pleasantly, you will find this behaviour will be returned. People will naturally speak kindly to you and with respect.

7. **Meaningful Speech:** By making effort to speak with intention and purpose, you are creating the causes to experience speech which is extremely meaningful and beneficial for your life. This can come in the form of spiritual teachings or valuable information that creates a positive influence on your mind.

8. **Contentment:** By learning to be content with whatever conditions you find yourself, you are creating the causes to discover your own wealth of inner resources. When you do this, you will see that there is nothing more that is needed and you will experience incredible peace of mind.

9. **Cultivating Good-Will:** This means to cultivate the desire for others to experience happiness and to be free from suffering. This attitude will lead you to work for the benefit of others and therefore will result in you receiving kindness from others and being held in high regard.

10. **Holding Correct Views:** By making the effort to develop greater intelligence and wisdom, you will be creating the causes for a clear and powerful mind. This mind will allow you to overcome all forms of ignorance and ultimately experience lasting genuine happiness.

The fundamental practice of ethical discipline is to maintain mindfulness of these twenty actions at all times during the day. It is generally easiest to start with the actions of the body as they are the most obvious and easy to control. You can choose one particular action to focus on or work with the entire set. In the morning, remind yourself of the actions that you wish to avoid and those that you wish to cultivate. Then during the day, try to maintain some degree of awareness of everything you are doing. If you notice you are about to commit one of the non-virtuous actions, then try to avoid it if possible. Likewise, if you see an opportunity to perform one of the virtuous actions, make the effort to do so where possible. As you develop greater familiarity with the actions, then slowly try to add more actions of which to be aware, until you have incorporated all twenty points into your behaviour.

Doorway	Non-Virtue	Virtue
Body	Killing	Saving Lives
	Stealing	Generosity
	Sexual Misconduct	Ethical Discipline
Speech	Lying	Speaking Truth
	Divisive Language	Reconciling Disputes
	Speaking Harshly	Pleasant Speech
	Worthless Chatter	Meaningful Speech
Mind	Covetous Thoughts	Contentment
	Harbouring Ill-will	Cultivating Good-Will
	Holding Incorrect Views	Holding Correct Views

Table 6-1 Virtuous and non-virtuous actions of the body, speech and mind.

Remember that the purpose of ethical discipline is to develop constructive habits. Don't beat yourself up if you find your existing negative habits overwhelm you at times. To actually be aware of your actions is an important and very positive first step. If you do recognise that the behaviour in question is not constructive, simply try to develop the desire to have the ability to avoid it in the future. In this way, you weaken the existing habit and give yourself a better chance to be successful in your training.

REVIEW OF KEY POINTS

- There are two types of causes: a substantial cause and a supporting condition. The substantial cause is what transforms into the result, while the supporting conditions help make that transformation possible.

- The Law of Karma is specifically focused on describing the causal relationships between our actions and our experiences. While actions can generate changes in the physical world, we are mainly concerned with changes in the mind.

- Actions are performed on the basis of intentions in the mind and these intentions leave a habitual propensity in the foundational consciousness which is known as a karmic seed.

- Karmic seeds ripen in the mindstream as the experience of suffering or happiness.

- The Four Natural Laws of Karma are that 1) karma is definite, 2) if there is a result, there must be a cause, 3) if there is a cause, there must be a result and 4) karma expands.

- Karmas have scope based on the interaction of the people involved in the action. This leads to a combination of both collective and individual karma.

- The intensity of karma is governed by the strength of the intention combined with the completion of an action.

- The magnitude of the result will be based on the nature of the object of an action and the type of action performed. Very powerful karmas can ripen in this same life, while others will definitely ripen within the next or subsequent lives.

- When we die, the karma which ripens at that time will determine the general shape of your subsequent experience. This is known as projecting karma. Those karmas which shape the specific details of your subsequent experience are known as completing karma.

- Every karma produces different types of results: there is the experience that is similar to the cause, the habitual tendency that is similar to the cause and the experience of one's environmental conditions.

- The basic framework for ethics in Buddhism revolves around developing greater mindfulness of the three doors of body, speech and mind.

- Virtue is any action that is motivated by a mind that is free from afflictions while non-virtue is an action motivated by an afflicted mind. The aim of the practice is to abandon ten non-virtuous actions and to cultivate ten virtuous ones.

The Wheel of Life.

CHAPTER SEVEN

The Suffering Nature of Cyclic Existence

The *Law of Karma* provides us with a detailed model for how our minds are conditioned by our actions, providing us with the basic mechanisms for explaining why we experience what we experience. In many ways, karma is like the fuel that keeps the flow of appearances arising in our minds, while also being the engine that perpetuates a particular type of relationship with those appearances.

When we consider the possibilities of how our mind can relate with any given phenomena, we can identify two basic relationships:

1. **Ignorance:** When appearances are interpreted based on the misconceptions of a deluded consciousness, then they can be considered to be distorted by ignorance.

2. **Wisdom:** When appearances are interpreted based on a clear awareness of reality *as it is*, then we can say they are arising out of wisdom.

As we have seen, anything which arises out of an afflicted mind such as ignorance, will either directly or indirectly generate the causes for suffering. Therefore, in order to remove all experience of suffering, we need to stop relating to the world on the basis of our deluded consciousness.

In this chapter, we will be exploring in detail the diversity of results that are produced by ignorance. In particular, we will be studying the nature of what is known as *cyclic existence* (samsara). Cyclic existence is not a place that you visit, it is a pattern for how we relate to the world. This particular pattern is rooted in ignorance and therefore by its very nature it is responsible for the generation of a wide variety of unsatisfying experiences. By understanding the dynamic components of this system, we can develop strategies for breaking free from this endless loop and thereby open the door to experiencing our lives on the basis of wisdom.

Through recognising and contemplating the suffering nature of cyclic existence, coupled with our firm understanding of the karmic law of cause and effect, we begin to see it is possible to make changes to our situation and we do not have to suffer in the ways that we do. On this basis, we develop the aspiration to seek a path that can lead us out of such suffering. It is this aspiration which provides us with a powerful motivation for developing the mind of renunciation and gives us confidence in our capacity to be free.

HOW KARMA GIVES RISE TO CYCLIC EXISTENCE

The first step then is to identify the causal relationships that give rise to cyclic existence. This broader understanding enables us to identify the creative potential this system has for producing different types of experiences. It also provides us with a context to then explore the various manifestations within that system.

The method for doing this is through the study of the *Twelve Links of Dependent Origination*. This teaching was originally presented by the Buddha in the *Rice Seedling Sutra*:

> *Because this exists, such-and-such will arise. Because that has arisen, such-and-such arises. Hence, because of ignorance karmic formations arise, because karmic formations arise consciousness arises, and so on and so forth. The same holds true for name-and-form, the six sense-bases, contact, sensation, craving, grasping, becoming and birth, down to old age, sickness and death. Sorrow, lamentation, misery, unhappiness and distress will then arise. Thus this great mass of total suffering arises... Similarly, the formations will cease because of ignorance having ceased and so forth, down to the point where, because of birth, old age and death having ceased, sorrow and so forth, this great mass of total suffering will also cease. Thus it has been taught.*

Simply put, the body and mind we inherit in this life and future lives depend on the karma we continue to create with our body, speech and mind under the influence of ignorance. The force of karma therefore propels us to be reborn again and again in cyclic existence, and for this reason we are completely dominated by our conditioning.

The Twelve Links of Dependent Origination

The twelve links are traditionally depicted in an image known as the *Wheel of Life*, which shows graphically how cyclic existence comes about. The outer circle represents the twelve links of dependent origination, while the inner circles symbolise the various realms into which sentient beings are born. The centre depicts the three poisons (attachment, aversion and ignorance) represented by a rooster, snake and pig, which cause one to take birth in cyclic existence over and over again.

The first seven of the twelve links describe the process by which new karma lay down propensities for a specific result, while the final five links show how those propensities are ripened into experience. Each of these two groups can be broken down further into links which are causes and links which are results.

Type	Relationship	Link
Projecting	Causes	1. Ignorance
		2. Karmic Formation
		3. Consciousness
	Results	4. Name and Form
		5. The Six Sense Doors
		6. Contact
		7. Feeling
Ripening	Causes	8. Craving
		9. Grasping
		10. Existence
	Results	11. Birth
		12. Aging and Death

Table 7-1: Divisions of the Twelve Links of Dependent Origination.

Projecting Causes

1. **Root Ignorance:** The first link of root ignorance is the basis for all the other links and is symbolised in the Wheel of Life by a *blind man holding a stick*. Because we do not see the true nature of things as they are, we project permanence onto all phenomena. We are under the delusion

that a truly existing and independent self exists, and we believe in false views such as the idea that material possessions can bring us genuine happiness. It is through this confusion that our samsaric world is generated. This deluded consciousness is the basis for all of our thoughts and emotions. While ignorance is considered the root, this link also represents all of the other afflictive states of mind which are derived from this ignorance.

2. **Karmic formation:** The second link of dependent origination is depicted by a *potter making pots on a wheel.* Due to our ignorance we engage in all manner of actions based on the belief that the world exists in the way it appears to us. For example, when our mind is overwhelmed by hatred, it only sees the negative qualities of a person or thing. This distorted perception lead us to lash out in harmful ways against that object. With every action we engage in, we lay down karmic propensities in the foundational consciousness. The result of these propensities produce future experience and habitual responses. This act of creating karmic propensities is what is referred to by the label *karmic formation.*

3. **Consciousness:** Due to our ignorance (the first link) we perform actions which plant karmic seeds in our mental continuum, creating the potential for future experience and for acting in particular way (the second link). This conditioned consciousness carries with it the potential to project the next birth and is thus known as the *impelling consciousness.* Once the conditions for rebirth have all come together, the result is called the *consciousness of the impelled result.* Both of these terms are referring to the same foundational consciousness at different stages of manifestation. Since it is the consciousness which provides the continuity from one life to the next, it is depicted as a *monkey in a fruit tree,* swinging from branch to branch.

Exercise 7.1—The Influence of Afflictions

- *In a relaxed posture, establish a neutral mind through the practice of mindfulness of breathing.*

- *Bring to mind an example where your mind was dominated by aversion. Spend some time establishing the details of the event as best you can. Observe how your aversion influenced your behaviour. What sort of thoughts were arising? What types of words were you saying? What physical behaviours did you exhibit? Based on your understanding of karma, consider the types of karmic propensities that you generated during this event. Think about the essential nature of these actions and how they could potentially manifest in the future.*

- *Now do the same exercise, but this time identify a situation in which the main affliction was attachment. Again, observe what was going on with your three doors (body, speech and mind) and identify the types of propensities that were generated in your mindstream. Recognise the potential suffering that these propensities could create for you in the future.*

- *For a third time, repeat the exercise using a situation where ignorance was the dominant affliction. For instance saying something hurtful because you did not fully understand what was going on. Consider specifically how assumptions based on wrong views can lead you to engage in many types of misguided activities. Consider the potential results that these activities can produce.*

- *Rest in any insights that arise.*

Projected Results

4. **Name and Form:** The karmic seeds carried by our mental continuum project our consciousness into a new rebirth. For a human rebirth, three components need to come together: a stream of consciousness, the mother's ovum and the father's sperm. From a Buddhist perspective, this is the moment in which conception occurs. It is the moment in which a mind (name) attaches itself to a body (form). These two are often referred to as the *psycho-physical aggregates*. As we will see

below, the coming together of a particular set of aggregates is dependent on the type of karma that projected them. The shape and subtlety of the body which develops, will therefore vary significantly. In the case of humans and animals, the body is very solid and physical in nature, while in the case of other non-human entities, their bodies are more ethereal or dream-like in nature. There are even entities that exist without any form aggregate whatsoever, existing as a purely mental being. This link is symbolised by *two men in a boat crossing the river* of existence.

5. **The Six Sense Doors (also known as the Bases):** After the moment of conception, depending on the type of being, the psycho-physical aggregates will undergo a process of evolution. In the case of a human being, this will normally involve the formation of six sense faculties: eyes, ears, nose, tongue, central nervous system and brain. These faculties provide the basis upon which gross forms of consciousness can arise. Not all beings will develop all six sense faculties. For instance, some humans are born without the faculty of sight or hearing. This will depend on the specific completing karma of the individual being. This link is depicted by a *house with six openings* (five shuttered windows and a closed door), representing the five physical senses plus the mental sense.

6. **Contact:** Once each faculty is developed fully, the being now has the capacity to perceive various types of objects. For instance, when a human fetus develops a basic nervous system, it can then sense tactile sensations. Likewise, when the visual faculty is complete, it can sense the darkness of the mother's womb. Contact represents the simultaneous meeting of three aspects: the object, the sense faculty and the consciousness. This union provides the basic mechanism of perception which is in turn the basis for all of our experiences. It is symbolised in the wheel of life by *two lovers in sexual embrace*.

7. **Feeling:** From this perception, the mind establishes the appearances of subject and object and when this happens, the mind also creates a relationship between the two. At its most basic level, this relationship manifests as a feeling that is either pleasant, unpleasant or neutral. This is the actual ripening of a karmic propensity as an experience. It is symbolised by a *man with an arrow stuck in his eye*.

Exercise 7.2—Different Bodies, Different Experiences

- *In a relaxed posture, establish a neutral mind through the practice of mindfulness of breathing.*

- *Bring to mind all of the different types of humans and animals which you are aware of on this planet. According to Buddhism, all of these beings possess a mind. If this is true, in what ways are they different?*

- *Consider the many ways these beings are conceived. Then consider how these different beings develop before birth. Bring to mind examples of different types of beings to illustrate each case.*

- *Now think about the different sense faculties that we all develop. For instance, consider the differences in a dog's faculty of smell or a bat's faculty of hearing. Within humans alone consider how the faculties of some people develop differently from the faculties of others.*

- *What effects do these different faculties have on the way we experience our world? What would it be like to be completely without one of your senses? What would it be like to have the senses of an animal like a dolphin or an eagle? What difference does it make to have the brain of an ant versus the brain of a human?*

- *Now think about our capacity to experience different feelings. Identify examples of objects which trigger pleasant feelings in your mind. Likewise those that trigger unpleasant and neutral feelings. Investigate whether animals also have this capacity to feel. For instance, are there things which a dog finds pleasant or unpleasant?*

- *Rest in whatever insights arise.*

Ripening Causes

8. **Craving (Involvement):** When an object makes contact with a sense faculty, a consciousness arises. This objective experience brings with it the subjective experience of a feeling. On the basis of this feeling, the mind either desires to be separated from an unpleasant feeling or desires to not be separated from a pleasant feeling, or develops indifference in relation to a neutral feeling. It is this basic relationship that drives our intention to either move towards or away from an object. This link is represented by a *man drinking wine*.

9. **Grasping (Adoption):** On the basis of craving, our mind develops a definite relationship with the object by reinforcing the initial reaction with conceptual overlays. Our mind uses concepts to give shape to our basic intention—telling a story to rationalise the acquisition of a desirable object or the rejection of an undesirable one. The moment the mind does this, it is laying down new karmic propensities that reinforce the existing habit, thereby creating the causes for a similar experience to arise in the future. Generally speaking, there are four types of grasping: grasping onto sense-pleasures, grasping onto wrong views, grasping onto rites and rituals and grasping onto a sense of self. This link is symbolised by a *man gathering fruit*.

10. **Existence (Becoming):** The more grasping that arises, the more a particular karmic pattern is strengthened. During the process of death, as our gross consciousness is starting to dissolve, the mind locks onto a particular train of thought. Through obsessively grasping at these ideas, it reinforces one specific karmic propensity to such a point that it completely dominates the mind. In this way the seed develops the power and the capacity to propel the consciousness into the next life. Because this particular ripening of karma is the cause for the next life, it is symbolised by a *pregnant woman*.

Exercise 7.3—The Mind of Grasping

- *In a relaxed posture, establish a neutral mind through the practice of mindfulness of breathing.*

- *Bring to mind an experience you can identify as either pleasant or unpleasant. Establish the details of the event in your mind as best you can.*

- *Mentally observe your initial reaction. When the feeling came up, what did you do? Did you recoil from the object or did you become more interested in it?*

- *Now think about the story that arose in your mind right after the initial feeling. What characteristics did you begin to focus on? How did your intention take shape? What plan formed in your mind?*

- *What sort of action resulted from this process? Did it remain purely mental or did your reaction get so strong it motivated you to say or do something? Maybe it was something subtle like a facial expression or a sound. Maybe it was more complex like stringing together words to communicate an idea, or physically engaging with the object in some way.*

- *Use different examples to get a sense for the way grasping adds power to craving, and generates actions.*

- *Rest with any insights that arise.*

Ripened Results

11. **Birth:** With the ripening of karma at the moment of death we are propelled into our next form of existence like a stuntman being shot from a canon. Without any sense of control or choice, we experience rebirth taking on a new set of psycho-physical aggregates, conditioned once again by the karmic seeds in our foundation consciousness. On

the basis of these aggregates we again experience the ripening of our karma which again propels us into another life. And so the wheel turns, an endless process of uncontrolled conditioning, perpetuating itself in each moment of experience. For this reason, we symbolise this link with a *woman giving birth*.

12. **Aging and Death:** When we look carefully at our different experiences within cyclic existence, we see that a life conditioned by karma is by its very nature unsatisfactory. While brief moments of pleasure may arise every now and again, they do not last. Life is always changing in dependence on a constant evolution of causes and conditions. The moment we are born, we begin to age. On the basis of aging we experience all kinds of sickness. On the basis of sickness, our bodies eventually lose their capacity to support life, leading to death. With death we once again experience the causes to propel us to a new birth. And so the cycle continues. This final link is symbolised by an *old man walking towards death with a bundle of sticks on his back*, for no matter how short or long our life, we continue to carry with us the weight of karmic seeds.

Exercise 7.4—The Nature of Existence

- *In a relaxed posture, establish a neutral mind through the practice of mindfulness of breathing.*

- *Consider your birth. Did you choose to be born? Did you choose your mother and father? Did you choose the time when you were born or the place? Did you choose to have the body that you have? What control did you have in this process? When did you start making choices about your own life?*

- *What types of experiences do you have because of your body? What differences does it make to have a male body or female body? Think of the full range of experiences that occur in life revolving around the shape and colour of our bodies.*

- *Now consider how this body has changed over time. Compare your body when you were a baby, your body as a young child, your body as a teenager, your body as a young adult and so on up to your present age. What sorts of experiences arose specific to these particular phases of your life?*

- *Think about the difference between growth and decay, health and sickness. Overall, is your body in a process of growth, or is it in a process of decay? If it is decaying, what are the consequences of this process? How will it end? At what point has the body decayed so much that it can no longer support your life?*

- *Now imagine repeating this cycle over and over and over again. Imagine having to experience all of these things whether you want to or not. Develop a sense of weariness of this process, a sort of boredom with the idea of doing it time and time again.*

- *Rest your awareness in any insights that arise.*

When we walk backwards through this sequence, we can see that each link is dependent on the link that precedes it. Without one, you cannot have the other. This means that if we do not wish to experience the suffering of aging and death, then we must stop uncontrollable rebirth. To do that we must remove the ripening of karma at the moment of death, which means that we must stop the grasping which empowers it. To cut the grasping we must cut the craving of acceptance or rejection. Craving will not arise without feelings, which cannot arise if there is no contact between subject and object. This contact will not arise if there are no sense faculties to sense objects. Those sense faculties will not arise if there is no coming together of mind and body. The aggregates will not form without a conditioned consciousness which relies on the presence of karmic propensities left in the mind by our actions motivated by the afflictions. The root of all afflictions is ignorance and therefore, by removing ignorance, none of the remaining links can develop and all suffering will cease.

While the twelve links describe how inner phenomena and suffering come about based on afflictions and karma, we can also understand the causes and conditions which give rise to outer phenomena by applying the principle of interdependence. We can observe the tendency of physical things to grow and change with time, just as a seed gives rise to a sprout, leaflets, stemmed plant, bud, flower and fruit. Each of these is regarded as a substantial cause for the following entity; just as wood is the substantial cause for a table. Contributing to this development are six conditions – earth, water, fire, wind, space and time. Earth stabilises, water causes cohesion, fire causes maturation and ripening, wind expands, space accommodates and time gradually transforms. The actions of living beings are also contributing conditions, such as a carpenter who intends to build a table or a bee which pollinates a flower.

Therefore, the arising of all outer and inner phenomena depends on their respective causes and conditions coming together in an appropriate manner. When these factors are complete, phenomena will arise, and when these causes and conditions are no longer present, phenomena will pass away. That is the nature of dependent origination. Since beginningless time there has been no creator of this continuous cycle, such as the self, God or others. Meaning, the causes do not conceive the thought, "I will produce this effect", and the effects do not conceive the thought, "I was produced from that", and yet they all arise with cause and effect being interdependent. Realising this, we can understand that all things are merely a manifestation of interdependence.

The process of the twelve links is usually described as occurring and being completed over three lifetimes, though we can also see the process operate over two lifetimes and in exceptional circumstances, during one lifetime. The causes from a past lifetime, ignorance and karmic formation, give rise to the present consciousness. In the present, the next eight links gather the karma that produces a rebirth, and we call this the second lifetime. From here, birth is taken and through that support one will undergo the samsaric suffering of aging and death which we call the third lifetime.

We are constantly involved with innumerable cycles of the twelve links, and in fact within every single action all of the twelve links are present. Every time we die we complete one cycle of links, and yet at each moment we are creating new karmic seeds for the links to arise again and again. In this way, cyclic existence will never end unless we do something about it.

UNDERSTANDING THE NATURE OF SUFFERING

What would motivate us to free ourselves from cyclic existence? Through our understanding of the twelve links, we can see that everything hinges on ignorance, but why would we want to remove it? You may like your life just as it is. Besides, developing the wisdom that is capable of removing ignorance will take a great deal of effort and determination, so why even bother?

These are important questions to ask ourselves at this critical point of our journey. If we don't establish our motivation on the basis of sound reasoning, it will be very difficult to develop the conviction necessary to progress much further in this process. So how can we approach these questions?

The key point to remember here is the need to develop a broader perspective of our situation. Just imagine you were on holiday, relaxing on a beach and sipping from a coconut, not a care in the world. Now imagine that this is the first time you have had a chance to take a holiday in more than fifteen years. You've been so busy with work you just couldn't get away. Finally, a weekend opened up and you have three days to enjoy yourself. Unfortunately, this holiday won't last and soon you'll be back at work, slogging away for who knows how long before you get this chance again. Fifteen years of blood, sweat and tears, versus three days of rest and relaxation.

Now imagine that while you were on this break, you totally forgot about work. You lose yourself in the holiday and you start to entertain the fantasy that this is what life will always be like. And yet, no matter how much you believe in your fantasy, eventually reality will catch up with you. There's no escaping it.

Right now we are on holiday. It is absolutely true that there are many wonderful things about this life. We are indeed very fortunate to be able to spend time with our friends and family and to experience an incredible array of sensory pleasures. But these are all temporary experiences and sooner or later they will pass. And when they do, we have to ask if we are prepared for what comes next?

In an effort to look beyond our present situation, Buddhism teaches that it is very important to understand the many forms that suffering can take within the cycle of existence. This is not to deny the existence of worldly happiness, but simply to highlight the many problems that we face because of the way that we relate to reality.

Acknowledging that there is suffering in our lives, gives us the opportunity to take the first steps to reducing it, rather than being carried along unwittingly by it. We may be able to see past the gross levels of suffering to its more subtle aspects, increasing our awareness of our samsaric reality. Cultivating an understanding that our suffering comes from the causes and conditions we create, that it is based on our attitudes, thoughts and ideas, encourages the development of mindfulness of our body, speech and mind. We can then be empowered to make changes to the way we think and act, working on the afflictive emotions that cause our propensities and hence our negative karma. It is this type of contemplation and action that characterises Dharma practice and allows us to move slowly in the direction of eliminating suffering completely.

Along with a more proactive attitude to our lives, understanding suffering can also help us grow our positive qualities and emotions. When we see that without insight into the primary causes of our suffering, most of us unknowingly continue to exacerbate the samsaric cycle by creating unecessary suffering for ourselves. This can arouse feelings of great empathy and compassion toward ourselves and others and we may not be so quick to judge or condemn those who behave badly. By acting completely under the control of their karma, they have no understanding of cause and effect and so do not realise the consequences of their actions. Additionally, when we realise we are only one being among countless other beings also experiencing suffering (and quite possibly far greater suffering than our own), we increase our sense of humbleness and reduce our self-cherishing. Ironically, by focusing on others we are actually helping ourselves as not only are we less distracted by our own suffering, we also create the opportunity to make merit and positive karma.

The Three Levels of Suffering

When referring to suffering, the Buddha would often use the term "duhkha". Duhkha has many translations including: "dissatisfaction", "stress" and "incapable of satisfying". The connotation is that some phenomena are simply unable to give us what we want. In the Buddhist context, what we want is long-lasting genuine happiness, and what we get is an endless stream of unsatisfactory, momentary experiences. On the basis of this broader understanding, we can begin to identify *Three Levels of Suffering*:

1. The Suffering of Pain

Of the three, the suffering of pain refers to the actual experience of suffering, comprising all physical, mental and emotional pain. It includes physical pain caused by injury, illness, heat, cold, hunger and thirst. It also includes the suffering of mental pain caused by sadness, dissatisfaction, confusion, anxiety, loneliness, depression or despair.

This is the grossest level of suffering which everyone can easily identify. We often believe that there is a simple way we can alleviate this gross level of suffering. "If only I could find a job where I was appreciated then I wouldn't feel so depressed", or "If only I could meet someone special, I wouldn't be so lonely". From a Buddhist perspective these are all only short term fixes that focus on the supporting conditions while ignoring the substantial causes. Since they do not address the actual cause of our suffering (karmic propensities in our mind), the effects can only ever by temporary in nature.

2. The Suffering of Change

This next form of suffering refers to the unsatisfactory nature of what we normally refer to as "pleasure" or "worldly happiness". A compounded phenomenon is something that arises out of the coming together of causes and conditions. All compounded phenomena have the nature of impermanence in that because they are dependent on conditions, they are subject to change. Therefore no experience that depends on compounded phenomena will last. Just when we think things are perfect they will inevitably change, and so cannot be relied upon for lasting happiness.

We usually have the perception that any kind of happiness we achieve will continue, not knowing that the suffering of change lies dormant within. If we sit in the same position for a long time our legs or back become sore, so we move into another position. Sooner or later this too will hurt, so we keep moving back and forth in order to avoid suffering and find some degree of comfort. This reactive approach to finding happiness only works for a short time at best. Take chocolate for example. It stands to reason that if chocolate was a true source of happiness then the more chocolate you eat, the happier you would feel. But what happens when you eat too much? Eventually you become sick and the chocolate that once made you happy turns into a condition for you to suffer.

This category of suffering arises from our mistaken belief that everything is lasting when in fact the opposite is true—nothing is permanent. We may have some happiness for a moment, a day or a year and then, in keeping with the transitory nature of all things, a change occurs which brings sadness and despair, and so the cycle continues. Rather than grasping onto the experience of pleasure, a wise person will cultivate a sense of resignation and acceptance, knowing that even enjoyable circumstances contain uncertainty and suffering. With reduced attachment and an awareness that all experiences change, when unfortunate situations inevitably occur, they will be less perturbed knowing that this is simply the nature of things.

3. All-Pervasive Suffering

The most fundamental level of suffering is known as all-pervasive suffering. We will always experience suffering as long as we remain under the control of karma and continue to take birth in the cycle of existence. In this situation, we cannot escape the pain of birth, sickness, old age and death. Since beginningless time we have endured this process, experiencing every kind of suffering imaginable. Every one of our past lives has contained endless hardships and sorrow, as this is the very nature of conditioned existence. As long as our aggregates remain tainted by afflictions and our perception of a self is based on ego and self cherishing, we will be immersed in an existence that has suffering at its core.

We habitually think that the causes and conditions for our comfort and happiness are objects like wealth, position, reputation and relationships, but these objects can only ever bring us temporary happiness. When the causes which give rise to these objects, and the conditions which support them are no longer present, change will occur and suffering will inevitably follow. All-pervasive suffering is embedded in the operation of cyclic existence and the presence of our afflicted physical and mental aggregates.

If we look deeply enough we will see that suffering and dissatisfaction are present in every form of conditioned existence, either in a manifest or potential way. Even if we feel happy and content with all the aspects in our life (a loving family and partner, a good job and a comfortable financial situation), we may find that we are actually linked to many interdependent processes which all involve suffering. The food we eat, for instance, may have been killed and brought to our tables by violent and inhumane means. Or the clothes we wear may have been produced by manufacturing processes which used a multitude of harmful chemicals. These examples illustrate how we are all connected in a chain of suffering that affects countless beings.

Suffering at this level cannot be avoided unless we really understand its nature and root source. When we unveil our true nature, eradicating our five afflicted and impure aggregates, we are no longer under the control of karma and the causes and conditions which give rise to cyclic existence.

These three levels of suffering operate in one form or another for every single life that arises within the pattern of cyclic existence. Depending on the karma of individuals, the mixture of manifest suffering and the suffering of change will vary. For some people, their lives are filled with pain and misery, while for others, worldly pleasures may be more dominant. For the latter, the suffering they experience is more internalised as they struggle with their attachments.

Type of Suffering	Examples	Primary Cause
Suffering of Pain	All forms of physical pain and mental or emotional anguish.	Aversion
Suffering of Change	All forms of worldly pleasure that are dependent on external causes and conditions.	Attachment
All-Pervasive Suffering	The systemic conditioning of cyclic existence.	Ignorance

Table 7-2: The Three Sufferings of Samsara.

The great Indian master Chandrakirti likened cyclic existence to a bucket moving up and down a well. Just as the bucket is bound by a rope, so beings are constrained by negative emotions and karma. As the movement of the bucket up and down the well is run by an operator, so too the process of cyclic existence is run by an untamed mind, fuelled by ignorance. Just as the bucket travels up and down the well over and over, so sentient beings wander ceaselessly in the great well of cyclic existence, requiring great effort to draw themselves up to happier situations, but descending easily into pain and suffering. The bucket does not determine its own movement, just as the factors which shape a person's life are the result of karma. Finally, just as the bucket bumps against the walls of the well when it goes up and down, so sentient beings are battered continuously by the suffering of pain, change and being caught in a process beyond their control.

The Individual Sufferings within the Six Realms

If we consider the full spectrum of experiences that are potentially possible within the context of cyclic existence, we can identify a number of general patterns for how an individual life manifests. We call these patterns, *realms of experience*. Each realm can be characterised by the dominant mental affliction which shapes a particular form of existence, as well as by the types of experiences that such a being would encounter once reborn in that form. In total we can speak of *Six Realms of Experience*:

Category	Realm	Causes	Dominant Experience
Lower Realms	1. Hell Realms	Hatred and resentment	Pain and torment
	2. Hungry Ghost Realms	Attachment, greed and miserliness	Hunger and thirst
	3. Animal Realms	Ignorance and stupidity	Fear and lack of control
Higher Realms	4. Human Realms	Desire	Variable
	5. Demigod Realms	Jealousy and competitiveness	Constant turmoil
	6. God Realms	Pride and complacency	All worldly pleasures

Table 7-3: The Six Realms of Experience.

Of these six, the first three are dominated by different forms of manifest sufferings and are therefore considered the *three lower realms*. In contrast, the last three are dominated by different degrees of worldly pleasure and therefore are referred to as the *three higher realms*.

Each realm exists at a different level of subtlety from the other realms. The grossest forms of existence are those of the human and animal realms. They share a similar degree of physicality, making it possible for us to directly experience beings at these levels. As we move towards the extremes though, the beings become increasingly more subtle, making them harder and harder to perceive. For most people, hell realms, hungry ghost realms and all of the demigod and god realms are beyond their capacity to experience. These realms can only be experienced by being born into them or by making the mind more subtle through meditation.

We will now explore each realm in greater detail, including the types of beings found in each realm, the particular sufferings endured and the path to follow in order to avoid or overcome these types of sufferings. While some of their descriptions may be challenging to accept, we must always remember the limitless creativity that the mind possesses.

One way to think about this is to ask yourself, what limitations do your dreams have? Consider how in a dream world, if you can imagine it, you can experience it. A dream can be wonderful, filled with every type of pleasure, or it can be horrific and filled with torments of all descriptions. Just imagine what it would be like if you couldn't wake up from your dream. What if the dream world that your mind created, became your reality?

We sometimes get so fixated on our present reality that we think that this is all there is. We close our minds off to the possibilities and limit our view to only one tiny portion of reality. By learning about these different realms, we expand our reality exponentially to include a much broader bandwidth of experience. This broader view gives us perspective on our present life and helps us develop a more realistic relationship with life.

The Hell Realms

Hell beings are those who have accumulated seemingly limitless stores of negative karma. Their minds are so dominated by intense mental afflictions of hatred, malice and paranoia that the worlds they create are equally twisted and filled with torment. Everything in these nightmare environments is designed to trigger such overwhelming pain, that the only thing a being born into these realms can do, is suffer through the agony until all of their negative karma is exhausted. While the suffering may appear to be eternal, eventually there will be an end, and the being will be reborn in a higher realm of existence. While there are infinite ways a being can torture itself, the scriptures generally speak of eighteen different levels that are representative of the different types of suffering experienced in these realms.

The Eight Hot Hells

These eight hells lay one above the other like the storeys of a tall building with the "lightest" form of hell on top and the "heaviest" form of hell below. These realms are described as being saturated by a blazing heat which makes every moment feel like you were standing on the sun. With each level of hell, the intensity of the heat and the duration of suffering increases. In the lower hells, beings must endure aeons upon aeons of constant pain and misery. The hot hells can be described as follows:

1. **Reviving Hell:** Here there are countless beings that are forced by their previous negative actions to fight, hacking and slashing each other until they have all suffered a horrible death. Once they have all died, the word "Revive!" is heard and they immediately come back to life, fighting to the death all over again. Unlike the other hell realms where the pain and suffering is continuous, this realm offers the mercy of death for just a brief moment.

2. **Black-Line Hell:** The inhabitants of this hell are laid out on metal slabs and sliced up into pieces by burning metal. Once they have been dissected, they instantly return to one piece, only to be sliced up all over again for what seems like an eternity.

3. **Rounding-Up and Crushing Hell:** In this hell, beings are thrown by the millions into vast mortars made from iron, the size of whole valleys. Monstrous hell guardians use huge hammers to relentlessly pound their victims for aeons.

4. **Howling Hell:** Here beings suffer by being roasted in buildings of red hot metal with no way out. They scream and cry, feeling that they will never escape as their flesh falls from their bones and they burst into flames.

5. **The Great Howling Hell:** In this level of hell, a vast number of hell guardians shove victims into metal sheds with outer and inner walls blazing with fire, where they are beaten with hammers and other weapons.

6. **Burning Hell:** Countless beings suffer in this hell by being cooked in unimaginably huge iron cauldrons, boiling in molten metals. Whenever they surface they are grabbed by the hell guardians with metal hooks and beaten on the head with hammers, sometimes losing consciousness. This rare moment is their idea of happiness as they temporarily feel no pain; otherwise they continue to experience this immense suffering for aeons.

7. **Intense Burning Hell:** The beings in this hell are trapped inside blazing metal houses, where they are impaled through their heels and anus with tridents of red-hot iron until the prongs push out through the shoulders and the crown of the head. This continues for an immeasurable length of time.

8. **Hell of Ultimate Torment:** This is called the Hell of Ultimate Torment because no worse torment could be found elsewhere. It is the hell where those who have committed the five heinous crimes with immediate retribution or those who have broken their sacred commitments with their spiritual teacher are reborn. No other actions have the power to cause rebirth here. In this hell, beings are cast into a red hot place of unspeakable agony. The only sound of life is the occasional cry from those trapped there for a seeming eternity.

The Neighbouring Hells

For those who have depleted the karma to be born into the intense heat of the hot hells, there are various neighbouring hells. Each of these hells represent different trials a hell being must go through in order to purify the remaining negative karmas that keep them bound to the hell realms. They include:

1. **The Hot Ember Pit:** When beings have purged most of the effects of the actions which have plunged them into the Hell of Ultimate Torment,

they emerge to see in the far distance what looks like a shady trench. They leap into it with delight, only to find themselves sinking down into a huge pit of blazing embers which burn their flesh and bones.

2. **The Swamp of Putrefied Corpses:** Released from the trench, they then see a river. After burning in a fire of the most intense heat for aeons, seeing water fills them with joy and they rush toward it. There is no water however; there is nothing but rotting corpses which give off a putrid stench. The would-be escapees sink into this swamp and are devoured by carnivorous worms.

3. **The Plain of Razor Blades:** Emerging from the swamp of corpses, the hell beings become ecstatic to see a beautiful green plain. As they step into the meadow, the blades of grass cut their feet as though they were sharp daggers.

4. **The Forest made of Swords:** As they cross the plain, they hear the sounds of wild beasts chasing them. In the distance a forest can be seen and they hurry toward it for cover. When they arrive there however, they find the branches and trees are like weapons, cutting into their bodies again and again.

5. **The Iron Salmali Tree Hill:** For those who have broken their vows of chastity or have given themselves over to sexual misconduct, they see all of their former lovers calling to them. They climb over trees and mountains in order to get to them, only to have their bodies cut into shreds. When they finally arrive at their destination, their loved ones disappear and their eyes are poked out by crows.

6. **The Boiling River:** Finally they reach a great river. Out of fear of returning to the hot hells, these beings jump in and try to swim to the other side. The moment they touch the water, they discover it is boiling hot and it burns away the skin from their bones. As they approach the far bank, hell guardians appear and block their way, throwing them back into the river.

The Eight Cold Hells

The cold hells are icy and dark landscapes, ravaged by freezing winds and ice. The beings born into these environments are born naked and alone and therefore suffer unimaginably. These hells include:

1. The Hell of Blisters
2. The Hell of Burst Blisters
3. The Hell of Clenched Teeth
4. The Hell of Lamentations
5. The Hell of Groans
6. The Hell of Cracks
7. The Hell of Popping
8. The Hell of Shattering

These names derive from the various agonies endured within them. These sufferings become more and more intense up to the Hell of Shattering, where the suffering is the greatest. In this hell, the flesh of the inhabitants is turned completely inside out, exposing even bone. No matter how cold it gets, the suffering does not end until the negative karma has been exhausted.

The Ephemeral Hells

The ephemeral hells exist in all sorts of different locations and the suffering entailed can include almost anything the imagination can conjure up. For instance, beings may be crushed between rocks, frozen in ice or trapped within objects that are constantly put to use such as brooms, doors and ropes. Any conceivable type of torture can occur in these places.

Exercise 7.5—The Suffering of a Hell Being

- *In a relaxed posture, establish a neutral mind through the practice of mindfulness of breathing.*

- *Imagine yourself opening your eyes to find yourself in the middle of some horrific nightmare world. Choose one of the descriptions of a hell realm and imagine yourself experiencing the extreme torment of that situation.*

- *Spend as much time as you can building up the details of this experience. Start with the environment, painting a picture of your immediate surroundings. Imagine the searing of the intense heat or the bite of an icy cold wind. Imagine the shadowy landscape and the frightening shapes of twisted metal and hellish silhouettes. Engage all of the senses, making the experience as real as you can.*

- *Then conjure up the different beings who are the main actors in this scene. Again, make them as scary as you can, with all of the things that would truly fill your mind with terror.*

- *Then imagine these beings inflicting unspeakable acts of torture upon you. Think not only about the excruciating pain, but also the mental torment of fear and paranoia that accompanies each moment.*

- *Imagine this torture going on over and over again, for countless aeons. Get a sense for the seemingly never ending stream of pain and suffering. Make it as extreme as possible, until the sense of aversion is simply too much.*

- *Let the images of horror fade into your mind and rest your awareness on the intense desire to never be faced with such an existence. Develop a strong resolve to do whatever is in your power to avoid the causes for such an experience, namely acts of hatred and resentment.*

The Hungry Ghost Realms

Rebirth in a hungry ghost realm is the result of extreme self-cherishing, greed, craving, miserliness and lack of generosity. In general there are two categories of hungry ghosts:

Hungry Ghosts Living Collectively

These ghosts share sufficient collective karma to experience a similar realm of existence. They can be divided up into three types:

1. **Those Suffering from External Obscurations:** These ghosts are obsessed with satiating their endless hunger and thirst. Their external

environment is such that these cravings can never be fulfilled. They spend their entire existence chasing mirages which promise food and drink, only to find them to be illusory. As a consequence, they spend their whole lives in a state of perpetual dissatisfaction.

2. **Those Suffering from Internal Obscurations:** These ghosts have mouths no bigger than the eye of a needle. If they happen to find a small enough morsel of food to fit in their mouth, it has to pass down a throat that is no wider than a single hair. Even if they were able to eat and drink enough to satisfy their bottomless hunger, their stomach burns away any food before it has time to nurture them. In this way, the very shape of their bodies prevents them from getting what they crave.

3. **Those Suffering from Specific Obscurations:** These ghosts have all sorts of different experiences which give rise to sufferings of varying degrees of intensity. For example, some have many creatures living inside their bodies, devouring them whole. The common theme across their sufferings is that they are prevented from fulfilling their desires— everything is an obstacle.

Space Going Hungry Ghosts

These include all the different ghosts, spirits and worldly deities who live out their existence in delusion and terror. They are subject to constant torture and are plagued, like all ghosts, with distorted perceptions. Hot seems cold and pleasure feels like pain.

Exercise 7.6—The Suffering of a Hungry Ghost

- *In a relaxed posture, establish a neutral mind through the practice of mindfulness of breathing.*

- *Begin by imagining the most barren of environments. Make every aspect of this landscape as inhospitable as possible. There is nothing here which provides any comfort whatsoever. It is harsh and dry.*

- *Now imagine that you can't remember the last time you ate or had anything to drink. Your body is completely malnourished and weak. Your skin hangs off your bones and every inch of your being aches with pain.*

- *What would it be like to always have to search for food and drink? You are always wanting but never getting anything. Imagine the agony of the situation. Imagine that everyone around you is experiencing the same thing. Even if you do find something to eat, you have to fight off countless others to keep it.*

- *Now imagine your actual body is an obstacle. So much effort is needed to just take in some food. And even when you do succeed, you are filled with pain and the food does not satisfy you. Imagine trying to eat something and failing over and over again. How agonisingly frustrating would this be?*

- *Allow the frustration, hopelessness and sorrow to build up in your mind. Hold onto this feeling and then develop the strong desire to be free from it. Recognise that this existence is the result of intense attachment and miserliness, and make the resolve to do whatever you can to avoid these harmful states of mind.*

The Animal Realms

The primary causes of rebirth in the animal realm are ignorance and an intense preoccupation with the pursuit of instinctual desires such as eating, sleeping and sexual gratification. This fixation causes a disregard for developing one's mind resulting in "dullness". There are two categories of animals: those living in the depths of the oceans and those scattered in different places throughout the lands.

1. **Animals living in the ocean depths:** The great oceans are full of creatures so numerous that we cannot conceive of their variety. All such creatures undergo intense suffering through being stalked, eaten, preyed upon and having their bodies used by other beings as a dwelling. They are ignorant of their situation and thus continue to live out their days in the darkened depths, oblivious to the suffering they endure.

2. **Animals scattered in different places:** Animals are generally so exploited by humans they are destined to suffer. They are often seen as objects rather than beings with feelings. There are animals that are hunted, slaughtered, enslaved, used for research and held captive. Wild animals fall victim to each other in a battle for survival and are seldom relaxed as they continuously fear for their own safety and that of their offspring. They also endure the suffering of hunger and thirst. Even animals that appear to live well with a kind owner are still subject to the whim of that owner.

We ought to carefully reflect on the sufferings of animals and endeavour to develop our mind rather than blindly pursue animalistic desires. It is also important to always try to avoid causing suffering to animals (including insects), meditating deeply upon the distress they endure and pray for their liberation. We can dedicate the merit of our meditation to release them from suffering.

Exercise 7.7—The Sufferings of an Animal

- *In a relaxed posture, establish a neutral mind through the practice of mindfulness of breathing.*

- *Bringing to mind the wide range of animals on this planet, start by considering those animals living in the ocean. Identify some examples and consider what their day-to-day experience is like. What challenges do they face? How do they respond to those challenges? Is there any time where these animals can just rest? Or are they constantly under imminent threat, having to fend for their lives from a variety of predators that want to eat them?*

- *Now consider those animals living on dry land. Start with the animals that live in the wild. Again, consider the sorts of lives that they lead. Imagine living such a life. Imagine the fear and overwhelming anxiety that comes with it.*

- *Finally, think of the lives of those animals who are controlled by humans. Consider the lives of the millions of chickens, pigs and cows that we breed for our food and the horrible things they must live through. Imagine yourself in those very situations, try to experience what it would be like.*

- *Allow the feeling to arise of having no control over anything, being subject not only to the whims of others but to your own instinctual responses, with no opportunity to make choices. Recognise the causes for these experiences as the habitual ignorance that doesn't think, but simply follows whatever urge arises. Develop the strong desire to not fall into this stupefying state and instead to cultivate greater intelligence and wisdom.*

The Human Realms

Although rebirth in the three lower realms is characterised by intense suffering, you might expect that the three higher realms would be happy and pleasant; however this is not the case, as even in these higher realms there is no real lasting happiness to be found.

As only virtues can project rebirth into the human realm, the most favoured of all the realms, it is a precious and rare occurrence (as we will learn more about in the following chapter). Despite this, humans undergo a wide variety of sufferings that includes physical pain and mental torment. Unlike the lower realms, this suffering is not always manifesting, and brief moments of respite exist that give the opportunity to gain perspective on our situation. The types of suffering experienced by a human can be understood generally and specifically by the following categories:

The Four Great Streams of Human Suffering

This first set of sufferings are closely tied to the cycle of life and represent the nature of our lived experience as humans. These sufferings are always with us from the moment we are born until the time that we die. The four great streams of human suffering are:

1. **The Suffering of Birth:** Within our mother's womb there is a considerable amount of suffering. When our mother moves we are thrown back and forth. When she lies down we feel the pressure of her form. When her stomach is full we are squashed. When she consumes hot or cold food and drinks we feel the pain of burning heat or freezing cold. If we could actually remember all this suffering it would surely make us wish never to be reborn again, yet we cannot recall this due to our ignorance and the trauma of childbirth. There is the pain of being squeezed from our mother's body and the distress as we meet the harsher environment of the outside world. From this moment on, we will now have to face the sufferings of a world dominated by our senses. By virtue of being born, we are now subject to these sufferings whether we like it or not.

2. **The Suffering of Aging:** After birth, we have the mistaken sense that we are growing and increasing in capacity, maintaining the delusion that we are gaining more life. The reality is however, that our life is shortening with every moment that passes. While we are consumed with living our lives we forget that we are ageing. Due to our lack of mindfulness and wisdom, we are unaware that we are racing towards death with every instant. Even the most skilled surgeon cannot make us younger, even though they may be able to improve our appearance temporarily. Eventually the reality of old age dawns upon us along with an ailing body, reduced energy levels and failing sense faculties. Aging is inevitable and we are unable to avoid it no matter how hard we try. As the body deteriorates our suffering can be considerable, not unlike some of the existences in the lower realms.

3. **The Suffering of Sickness:** As the body ages it becomes susceptible to imbalances arising. We call these imbalances "sickness" and they can strike us at any moment. Most of the time we don't pay much attention to our health. It is only when we are inflicted with a serious illness that we are shocked into recognising the fragile nature of our life. While we may be able to avoid some symptoms for some of the time, eventually sickness catches up with us. The more we age, the less our body is able to support our life and the more sickness arises.

4. **The Suffering of Death:** Eventually, our body completely breaks down and sickness overwhelms us, causing our mind to be separated from our bodies. We call this process "death". It can be extremely painful to helplessly watch as your body shuts down and you are uncontrollably thrust into the unknown. The fear that arises in this moment can truly be terrifying. For some, this process will occur over a short period of time (for instance in the case of accidental death). For most though, it will be a protracted process, filled with many forms of physical and mental sufferings. As the moment of death draws near, a person will often reflect back on their lives. They can feel an intense sensation of regret and sadness regarding their actions. They may even become frightened when they think of the consequences those actions will bring in the future. Those with no belief in an afterlife will often experience an overwhelming fear of annihilation which only serves to ripen negative karmic propensities.

Exercise 7.8—The General Sufferings of Humans

- *In a relaxed posture, establish a neutral mind through the practice of mindfulness of breathing.*

- *Imagine you are currently in the womb. Spend some time thinking about this environment. What would it be like? Now imagine the feeling of being born. What would it be like to have your body squeezed through a tiny opening? How disorienting would this be? Imagine what it would be like to be thrust into a world with all sorts of unfamiliar sights, sounds and feelings. Consider how confused you would be by all these strange experiences.*

- *Now walk through the phases of life from birth until natural death. Consider the experience of being a young child, with all of the challenges a young child faces. Then consider the experience of an adolescent, a young adult, an adult and an elderly person. Bring to mind all of the different problems we face at each stage of our lives. Specifically take note of the relationship we have with our body during each stage.*

- *Imagine that you are sick. What does it feel like when your body isn't working properly? Consider the different types of illnesses you have experienced so far, from a relatively minor lack of energy to a very serious or life-threatening disease. Think about all of the different illnesses you could potentially encounter.*

- *Imagine you are on your deathbed, with your family and friends gathered around you. You know you are going to die and there is nothing you can do about it. What state of mind would you have? What sorts of things would frighten you? What would give you comfort?*

- *Allow a general sense of dissatisfaction to arise with being subjected to these sorts of sufferings. Rest your awareness in this feeling.*

Four Other Natural Human Sufferings

The next set of sufferings are related to the turbulent nature of our lives and the many problematic situations we find ourselves in. These kinds of sufferings are constantly generating difficulties in our lives and creating the conditions for dissatisfaction to arise.

1. **The Suffering of Meeting Enemies:** No-one wishes to meet harmful enemies or people who are against us. If however we fail to maintain good moral conduct and instead devote our attention to acquiring wealth, fame or status, driven by a greedy motivation, then we will naturally develop opponents. It is then much harder to have a truly peaceful mind. Our suffering is often in direct proportion to our accumulated wealth and status, as we feel we have to guard these from people who are against us. We should therefore reflect and meditate on the importance of living in peace and strive to decrease our attachment, especially to wealth and fame.

2. **The Suffering of Separation from Loved Ones:** Living in the world as we do, we develop great attachment to various people and often to animals as well. As no being can live forever, at some point in our lives we will experience the loss of loved ones in some form, be it through separation or death. Furthermore, there is no guarantee that we will always be close to our loved ones. Friends and family that claim to love us can become unsupportive or antagonistic in certain situations. Think of a husband and wife who have separated with ill feeling. Once these two were deeply in love, yet now they behave like deadly enemies. Even harmonious relationships will end, as death is the ultimate point of separation and will definitely occur for every person.

3. **The Suffering of Not Getting What You Want:** It is human nature that everyone desires to be happy and to have everything they want. This very desire means that anytime we are faced with obstacles to having our wants fulfilled, there is certain to be some form of suffering. Even if our desires are fulfilled, we often still want more and consequently, we are never truly satisfied. We should therefore meditate on the benefits of practising the Dharma, and try to lessen our reliance on samsaric enterprises, such as those outlined by the eight worldly dharmas. Eventually we will come to understand that they are not a reliable source of true and lasting happiness.

4. **The Suffering of Getting What You Do Not Want:** While we all desire to avoid certain unpleasant or unwanted things, throughout our lives we will surely encounter situations we would do almost anything to avoid. This is one of the most common sufferings we face in life. Failing to understand that everything we experience is the result of our past actions, even though we do not want to suffer, we constantly create the causes of suffering. Similarly, although we long for happiness and prosperity, we often fail to cultivate the causes necessary for happiness.

We should not take good fortune for granted. We should instead appreciate the numerous positive aspects in our lives, especially if we have taken birth in a wealthy country, with a healthy body and with all our sense faculties intact.

These fortunate conditions enable us to live a prosperous life and provide the incredible opportunity to study the Dharma. At the same time however, we should understand that this is all the result of specific causes such as generosity and virtuous moral conduct. This kind of insight helps us to create a happy future for ourselves and recognise why less fortunate circumstances arise, and consequently we can begin to reduce the level of suffering we experience.

The degree to which we suffer is also determined by our mental attitude. If we can develop wholesome ways of thinking such as patience and flexibility, we are more likely to have realistic expectations and be more accepting of challenging situations that arise. We thereby develop wisdom, which can help us reduce this kind of suffering.

In summary, we can't always get what we desire or avoid what we don't want as this is the nature of samsara. It is better therefore to change our attitude and cultivate as much merit and positive karma as we can, rather than leading a life controlled by craving and desire.

Exercise 7.9—The Specific Sufferings of Humans

- *In a relaxed posture, establish a neutral mind through the practice of mindfulness of breathing.*

- *Bring to mind different events where you were faced with someone who prevented you from doing something. They may have inadvertently created obstacles for you or they may have intentionally tried to harm you in some way. Think of how these people show up in your life over and over again. Think of the frustration that arises in relation to these people.*

- *Now consider the pain of being separated from a loved one. Think back through your past relationships and identify all those people you previously felt very close to and yet are now no longer a part of your life. Consider all of the different circumstances that contributed to these relationships falling apart. Make a note of all the people you come in contact with and the duration that these relationships last. Get a sense for the role that attachment plays in the suffering that is experienced during separation.*

- *Consider all of the things you have desired in this life. Identify the people, places and situations you have longed for and yet have been unable to experience. How does it feel to want something so badly and yet not be able to fulfill that desire?*

- *Now consider all of the things you didn't ask for, but had to experience nonetheless. Think about the different times when you got sick or experienced some sort of misfortune in your life. Think of the problems you encounter every day, the little things that make your life difficult. Think of the moments of crisis you have gone through and the suffering of not knowing what would happen.*

- *Allow a general sense of dissatisfaction to arise. Rest in the desire to be free from these forms of suffering. Make a resolve to abandon the mental states of craving and desire which are the causes for these sorts of experiences.*

The Demigod Realm

A Demigod is a very powerful being that is completely dominated by feelings of jealousy, inadequacy and competitiveness. Even though their environment is filled with numerous pleasures and riches, they pale in comparison to the god realms and this brings the demigods no end of suffering. Their jealous desire to have what the gods possess, leads them to wage endless wars against the gods in the wish of acquiring all that they want. But as the gods are even more powerful, the demigods are always defeated and therefore their ambitions are never fulfilled.

In such a realm of constant fighting, there is no opportunity for rest. To avoid being born here we must always avoid jealousy and envy. Instead, try to develop compassion for others by reflecting on their plight from the depth of your heart.

Exercise 7.10—The Sufferings of a Demigod

- *In a relaxed posture, establish a neutral mind through the practice of mindfulness of breathing.*

- *Imagine you were born in a city on the side of a river. Everything you needed was available to you: food, clothing and companions.*

- *But imagine across the river, there was another more magnificent city. Everything about this place was bigger and better than where you lived. Each day you would sit on the bank of the river and look over at the people enjoying themselves. Each day you developed your desire to have what they had. Imagine the envy and desire arising in your mind.*

- *Now consider what you would do if that envy was so strong that you could not take it anymore. And not just you alone, but everyone in your city is filled with an intense desire for what the neighbouring city has.*

- *Imagine that you go to war, convinced that the only way to get what you want is to take it. Try to experience the savagery and brutality of fighting a foe who is bigger and stronger then you are. Every time you lash out, they beat you back, mocking you and denying you everything you desire. Imagine the resentment and frustration that would arise.*

- *Recognise this form of existence is the result of cultivating the minds of jealousy and desire. Develop a strong resolve to abandon these destructive states of mind and to instead cultivate a sense of inner contentment with what you have.*

The God Realms

Within the context of the Buddhist worldview, the term "god" is used to describe an increasingly subtle form of existence that is characterised by immense pleasure and absence of manifest suffering. These gods are not enlightened and are still trapped within the cycle of existence. While they may live for unimaginably long periods of time, they are still subject to causes and conditions and therefore the nature of their existence is impermanent. Eventually, their existence will come to an end and they must take rebirth in one of the other realms, where they will once again experience different degrees of suffering and create the causes to perpetuate that suffering.

When speaking about the god realms, we can establish three types of realms that correspond to three levels of subtlety:

1. **The Desire Realm:** These gods exist within the physical dimension that is shared by the other five realms of existence. While their bodies are more subtle than a human or animal, they can still interact with other types of beings. Their lives are characterised by intense pleasure and a complete absence of manifest suffering.

2. **The Form Realm:** This is a predominantly mental sphere of experience with a very subtle body that is produced through the power of meditation. Since this realm can only be experienced by those in meditative absorption, it is not directly accessible from the desire realm. It is characterised by increasingly subtle forms of bliss, non-conceptuality and vividness of mind.

3. **The Formless Realm:** Through the power of their concentration of mind, the being is able to transcend all semblance of subtle form and abides in a purely mental sphere. They remain in a blissful state of suspended animation for countless aeons, oblivious to all other sentient beings.

While gods do not experience the suffering of pain, they do eventually experience the suffering of change and the all-pervasive suffering. Specifically we can speak of the following sufferings for each of the three types of god:

The Six Desire God Realms

In total, there are six distinct levels of desire realm gods. Each level is more subtle and more powerful than the ones below it creating a sort of hierarchy within the different god communities. To project a rebirth in one of these realms, one needs to have performed a large amount of meritorious deeds. These gods have incredibly long lives during which they enjoy a constant stream of perfect health, comfort, wealth and happiness. Until the time of their death, they never experience gross suffering, while the suffering of change and all-pervasive suffering are not at all evident to them, and as a result, they have little reason to practise Dharma. Every moment is enjoyable for them, but as they are preoccupied by this continuous stream of pleasure, they fail to apprehend their approaching death and therefore never consider preparing for it. As such, a god may die in great sorrow and suffer in a way likened to the suffering of some of the hell realms, as their death is incredibly long-lasting and painful. At the time of death they see by clairvoyance the place of their next birth, and they are often consumed by remorse when they realise how they have wastefully exhausted all their stores of positive karma during their current lifetime, only to be reborn in the lower realms.

The Seventeen Levels of the Form Realm

The form realms occupy a more subtle state of existence than the desire god realms, yet unlike the formless realms they still contain some element of form such as colour, shape, sound, smell, taste or tactile sensation. To be born in these seventeen form realms, one needs more than just an accumulation of virtues. The minimum requirement is to have accomplished Shamatha, the complete stabilisation of the mind. This establishes what is known as fixed or unchanging karma as it cannot be changed until the result is exhausted. There are seventeen different form realms with one peak level and sixteen levels of increasing subtlety. These sixteen are grouped into four distinct levels representing four different mental states or types of meditative absorptions of single-pointed concentration known as the jhanas. The beings from these sixteen form realms can remain for aeons in the particular form jhana or meditative absorption which represents their state of mind.

Such beings have not escaped from all-pervasive suffering, and so when the unchanging karma that keeps their minds in the state of Shamatha is exhausted, they begin to arouse emotions and eventually take rebirth in one of the other six realms, depending on which of their karmic imprints arises next.

There are some exceptions to this scenario as some beings are born in the form realms with the purpose of attaining certain practices on the path to enlightenment. The quality of the mental state of beings in the form realm is very conducive to effective meditation and the possibility of achieving enlightenment exists, nevertheless, the mind of Shamatha can be achieved while in human form, and if directed towards enlightenment this is a far more effective method than being karmically driven towards rebirth in the form or formless realms.

The Four Levels of the Formless Realm

As with the form realm, rebirth in the formless realm requires the minimum achievement of Shamatha. Also similar to the form realm, these realms are comprised of four levels representing different mental states or meditative absorptions; although in this instance they are known as the formless jhanas. Beings within the formless realms do not perceive any kind of physical subject or object, nor do they possess any of the five sense faculties. This is why these realms are called formless. Although they have no feelings, beings in the formless realms do have perception of some of the more subtle aspects of the mind.

1. At the first level, beings are able to perceive space.

2. At the second level, beings have a more subtle perception, with the ability to perceive the mind but no perception of space.

3. At the third level, beings only have perception of nothingness and no perception of mind.

4. At the fourth level, beings dwell in an extremely subtle state of mind, even without a perception of nothingness.

All this means that the minds of beings in the formless realms are very insubstantial and therefore too weak to serve as an adequate foundation for eliminating the seeds of mental afflictions. All four types of beings within the formless realms have attained a Shamatha state of mind, but have not achieved any degree of insight. Bodhisattvas therefore avoid being born in the formless realms since they are unable to achieve the mental states required to attain enlightenment there.

Exercise 7.11—The Sufferings of a God

- *In a relaxed posture, establish a neutral mind through the practice of mindfulness of breathing.*

- *Imagine you are living in an opulent pleasure palace. You are able to experience whatever you want, without boredom or dissatisfaction. Throughout your whole life, you have merely to make a wish and your every desire is fulfilled. Spend some time, imagining the luxury and bliss of such a situation.*

- *Now imagine that after thousands upon thousands of years, all of the riches, all of the opulence all of the sensual pleasure is taken away from you. Where once there were pleasant fragrances, now the stench of body odour arises. Where once your skin shone with a golden radiance, now that light begins to fade. Where once you were surrounded by beautiful companions, now you are isolated and alone. Try to get a sense for what it feels like to lose it all. This is the suffering of the desire realm gods.*

- *Now imagine you took a powerful drug that put you into a blissful stupor. Imagine staying like this for billions of years. And then the drug wears off and you come crashing down, back into the dirt and grime of cyclic existence. This is the suffering of the form realm gods.*

- *Now imagine that you space out. Your mind frozen in a seemingly endless stream of bliss. Absolutely no movement whatsoever. And then, without really noticing, the stream breaks down and once again you must face the harshness of reality, only now all of your virtuous karma has been depleted and you must experience the intense suffering of the lower realms. This is the suffering of the formless gods.*

- *Recognising that none of these forms of existence are permanent solutions to your suffering, develop the strong desire to avoid getting caught in their enticing web. Develop the strong resolve to abandon being proud and complacent, instead focus on cultivating virtue that is driven by compassion and wisdom.*

As we can see, no matter where you may be born within these six realms, there will always be some form of suffering. If you are born in the lower realms, the suffering is so intense you have no chance to cultivate virtue and instead will only experience pain and hardship. And yet, if you are born in the higher realms, you are still not free from karmic causes and conditions, and therefore you will inevitably experience unsatisfying situations.

Three Realms	Six Realms	Type of Existence
Desire Realm	1. Hell Realms	Hell beings: 1. Hot Hells 2. Cold Hells 3. Neighbouring Hells 4. Ephemeral Hells
	2. Hungry Ghost Realms	Hungry Ghosts: 1. Those living together 2. Those living in space
	3. Animal Realms	Animals: 1. Those in the depths of the ocean 2. Those scattered on land
	4. Human Realms	Humans
	5. Demigod Realms	Demigods
	6. God Realms	Desire Realm Gods: 1. The Four Great Kings 2. Heaven of Thirty-three 3. Non-Combat 4. Tushita Heaven 5. Enjoying Emanations 6. Controlling Others' Emanations
Form Realm		Form Realm Gods: 1. First Stabilisation 2. Second Stabilisation 3. Third Stabilisation 4. Fourth Stabilisation 5. Pure Realms
Formless Realm		Formless Realm Gods: 1. Sphere Beyond Perception 2. Sphere of Nothingness 3. Sphere of Limitless Consciousness 4. Sphere of Limitless Space

Table 7-4: The full range of experience in cyclic existence.

REVIEW OF KEY POINTS

- Cyclic existence arises due to the interdependent relationship between twelve causal links: ignorance, karmic formation, consciousness, name and form, the six sense doors, contact, feeling, craving, grasping, existence, birth, and aging and death.

- There are three levels of suffering: the suffering of pain, the suffering of change and all-pervasive suffering.

- There are six realms of existence: the hell realms (aversion), the hungry ghost realms (attachment), the animal realms (ignorance), the human realms (desire), the demigod realms (jealousy) and the god realms (pride).

- There are eighteen hell realms described traditionally: eight hot hells, the neighboring hells, eight cold hells and ephemeral hells.

- The hungry ghost realms are divided based on the types of obscuration these beings face: those facing external obscurations, those facing internal obscurations and those suffering from specific karmic obscurations.

- The animal realm is divided by where the beings abide: there are those in the ocean and those on land. Of those on land, there are those who are wild and those who are controlled by humans.

- The human realm is divided based on the types of sufferings that we experience: there are four great streams of suffering (birth, aging, sickness and death) and the other natural sufferings of humans.

- The demigod realm is characterised by the suffering of never being content with what you have and always wanting to fight others and take their things.

- The god realms are divided into three sub-realms: the desire realm gods, the form realm gods and the formless realm gods.

Khentrul Rinpoché meditating in the hills of his homeland of Tibet.

CHAPTER EIGHT

The Precious Opportunity Offered by a Human Life

When we study the cycle of existence, we develop a much vaster understanding of a universe that functions on many different dimensions. It is a universe teeming with life-forms of all shapes and sizes, where human beings are just one possibility among many. Having mapped out the full range of this spectrum of potential, we can now focus on the specific situation that we find ourselves in right now.

Of all of the six realms of existence, we currently inhabit the most moderate of the six; the human realm. This realm is unique in that it is not dominated by extreme suffering nor extreme pleasure. It is generally a middle ground of sorts, where it is possible to experience a wide range of both pleasant, unpleasant and neutral feelings, without being completely overwhelmed and saturated by these experiences. These feelings come and go in a noticeably transient way that allows those who are paying attention to reflect upon their nature. In such an environment, it is possible to develop insights into phenomena and in doing so to develop greater intelligence and wisdom. This is something (as we will see below) that is extremely unlikely in any of the other realms.

It is this capacity to actively develop our minds that makes the human realm such an important form of existence in the context of practising Dharma. When we begin to look honestly at its characteristics, we see that we have everything we need to achieve all that we ever wanted. This is possible because right now, in this very moment, we have the capacity to choose. We can choose to either create the causes of suffering or we can choose to create the causes of happiness. It is entirely up to each of us, how it is we spend our time.

The following teachings are all designed to help us develop insight into two key aspects of our human life:

1. The incredibly *precious opportunity* this life presents us with

2. The unbelievable *rarity* of having encountered such an opportunity

When you combine these two qualities, they help to develop a sense of appreciation for your present situation which acts as a strong motivator for practising Dharma. Instead of wasting this opportunity, you can instead choose to make the most of each second and thereby convert a regular human existence into what is known as a *"precious human life"*. It is this precious human life that is the perfect platform for achieving spiritual realisations.

THE CHARACTERISTICS OF A PRECIOUS HUMAN LIFE

We will begin by first distinguishing clearly what makes a precious human life distinct from all other forms of existence. Traditionally we can do this through the study of eight characteristics that we are free from and ten characteristics we are endowed with. These eighteen points highlight the supporting conditions that, when used skillfully, can lead to lasting genuine happiness.

Simply being born as a human being does not automatically guarantee that we have a *precious* human life. Whether we make this life precious or not will depend on the choices we make. Unfortunately many human beings live unwisely, creating negative karma and causing suffering for themselves and others, which inevitably leads to further suffering in the future. As we read through the following characteristics, it is important to contemplate and analyse whether we actually possess them and if we don't, we then need to consider how to go about gathering the missing conditions.

The Eight Freedoms

We can begin by first analysing the absence of eight situations that make it impossible to practise Dharma. These conditions are known as "freedoms" because as long as they are absent, then we have the freedom to engage in spiritual practice. The first four conditions are related to the non-human states which offer no opportunity for practise:

1. **Being born in a hell realm:** As we have seen, hell beings are incessantly tormented by intense heat or cold and various unbearable methods of torture. This incessant stream of pain and suffering means that a hell being has absolutely no opportunity to practise Dharma. Enduring the results of their negative karma, they are simply too overwhelmed by their agony to even be able to develop a positive intention.

2. **Being born as a hungry ghost:** Like hell beings, hungry ghosts also have no opportunity to practise the Dharma because of the ceaseless torment of hunger and thirst that they must endure. They are so consumed by the longing for sustenance, their minds cannot fathom practising for even one second.

3. **Being born as an animal:** An animal's mind is constantly reacting to the push and pull of their habitual tendencies. Such a mind doesn't make choices, it reacts on an instinctual level. This is a sign of their deep seated ignorance which blinds them to the meaning of the teachings and this inability to understand the teachings, means they have no opportunity to practise Dharma.

4. **Being born as a long-lived god:** The gods live a life of extreme luxury and pleasure, they therefore have very little incentive to question the nature of their reality. This blinds them to the disadvantages of cyclic existence and prevents them from seeking out the Dharma. Those who are lost in the higher states of absorption have minds that are so subtle, they do not have the capacity to reflect on their conditions and consequently waste a seeming eternity depleting all of their positive propensities, until they eventually fall to the lower realms.

Exercise 8.1—Free from Having No Chance to Practise

- *In a relaxed posture, establish a neutral mind through the practice of mindfulness of breathing.*

- *Bring to mind an event where you felt substantial pain or where you experienced some sort of intense hardship. Now amplify that feeling by a thousand to develop a sense for the intensity experienced by hell beings. What kinds of thoughts would you be thinking in such a situation? How disturbed would your mind be? Can you imagine sitting down to meditate in such a situation?*

- *Now think back to a time when you hadn't eaten for a while. How did your hunger affect your mood and state of mind? Imagine going two or three days without food. How would your mind deteriorate in such a situation? Consider that hungry ghosts can go hundreds of years without finding a single morsel to eat or a drop of water to drink. How could they possibly practise the Dharma?*

- *Try to remember a time when you were filled with a great deal of fear or anxiety. You were so worried about something happening, you did everything you could to avoid it. Now imagine living your whole life in this state. Imagine that the danger was very real and letting your guard down for even just one moment meant you could be killed. Think about the state of mind of such a being. Does it have the necessary space to practise?*

- *Now think about those times in your life when everything was going well. You were in a great relationship, you had all the money you needed and you were surrounded by wonderful people. Everything was perfect. Would you want to change your life? Imagine this state of perfection multiplied by a thousand, a constant flow of pleasure and satisfaction. What would motivate you to make the effort to practise?*

- *As you contemplate each of these points, recognise that you are free from these types of existence. Of course you experience ups and downs, but there are many spaces in between. Allow a sense of relief to build up in your mind. Rest in this sensation.*

The next four conditions are all related to different forms of human beings who do not have the necessary supports for practising Dharma:

5. **Being born in a time where no teachings exist:** According to Buddhism, the universe cycles through periods of increasing darkness and periods of increasing light. The light here refers to the presence of the teachings which rely on the appearance of a teacher (ie. an enlightened being). During the periods where no teacher arises, there are no teachings to practise, these are therefore considered dark aeons.

6. **Being born in remote regions:** Even if the teachings exist in our world, we can be born into remote regions where they are not present and there is no Dharma community to give encouragement or inspiration. In such a place there is very little chance to practise the Dharma. Often local values and customs will be excessively worldly in nature making it very difficult for a person to find the opportunity to even learn about the idea of seeking genuine happiness.

7. **Being born without the mental capacity to understand the teachings:** Even if we are born into a region where the Dharma exists, we may not have the mental capacity that allows us to understand the meaning behind the teachings. Our intellect may be severely limited or we may have sensory impairments that prevent us from accessing the teachings fully. While this condition is normally not insurmountable, it does add an additional layer of obstacles that need to be overcome.

8. **Holding wrong views:** Even if we are capable of understanding the teachings, we may have developed mistaken beliefs that prevent us from practising the Dharma. These beliefs may have been passed down through our parents or through the society in which we live. However they were acquired, they serve to limit one's receptivity, thereby closing one off to the full range of their potential.

Exercise 8.2—Free from Having No Capacity to Practise

- *In a relaxed posture, establish a neutral mind through the practice of mindfulness of breathing.*

- *Consider all of the great sages of the past. Imagine what this world would be like if none of them ever existed. Think of all of the teachings that would never have been given, and all of the wisdom that never would have been shared. Imagine a world devoid of Dharma. How could you practise something that didn't even exist?*

- *Now imagine you live on an island, completely isolated from the rest of the world. Even if the teachings did exist, you couldn't know them. How do you practise something you have never encountered? How do we learn about something if there is no one to teach us?*

- *Then consider what it would be like be unable to see the written word of the teachings or to hear the sounds of the words if they were spoken. What would happen if you couldn't understand what those words were saying? If the meaning was so hidden from you, what benefit could you draw from them? Imagine living in a culture that lacked the support to help you overcome these obstacles.*

- *What would happen if you lived in a culture that did not value spiritual development? What sorts of beliefs act as barriers to practising Dharma? Think about the different ways our beliefs can prejudice us from engaging in constructive behaviours.*

- *Check up on your own life to see if any of these situations are present. If you are free of all four, then allow that feeling of relief to arise again, and rest in the sense of freedom and possibilities.*

The Ten Advantages

Having established the conditions which are not present in your life, we can now look at the conditions which are. With the ten advantages present in our life, we have everything that is needed in order to engage in practising Dharma. Through practising Dharma, we are able to generate the causes for genuine happiness in our lives and ultimately be free from all forms of suffering. Therefore, if we find we have all ten of these points, it is a great cause for rejoicing.

If we find we are lacking one or more, it is important to do whatever we can to change the situation. These ten points are grouped into two sets:

The Five Individual Advantages

This first set focuses primarily on your own personal karmic conditions that provide you with the basis for engaging in the practise of Dharma. The five individual advantages are:

1. **Being born a human:** As we have seen, of all the different forms of existence, being born a human is the only form that provides the right balance of moderation that is conducive to spiritual contemplation.

2. **Being born in a spiritually central place:** Traditionally, a "central" place is described as any place where the Buddha's complete teachings have been established (especially the monastic code). If we extend this to other wisdom traditions, we could say that a central place is anywhere with access to authentic spiritual teachings (whether Buddhist or otherwise). For many years, Tibet was considered to be a border country that lacked spiritual teachings. It wasn't until the reign of several influential kings that Buddhism was established in the country and Tibet was transformed into a central land.

3. **Having one's faculties intact:** Cognitive and sensory impairments impede the practise of Dharma. This includes those who do not have the good fortune to be able to see representations of the Buddha to inspire their devotion, or to read or hear the precious and excellent teachings. As it would be more difficult to engage in study and reflection it is therefore considered an advantage to have all of one's faculties intact.

4. **Being without a conflicting lifestyle:** Immersing oneself in unvirtuous activity which contradicts the Dharma can be considered a conflicting lifestyle. This includes committing heavy karmic actions such as breaking essential vows, abandoning the Dharma, committing the five heinous crimes or being involved in a livelihood where negative actions cannot be avoided. Although we may not be born into such a lifestyle, we could easily fall into one later in life.

5. **Having faith in the Dharma:** Finally, it is essential to have faith in an authentic source of Dharma (such as the Buddha's teachings). Without faith, we have no inclination to practise. If through contemplation, analysis and meditation we develop a properly reasoned faith in the teachings, we are without doubt a fit vessel for the true Dharma. This is the greatest of the five individual advantages.

Exercise 8.3—Your Personal Capacity

• *In a relaxed posture, establish a neutral mind through the practice of mindfulness of breathing.*

• *First, recognise that you have indeed been born a human. You have a human body and a human mind. Consider the characteristics of being human and how they are particularly useful. In particular, focus on the benefit of having the capacity to distinguish between constructive and destructive actions.*

• *Now consider your physical location. What are the characteristics of the place where you live? Do you have access to spiritual teachings, either through books or through a local community you can visit? Is information available to you? If so, you live in a central land. Consider the benefits of living in such a place.*

• *Next think about the quality of your mental and sensory faculties. Are you able to fully experience all aspects of the teachings? In what ways are you able to interact with them?*

• *Consider your personal livelihood. Is it conducive to spiritual practice? Can you engage in your day-to-day activities without needing to commit negative actions? What sort of minds does your personal routine promote? Think of the types of habits that your lifestyle reinforces. If there are negative influences, can you change anything?*

• *Do you see value in spiritual practice? Can you see the benefit that comes from training your mind? Are you interested in developing your personal capacity for love, compassion and wisdom? How important is spirituality in your life?*

- *After carefully reflecting on whether these conditions exist in your life, recognise that you have everything you need to engage in spiritual practice. Develop a joyful mind that celebrates this present situation. Rest your awareness in this feeling.*

The Five Circumstantial Advantages

The second set, looks at the collective karma of the particular time and place into which you have been born, highlighting what makes this environment so well suited for practise. The five circumstantial advantages are:

6. **An enlightened being has appeared in the world:** If we look back at our history we can see that we live in a time when many enlightened beings have appeared in our world. These beings were endowed with extraordinary wisdom and possessed the capacity to teach us.

7. **This being has given teachings:** Even though an enlightened being may have appeared in our world, there is no guarantee that we have the karma to receive teachings from them. Fortunately though, at the time of the great sages such as the Buddha or Jesus, there were those who requested them to teach. Because of these teachings, we have the incredible opportunity to put them into practise.

8. **Those teachings remain in this world:** We live at a time when the five degenerations are increasing: our life spans are shorter (in terms of Buddhist cosmology), our beliefs and emotions are deteriorating, times are becoming increasingly difficult and beings are harder to help. Despite all this, the teachings continue to persist in the form of textual transmission and the realisations in the minds of practitioners. This means that even though we may not have been around at the time of the Buddha, we are still able to access his wisdom.

9. **There is recognition and cultural acceptance of the teachings:** This means that not only are the teachings with us today, they are also accepted in many parts of the world as being authentic and valuable. In a vast majority of places, there are sufficient religious and governmental freedoms allowing people to practise the teachings and to support each other in the form of spiritual communities.

10. **You have encountered a spiritual teacher:** While we may have the good fortune to live in place where the teachings are accessible, we must also recognise our great fortune in having actually encountered these teachings in the form of a living spiritual teacher. Through such a teacher, we are given the guidance we need to fully comprehend the teachings and actualise them in our mindstreams.

Exercise 8.4—Your Present Opportunity

- *In a relaxed posture, establish a neutral mind through the practice of mindfulness of breathing.*

- *Bring to mind the many wisdom traditions that currently exist in this world. Consider the incredible benefit that billions of people have received through the practise of these traditions. Recognise that none of this benefit could have been possible without the original founder of those traditions being born into this world. Allow a sense of joy to arise that these beings have indeed appeared on this earth.*

- *Now consider what would have happened if those great sages had never shared their wisdom with others. If they had not given their teachings to us, then we could never have received the benefit. Give rise to a sense of deep gratitude to those beings who were moved by compassion to share their wisdom with us.*

- *Consider the ways in which those teachings have come to be with us at this time. Think of all of the great adepts and saints who valued these teachings and dedicated their lives to actualising them in their minds. Develop a sense of great appreciation for the incredible efforts they made to preserve this wisdom.*

- *Think of the attitudes towards spirituality that exist within your particular society. Consider the freedoms you enjoy in relation to practising the Dharma. Imagine what it would be like to live in a place where you didn't have that freedom. Give rise to an attitude of gratitude for the tolerance and support that you receive from your community or society.*

- *Bring to mind the various teachers you have encountered during your life. Consider the impact these people have had on you. Recognise how they have helped you to work with your mind and to grow as a person. Nurture your sense of gratitude for having these people in your life.*

- *Reflect on the incredible opportunity these conditions present to you. Generate an intense sense of joy at having recognised this precious opportunity. Rest in this feeling.*

Group	Category	Characteristic
Eight Freedoms	Freedom from Non-Human States	1. Free from being born in a hell realm.
		2. Free from being born as a hungry ghost.
		3. Free from being born as an animal.
		4. Free from being born as a long-lived god.
	Freedom as a Human	5. Free from being born in a time where no teachings exist.
		6. Free from being born in remote regions.
		7. Free from being born without the mental capacity to understand the teachings.
		8. Free from holding wrong views.
Ten Advantages	Individual Advantages	1. Being born a human.
		2. Being born in a spiritually central place.
		3. Having one's faculties intact.
		4. Being without a conflicting lifestyle.
		5. Having faith in the Dharma.
	Circumstantial Advantages	6. An enlightened being has appeared in the world.
		7. This being has given teachings.
		8. Those teachings remain in this world.
		9. There is recognition and cultural acceptance of the teachings.
		10. You have encountered a spiritual teacher.

Table 8-1 The characteristics of a precious human life.

THE RARITY OF ATTAINING THIS PRECIOUS HUMAN LIFE

Once we have identified the specific conditions which are present in our lives, we must then recognise how incredibly rare they actually are. Only then can we develop a sense for the preciousness of their potential. We can do this by way of the following contemplations:

The Causes for Attaining a Precious Human Life

To get a sense for how amazingly difficult it is to actually be born with a precious human rebirth, we must first consider the specific causes and conditions that are required to produce it:

1. **Ethical Conduct:** The main cause for attaining a precious human birth is having engaged in good ethical conduct previously. This means having kept at least one form of vow or precept for some period of time without breaking it. In Buddhism we can speak of holding the eight precepts of abstaining from: harming living beings, stealing, sexual misconduct, lying, taking intoxicants which cloud the mind, taking untimely meals, dancing and singing, and adorning oneself or using high seats. The most basic form of ethical conduct is to uphold the *Ten Virtuous Actions* (as outlined previously in Chapter Six).

2. **Lots of Merit:** You must have performed oceans of meritorious actions in the past. These may include acts of generosity, discipline or patience.

3. **Strong Aspiration:** Merit alone is not enough to attain a precious human life. Secondary causes must also be created, such as having a constant aspiration to achieve such a life and dedication of any meritorious actions towards being reborn as a human.

Without these three factors it is impossible to obtain a precious human life.

Exercise 8.5—The Difficulty of Creating the Causes

- *In a relaxed posture, establish a neutral mind through the practice of mindfulness of breathing.*

- *What is the difference between simply acting in an ethical way and taking a vow to act in an ethical way? What effort is required to keep such a vow? What vows do you hold? How common is it for people to hold such vows?*

- *What types of actions are you habituated to? Is it easier to engage in a non-virtuous action or a virtuous action? Why do you think it takes such effort to do something virtuous? Does our society encourage virtue or non-virtue? How does this bias influence your ability to practise?*

- *How strong is your conviction in the existence of future lives? Can you recognise the value in obtaining a precious human birth? Recognising its importance, how much of your day do you spend creating the causes for such a birth? How much effort would it take to constantly reinforce this aspiration and direct your life towards this attainment?*

- *Consider that right now you have attained a precious human rebirth. This fact means that in a previous life you exerted incredible effort to generate the causes for this present situation. Your previous self lived his life in accordance with a code of ethical conduct. He spent all of his time accumulating merit through engaging in virtuous actions. He also made strong aspirations and dedicated all of his energy to this goal. How would he feel if you threw all of that effort out the window and wasted this life?*

- *Develop a strong resolve to not let this life slip through your fingers. Rest your awareness in this feeling.*

Examples Illustrating the Rarity of Attaining a Precious Human Life

There are several examples found in the Buddha's discourses that are traditionally used to illustrate the incredible difficulty in attaining a precious human birth:

1. **The Example of the Blind Turtle:** Imagine there is a piece of wood with a hole in it floating on the surface of a great ocean. This piece of wood is at the whim of the waves, being randomly tossed about, never staying in the same place for any given moment. At the same time in the depths of this vast ocean, there lives a blind turtle. Due to its meagre accumulation of merit, the turtle can only rise to the surface of the ocean once every hundred years.

   The chance of this blind turtle rising to the surface in the exact place as this piece of wood so as to fit its head through the hole, is virtually impossible. If the turtle wasn't blind and could actually search out the piece of wood, the situation would be quite different. But as it is, an incredible ripening of fortunate karma would be necessary for this to happen naturally.

   The vast ocean represents the seemingly infinite forms of existence that arise on the basis of ignorance. The turtle represents any single being that is trapped in this cycle of existence. The depths of the ocean represent the time this being spends in the lower realms, while the opportunity to travel to the surface represents the relative time spent in the upper realms. The piece of wood represents the possibility of finding a precious human life.

2. **The Example of the Mustard Seeds:** Also consider the following illustration. Imagine a bowl capable of containing an infinite number of mustard seeds, with hundreds of different varieties. Within this bowl is a solitary seed that represents the scarcity of a precious human birth. Think of the odds of randomly selecting this single seed from the bowl while looking in the opposite direction.

What both of these examples point to, is the culmination of an unbelievable amount of positive karma ripening in exactly the right way to generate a precious human rebirth. Recognising this, how foolish would we be to not take advantage of it?

Comparing the Numbers of Beings in the Six Realms

Another way to get a sense for the extreme rarity of this human life is to look at the number of humans there are in comparison to all of the other realms. If we actually stop to reflect on the sheer volume of beings in the six realms, we will realise that the number is immense. As we have seen, each of these realms is generated by specific states of minds. Therefore, the numbers of beings born into these realms will be directly proportionate to the commonality of those mental states.

In general, virtue gives rise to the three higher realms of the humans, demi-gods and gods, while non-virtue gives rise to the three lower realms of the animals, hungry ghosts and hell beings. If we consider whether virtue or non-virtue is more common, we will see that the vast majority of beings are very strongly habituated to non-virtue. This means that this vast majority of beings are creating the causes to be born in the lower realms. The classic example given, is that the number of beings in the lower realms is likened to all of the sand on the floor of the ocean, while the number of beings in the higher realms is like the dust that fits on the tip of a fingernail.

To get a sense for this, compare the number of humans to the number of animals. Which is there more of? On this planet there are something like 7 billion human beings. How many ants are there? How many birds? How many fish? How many tiny micro-organisms are there floating around in the sea? Very quickly we can see that many more beings had the karma to be born as animals then had the karma to be born as humans. And this is just considering one planet in one solar system of one galaxy. It is difficult to even imagine the vast number of beings living on other planets, and in other galaxies.

We can then consider all of those beings that we cannot even see right now. It is said that every single piece of space is inhabited by some sort of being. According to the Buddhist teachings, the hungry ghosts vastly outnumber the animals, while the hell beings vastly outnumber the hungry ghosts. So as we expand our perspective, the percentage of beings born into a human realm becomes exceedingly tiny and rare.

To attain a birth as an inhabitant of a higher realm is already difficult enough, but rarer still is a precious human life replete with all the good conditions required for the attainment of freedom from samsara. This means we are born in a place and a time when the Dharma is understood and we have the opportunity to practise the teachings in an authentic way. If any of these conditions are incomplete, then it is not possible to consider your human life as a precious one regardless of how extensive your skills, abilities and knowledge may appear.

We already considered how many humans there are on this planet compared to other life forms, from the most simple to the most advanced form. Now try to contemplate the small number of humans fortunate enough to be born in places where the Dharma is understood and practised. You will realise there are very few humans who can even be considered to possess a precious human life.

THE GREAT BENEFIT OF ATTAINING THIS PRECIOUS HUMAN LIFE

The eight freedoms and ten advantages help us to identify the uniqueness of our present situation, while by studying the rarity of the situation we recognise that these conditions do not come around all the time. The question then arises, "What should I do with this precious opportunity?" According to Buddhism there are three meaningful ways that this life can be used to bring you and those around you greater peace and happiness:

1. **Definite Goodness of Higher Rebirth:** The first thing you can do is to use this life in order to create the causes for a higher rebirth, free from the intense suffering of the lower realms. While you could aim to achieve rebirth in a god realm, from a Buddhist perspective, it is more worthwhile to create the conditions for another precious human birth in which you can continue your spiritual practice. In this way, you can move from life to life, evolving your capacity and eventually developing all good qualities.

2. **Liberation from Suffering:** For those with a particularly strong disenchantment with the cycle of existence, you can use this life to develop the wisdom of reality that acts as an antidote for ignorance. By removing ignorance you can break the chain of the twelve links and thereby stop the process of uncontrolled conditioned rebirth. In doing so, you achieve a state of lasting genuine happiness that is free from suffering. This state is commonly referred to as nirvana.

3. **Complete Enlightenment:** And finally, for those who are not satisfied with only achieving their own welfare, but instead are determined to bring benefit to all sentient beings, this life can be used to achieve the greatest of all accomplishments; full and complete enlightenment. By doing so, you not only remove the gross obscurations which cause your own suffering, you also remove the subtle obscurations thus enabling you to manifest in an infinite number of ways, so as to bring benefit to others.

Which of these motivations you choose, depends on where you are right now in your own personal spiritual development. It is useful to note that through working to attain a higher aim, you automatically gain the benefits of seeking the lower aims. In this way, if you choose to dedicate your life to achieving enlightenment, you will also attain personal liberation and definite goodness. The main thing to remember is to try and look beyond our immediate life and consider the broader scope of our situation. If we only work for the benefit of this life, we then fail to create any causes for genuine happiness, meaning that when we die, we will lose everything we have worked so hard to acquire.

Exercise 8.6—A Question of Priorities

- *In a relaxed posture, establish a neutral mind through the practice of mindfulness of breathing.*

- *Bring to mind the various activities you engage in throughout the day. Identify your dominant habits. How much energy do you spend engaging in these actions?*

- *Now consider the types of results that are produced by these activities. Are these results focused on this present life or are they focused on future lives? How much of your time is spent in spiritual pursuits versus worldly pursuits? Get a sense for the balance of how your time is being spent.*

- *Now think about how you could be using your time. Are there any habits that are not bringing long lasting benefit to your life? Are there any habits that are actively contributing to your suffering (either now or in the future)? What can you do to reduce the energy you give to these activities?*

- *Think of the benefits you could achieve if you shifted your priorities even just a little. What effect would it have on your life and on those around you? What effect would it have on your future lives?*

- *Identify a few simple changes you could introduce into your life in order to give greater priority to your personal spiritual development.*

OBSTACLES FOR PRACTISING THE DHARMA

With an appreciation for your present circumstances and the desire to make the most of this opportunity, you have everything you need to practise Dharma. That being said, you must remain alert to the fact that these conditions can deteriorate at any moment. The following are two sets of conditions which can act as obstacles to your practise. They should be avoided as much as possible as they have the capacity to destroy your resolve and reinforce the bad habits which fuel cyclic existence.

The Eight Temporary Circumstances

Also known as the eight intrusive circumstances, this subject was first taught by the great Tibetan master Rigdzin Jigme Lingpa. His original teachings have been expanded upon and nowadays are presented as follows:

1. People in whom the five poisons (ignorance, attachment, aversion, pride and jealousy) are too strong, cannot practise pure Dharma. Even if they have the desire or interest to do so, these mental afflictions are too dominant in their minds. Therefore, we must do what we can to remove these afflicted mental states.

2. People with limited intellect, even though they have the opportunity to practise Dharma, cannot do so properly because they are unable to understand the deeper meaning of the teachings. Therefore, we must exert great effort to sharpen our minds through study, reflection and meditation.

3. Students who are disciples of teachers who are "false spiritual friends", are guided towards distorted views and actions which lead onto wrong paths. As they do not learn the pure Dharma, they cannot progress in their practise. Therefore, we must carefully investigate our spiritual teachers to ensure that the Dharma they teach is authentic.

4. Complacent or lazy people can never learn about and practise the Dharma authentically because they lack the perseverance to accomplish the required study. These people will always procrastinate, thinking, "I will do it later." However, later never comes. Therefore make great effort to apply the antidotes to laziness.

5. Due to the magnitude of obstacles accumulated over many lifetimes, some people will find it very difficult to develop the correct qualities to practise the Dharma. They become overwhelmed by a back log of negative karma, and become disillusioned by their lack of progress. They fail to perceive that it is all a result of their own actions. Therefore, make effort to purify one's negative karma as much as possible.

6. Those enslaved by worldly pursuits or have unbreakable commitments that serve as obstacles to the Buddhist path, have lost their freedom to practise the Dharma, even if they desire to do so. Therefore, meditate on the faults of cyclic existence and develop a strong mind of renunciation.

7. Some people study the Dharma due to fear or to try and escape their present life situation. They may even live as a monk in a monastery and may appear as a good practitioner, but in truth they are unable to progress since their intentions are not genuine. Therefore, develop mindfulness of your true intention and work hard to choose a meaningful motivation for this life.

8. Some people have the outward appearance of being a Dharma practitioner, but their minds are more interested in worldly concerns such as prestige and power. They are too far from the path to truly engage with the Dharma. Therefore, meditate extensively on the *Eight Worldly Dharmas* and the *Four Convictions of Renunciation*.

The Eight Unsuitable Attitudes

These are also known as the eight incompatible propensities that lead one away from the Dharma. They include:

1. Some people are so consumed and preoccupied by their wealth, family, possessions and business life that they have no opportunity to practise the Dharma. These people may wish to practise, but they are held captive by their worldly commitments. Therefore, establish meaningful priorities in your life.

2. Some people have personalities which are so arrogant and selfish that they lack the humility to consider improving themselves. Even if they have the good fortune to meet the most wonderful teacher and spiritual community, they will not change for the better. Therefore, develop a mind that is open and receptive to learning from others.

3. No matter how often and how well a person is taught about the faults of samsara and the incredible suffering of the lower realms, they may still lack any true understanding. They have no determination to free themselves by engaging in Dharma practise. Therefore, continually study and contemplate the *Four Convictions of Renunciation*.

4. People who have no faith in the teacher and the teachings have no key to open the door of Dharma. Therefore, spend time to contemplate your potential and to develop faith in the Dharma's capacity to help you achieve that potential.

5. Some people actually take pleasure in acting non-virtuously with their body, speech and mind. Failing to control their thoughts, words and actions, they cannot practise the Dharma as they have turned away from it. Therefore, always be mindful of your actions, conscientious of what effects they will have on yourself and others.

6. Other people are so apathetic about the value of cultivating virtue or the importance of the teachings that they can never bring themselves to practise Dharma. They are likened to a dog being offered grass to eat; they will simply never be interested. Therefore, focus your studies on understanding the *Karmic Law of Cause and Effect*.

7. Anyone who has entered into Buddhist practice and then breaks the vows of moral conduct, with no genuine intention of repairing them, will be reborn in the lower realms. Then there will be no chance to practise the Dharma. Therefore, whatever ethical guidelines you decide to integrate into your life, be sure to safeguard them at all times.

8. Any advanced spiritual practitioner who breaks their sacred commitments to their teacher or to their spiritual brothers and sisters, and who has no genuine remorse within a certain time period, will bring about the downfall not only of themselves, but also of others in the spiritual community. Therefore, take your spiritual commitments seriously and strive to keep them pure.

Making the Most of This Opportunity

Right now, at this moment, you have been blessed to encounter authentic Dharma teachings. What you do next is your choice alone. If you walk away from this chance, you are wasting your human life and putting yourself at a disadvantage by not cultivating virtues and following a spiritual path. Therefore decide wisely, for to be awakened to the preciousness of our lives and to then turn our backs on this opportunity is a great misfortune.

As the great saint Milarepa said:

Used well, this body is our raft to freedom,
Used poorly, this body anchors us to samsara,
This body does the bidding of both good and evil.

Now is the time to make a sincere effort to live a meaningful life by following a spiritual path, and to dedicate our merit to attaining future rebirths through which we can benefit ourselves and others through genuine Dharma practise.

As it says in The *Way of the Bodhisattva*:

Thus having found the freedom of a human life,
If I now fail to train myself in virtue,
What greater folly could there ever be?
How could I betray myself?

REVIEW OF KEY POINTS

- There are two qualities that we need to recognise about our present situation: that it presents us with a precious opportunity and that this opportunity is exceedingly rare.

- There are eighteen conditions which define a precious human rebirth: eight freedoms and ten advantages. The freedoms describe the absence of certain obstacles that prevent practice, while the advantages describe the conditions which support our practice.

- The eight freedoms are broken into two sets of four: the four non-human states that lack any leisure due to the extreme experiences of either pleasure or pain, and the four human conditions which directly prevent one from fully engaging with Dharma practice.

- The ten advantages are also broken into two sets of five: the five individual advantages describe specific characteristics that a person can possess which make them particularly suited to practising Dharma, and the five circumstantial advantages which relate to the characteristics of being born at a particular time and place.

- Appreciation for the rarity of this precious life is developed by contemplating the causes that are required to generate such a life, various examples that illustrate the rarity of attaining such a life and an analysis of the relative numbers of beings in order to establish the improbability of attaining this life.

- In order to recognise the potential that we have, we contemplate the benefits that can be achieved on the basis of this life, namely: a higher rebirth, liberation from cyclic existence and complete enlightenment.

- There are various obstacles that can arise to weaken one's capacity to practise. There are eight temporary circumstances that should be avoided and eight unsuitable attitudes that should be abandoned.

CHAPTER NINE

Reflecting on Death and Impermanence

Practising Dharma often requires us to go against the flow of our own habitual tendencies and the generally accepted priorities of the societies in which we live. By recognising the precious potential that this life has to offer, we gain new perspective on what is important, but this does not always agree with the common view.

In many countries, you go to school, get a job, fall in love, have a family, work, retire and die. That's the pattern repeated over and over again all around the world. While there is nothing inherently wrong with such a pattern, as we have seen previously, it is a limited perspective and one which only takes into account this present life.

So, as we begin to turn our mind towards Dharma, we enter into a process of reconciliation between this worldly view, which has been with us since we were small and a spiritual view, which we are presently developing. At first it can feel like a tug-of-war between the two, as our habits continually and repeatedly assert themselves again and again. More often than not, our habits win out. We start making excuses such as not having enough time or being surrounded by too many distractions. We tell ourselves that right now it is just too difficult, but as soon as such and such or this and that is complete, then we will practise. We start creating for ourselves all kinds of conditions and requirements that we feel are necessary for us to be able to practise. Each time we do this, we push practise out of the present and into the future.

The Dharma can be incredibly transformative in your life, but it won't do you any good if you confine it to a fantasy world which may or may not happen. We need to bring it into this present moment so we can truly benefit from it. To do this, we need a sense of urgency that counteracts our tendency to procrastinate—a strength of mind that allows us to swim against the current. This strength comes through meditating on the topic of death and impermanence.

Whether we know it or not, most of us operate under the assumption that there is still time left to do the things we want to do. Our culture has become quite good at helping us plan out our lives in different ways. All of these plans assume that you will be around to experience them. It is this assumption that we need to analyse. For on the basis of this assumption, we often put off what is most important to us, in favour of engaging in some temporary action that may or may not lead to the results that we desire. We do this so much, we can spend our entire lives in a sort of holding pattern, always working towards a result, but never actually experiencing it. In this way, our life can literally flash before our eyes and before we know it, we have just squandered this precious human rebirth.

For some, the idea of thinking about death is a scary and unnecessary thing to do. Western culture tends to have a great deal of fear connected with this subject. This is probably most closely related to the dominance of a rather nihilistic viewpoint which views death as the same as annihilation. For these people, it is the end of everything and therefore it should be avoided at all costs. Our culture reinforces these ideas by promoting the value of staying young and beautiful. They attempt to hide death behind a brick wall in the hope that it will just go away.

From the Buddhist perspective, there is no benefit in taking this view. Through understanding karma and cyclic existence, we come to realise that death is not an end, but merely a transition. Rather than something to be feared, it is actually filled with great potential and can be used in extraordinary ways to develop ourselves spiritually. By reflecting on the nature of death and impermanence, we are able to lessen our attachment to the things of this life and therefore cultivate a more realistic and pragmatic approach to how we live our lives. Most importantly though, death reminds us that life is short and we cannot afford to waste even one second in trivial activities. For this reason, it stokes the fire of our determination and drives us forward, giving us the strength that is needed to overcome whatever obstacles we face.

GROSS AND SUBTLE IMPERMANENCE

The nature of our external reality is that it is impermanent—constantly changing from moment to moment. There is nothing in this reality that does not change. This is because everything we experience at this level, is a *conditioned phenomenon*. That is to say it arises in dependence upon the coming together of causes and conditions.

1. **Gross Impermanence:** On a very obvious level, we can see how phenomena arise, abide for some time and then cease. For instance, we are born, we age and then we die. Likewise a seed grows into a sprout, which grows into a tree, which produces fruit, which eventually decays and dissolves back into the earth. Often this process is playing out over extended periods of time and we do not notice it until we compare the present state of a phenomenon with a previous one. Think of comparing how you look now with how you looked as a child. This obvious process of change is known as *gross impermanence.*

2. **Subtle Impermanence:** On a deeper level though, we can speak of *subtle impermanence* which relates to the basic mechanism that drives the more obvious forms of change. Change does not occur abruptly. We don't shift from being young to being old in the blink of an eye. It doesn't work like that. Instead we evolve in a constant stream of very small increments at the level of a microsecond. With each moment that arises, it carries with it the causes for its own cessation. Because it only exists for a single moment, then it creates the opportunity for another moment to arise in its place. That new moment though, is established by a slightly different set of conditions, leading to extremely subtle variations in the resultant phenomena.

To the naked eye, everything looks as though it stays the same, while on a very subtle level everything has shifted. Over time, these tiny changes accumulate until there is now a noticeable change at the obvious level.

Since we normally only perceive the obvious changes, we develop the belief that phenomena persist over time. We attribute to them a sense of permanence in which we can clearly identify an object as being the "same" object as the one encountered previously. This is an illusion. While we can conceptually label them as part of the same continuum of changes, nothing of a previous moment persists into the present moment. They may be similar, but they are not the same.

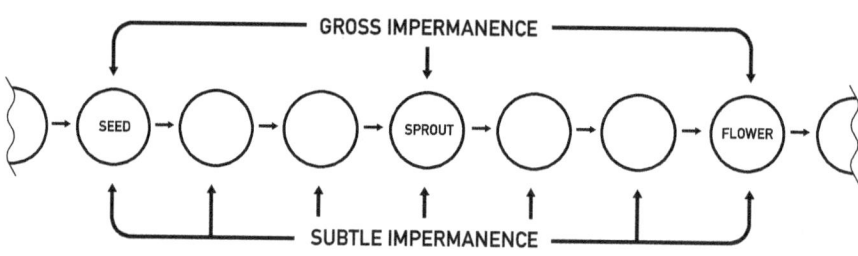

Figure 9-1: Gross and subtle impermanence over time.

A good example of how this works is to think of a river. When we encounter this river we can see the water flowing past. If we fix our gaze on a particular portion of the river, we can see that the water passing through that section is constantly changing. There is never a moment where the river freezes. If we come back the next day, we can be sure that the water of that same section of the river will be completely different from the water of the previous day. The river just keeps flowing in a steady stream of change. While we can label this collection of changes "river", there is however nothing fixed or stable for that label to refer to.

Subtle impermanence is only directly perceivable by those who have attained a high degree of contemplative realisation. Through the practise of placement meditation, it becomes possible to focus the mind to such a degree, it is able to pick up on the subtle flow of momentary change. Such a realisation gives the practitioner direct insight into the nature of their reality and can lead to a significant shift in the way that person relates with the external world. For those of us who have not reached such levels of realisation, we need to rely on an indirect knowledge of this phenomenon through concepts.

SEVEN CONTEMPLATIONS ON GROSS IMPERMANENCE

Even if we find it difficult to understand subtle impermanence directly, an understanding of gross impermanence is extremely helpful in order to reduce attachment to worldly phenomena, such as material possessions, relationships and status. Grasping onto these aspects as lasting sources of happiness will only result in suffering and dissatisfaction. It is therefore important to carefully investigate and analyse the gross level of impermanence, and to reflect upon how it impacts on our own lives as well as the world in which we live. According to the glorious *Nyingthig* lineage of Tibetan Buddhism, there are seven contemplations on gross impermanence. We will now explore each of them in detail.

1. The Evolution of the External World

The easiest place to notice the constant flow of impermanence is to look at the evolution of the natural world. In nature, we can see the cycles of time playing out in all manner of phenomena such as the four seasons, the ebb and flow of the oceanic tides and the swirling weather patterns that shape our day-to-day experience. All of this is happening due to the movement of this planet in relation to the other planets in this solar system, which in turn is moving in relation to the planets in other solar systems, which move in relation to the planets in other galaxies. Everything moving and changing in an endless cosmic dance.

So how does this vast universe take shape? It will depend on who you ask. For some, this universe was created by an omnipotent being. Others believe it arose out of nothingness. If we ask scientists, there are different opinions, but most believe in the theory that it began with a singularity of super condensed matter exploding outward in a rapid expansion, known as the "big bang". From a Buddhist perspective, this theory is not incorrect, it is simply incomplete. What it fails to identify is why this singularity occurred in the first place.

Based on the understanding of the mutual influence between mental and physical reality, Buddhism posits that the universe began out of the collective karmic propensities of the sentient beings that dwelled in that space. While there was no physical basis for gross beings such as humans or animals, purely mental beings such as form and formless realm gods still existed. It was their karma that catalyzed the condensation of energy which eventually lead to the big bang.

In the early phases of the cosmos, the various elements began to manifest. This created the conditions for sentient beings to take birth in increasingly grosser forms. The very first humans were therefore the spontaneous result of the ripening of the beings in the god realms. Of course these humans carried little similarity to ourselves. They were much more pure with subtle bodies made of energy.

Once they had taken bodies, then they began to react to the sensations that arose in their minds. Initially these humans were not possessive, sharing everything they had with each other. Merely looking at each other was enough to give them complete sexual satisfaction. But over time, their sense of craving and desire grew, leading to their view of reality becoming more solidified and coarser. Subsequently, they now required more effort in order to experience gratification. Where once a look was sufficient, they now needed to see a smile and then eventually to experience physical contact.

The more their desire grew, the more substantiated their world became. Stars began to form and orbiting planets emerged. The more solid their bodies, the more individuated they felt. People developed a sense of possessiveness towards different types of objects. They began to engage in negative actions in order to acquire these objects. On this basis, disharmony arose in their communities. To avoid conflicts, they established social rules and chose leaders to enforce them. People who disobeyed these rules were punished.

As the various afflictions became stronger, sentient beings began taking on new forms. At first there were just a few animals, but eventually that number grew. Each of them fueled by ignorance, attachment and aversion. These states of mind gave rise to beings taking birth in the hungry ghost and hell realms. In this way, the six realms emerged.

At some stage, the minds of the human beings had degenerated to such a degree that they took on a form that was very similar to the animals around them. What we call the evolution of man is actually the progressive ripening of human karma over the course of thousands of years. While it may appear externally as though we have improved significantly from our neanderthal ancestors, when compared to the purity of our previous form of existence, we have degenerated considerably.

This process of evolution represents a period of degeneration. When seen from the perspective of cosmic cycles, it is just one portion of a continual process of creation and destruction. As this present universe degenerates further, it will eventually start to disintegrate. This process begins when many beings start achieving advanced stages of meditative absorption. This will lead them to take rebirth in the form and formless realms. For those whose negative karma is too strong, increasing numbers will start taking rebirth in other solar systems, effectively emptying out this particular physical realm. Without the collective karma to perpetuate it, the atmosphere of this world will collapse and the sun will expand, effectively consuming the world in a blazing supernova.

The first wave of the sun's expansion will burn up all fruit-bearing trees and forests. The second wave will evaporate all streams, creeks and ponds, while the third and fourth waves will dry up all the rivers and the great lakes. During the fifth phase, all the vast oceans will then progressively evaporate to varying degrees. The seawater that is left will shrink to such a small area that not even a footprint can be filled. By the time the six waves of the sun's expansion has occurred, the entire earth and its snow-covered mountains will have burst into flames. With the seventh expansion, even the most subtle essence of the earth will be engulfed by flames, together with every remaining trace of the physical world.

With the destruction of the gross physical realm, the energy of the fire will continue to expand and consume even the subtler realms: first the hungry ghosts, then the hell beings and finally the various levels of gods. At this stage, all that will remain are those who have transcended the desire realm and have taken refuge in the form and formless realms.

The cause of the destruction of the form realm is the inability of these beings to maintain a subtle mental state, as well as the abandonment of investigation and analysis by beings up to the first form realm. As this state is characterised by a fire-like energy, they are then susceptible to destruction by fire in seven waves of destruction. Storm clouds will then form in the realm of the gods of the second form realm and a tremendous torrential rain will fall. Like salt dissolving in water, everything up to and including the realm of the gods of the second form realm will disintegrate. This again is caused by the inability to maintain a subtle mental state and failure to abandon worldly joy and bliss by the beings of the second form realm. Since this mental state has a water-like energy, they are not spared from destruction by water.

After seven devastations by water, an all-pervasive wind will rise up from the base of the universe. Like dust scattered by the wind, everything up to and including the realm of the gods of the third form realm will be blown away completely. This occurs as a result of a lack of subtlety in meditative stabilisation and the non-abandoning of equanimity by the beings of the third form realm. This meditative state is characterised by wind-like energy and these beings are therefore susceptible to destruction by wind.

By the end of this process, all that is left is space and the formless realm beings. They will remain in their extremely subtle mental stabilisation until such point as their karma runs out, which then triggers the whole process to begin again. In this way, sentient beings are constantly driving change at both an individual and collective level.

Exercise 9.1—The Impermanence of the Environment

- *In a relaxed posture, establish a neutral mind through the practice of mindfulness of breathing.*

- *Focusing on the natural world around you, identify the different patterns of change that occur over the course of a year. For instance, consider the signs that indicate to you each of the different seasons. Are these signs consistent across the globe or are they experienced in different ways? What drives these seasonal changes? Consider both the physical causes and the karmic causes for this variation in experience.*

- *Now consider the variation in landscapes on this planet. Think about the different habitats and how they are each capable of supporting a different form of life. Think about the relationship between a being and the environment they inhabit. How do they influence each other? When a being is in harmony with its environment what is the result? Likewise, what happens when a being is in disharmony?*

- *Broaden your scope to consider the ways in which our environment is influenced by the planetary bodies around it. For instance, what effect does the Moon have on Earth? What signs do we have to indicate this effect? Consider how the Sun has changed over the years. Think of the evolution of a star and what that means for life on this planet.*

- *Try to get a sense for the incredible interconnection of causes and conditions that are driving the constant evolution of this world. Recognise its impermanent nature and rest your mind in this certainty.*

2. The Impermanence of Worldly Beings

From the highest heaven of Akanistha to the lowest hell, not a single being is able to escape death. As the *Letter of Consolation* says:

On earth or in all the heavens,
Has there been a being who will not die?
Or even heard of this happening?
Or imagined that it could?

In all of the realms, no-one has ever encountered a being that was born and did not die. Death is a certainty, and we live during a time where the length of life is quite unpredictable. We don't know how we will die, what day or what hour, nor do we know where we will go after we have died. Death occurs between the inhalation and exhalation of our breath and can happen at any time. As it said in *The Collection of Deliberate Sayings*:

Who can be certain he will live until tomorrow?
The time to be ready is now,
For the messengers of the Lord of Death;
Are they your friend?

Nagarjuna too, says:

Life flickers in the wind of a thousand ills,
More fragile than a bubble in a stream.
In sleep, each breath comes and goes;
How amazing that we wake up with life!

Although we know we are going to die one day, we generally don't talk about it and we seldom reflect upon it. We continually plan and worry about our future and act as if we are going to live forever. We work tirelessly to achieve a happier life until suddenly the reality of death confronts us. At this time nothing can help us – power, wealth, intelligence, beauty or health will be of no use whatsoever. When our karmic life force has expired, the world's most powerful army cannot protect us, nor could the Medicine Buddha or any god delay our death even if they were to appear in person. Once death occurs our skin begins to fade, our eyes glaze over, our head and limbs become limp, and under the control of our karma, we are swiftly swept along towards our next rebirth.

3. The Impermanence of Great Rulers

There are gods and rishis who can live for as long as an aeon, but eventually they too must experience death. Even those who rule over beings, such as Brahma, Indra, Vishnu, Ishvara and other great gods, are not beyond karma and the reach of death. Throughout history there have been many powerful emperors and influential rulers such as Julius Caesar, Alexander the Great, Genghis Khan and Napoleon. They accomplished great things, achieved immense fame and incredible material wealth, but eventually they succumbed to death just like all other beings and could take none of their worldly accomplishments or power with them.

The history of Tibet is a perfect example of impermanence. Tibet carries a colourful past spanning thousands of years, especially from the time of King Nyatri Tsenpo, who is considered an emanation of a great Bodhisattva. Forty-four kings reigned, spanning various dynasties, all with different policies. There were times during which Tibet ruled over many neighbouring countries such as China, Mongolia and some parts of India and Burma, but true to the nature of inevitable change and impermanence, these glorious times are now just a memory and the Tibetan people are presently struggling with the loss of political freedom and even their own cultural identity. The former glory of Tibet seems like a dream to most Tibetans as their situation is now completely reversed. This pattern has been repeated countless times throughout world history.

Contemplating such matters can help us to understand the futility of holding onto anything with the idea of it being permanent or unchanging. The greater our attachment to worldly aspects such as material possessions, relationships and status, the more we will experience sorrow and painful loss.

4. The Impermanence of Enlightened Beings

All that remains of the exalted holy beings from the world's great spiritual traditions, such as Jesus Christ, Abraham, Mohammed and Krishna, are their stories. In the present aeon four Buddhas have already appeared, each with their own vast number of Shravaka and Arhat disciples; beings that have accomplished liberation from cyclic existence. Nowadays all we have are what remains of the teachings of the most current Buddha—Buddha Shakyamuni.

In India, these words of Buddha Shakyamuni were compiled by five hundred Arhats. Since this time there have been many great practitioners such as the *Two Supreme Ones* (Nagarjuna and Asanga), the *Six Ornaments*, the *Eighty Mahasiddhas* and many others. They mastered all elements of the paths and all possible levels of attainment, achieving unlimited clairvoyance and miraculous powers. Now however, all that remains of them are the tales of how they lived. In Tibet there were also many exceptional practitioners such the great Padmasambhava and the Mahasiddha Panchen Dawa Gonpo, who attained extraordinary enlightened qualities and miraculous powers. All the Tibetan Buddhist lineages flourished and the Kalachakra Wheel of Dharma was turned to ripen and liberate beings.

All over the world there have been many beings who attained miraculous powers, but in the end they all chose to demonstrate that everything is impermanent and today we only have their stories to remind us of their achievements. If all that remains of such great beings are the tales of how they lived, how can we, carried along by the wind of our negative actions, hope to achieve any lasting freedom? Bearing this in mind, we should again contemplate our own impermanent nature.

Exercise 9.2—The Impermanence of Sentient Beings

- *In a relaxed posture, establish a neutral mind through the practice of mindfulness of breathing.*

- *Bring to mind, anyone you knew who has passed away during your life. Now consider all those who have died that you did not know. Reflect upon the sheer number of people who die each day.*

- *Then expand your scope to include all of the animals. Consider those who die through natural causes, who are killed by others or whose lives are taken accidentally.*

- *Think back through history and identify the most famous people you can think of. Where are they now? Do you know of anyone who has escaped death? Consider those who held great political power or those who were wealthy. Were any of them able to avoid dying?*

- *Think back to all of the world's great sages. What remains of them today? Consider all of the saints that came after them. Have any of them survived?*

- *Recognising that all sentient beings will die at some point, rest your awareness in this certainty.*

5. Further Examples of Impermanence

The four seasons are a continuous lesson in impermanence as is the rise and fall of governments and leaders. The ageing process also gives us constant evidence of the passage of time. Of all our family members who were living one hundred years ago, fulfilling all their commitments to work and family life, who now remains? All our human relationships are subject to change. Lovers come and go; old friends drift away over the years and new friendships are forged. Even if we are happily married and it seems like we'll be together forever, eventually one person will die and therefore we are still at the mercy of impermanence. Nothing therefore, is guaranteed.

In a hundred years who will remain of all the so-called famous people of our time? These people may seem to have everything that is coveted by the masses. People wish to be like them and own what they possess, yet in a hundred years these people will certainly have died and where will they be then? Perhaps if they committed many negative actions, they could be wandering around in the hell realms, or if they had great attachment to worldly possessions they may be relegated to living as a bird making nests under the eaves of a rich man's house.

To understand the vast display of impermanence more deeply, we only need to contemplate the cycles of ascension and decline, or the ebb and flow of life over millennia. In the distant past, during the beginning of this aeon, according to the Buddhist perspective, humans were completely reliant upon the light from their own intrinsic nature. No external celestial bodies, such as the sun or the moon, were required to bestow light and warmth upon these beings. They could move at will through time and space and they were six times taller than the average humans of today.

These beings prospered in an environment of peace, compassion and contentment and they lived like the gods themselves, being nourished by heavenly ambrosia. True to the nature of impermanence, disharmony eventually took root among these humans and they fell victim to the errors of judgment and other negative emotions. They gradually deteriorated into the flawed human beings of today.

It is said in Buddhist doctrines that this cycle of degeneration will continue, with the Dharma ceasing to exist after several thousands of years, with many humans dying in times of war and epidemics of disease. At that time the remaining humans will be a mere three feet tall and have a lifespan of only ten years. An emanation of the Buddha Maitreya will then appear, guiding the survivors away from behaviours that are not conducive to enlightenment. Due to the blessing and guidance of Buddha Maitreya, humans will begin to resurrect themselves as a people. They will gradually increase their lifespan again from ten years to twenty years and onwards until it reaches eighty thousand years. Lord Maitreya will then appear in the flesh, manifesting as a Buddha and turning the Wheel of Dharma.

When eighteen such cycles of growth and decline have occurred, the Buddha of Infinite Aspiration will appear and live for as long as all the other thousand Buddhas of this Good Aeon combined. Finally, even this aeon will end in destruction. Nothing, therefore, is beyond the reach of impermanence.

6. Death

Contemplating the above points will help you to develop a general understanding of the pervasiveness of impermanence in all aspects of our lives. However, most people still hold tightly onto the notion that somehow, they will be the exception to the rule. We wake up in the morning, expecting to survive the day. We make extensive plans for the future, expecting to be around to enjoy them. In order to overcome this deep rooted grasping onto our own permanence, we need to specifically meditate upon the reality of our own death.

The Certainty of Death

There is very little that is certain in life, except for death. Nothing at all, whether animate or inanimate, can escape the fact that everything which arises will eventually cease. There is nothing in the entire universe that can be called a truly permanent entity. Everything changes.

This precious body which we feed, clothe and care for, will also fall away and be left behind at the moment of death. It is the mind alone that will travel through the intermediate stages after death. There are no companions at this time as all our relationships will have been set aside. Our only refuge will be the accumulated propensities we have collected through our altruistic or self-centred intentions. These are the only things that travel with us wherever we go.

Our lives are filled with an endless stream of ups and downs, where no single situation is immune to the ravages of time. There is so much that is beyond our control. Therefore encourage yourself to loosen your attachment and instead cultivate loving-kindness and other good qualities. This will naturally draw your attention towards the Dharma. If we genuinely aspire towards enlightenment, we should meditate on the true nature of impermanence so that our devotion to achieving worldly accomplishments can transform into devotion towards our teachers and the teachings that will liberate us.

With the certainty of death looking over our shoulder, we should seize every opportunity to fulfil our highest purpose while we still have this rare and precious human life. It is highly possible that in old age we will no longer have the faculties that give us the ability and the desire for liberation. Therefore, don't procrastinate! Everything is subject to change, so we need to consider the consequences of delaying our commitment to a path that will lead to the ultimate benefit for ourselves and others. Now is your chance to practise Dharma and discover your sacred truth!

Exercise 9.3—Nothing Lasts Forever

- *In a relaxed posture, establish a neutral mind through the practice of mindfulness of breathing.*

- *Looking back through time, identify the people who were close to you at different stages of your life. How many of them are still present? Think of childhood friends, co-workers and romantic relationships. Review how each of these relationships have changed over time.*

- *Now consider the person you were at different stages in your life. Think of the things you were interested in at those times. How have your likes and dislikes evolved over time? What activities did you previously enjoy that now no longer interest you? If you compare the person you were then, to the person you are now, how similar are you?*

- *Think about the changes in your body. Bring to mind how you looked and felt at different stages. How are you physically different? What part of your previous bodies still exist in this present body?*

- *What makes you different from other people? Can you think of any good reason why you won't die? Recognising that you are just as impermanent as they are, rest in the certainty that sooner or later you're life is going to end.*

Uncertainty of the Time of Death

Having been born, it is certain we will die and every moment following birth we are getting closer to our death. We are never certain of the time or place that death will occur nor will we know the cause. There are few things in this world that favour life and many that threaten it. As the master Aryadeva points out,

Causes of death are numerous;
Causes of life are few,
And even they may become causes of death.

There are countless circumstances that can lead to our death, such as car accidents, heart attacks, fires or floods. Even things which normally benefit us, such as food or medicine, can kill us. We can choke on the food we consume or we could experience an allergic reaction to a particular medicine that causes us to stop breathing. Similarly, desire for fame, wealth and honour may lead to disputes or even wars that could cause the death of many people.

We are never sure when any of these causes of death might descend upon us. Some die in their mother's womb or at birth, while others are born into poverty and die young unable to get the medical assistance they need. Many people die suddenly while eating, talking, working or travelling, while others endure a long and painful process, dying old and decrepit. Some even take their own lives, driven to despair by the circumstances of their life. Given this great uncertainty, there is absolutely no guarantee that death will not strike us suddenly. It is totally possible that tomorrow we might wake up in the body of a hungry ghost or an animal. Death is unpredictable and can strike at any time.

Exercise 9.4—Living Each Day Like it was Your Last

- *In a relaxed posture, establish a neutral mind through the practice of mindfulness of breathing.*

- *Since each life is projected by a single karma, we all have a maximum lifespan. Sooner or later, the energy which sustains this life will be used up. This means that every second, we are moving one second closer to our death. Consider the time it takes to perform the various activities in your daily routine. As you perform these actions, you are moving that much closer to death. Like an arrow shot from a bow, the end is fast approaching. Get a sense for the uncontrollable march of time.*

- *Now consider the many ways that people die. How much damage does the body need to take before it stops working? What sorts of things can cause this damage? Think of the many things around you and how they could all become conditions for your death.*

- *Consider the things which we rely upon to protect our bodies. Can any of these things be used to kill us? For instance food is normally necessary to sustain the body, but if it gets caught in our windpipe, we can die from choking to death. Identify a number of other examples.*

- *Now, what guarantees do we have that we will not die within the next twenty-four hours? Do you know what is going to happen in the future? If you are surrounded by things that have the potential to kill you, what makes you so sure they won't? Consider all of the people that have died unexpectedly due to accidents or other unforeseen events.*

- *Recognising that death is imminent and can happen at any moment, develop the resolve not to waste a single second of the precious time you have left. Rest your awareness in this conclusion.*

7. Constant Recognition of Impermanence

The seventh and final contemplation on gross impermanence considers the benefit of meditating single-pointedly on death at any time and in every circumstance. Whether we are lying in bed, going to work or enjoying a coffee with our friends, we can never be sure that we won't die at that moment. To maintain a recognition of the constant possibility of our death is to be like the Kadampa Geshes who were aware of death at all times. At night they would turn their bowls upside-down and leave the embers of their fires uncovered, knowing that the next day, there may be no need to light a fire or prepare a meal.

Focusing on the uncertainty of the time of death can gives us a sense of urgency in our practise of authentic Dharma. It can impel us to contemplate the transience of worldly activities and the impermanence of our body and mind, heightening our awareness of the preciousness of each moment.

Spurred on by the thought of impermanence, we can try to view every situation we encounter with humility, gratitude and pure perception. This will help us develop profound concentration, nourishing our mindfulness and awareness which can even be present during sleep, warding off nightmares caused by ignorance.

Remember that even loved ones, friends and family are impermanent, so in a solitary place arouse the desire for liberation. Name and fame are impermanent, so always take a lowly position. Speech is impermanent, so inspire yourself to recite prayers and mantras. Ideas and thoughts are impermanent, as are faith and the desire for liberation, so work to develop a good nature and make your commitments resolute.

Sometimes people feel proud of their experiences in meditation but these too are impermanent. Practise diligently until everything dissolves into the true nature of reality. At that time, the cycle of death and rebirth will cease and we will then be completely prepared for death. In fact, we will even look forward to it as an incredible opportunity for liberation. Meditate single-pointedly on death and impermanence until you reach this stage and all fear of death will be overcome.

As the great Tibetan saint Milarepa sang:

Fearing death I went to the mountains,
Meditating intensely on the uncertainty of the moment of death,
And discovering the fortress of the deathless unchanging nature of mind,
Now I have gone beyond all fear of dying!

For a follower of the Buddha-Dharma, of all subjects of meditation, the focus on impermanence is the most essential. As Lord Buddha said:

To meditate persistently on impermanence is to make offerings to all the Buddhas.
To meditate persistently on impermanence is to be rescued from suffering by all the Buddhas.
To meditate persistently on impermanence is to be guided by all the Buddhas.
To meditate persistently on impermanence is to be blessed by all the Buddhas.

Padampa Sangye explains how this contemplation is essential through every stage of the spiritual path:

At first, to be fully convinced of impermanence makes you take up the Dharma;
In the middle it whips up your diligence;
In the end it brings you to the radiant Dharmakaya.

There is much to be gained in our worldly lives from contemplating deeply on impermanence and taking its message to heart. It is also important to realise that without a sincere conviction in the impermanent nature of all things, we will not penetrate the true meaning of Dharma, as meditation on impermanence is the door that opens the way to all Dharma practice.

We should be like Geshe Kharak Gomchung, who went to meditate in the mountains of Jomo Kharak in the province of Tsang:

In front of his cave there was a thorn-bush which kept catching on his clothes.
At first Geshe Gomchung wondered whether he should cut it down. He thought
to himself, "But after all, I may die inside this cave. I really cannot say whether
I shall ever come out again alive. It is more important to get on with my
practise." When he did come out he had the same problem with the thorns.
This time however he considered, "I am not sure that I shall ever go back
inside" And so this went on for many years until he became an accomplished
master. When he left the cave for the last time, the bush was still uncut.

Exercise 9.5—Packing Your Bags

- *In a relaxed posture, establish a neutral mind through the practice of mindfulness of breathing.*

- *Imagine that you are on your deathbed. As you prepare yourself for the final moment of your life, consider the nature of this transition. Start by asking yourself, what will happen to your physical possessions? Can you take any of them with you? What benefit will you get from them after you are dead? How could attachment to these items affect your next rebirth?*

- *Now consider what will happen to your relationships. Can any of your family or friends come with you on this journey? Again, what effects would your attachment to these relationships have on your mind?*

- *Now think about the foundation of your consciousness. Think about all of the different karmic propensities you have created in this and beginningless past lives. Will these propensities just disappear after death? If you think they will, what would cause them to disappear? If not, then how will they affect your mind after death?*

- *Recognise that the only thing which continues on after death is the mindstream and its karmic conditioning. The most important thing to do with this life then is to ensure that we generate as many positive propensities as possible. For this reason, develop the resolve to not give in to laziness and to practise the Dharma as much as possible. Rest your awareness in this resolve.*

REVIEW OF KEY POINTS

- Reflecting on death and impermanence is the best way to counteract laziness and to bring urgency into our practise.

- There are two forms of impermanence: gross and subtle. Gross impermanence includes the obvious changes that are visible to our senses, while subtle impermanence refers to the continual stream of change occurring on a moment to moment basis.

- The external world is pervaded by impermanence, fueled by the mutual interaction of the minds of sentient beings and the physical environments that they inhabit. The universe is cyclical in nature, evolving in a never-ending process of growth and decay.

- Death is a natural part of all conditioned phenomena. Since the form of a sentient being is conditioned by its karma, then it too will eventually die. Everyone who is born in this world, will eventually die. It doesn't matter how powerful or famous you are. Even enlightened beings manifest death.

- There are two realisations you need to develop regarding your own mortality. Firstly, you are definitely going to die and secondly, you have no idea when that death will occur.

- By constantly reminding yourself about death, you can be sure not to waste your time with trivial matters. This will keep your mind focused on the Dharma.

A lone monk walking through the forest.

PART THREE

Developing Faith in a Path

CHAPTER TEN

Choosing a Spiritual Path

The *Four Convictions of Renunciation* are specifically designed to help turn our minds towards the practice of Dharma. They highlight the characteristics of our present situation and show us the ways in which our minds perpetuate our own suffering. On the basis of this, we are able to see that we have options and we do not have to blindly follow our habitual modes of thinking. Instead, the four convictions show us that we have a choice. We can choose to continue as we are or we can choose to change. It's entirely up to us.

Deciding to set out on a spiritual journey is a great first step. It can act like a sort of compass, orienting your mind and guiding you towards your goal. Unfortunately, merely knowing the direction you wish to take is not enough. Eventually, you have to start taking actual steps and this is where a spiritual path is vital.

As we have seen, there are many different types of dharmas. Some can help you achieve greater success in this life; some can bring you greater harmony in your relationships; some can reduce afflictive states of mind; some can cut through ignorance and some can reveal your true nature. Although we might know we want to practice Dharma, it may not always be clear which dharmas to practice and in what order.

To eliminate this uncertainty, we need to rely on the maps that have been left to us by the great sages of our world. These maps encapsulate timeless wisdom in specifically defined paths that we can each use to help us transition from a life filled with disatisfaction, to a life filled with genuine happiness. They are the keys to actualising meaningful transformation in our lives.

TYPES OF PATHS

If this is the case, then we must ask ourselves, "Are all paths the same?" The answer is no. Since each path has arisen out of the coming together of specific causes and conditions, then the form they have taken is necessarily different. The following are just a few ways that we can distinguish between paths.

Paths Based on Scope

The scope of a path refers to the potential results which that path is capable of producing; you can think of it as its maximum capacity. Some paths are by nature, more limited than others due to the types of phenomena they focus on. When considering scope, we can identify two broad categories of paths:

1. **Mundane Paths:** A mundane path is a path which focuses on the application of conventional wisdom in order to produce results that transform one's gross level of experience. An example of such a path is a four year undergraduate degree. When you begin such a path, you lack certain knowledge. By the end, you will have developed the knowledge and skills that allow you to function as a professional in whatever field you have studied. While this type of path is not capable of bringing you lasting genuine happiness, it is capable of helping you to create conditions for temporary worldly happiness. Unfortunately, because this knowledge is superficial in nature it is only beneficial during this life and will largely be lost during the dissolution process between this life and the next.

2. **Spiritual Paths:** A spiritual path is a path that is focused on developing wisdom in relation to the nature of reality. Through this wisdom, one is able to purify the mind and thereby create the conditions for the experience of genuine happiness to arise. The degree to which the mind is purified will depend on the path being used. Because these paths work by bringing the practitioner closer to reality as it is, then they are capable of producing a more profound degree of transformation than a mundane path. The changes they generate are generally more long-term in nature, taking into consideration the continuation of experience after the moment of death.

Since our aim here is to experience genuine happiness, I will be focusing primarily on spiritual paths from this point on. That being said, be aware that mundane paths can be very useful for creating the conditions to support your practise of a spiritual path and should therefore not be disregarded completely. Instead, we simply need to recognise their limitations and to focus our attention on those paths that are capable of providing the results we are ultimately looking for.

Paths Based on Motivation

Within the category of spiritual paths, we can distinguish a number of different types based on the different motivations that are held by different practitioners. These motivations act to further limit the potential a path has for producing certain results within the mind of an individual. Generally speaking, we can identify three types of spiritual motivations:

1. **Aspiring to improve the conditions of one's next life:** This motivation is focused on the life that immediately follows after death. Paths based on this motivation tend to emphasise engaging in virtuous activity that will create the causes to be reborn in a heavenly realm.

2. **Aspiring to remove the causes for one's own suffering:** This motivation seeks to attain what is known as liberation from cyclic existence. Paths that are designed around this motivation will generally emphasise the cultivation of a wisdom that removes the causes of suffering. Different paths will define what liberation means in different ways, leading to further variations in the methods used to achieve that state.

3. **Aspiring to remove the causes for the suffering of one's self and others:** This final motivation not only seeks to end one's own suffering, but also to end the suffering of everyone else in cyclic existence. This type of altruistic aspiration is extremely rare and likewise the number of paths that promote it are also rare. It is based on a profound understanding of the interdependent nature of our reality and is fueled by compassion for sentient beings. These sorts of paths can be considered paths to enlightenment.

From a Buddhist perspective, the first motivation is the most limited, while the third is the most expansive. Fortunately, motivations are not fixed and therefore they can change over time. While a practitioner may only be able to go so far with a particular way of thinking, they can still develop the foundations that will allow them to later adopt a broader motivation that will in turn give them the opportunity to actualise more of their potential. In this way, we may find that during the course of our lives, we might engage with multiple paths that fulfill our specific needs in accordance with where our spiritual development is currently at.

Scope	Motivations	Examples
Mundane	Benefit for this life	• University degrees • Professional apprenticeship
Spiritual	Benefit for next life	• Extrinsic belief systems (such as Hinduism, Judaism, Christianity and Islam) • Intrinsic belief systems (such as Jainism, Buddhism, Taoism)
	Personal Liberation	
	Enlightenment	

Table 10-1: Motivations for different types of paths.

Paths Based on Authenticity

While scope limits the maximum potential of a path and motivation limits the potential of an individual practitioner, they do not indicate whether the path actually has the capacity to realise that potential. The whole point of relying on a spiritual path is to help us produce wisdom more efficiently. If the path is not capable of doing this, then there is no reason to follow it. If we therefore analyse the efficacy of a path, we can identify two categories:

1. **Authentic Paths:** An authentic path is any body of knowledge that has arisen out of wisdom and relies on methods that have been proven to cultivate that wisdom. It is authentic in that it has the legitimate capacity to produce the results it claims to be able to produce.

2. **Corrupted Paths:** A corrupted path is a body of knowledge that has arisen out of ignorance or has been distorted by ignorance and therefore is only capable of generating more ignorance. These paths may have originally started out as authentic paths but over time, mistaken

interpretations evolved serving to distort the teachings and thereby limit their potential.

Judging whether a path is authentic or not can be quite difficult. It is therefore important to use our understanding of valid perception to help us evaluate the authenticity of a given path. As we will recall from Chapter Two, there are three ways we can know something:

1. **Faith in Authority:** We normally start our spiritual journey by relying on the authority of other people (such as friends, family or the greater society) to help suggest different paths we could potentially follow. While this may be sufficient to introduce us to a path, eventually we need to develop our own criteria for how to evaluate its authenticity.

2. **Logical Reasoning:** Initially we can do this by studying the teachings of the path we are considering to follow. It is important at this stage to be as inquisitive as possible in order to test the qualities of that path. Through actively questioning what is being said, we can develop greater clarity regarding whether it is actually capable of producing the desired results. If the path is authentic, it will then stand up to analysis as it is based on a wisdom that accords with how things actually exist.

3. **Direct Experience:** On the basis of your conceptual analysis of the path, you may find you have developed sufficient confidence to at least give it a try. You may not be totally convinced, but you can at least recognise the potential for receiving benefit. By putting the methods of the path into practice, you start to actually experience the teachings and on the basis of that experience you can establish whether the teachings are authentic or not.

Exercise 10.1—Identifying Authentic Spiritual Paths

- *In a relaxed posture, establish a neutral mind through the practice of mindfulness of breathing.*

- *Begin by first distinguishing between mundane and spiritual paths. Think of a few examples of knowledge or skills you would find useful to have in this life. Now consider the different ways people can go about acquiring this knowledge or learning these skills. These are mundane paths.*

- *Likewise consider the type of knowledge that is needed in order to transcend suffering. What paths can you think of for doing this? How do you distinguish them from mundane paths? What qualities do they have that a mundane path doesn't? These are spiritual paths.*

- *Now consider some of the spiritual paths you know about. What is the dominant motivation behind these paths? What are practitioners of these paths aiming to do? What sort of result can they expect to achieve? Choose a number of examples and see if you can match them to at least one of the three types of motivation. Can you think of different motivations that practitioners can have within a single path? Identify examples.*

- *Using the spiritual paths you have already identified, consider ways in which they can be either authentic or corrupted. Try to distinguish between the essential message of the path and the distorted ways in which that path can be understood. Recognise the different effects these distortions produce.*

Having developed our capacity to identify whether a path is authentic or not, you are now faced with a new challenge. Of the available authentic spiritual paths that exist in this world, which one will be best suited to your specific needs? To answer this question you will need to learn how to evaluate a wide range of beliefs in order to identify the overall suitability of a given path.

This process will rely on your ability to recognise the benefits that a diversity of beliefs can offer you. Through introducing yourself to multiple perspectives, you are able to develop a very broad panorama of your available options. You can then compare these options and gain insights into how these different approaches work and where they place their emphasis.

As you do this, some ideas may really jump out at you. You may find your interest is roused and you are drawn to know more. This is a good sign that may indicate you have existing karma with a particular path. Based on the strength of your intuitive connection, you may develop a significant degree of conviction about wanting to engage more in this path.

By engaging in such an analysis, your choice of path will be grounded in a combination of intuitive and reasoned faith that will bring greater strength and determination to your practise. Without such faith, you may find it hard to really commit to any one tradition. This will lead to a sort of mix-and-match approach where you keep jumping from one path to another, never really progressing very far in any one direction. This sort of approach can also increase the potential for distortions to creep into your practise which can reduce the general efficacy of the paths you are following.

ESTABLISHING A RIMÉ PHILOSOPHY

In Tibetan, we use the term "rimé" to describe a mind "free from bias". It is a particular attitude which helps people work with diversity in a way that supports their own personal development, while at the same time, promoting greater harmony with those who hold different views. We can call this attitude the *Rimé Philosophy*.

When we first begin a spiritual journey, having a Rimé Philosophy can provide you with a basis for choosing a path. Then, as you begin to progress along that path, it can help you overcome obstacles by showing you alternative ways of thinking about a given situation. And finally, when you reach more advanced stages, it provides you with a greater flexibility of mind that can be used to adapt to a wide variety of situations and thereby helps you to bring greater benefit to those around you. In this way, the Rimé Philosophy is helpful in the beginning, middle and end.

We can break this attitude down into four distinct qualities that develop in a gradual process over time. As you strengthen one quality, it naturally creates the conditions for the next quality to arise. In this way, we can think of the Rimé Philosophy as being like a flower that starts off as a seed and eventually blooms into a beautiful display of colour.

Tolerance

The first quality we need to develop is tolerance, built on a basis of mutual respect. A mind that lacks this type of tolerance is openly antagonistic towards people who hold different views. It is a mind that grasps very strongly to one's own beliefs and feels threatened by the mere presence of other viewpoints. We need to loosen this grip in order to be able to communicate in a meaningful way.

Developing tolerance for a view is based on developing respect for a person. Respect means being able to connect with a person in such a way, that even if we don't agree with their views, we can still value their right to hold those views. The key to developing this sort of tolerance is to separate the validity of an idea, from the validity of the person holding the idea. Behind every idea is a motivation that is shaped by hopes and fears. If we are able to identify this underlying motivation, we will see the wish to find happiness and to be free from suffering. Ultimately we all want the same thing; we just have different ways of going about it. Mutual respect can grow from understanding this basic commonality of motivation that unites us as people. If you connect with that basic motivation, then you establish a working basis for dialogue to occur.

Exercise 10.2—A Foundation of Respect

- *In a relaxed posture, establish a neutral mind through the practice of mindfulness of breathing.*

- *Spend some time thinking about views that you strongly disagree with. Bring the idea to mind and note any aversion that comes up. If you find the aversion too strong to work with, look for some other examples.*

- *When you have found a subject, imagine a situation where you might encounter a person who holds this view. Imagine that this person starts telling you about what they believe.*

- *Regardless of what your initial reaction is, take a moment to step back and consider what this person is saying. Consider why they might hold such a view. Even if you know it is wrong, what reasons might lead someone to believe in this way? Keep probing into their motivation, asking yourself, why, why, why? Try to reduce the motivation down to its most essential form.*

- *Now consider, is this a motivation that you could have? Is this something that you can relate to? Think of examples from your own life where you acted with a similar motivation.*

- *Having connected with this deeper motivation, can you detect a shift in how you perceive this person? If you perceive the person differently, does it change the way you relate to the view itself?*

- *Rest in any insights that arise.*

Receptivity

Tolerance makes it possible to establish a basic connection with another person. On the basis of that connection, you can then begin to open up to the possibility of communication. All forms of communication involve the transmission of ideas and the reception of those ideas. At this point, our main focus is on acquiring new information and therefore we need to cultivate a greater quality of receptivity.

The basic idea behind receptivity is to create space in the mind for new ideas. As long as our mind is full, it will be unable to acquire anything new and therefore we will be unable to learn anything. Fortunately the mind is infinite in nature and it therefore has the capacity to accommodate as much as we like. It is only due to our grasping that we effectively limit that capacity. We box it in and solidify it, making it difficult for us to grow.

To counteract this tendency of closing ourselves off, we need to cultivate a mind of humility and non-grasping. The humility counteracts the pride that tells us we know everything. This can be developed through contemplating the uniqueness of the conditions that give rise to a particular situation. When we are able to recognise the potential for learning provided by such a situation, it becomes much easier to open ourselves to what is being communicated.

Meanwhile, adopting a mind that is free from grasping is a direct antidote to a narrow and fixed perspective. This mind can generally be developed either formally through awareness meditation or informally through mindfulness of the present moment. Either way, the essence of this practice is to adopt the capacity to simply observe what is happening without getting carried away by excessive judgements or other discursive thoughts.

Exercise 10.3—Opening Up to Others

- *In a relaxed posture, establish a neutral mind through the practice of mindfulness of breathing.*

- *Begin by identifying a person that holds views different from your own. They can be anyone with whom the thought of speaking with, raises a degree of aversion. Imagine this person approaches you in the street and starts a conversation. Observe how you would feel. Can you detect any barriers between you? Any resistance to listening? Try to get a sense for this closed off mindset.*

- *Now bring an awareness of the present moment into the scenario. When you encounter this person, focus on what is happening here and now. Release the history you have with this person, and simply observe what is being said in this moment. Similarly, let go of any expectations for where this conversation may lead. Stay in the present, engaged and aware of what is going on. How does this change the way you experience the scenario?*

- *Now consider what is appearing to you. Here is a person. A person who has unique hopes and dreams. A person who has unique experiences. This person is one of a kind. There is no one else who has the exact perspective on life that this person has, and right now, this person is here, talking with you. In what ways could this encounter teach you something? Think of the potential, not merely in terms of factual information, but also in terms of who you are as a person and how you react to different things. Run through the scenario again and imagine different ways you could really make the most of this situation.*

- *Rest in any insights that arise.*

Curiosity

As you begin to open yourself more and more to the lessons that life has to offer, you will naturally be influenced by the information you take in. When new ideas are introduced into the mind, they go through a process of integration in which the mind tries to reconcile what this new information means in relation to existing ideas.

At this point you have a choice. You can choose to disregard the new information, in which case you are left no better off than when you started, or, you can choose to actively seek to understand the implications of this new information, leading you to a more robust and integrated mind. If you choose the latter, you will need to develop the quality of curiosity.

Curiosity is an inquisitive mind that desires to understand. In a way we can say that curiosity is a reaction to uncertainty. When such a mind sees two conflicting ideas, it desires to reconcile the uncertainty regarding which idea makes more sense. This leads to the asking of questions and when we ask questions, we get answers. The new information these answers provide, helps us to fill in holes in our understanding, leading to the removal of uncertainty.

To cultivate such a mind we need to nurture our thirst for understanding. We need to counteract the passive mind which complacently just absorbs things. This can be done by engaging with each opportunity as though it were the missing piece in a great puzzle. We develop joy in the very process of working things out and revel in the challenges that life presents us with. In this way, everything becomes fascinating because everything has the capacity to teach us something. This is the mind of curiosity.

Exercise 10.4—The Wonder of Life

- *In a relaxed posture, establish a neutral mind through the practice of mindfulness of breathing.*

- *Imagine that you are setting out on a great adventure in search of an incredible treasure. You have no idea who you will encounter or what will occur along the way. Allow the anticipation to arise in your mind, the thrill of not knowing what will happen.*

- *Now imagine going about the various activities of your day. Pick a scenario to work with. For instance, playing with your child or driving to work. Imagine that there are clues hidden within this experience. Clues that will point you towards the treasure. Like a young child on an easter egg hunt, take an intense interest in what is going on. Look at every detail, soaking in the experience on as many levels as possible.*

- *Now start thinking about the different patterns that you observe. Like a big jigsaw puzzle, start putting the pieces together. See what sort of image emerges. What does this image tell you about the nature of the situation?*

- *Reflect on the implications of your observations. What sorts of questions arise? Imagine that each question is a breadcrumb, leading you closer and closer to the treasure. How could you go about finding answers to these questions?*

- *Nurture your desire to uncover the mystery, to follow the breadcrumbs, to reveal the treasure. Rest your awareness in this desire.*

Flexibility

The previous three qualities of tolerance, receptivity and curiosity combine together to form a powerful engine for the acquisition of information. A person who has cultivated all of these qualities will be very much like a sponge.

They will pull in as much as they can whenever they can, and because they actively engage in clarifying their understanding, the quality of their view will be very strong and very broad.

Having such a view provides a practitioner with a very unique opportunity. The more you learn about diverse approaches to similar problems, the more flexibility of mind you are able to exhibit. You can start to see how different ideas are more suited for different conditions. So when those conditions arise, you are able to respond in an appropriate manner that is capable of optimising the benefit for yourself and others.

This sort of flexibility arises out of an awareness that clearly perceives what is going on in any given moment. This discriminating awareness can be cultivated by exposing the mind to a wide variety of circumstances and then looking at those circumstances from many angles. Doing so reduces grasping onto reality as being just one way and promotes a malleable mind that can adapt very easily to variation.

Exercise 10.5—Shifting Perspectives

- *In a relaxed posture, establish a neutral mind through the practice of mindfulness of breathing.*

- *Bring to mind some different events from your recent history in which you were interacting with another person. Select an event and establish the details of the scenario in your mind. Making it as vivid as possible.*

- *Run through the scenario from different perspectives. First re-create your own experience of the event. Try to get a sense for how you reacted, both the thoughts which arose in your mind and the subjective feelings.*

- *Now pull out of your perspective and observe the event from the perspective of a third person (like a fly on the wall). Run through the sequence again. Watch how both people react. What actions do they do? How do the different actions relate?*

- *Now take on the perspective of the other person. Try to get a sense for the states of mind that would have motivated the different actions that you previously observed.*

- *Based on your observations of this event, consider what you could have done to optimise the interaction. Was there a different way you could have said what you said? Were there actions that you could have avoided? Were there other actions that would have been helpful? Use as much of your knowledge as possible to take full advantage of the opportunities this event has presented you with.*

- *Repeat this last step as many times as you can, thinking about different ways this scenario could have played out in a beneficial way. There are always options. Explore the potential of the situation.*

Developing an unbiased attitude does not mean we have to think of all paths as being equally the same, as this is simply not true. Each has its own flavour and strengths and therefore what we are trying to do is to develop greater awareness of what this diversity has to offer. Our aim is to clearly distinguish between their differences, respecting each as a skillful means to guide different sentient beings towards greater happiness.

We can think of these paths as being like medicine. Right now, we are sick with many illnesses such as ignorance, attachment and aversion. We need help and so we turn to the great teachers of this world who are like doctors. These doctors look at our specific conditions and prescribe to us a set of remedies that are designed to alleviate our suffering. They recognise our uniqueness as individuals and therefore teach us accordingly.

Similarly, when a doctor is presented with two patients that are exhibiting different symptoms, she gives each a medicine that is suited to their needs. For instance she won't give headache medicine to a person who is suffering from an upset stomach. She also doesn't consider that headache medicine is the best medicine and that all other medicines are useless. Instead, she sees that each has its benefits and within the right circumstances, all medicines can be useful. This is the sort of attitude we need to develop in relation to our spiritual path.

The bias we are trying to avoid is the bias that holds tightly to one's own view as superior to all other views. This kind of attitude only serves to fuel our pride and to bring us into conflict with other people. Instead of seeing different views as being opposing, we can instead see them within the context of a dynamic ecosystem of belief that helps each of us adapt better to our unique circumstances.

In this way, it is possible to cultivate greater respect for the belief systems of other people while at the same time developing profound faith in one's own spiritual path. You can see that they are not contradictory. While we use one path as the core of our practice, we can skilfully integrate ideas from other traditions to help us develop a more rounded and robust understanding of reality. Not only does this stimulate us to think more profoundly about our favourite approach, it also helps us to connect with others and to understand how they see the world. This connection is vital considering the fact we do not live in isolation. For better or worse, we all share the collective karma to be born in the same world and therefore it is in our interest to find meaningful and harmonious ways to relate with one another. Developing the qualities presented above is a wonderful way to do this.

Exercise 10.6—The World's Belief Systems

- *In a relaxed posture, establish a neutral mind through the practice of mindfulness of breathing.*

- *Spend some time carefully reading about a belief system (other than Buddhism). Start by studying the historical context in which that belief system evolved. What were the main events that influenced how the system developed? Think about the various geographical and political influences that also influenced where emphasis was placed within the system.*

- *Now look at the core beliefs that define the view of the system you are studying. How are these beliefs structured? What sorts of topics do they explore? Why is knowing about these particular phenomena important to the system?*

- *Based on their view, research the various methods that are used within this system. Consider the types of qualities that these practices produce in the practitioner. What sort of transformation is being developed?*

- *Finally, analyse the internal diversity within the system, looking for the different ways in which the core beliefs or common practices are interpreted. In what ways do practitioners divide themselves? Try to understand the motivation behind these divisions. What benefit comes from these alternative modes of engaging with the system?*

- *Based on what you have read, consider the main themes that you feel characterise the system. How important are these themes to you? What sort of connection do you feel towards them?*

THE IMPORTANCE OF RELYING ON AN AUTHENTIC LINEAGE

As we begin to expand our understanding of the paths that make up our spiritual landscape, we will be exposed to a wide diversity of ideas and methods. You may be tempted to start collecting practices based on whatever is most "attractive" to you. This will lead to a sort of custom belief system that borrows a little from here and a little from there. I would recommend against this approach for the following reasons.

Firstly, choosing a practice merely on the basis of what you like is a good way of never really challenging yourself to change. You end up practising only those things which reinforce your present state of mind and therefore your understanding tends to remain at a rather superficial level. Remember that practising Dharma is about taming the mind and that means we have to face our bad habits and learn to work with them. Yes, it will be uncomfortable at times, but that discomfort is proof that the medicine is working.

Secondly, in western society there is a heavy emphasis on individualism. We are deeply habituated to believing we know what is best for ourselves. This leads to the belief that our judgement is always "right". Now in the context of spiritual development, this sort of view creates problems. We are engaging in spiritual practice to help us get over our neurotic way of relating to the world, and yet we trust our neurotic mind more than we trust the wisdom of the great sages who have gone before us. This unbroken stream of wisdom is known as a lineage. When we choose our own "custom" approach, we are disregarding the lineage and instead relying on our own confused state of mind. It would be like a patient deciding to mix alcohol with his painkillers, contrary to the instructions given to him by the doctor. The results of doing so can only lead to suffering.

Thirdly, we all want gain and we don't want loss. The wisdom that has been embedded within the various belief systems of this world have been developed over thousands of years to be the most effective methods for achieving profound spiritual transformation and for avoiding the many pitfalls. The combined body of knowledge that they represent is truly remarkable. If we choose to disregard this collective wisdom, then we are essentially attempting to reinvent the wheel. While there is nothing to stop you from doing so, it is an enormous waste of time. And time is something that none of us have to waste. This life is unbelievably precious, but it is also unbelievably fragile. Like a flash of lightning it will soon be over. We therefore need to make use of every tool we can to help us progress along the path as quickly as possible.

Relying on an authentic lineage is the best method to do this. Because the path structure has been previously established, we can take the guesswork out of the equation. We can focus on putting the teachings into practice and getting on with the task of taming our minds. Others have walked this path before us, so we can rely on their wisdom to help us find the most effective methods for overcoming the different obstacles we are sure to face. We can also more clearly identify the areas of our minds that need the most work. Instead of simply maintaining the status quo, we can courageously dive into the muck and actually start the process of healing.

ESTABLISHING A CONTEXT FOR THE KALACHAKRA PATH

The path that we are exploring in this book series is the *Kalachakra Path* in accordance with the *Jonang-Shambhala* tradition of *Tibetan Buddhism*. This extraordinary lineage has provided guidance to spiritual practitioners for more than 2500 years and has been responsible for producing a steady stream of highly realised beings.

In Books Two and Three of this series we will be exploring this lineage in significant detail, looking at the unique philosophy and practices which can lead a practitioner to the state of enlightenment. Before we do that though, it is necessary to get a sense for the context of this path within the greater scheme of the world's wisdom traditions.

For this reason, in the following chapters, I will give a general introduction to Buddhism, followed by specific presentations of the three main styles of Buddhist practice. By looking at Buddhism from these different perspectives, we will develop a broader and more robust understanding of where Kalachakra actually fits in.

REVIEW OF KEY POINTS

- A path is a sequence of practices that can be used to develop desirable qualities.

- There are two types of paths based on scope: mundane paths which focus on acquiring knowledge and skills that are capable of supporting worldly happiness; and spiritual paths that provide knowledge and skills for cultivating genuine happiness.

- Spiritual paths can be divided into groups based on the motivation of their practitioners: there are those that aspire to improve the conditions of their next life, those that aspire to remove the causes for their own suffering and those that aspire to remove the causes for the suffering of themselves and others.

- Spiritual paths are considered to be authentic if they are consistently capable of producing the effects they claim to be able to produce. A path can become corrupt when misconceptions distort the teachings in such a way that prevents them from producing the desired results.

- We can only judge the authenticity of a spiritual path through valid perceptions. We first rely on trusted authorities to help us identify potential paths, then through study we develop greater confidence in the capacity of the path and finally after putting the teachings into practice, we are able to see if the path actually produces the results we are looking for.

- Choosing a spiritual path is about finding which approach to practice is best suited to your specific conditions. This requires developing a broad understanding of what your options are and then developing criteria for making a choice.

- The Rimé Philosophy is a specific attitude we can develop in order to facilitate working with a diversity of views. It consists of the cultivation of four qualities: tolerance, receptivity, curiosity and flexibility.

- Developing an unbiased view is about being able to clearly distinguish between the characteristics of different views and to understand how each view can be beneficial for specific types of people.

- It is important that we develop faith in an authentic lineage in order to most effectively develop the qualities we need to fulfill our temporary and ultimate aims.

The Mahabodhi Stupa built on the site of the Buddha's enlightenment in Bodhgaya, India.

CHAPTER ELEVEN

Introduction to Buddhism

The term "Buddhism" is somewhat of a misnomer in that it tends to position the tradition as a purely religious system. As we have already seen, the Buddha gave many different types of teachings on the basis of the needs of his students. It is true that some of those teachings can be considered religious in nature as they focus on acts of devotion or faith. But as we also saw in the first part of this book, other teachings are focused on developing a robust science of the mind, providing a detailed psychology and methodology for contemplative research. Still other teachings are more philosophical in nature, making extensive use of logic and epistemology. So while we can say that Buddhism does have religious aspects, we cannot say that it is a religion *per se* in the Judeo-Christian sense of the word.

A more accurate way of referring to the teachings and practices proposed by the Buddha is to use the term "Buddha-Dharma". Literally speaking this means, "the teachings of the Buddha". In this way, we can speak of Christian-Dharma when referring to the teachings of Jesus, Muslim-Dharma when referring to the teachings of Muhammed and so on and so forth. That being said, since the western world is so accustomed to using the suffix "ism" to describe wisdom traditions, for the sake of simplicity we will continue to use the term "Buddhism". Just remember that we are using it as a synonym for the more accurate term of Buddha-Dharma.

In Tibetan, a follower of the Buddha-Dharma is known as an "nangpa" which means insider. In this context we are referring to the fact that the person has turned inwards in their search for greater happiness. Instead of looking for happiness in the temporal phenomena of the external world, they recognise that genuine happiness arises inside the internal world of the mind. For this reason, they make it a priority in their lives to study and practise the Buddha-Dharma in order to tame their minds.

Throughout this book we have been relying on some of the more universal aspects of the Buddha's teachings in order to gain greater insight into how our mind works and how training our mind can lead to a life with greater meaning and purpose. While we have already explored a considerable amount of the Buddhist worldview, we have done so from the general perspective of an outsider looking in. This approach has allowed us to gain the greatest benefit from the techniques while not requiring us to adopt any particular system of beliefs.

Moving forward though, we may find that our relationship with these teachings begins to shift. As we continue to learn more about the way the Buddha understood reality, we may begin to identify more strongly with this material. Rather than merely connecting with these ideas on a purely intellectual level, our minds may become so inspired that we now actively look for ways to engage with these teachings in a more profound way.

The following chapters will provide you with a detailed overview of the broad range of teachings that can be considered Buddhist in origin. This information is meant to give you a contextual understanding for how the different teachings fit together and relate to each other. As you will see, there is a significant amount of diversity within the Buddha's teachings providing a Buddhist practitioner with many options for how they actually engage with practise. By understanding the bigger picture, you will be better equipped to determine if you would like to make Buddhism your primary spiritual path.

THE LIFE OF THE BUDDHA

Buddhism in the form that we recognise, begins with the story of its founder; the historical Buddha of this fortunate aeon, Buddha Shakyamuni. The very fact that we have Buddhist teachings in this world, at this time, is only made possible by the appearance of this great teacher. By following in his footsteps we have a rare opportunity to make our human lives truly meaningful.

While there is some debate among historians as to the exact dates in which events occurred, most people accept that the historical Buddha was born

Figure 11-1: Important events from the life of Shakyamuni Buddha.

approximately three thousand years ago in a garden called Lumbini Park (in what would now be considered a part of Nepal). His mother, Queen Maha Maya was travelling on her way to Koliya (her ancestral home) in order to give birth to her son. She stopped briefly to rest in a beautiful park and there underneath the sala trees, she went into labour. The day was a very auspicious one, marked by a full moon.

Overjoyed, the Buddha's father, King Shuddhodhana celebrated his child's birth with a naming ceremony in accordance with the custom. Various wise men who attended the ceremony, examined the child and found his body to be adorned with a number of very auspicious marks. One in particular recognised him to be a very special child indeed and predicted that if he became a ruler, he would be the greatest of all kings. Likewise, if he chose a religious path, he would then achieve the ultimate attainment and become a Buddha (awakened one). The child was given the name Siddhartha, which meant "the one who has fulfilled his wishes".

The young prince began his education at a very young age and quickly showed a high aptitude in every subject he studied, learning at a much faster rate compared to his fellow school mates. No matter what the contest, Prince Siddhartha was always the best, the fastest, the strongest and the smartest. He was also the wisest, earning him a great deal of respect from his teachers and his incredibly kind heart and caring nature meant he was much loved by everyone that knew him.

As Siddhartha began to display his many talents, the King began to fear the prophecy made by the wise men. They had warned him that if the prince encountered suffering, he would most surely be moved to take up a religious path. Fearing the loss of his only heir to the throne, the King resolved to shield the young prince from all forms of unpleasurable experience. He built various palaces designed specifically to prevent Siddhartha from encountering suffering in any form. But despite his extravagant and luxurious lifestyle, the prince was notably dissatisfied.

To brighten his son's disposition, the King arranged for him to be married. He presented him with a selection of the most beautiful girls, drawn from all across the country. Among them was a young girl named Yashodhara.

Siddhartha was so moved by her beauty, he gave her an engagement gift and soon they were wed.

Eventually the palace walls which enclosed Siddhartha began to feel like a prison to him and he begged his father to be allowed to visit the neighboring villages. His father was hesitant but finally agreed. When the prince left the palace, he was struck by the image of an elderly man. He had never seen the effects of old age before and was astonished to hear that everyone grows older. Returning to the palace, Siddhartha became depressed by the inevitability of aging.

Once again the prince requested to leave the palace and his father, knowing it was useless to resist, conceded. This time as Prince Siddhartha travelled through the town, he saw a man who was ravaged by sickness. He could not believe such suffering was possible and that it could not be escaped by anyone. Thinking about this man, Siddhartha returned to the palace and became even more despondent.

The King could see that his son was changing but could not refuse his request to go beyond the palace walls once again. As the Prince walked through the village streets, he came across a funeral procession in which a group of men carried a dead body to the cremation grounds. His curiosity aroused, the Prince watched as the body was burnt, but he could not understand why the people were doing this and why the body did not move. Turning to his attendant for an explanation, he then learned of the reality of death. Distraught, the Prince returned to the palace and began to contemplate what he had seen. As a result, a great desire arose within him to find a way to stop this suffering.

On his fourth excursion out of the palace, Prince Siddhartha was travelling to a park when he saw a man dressed in robes sitting on the side of the road. This man looked very happy and so Siddhartha asked who he was. The Prince's attendant explained that he was a spiritual renunciant who had dedicated his life to exploring how to achieve peace and freedom from suffering. The Prince immediately knew this was what he wanted to do with his life and realised that as long as he remained in the royal palace, surrounded by everything he needed, he would never have the conditions to fulfill this spiritual aim. From this came a resolve to abandon everything his sheltered life provided, as well as the strong intention to find the answers he sought and share them with everyone he could.

Soon afterwards, he chose to depart from his royal life, fleeing the palace on horseback in the dead of night. With an intense determination, he left behind his loving wife, their newborn son and all of his other friends and family. He gave up his royal title and the privileges that came with it, including all of his luxurious estates. He chose to focus his mind single-pointedly on the task of achieving liberation. Shaving his head and donning some tattered rags as clothing, he embraced the life of a wandering ascetic. Soon he became known throughout the land as the *Shakyamuni,* meaning "Sage of the Shakya Clan".

With his mind focused on attaining freedom from suffering, Siddhartha sought out the most highly respected meditation masters in the land: Alara Kalama and Uddaka Ramaputta. Under their guidance he quickly progressed along the path, equalling their realisations and attaining advanced stages of meditative equipoise. And yet, no matter how absorbed his mind became, he was still not satisfied.

Siddhartha then decided he would engage in the practice of extreme asceticism and self-mortification. Along with five other ascetic practitioners, he practised intensely for six years along the banks of the Nairanjana, eating only a handful of food each day. As his body wasted away Siddhartha came to understand that this path he had chosen was a mistake. He recognised that the mind and body formed a single reality which could not be separated and therefore to abuse the body was only serving to harm the mind.

In a moment of utter exhaustion, he was offered a bowl of sweet rice milk porridge with honey by a young Brahmin's daughter named Sujata. Upon eating the meal, Siddhartha's body was revived and his complexion took on a golden shine. He immediately noticed the quality of his meditation improved, having greater clarity and becoming more peaceful. Believing Siddhartha had become corrupt, the five ascetics abandoned him and they parted ways.

At the age of thirty-five, Prince Siddhartha travelled to Bodhgaya in Northern India and sat beneath the Bodhi Tree, vowing to remain there until he attained full enlightenment. It was there that he confronted all the forces of negativity in the mind, remaining unharmed and unmoved by their terror and seduction. With the earth as his witness he conquered all his demons.

At dawn of the next morning, Siddhartha overcame the subtlest cognitive obscurations and attained complete enlightenment. Overcoming ignorance of the true nature of reality, he felt as though he had been released from a prison which had confined him for thousands of lifetimes. The endless wave of deluded thoughts that supported his ignorance, obscuring his mind just like the moon and stars hidden behind clouds, had been dissolved and defeated. He saw directly the interdependence of all things in the universe, and how beings suffered endlessly by falsely dividing reality into subject and object. This mistaken view lead to attachment, aversion and countless harmful actions that only created more and more suffering. He also saw the potential for enlightenment in each living being. From this time on he was known as the Buddha— the Awakened One.

To demonstrate the profundity and preciousness of his realisation, the Buddha decided initially not to teach until seven weeks later, when the great gods Brahma and Indra requested him to turn the Wheel of Dharma, setting in motion a new cycle of teachings.

Many days later the Buddha met his five ascetic friends at Deer Park in Varanasi. Despite their initial reluctance to greet him after his abandonment of the ascetic path, they were stunned by his radiant appearance and became his first followers. The Buddha turned the First Wheel of Dharma by teaching the *Four Noble Truths* and each of his followers, under his guidance, attained the state of *Arhat* in three months. It is also said that multitudes of "unseen" beings attended these teachings and benefited immensely. Thus for the first time, the precious Three Jewels: the Buddha (teacher), the Dharma (teaching) and the Sangha (community) were known in this world.

Until his passing, the Buddha held forty-five summer retreats and turned the Wheel of Dharma innumerable times, expounding teachings of both definitive and provisional meanings, according to the needs and dispositions of his followers. His teachings were given to his chief disciples Shariputra and Maudgalyayana, along with a large assembly of monks, nuns, lay practitioners,

Bodhisattvas and non-human beings. His teachings always demonstrated impermanence and inspired true renunciation among his followers.

As an honourable monk, Shakyamuni taught in accessible places like Rajagriha, Vulture's Peak Mountain and Vaishali in Northern India, and through his miraculous abilities, he taught in other realms for non-human beings such as gods, nagas and spirits. He also appeared in different pure forms in order to mature more advanced disciples along their spiritual path. For example, he emanated as the deity Kalachakra to teach King Suchandra and a great entourage at Amaravati in Southern India.

At the age of eighty, in the city of Kushinagar, the Buddha lay down on his right side between a pair of sala trees and gave his final teaching in his physical form. He then passed into parinirvana.

From one perspective, we can speak of the Buddha as a single man who in the course of his life completed his training and achieved enlightenment, this is however only one interpretation of the Buddha's story. From another perspective, Siddhartha was already a fully enlightened Buddha who was now manifesting as a human being, descending to the human realm from the pure realm of Tushita. The person we know as the historical Buddha Shakyamuni manifested to teach us the Dharma and show us how to overcome afflictive emotions and hidden obscurations. In reality however, Buddha has no ageing, no sickness, no death and no karmic rebirth. He merely came in a dream-like manner to teach a dream-like Dharma in a dream-like world. We all have this reality; it is our enlightened nature. Until we discover this sacred truth, Buddha manifests spontaneously for us in various ways, in both ordinary and miraculous forms.

THE THREE TURNINGS OF THE WHEEL OF DHARMA

When we consider all the teachings the Buddha gave during his life, it is possible to identify a number of recurring themes. The Buddha would teach these themes based on the capacities of his particular students as he recognised that not everyone was ready for the profundity of certain ideas. So instead of confusing them unnecessarily, he chose to provide them with teachings that would best clear away the obscurations in their minds, which prevented them from experiencing the truth.

When we consider the teachings in this way, we can organise them into three progressive stages that represent how a single practitioner removes coarse and then increasingly subtle obscurations leading eventually to the realisation of their own pristine nature. These stages are referred to as the *Three Turnings of the Wheel of Dharma*. Remember that this is a thematic sequence and not a chronological one. For instance, in the period directly following his enlightenment, the Buddha gave many teachings to advanced human and non-human disciples, from the Second and Third Dharma Wheels. Likewise, one of the most famous teachings of the First Dharma Wheel was given on his deathbed. What is most important to know, is the subject matter each wheel focuses on and the way in which these teachings help students to remove obscurations. The Three Turnings are as follows:

1. **The First Turning of the Wheel of Dharma** revolves around the subject of cause and effect, particularly in relation to how suffering arises and how liberation is achieved. The most fundamental teaching in this cycle is known as the teaching on the *Four Noble Truths* as it was expounded in Sarnath, India. Through developing an understanding of cause and effect, the practitioner is able to abandon the causes of suffering and to cultivate the causes for genuine happiness. This orients our mind to the Dharma and helps accumulate merit so that we can penetrate deeper into the nature of our experience.

2. **The Second Turning of the Wheel of Dharma** is focused on the subject of emptiness. These teachings are most closely tied to the *Perfection of Wisdom Sutras*, which were taught to a host of bodhisattvas on top of Vulture's Peak Mountain in Rajagriha. In these teachings, the Buddha discusses how the phenomena we perceive are empty of the inherent existence that we project onto them. He very clearly shows how our ignorance to this true nature of phenomena, is the root of all of our suffering and therefore through meditation on emptiness, it is possible to clear away this misconception.

3. **The Third Turning of the Wheel of Dharma** presents the definitive teachings on the most profound of topics—our innate *Buddha-Nature*. These teachings were given on rare occasions in a variety of locations over the course of the Buddha's lifetime. They describe in great detail the innumerable sublime qualities of the enlightened mind, which are present in each and everyone of us. It is this mind that when separated from the temporary obscurations, is capable of manifesting as a fully enlightened Buddha. At this stage, there are no more obscurations to remove.

CATEGORIES OF BUDDHIST VEHICLES

A vehicle is a device which transports someone from one place to another. For example a bicycle, a car and an airplane are all examples of vehicles. While their basic function is the same, they are different in that they can achieve the same result in different ways.

Let's say you wanted to travel to a nearby city. You could ride your bike there, but it would take a long time. It would be faster to take a car. If the city you wanted to go to was on the other side of the country, a car would take a long time. Instead, if you took a plane you could get there in a single day.

How quickly we progress along our spiritual journey and how far we actually get in that time will depend on the vehicle we choose. The vehicle that is right for us will depend on our personal motivation and spiritual maturity. Anyone can pick up a bike and get across town. To drive a car however, you need to develop a particular skill set before getting behind the wheel. Likewise with a plane, you can travel much faster, but if you are not properly prepared you could very easily crash and burn.

When we consider the broad range of teachings the Buddha gave, we can see he was presenting different types of vehicles for different types of practitioners. He could see that we all come into this life with different karmic propensities and therefore some are ready for a bike, while others are ready for a plane.

That being said, just because we are currently at one stage in our spiritual development, doesn't mean we will always be this way. Over time, as we familiarise ourselves with one vehicle, we may find we are now ready to move on to another. In this way, the vehicles represent a progressive path that helps us to focus on a particular stage of our spiritual journey.

The following sections describe different ways we can divide the teachings in order to help distinguish the emphasis that is being cultivated at any given moment. Don't think of these categories so much as a hierarchy between vehicles, instead think of them as different slices of the same cake. Which slice you choose will depend on which appears most appetising to you.

Vehicles Based on Propagation

The Buddha gave all three turnings of the teachings during a span of fifty years or so. Not all of these teachings were immediately propagated in public. It took time for the general population to mature enough spiritually to be able to grasp the more profound teachings. This lead to a gradual revelation of the teachings into two main vehicles:

1. **The Foundational Vehicle (Hinayana):** The teachings of the First Turning were easily accessible to everyone and therefore they were taught publicly since the time of the Buddha. These teachings formed the foundations of all Buddhist practice and tended to emphasise the monastic code of conduct (vinaya) as the most effective method for achieving personal liberation from cyclic existence.

2. **The Great Vehicle (Mahayana):** The teachings of the Second and Third Turning were mostly taught to a limited number of advanced students in private. This meant they were not propagated widely until many centuries after the Buddha's death. These teachings became very popular within the lay communities as they tended to emphasise the ideal of altruistic social engagement and the achievement of enlightenment for the sake of all sentient beings. In this way, Buddhism grew to become fully integrated with all levels of Indian society.

The terms Hinayana (literally meaning "lesser" vehicle) and Mahayana (meaning "greater" vehicle) are used to indicate the scope of the vehicle. Because the Hinayana teachings focus on personal liberation and the

Mahayana focuses on enlightenment for the sake of others, we can say the Mahayana has a greater scope. This does not mean the quality of the teachings in one versus the other is more superior, simply that one has a more narrow focus.

Tradition	Turning of the Wheel	Main Emphasis
Hinayana	First Turning	Cause and Effect
Mahayana	Second Turning	Emptiness
	Third Turning	Buddha-Nature

Table 11-1: Vehicles according to propagation.

Vehicles Based on Approach

For his most advanced disciples, the Buddha manifested himself in a wide variety of pure forms in order to transmit the esoteric teachings that describe how to skilfully use one's own Buddha-Nature as a basis for rapidly progressing along the path. These extraordinarily powerful methods were passed down in strict secrecy from teacher to disciple for many generations.

Collectively these teachings became known as the *Buddhist Tantras*, while the public exoteric teachings were known as the *Buddhist Sutras*. Both of these groups of teachings have the same capacity to bring a practitioner to enlightenment. Where they differ is in the efficacy of the approach they use to produce the desired result of Buddhahood. If we divide the teachings between sutra and tantra, we arrive at the following vehicles:

1. **Causal Vehicles (Sutrayana):** These vehicles rely primarily on the sutric teachings. They emphasise practices from the perspective of a sentient being. In this approach, a sentient being is seen to be impure in nature, dominated by its own afflicted mind. In order for such a being to achieve enlightenment, it is necessary to first abandon all negative states of mind, while at the same time cultivating all positive qualities. The sentient being slowly develops their mind until they have achieved the state of Buddhahood. This process generally takes more than three countless aeons to achieve.

2. **Resultant Vehicles (Tantrayana):** These vehicles rely primarily on the tantric teachings. They work from the premise that our fundamental nature is Buddha-Nature. This nature is primordially pure and therefore there is actually nothing that needs to be done to it. Instead of working to develop qualities, the focus is on removing obscurations that prevent our pure nature from naturally manifesting. In this approach, the practitioner recognises the enlightened nature of their present experience and is able to skilfully use those same experiences as supports for their practice. Because they are working with the result (Buddha-Nature) in the present moment, these vehicles are referred to as *resultant*. Through these methods it is possible for a practitioner to achieve enlightenment within a single lifetime.

Based on where the greatest amount of emphasis is placed, we can summarise these vehicles and their relationship with the three turnings in the following way:

Type	Turning of the Wheel	Main Emphasis
Causal	First Turning	Cause and Effect
	Second Turning	Emptiness
Resultant	Third Turning	Buddha-Nature

Table 11-2 Vehicles according to approach.

Vehicles Based on Emphasis

Based on the previous categories, we can see that while the Hinayana is entirely based on the sutra teachings, the Mahayana includes aspects of both sutra and tantra. This has lead to the development of three distinct styles of practice that were each propagated during different periods of time and geographical regions:

1. **The Foundational Vehicle (Hinayana):** The Hinayana teachings were the first teachings of the Buddha and are associated mostly with the style of Buddhist practice followed today in Thailand, Sri Lanka, Cambodia, Burma and Laos. This style of practice is most commonly known as *Theravada*

Buddhism, named after the only surviving school to uphold this form of practice. They follow the teachings as recorded in the Pali Canon—the earliest recorded collection of scriptures from the First Turning.

2. **The Great Vehicle (Mahayana):** The common teachings of the Mahayana evolved more gradually and are generally associated with the styles of Buddhist practice followed in Tibet, China, Korea, Japan and Vietnam. They follow the Sanskrit Canon and mostly adhere to the system of graduated study and practice established in Nalanda University in central India. Often referred to as the *Nalanda Tradition*, it is this system which is followed closely in the Tibetan schools of Buddhism. Some of the other traditions which evolved in countries like China and Japan (notably Chan and Zen Buddhism) follow an approach which focuses less on study and more on closely guided meditation practice, designed to empty the mind of all concepts.

3. **The Vajra Vehicle (Vajrayana):** The Vajrayana teachings are almost exclusively found in Tibet and are generally accepted to have emerged out of the uncommon teachings of Mahayana Buddhism. It is also known as the *Thunderbolt Vehicle* as it is considered the fastest path to awakening. Vajrayana offers innumerable skilful methods, such as visualisations, mantras and techniques to channel the internal energies of the body, to enable the practitioner to directly connect with their Buddha-Nature. To remove the obstacles to enlightenment, Vajrayana focuses on seeing, knowing and eradicating any problems or limitations in the mind, whereas Sutrayana focuses on the cultivation of good qualities. As Vajrayana can be a difficult path, it is not recommended for all Buddhist students.

Although Mahayana and Vajrayana place greater emphasis on the Second and Third Dharma Wheels respectively, they are not contradictory to the teachings found in Theravada Buddhism which focuses on the First Turning. The Theravada teachings are fundamental to Buddhist practice and it is therefore essential to have a thorough grounding in this system in order to successfully practise the Mahayana Buddha-Dharma. The Tibetan Buddhist traditions for example study the Theravada Vinaya comprehensively as it demonstrates the moral code required in monastic communities. Likewise, the teachings of the Vajrayana depend heavily on the teachings of the Mahayana. Without establishing the foundation of a Mahayana motivation and view, it is impossible to achieve the result of enlightenment through Vajrayana practice.

Teaching	Tradition	Emphasis	Practiced In
Sutra	Foundational Vehicle	First Turning	Sri Lanka, Burma, Thailand, Cambodia and Laos
	Great Vehicle	Second Turning	China, Korea, Japan and Vietnam
Tantra	Vajra Vehicle	Third Turning	Tibet, Mongolia and Himalayan Region

Table 11-3: Vehicles according to emphasis.

GROUND, PATH AND RESULT

When analysing different vehicles, it can be helpful to use a simple framework to focus our analysis and provide us with a basis for comparison. All vehicles can be understood in relation to three aspects:

1. **Ground:** The foundation of any vehicle is the view used for describing the nature of reality. It is through this view that a practitioner is able to identify which aspects of their reality are unsatisfactory and how they can work with this reality to produce a desirable result. It is known as the *ground* because all of the practices are built on top of this understanding and it is this reality that we work with through the path.

2. **Path:** Once you have identified a problem, you can then begin to implement strategies for changing the situation. The *path* represents all of the methods that are provided by the vehicle for the purpose of transforming the practitioner's experience of the ground. Paths are usually designed to be gradual in nature—like a ladder, where each step brings you closer to the desired result. The two main ways to do this are through the different practices of meditation and conduct.

3. **Result:** Through engaging with a path, a variety of specific *results* are produced. Each vehicle is designed to bring you to a certain point. Once you have achieved the maximum result a vehicle can offer, you need to switch to another vehicle in order to go further. In this way we can speak of some vehicles being relatively "higher" than others, in so far as they are able to guide you to a more profound experience of reality. The ultimate result of using these vehicles is fully actualised enlightenment.

In order to illustrate these principles, we will now look at the ground, path and result that is held in common across all forms of Buddhism. These topics form the most fundamental understanding of the Buddha's teachings and will be further expanded upon in the coming chapters.

Ground—The Four Seals

The Four Seals are the very essence of the Buddhist view. No being has, or ever will, reach enlightenment without an understanding of them and so if we truly realise them, we cannot fail in the Buddhist path. The Four Seals are so named because so long as a document has a seal on it, it can be trusted to be authentic. In the same way, for a view to be truly Buddhist, it must contain these seals. If we correctly comprehend them, we can then know what makes the Buddha-Dharma unique, and we can clearly recognise the difference between the Buddhist view and all other philosophies, belief systems or religions.

As we examine each of these seals, you may notice that you have encountered some of the themes before in earlier chapters. This is a common feature in the Buddha-Dharma. Often a single theme will be analysed from multiple angles in order to develop a more complete understanding of the phenomena. Therefore, this is not repetition for the sake of repetition. Instead it is a skilfull means to help us progress along the path. The more we reflect on these topics, the more our view will evolve. As your view changes, you are provided with a new perspective with which to understand reality. This encourages greater contemplation which ultimately leads to the potential for greater wisdom to arise.

1. All Compounded Phenomena are Impermanent

Everything which exists and is knowable by the mind can be perceived to be compounded. This means that even though something may appear to be solid and real by itself, it is actually made up of many parts and depends on causes and conditions for its existence. All such compounded phenomena are therefore subject to change and impermanence.

For example, a wooden table is dependent on the pieces of wood from which it is made and the trees which provided the timber. Each tree depends upon a seed, as well as the soil, water and sunshine that help it to grow. Without any of these conditions, it would not exist. When we consider how those trees are cut down and transformed into planks of timber, and then transported and assembled by people in a factory, we can see how the chain of interdependence includes many other supporting factors. We can think about everything that is needed to make the trucks that transport the timber. Or all of the conditions which created the people who work in the factory. The manufacture of the table is dependent on all of these factors, and if one of these causes was to be absent, there could be no table.

Because all existing things depend on causes and conditions in order to come into being, and because these causes and conditions do not last forever, anything that comes to exist, must naturally decline and perish and is therefore impermanent. While the table might be an obvious example of an impermanent phenomenon, we can also see more subtle examples of impermanence in such phenomena as our personality traits, thoughts or emotions.

Do you know where you will be in ten years time? Will you still be living in the same house or still wearing the same clothes? Think about it. Ten years ago you might have had different ideas or views compared to now. Maybe you were full of youth and vigour, but now you may be starting to age and developing wrinkles. If you were once twenty and are now in your thirties or forties, then what kind of differences can you observe in your body? These are examples of obvious or gross level impermanence, which everyone can easily observe.

On the subtle level of impermanence, all compounded phenomena are in a state of constant transition, with each change occurring in a very small interval of time. The Buddha's teachings speak of 160 moments passing in the time it takes to snap your fingers. This means everything we perceive is changing many times every second. If things didn't change over such a tiny interval how could they change in a second, a minute, an hour or even a whole year? It is this aspect of constant change which explains how everything becomes old, decays and passes away.

Normally though, we are unable to see that an object like the palm of our hand is mostly different today compared to yesterday. This is because at the moment we can only perceive gross phenomena. If we go to a river, although we know it changes the moment we see it, we have developed a habit of thinking that it is the same river we saw last year. We think we have the same hand, the same parents and the same "everything" but in reality it's always changing. Scientists are coming to a similar view as advances in technology have made it possible to observe things on a very small scale. Highly realised beings who have developed their minds through meditation practice, are actually able to directly perceive phenomena continuously changing from moment to moment.

Exercise 11.1—The Instability of Causes and Conditions

- *In a relaxed posture, establish a neutral mind through the practice of mindfulness of breathing.*

- *Choose a phenomenon you would like to analyse. Take a moment to reflect on the characteristics of this phenomenon. Try to be as thorough as possible.*

- *Now consider the causes and conditions that had to come together for this phenomenon to arise in the state you are able to observe right now. First identify the substantial cause of the phenomenon, and then consider the different supporting conditions which influenced how the phenomenon evolved over time.*

- *Reflect on how this phenomenon would change if any of those conditions were different. Would the phenomenon be exactly the same, similar or would it become totally non-existent? Choose a number of conditions and play around with all of the possible outcomes.*

- *Now think about the conditions which maintain this phenomenon in the state that you are observing right now. Consider the shifting influences that are causing this phenomenon to decay over time. Will the phenomenon last long? Or will it dissolve in a relatively fast process?*

- *Think of different ways you could change the conditions to either prolong or catalyse the transformation of the phenomenon. For instance, what would happen if you added heat to the phenomenon? How about cold?*

- *Repeat this process of analysis with multiple types of phenomena. If a certainty arises regarding the impermanent nature of compounded phenomena, then simply rest in that certainty.*

2. All Conditioned Phenomena are Unsatisfactory

Any phenomena we experience through the distorted lens of our mental afflictions will by its nature be unsatisfactory—that is to say, their nature is suffering. This truth follows very closely behind the reality that anything which is impermanent is by nature unstable. When something is unstable, it creates uncertainty in our minds. This inevitably leads to anxiety, dissatisfaction and suffering of different degrees. Because all of the causes and conditions that gave rise to a particular phenomenon are beyond our present capacity to know, then each phenomenon represents a significant degree of uncertainty for us. This pervasive uncertainty means that there is always the potential for a phenomenon to act as a condition for suffering to arise in our mind. This is also known as all-pervasive suffering.

For instance, imagine you owned an expensive car and expected it to always remain pristine. You would be ignoring the uncertain (or unsatisfactory) nature of the car. Inevitably, the car will get scratched, the metal will corrode or the engine will wear out. No matter how much you long for it to remain as it is, the reality is that the car does not have that capacity. This experience of dissatisfaction is known as the suffering of change.

Likewise, when we make the effort to smile at someone, we often have an expectation that they will smile back. But if they don't, we may experience a level of dejection. How much dejection we feel, relates to how much we expected a smile in return. So in general we could say that we feel more or less mental anguish depending on how strong we wanted a particular outcome. This is known as the suffering of pain.

The term suffering is widely used to describe this idea, but these examples show that its complete meaning not only encompasses gross suffering such as intense pain, depression or sickness, but rather a more general "degree of dissatisfaction" which describes the nature of life itself. It is better to say "life is unsatisfactory" than to proclaim "the nature of life is suffering", as misunderstanding the term "suffering" and can lead one to think Buddhists are being overly pessimistic.

This view is mistaken however, as Buddhists strive to be neither pessimistic nor optimistic, but rather to see reality as it is more clearly. Buddhist teachings can be considered "realistic" as they show us the interdependent nature of our experience. Through them, we can see that our present is a result of our past and likewise that our future will be a result of our present. Although contemplating the nature of this reality can give birth to an intense feeling of sadness, as we see all the suffering and futility of the many things in this world, it also leads to an uncontrived gratitude and appreciation for the many wonders that the world has to offer; as well as for the precious opportunity we have to improve our situation and help others to do the same. In this way, Buddhists do not think that life is always unjust, but rather see it as filled with possibilities.

You may question the idea that "life is unsatisfactory". For people who have experienced pain and torment in their lives, it is a concept that is not difficult to understand, but for others, who feel they have a great life, it is much less obvious. Since it is certainly true that such people are experiencing degrees of happiness, they will need to look deeper in order to comprehend that things are unpredictable and temporary and so are not as attractive as they may think.

The best way to analyse this, is to investigate our everyday life, observing how we are continually chasing after happiness. Take a close look at your actions to see what motivates you. Why do you constantly shift from one activity to the next? Why can't we simply stay still? Something about this present moment is unsatisfactory, something is not quite right. Despite our constant shifting of effort to find happiness in what we are doing, eventually we end up dissatisfied in one way or another. This restlessness is the very nature of dissatisfaction.

Whatever actions we do, no matter how realistic or unrealistic they may be, and no matter how wise or foolish our intentions, our ultimate purpose is always happiness. The problem is that most of the ways in which we pursue happiness, depend on something external—something outside of ourselves. We can never be completely satisfied or find a stable, lasting happiness when that happiness depends on unstable phenomena.

Fortunately the Buddha did not stop at merely identifying the problem. He went on to give us a path which provides us with methods to relieve suffering and ultimately free us from it altogether. While everything is unsatisfactory by nature, this state of affairs, like all things, is subject to change and therefore there is a real possibility we can do something about it.

Exercise 11.2—The Experience of Never Being Satisfied

- *In a relaxed posture, establish a neutral mind through the practice of mindfulness of breathing.*

- *Choose a day from your recent past to analyse. Start at the beginning and slowly work your way forward. Sketch out a number of key activities that you engaged in during this time.*

- *Now go back through each of these activities and consider why you were doing them. First think of what you wanted to achieve with the activity. Then think of why you wanted to achieve this result in the first place. What was missing or lacking from the present moment that made you want to change something?*

- *For instance, if the activity was making a meal, the unsatisfactory condition was the suffering of feeling hungry. Since you didn't like this feeling, you wanted to eat as you knew this would reduce your hunger.*

- *Continue on through each moment of your day. Ask yourself why you chose to stop a particular activity. At what point did the activity itself become unsatisfying? Again, what motivated you to shift your focus?*

- *Continue to analyse different experiences you can remember from your life. When a certainty regarding the restless nature of your life begins to arise, rest your awareness in this feeling.*

3. All Phenomena Lack True Existence

In the previous two seals, we saw how all conditioned phenomena are impermanent and therefore uncertain. This uncertainty leads to an inevitable experience of dissatisfaction as we search for lasting, genuine happiness. Now we need to look more deeply at this situation and ask ourselves why these phenomena are impermanent in the first place and why is it we experience so much suffering in relation to this reality?

The answer is because we grasp onto this impermanent reality as though it were permanent. We then see these phenomena as inherently existing sources of genuine happiness. Both of these are misconceptions, or distortions that lead us to form a wide range of false expectations of reality that cannot be fulfilled.

Of all the phenomena that we perceive in this way, the most powerful misconception is the perception of a singular, substantial and inherently existent self. It is this self that we use as the reference point for understanding everything about our experience and for this reason, if we misinterpret how our self actually exists, then that misunderstanding will be projected onto everything else.

The first aspect of this misconception is the belief that phenomena are singular in nature. When we look at a table with things on top of it, we can identify those various individual objects, such as a book, a jar of pens or vase of flowers; each thing existing separate from the others. Likewise, when we look at our self, we see a single person. It is one thing, that is different from other things. You are here, while other people are there.

When we investigate this notion, we can actually see that it is false. While we may think we are one thing, we are actually made up of many things. As we saw in previous chapters, we have a body and we have a mind. The body can be broken up into a head, a torso, arms and legs. The mind can be broken up into eight forms of consciousness and fifty one mental factors. They can also be broken up into the five aggregates: form, perception, feeling, mental formations and consciousness. No matter how we divide things though, the main point is that we are not singular in nature. This collection of phenomena that we experience is merely the basis for us to label "self".

The next aspect of our misconception is the belief that we are substantially the same person over time. When we wake up in the morning we have the feeling that we are the same person we were when we went to sleep the night before. There is a sense of a continuity, a thread which binds all of these experiences together.

Again, if we investigate this belief, we find that each moment arises and dissolves in the same instant—each moment giving rise to a similar and yet different moment. What we label as a phenomenon "abiding" is merely a series of similar moments that we cannot differentiate in any substantial way. For this reason, when we look only superficially at the person of today and the person of yesterday, most aspects seem similar. On a much more subtle level though, we cannot find anything which is exactly the same.

Finally, the third aspect of our misconception is our belief that this self that we perceive, exists inherently from its own side. This idea fuses the perceived quality of a phenomenon with the phenomenon itself, thereby solidifying it into a self-existent entity. When we see a cup, we believe this object's nature to be a cup—it has an inherent "cupness". Likewise a flower is inherently a flower, an elephant is inherently an elephant and a person is inherently a person.

When we actually search for this inherent nature, we are unable to find it. Take a table for example. We see the table and we think, "This is definitely a table". But where is the table that we are perceiving? The table is made up of parts, so it stands to reason that the table must be the same as the parts or separate from them. We can begin by first looking at each part and trying to find anything we can identify as a table within those parts. When we look at the legs, we don't find a table, we find legs. Likewise, when we look at the frame we don't find a table, we find a frame. When we look at the top, we don't find a table we find a top. No matter where we look in the parts, there is nothing we can clearly identify as a table. So if the parts are not the table, then the table must exist separately from these parts.

To test this, simply start subtracting parts of the object until it stops being identifiable as the object. Start with one of the table's legs. While a three-legged table is rather unstable, it is still a table. When we take away another leg, one side falls down and it now looks like a broken table. Because it doesn't lie flat, it is no longer capable of fulfilling the function of a table which is to support things. Take away the top and now we are left with something that only hints at a table. Remove the final two legs and the appearance of a table completely disappears. This process shows us that the "table" we are so sure exists inherently, is merely a label we project onto a collection of objects or in other words, onto a specific type of appearance arising in the mind. The table we have been looking for does not exist in the object, it only exists in the mind depending on causes and conditions. We call this mere absence of inherent existence, the "emptiness" of the object. All phenomena have this quality and therefore we can say that emptiness is their nature.

On the surface these ideas can seem quite logical, and therefore you may not experience the great profundity that they describe, for when we actually realise emptiness, it has a dramatic effect on how you perceive the world of your experiences. Everything will become dreamlike in nature and the notion of "true" reality will subsequently dissolve. As the obscuring misconceptions are removed, our sacred truth will emerge, unaffected by the endless stream of projections—like the ocean depths which are undisturbed by the waves on the surface. When we truly understand emptiness, we will no longer be under the control of our afflicted states of mind and therefore we will be free from creating karma. When we stop karma, we stop cyclic existence and all of the unsatisfying experiences that this engenders.

Exercise 11.3—Searching for a Self

- In a relaxed posture, establish a neutral mind through the practice of mindfulness of breathing.

- Start by first establishing the way in which we perceive reality. This person that is sitting here meditating, is it one or is it many? Do you feel like multiple people? Or do you feel like a single person, separate from everything around you?

- Now consider this person over time. Do you feel like the same person that woke up this morning? Are you the same person from a week ago? Do not worry about analysing right now, just get a sense for how you feel.

- Now consider your qualities. What makes you you? Do you have the feeling that there is something in you that is unique from everyone else? Something that makes you different? Are there specific traits that you feel define you as a person? Bring these qualities to mind and observe how the self appears to you.

- Having developed a strong experience of the self, we will now start looking for where this self exists. When you think of a self, what are you referring to? Think of everything that this self has. For instance, your self has a body and mind. The self that we are looking for can only exist in two ways: either it is part of the body or mind, or it is separate from these. There are no other options.

- Start looking for the self in your body, selecting different parts to examine. Pose the question, "Is this part me?" If you answer yes, then investigate this phenomenon and consider whether it too is made up of parts. If it is, then go through each part and try to find which one is you. Keep doing this until you cannot divide up the phenomenon any more or you simply cannot find anything you could say is you.

- *As you begin to eliminate potential places to find the self, you may start to feel doubt about whether this self even exists. The more you investigate, the stronger this feeling may arise. When it does, simply rest in this feeling for as long as it lasts.*

- *Now search for the self as something separate from all these parts. Imagine dividing up your body into all its parts. Go through each piece, isolating it and placing to the side in little piles. As you remove pieces from your body, keep asking yourself the question, "Am I still me?" Explore how long it takes before you stop feeling like there is enough to actually identify yourself. Once you completely disassemble the body, also go through the different parts of your mind, looking for something that is independent and separate from all of these things.*

- *At some point in this process, you may have the experience of the self just vanishing. There's nothing to grab on to. Don't be afraid of this feeling, it is natural. Just rest in the mere absence of self.*

4. Nirvana is Total Peace Beyond All Extremes

When we investigate how we normally experience things, we can see we are projecting a level of existence onto reality—freezing it into this shape or that. This is known as taking the *view of eternalism*. It is from this view that we conceive of an eternal creator God or the idea of an unchanging soul.

However, when we start to look closely at our experience, we start to see how our perceptions are mistaken. Many of the assumptions we make, turn out to be false and begin to dissolve under the weight of our analysis. Things stop feeling so solid and become more dreamlike in nature. Unfortunately, as the bottom falls out of our world, we tend to swing too far in the other direction, taking on a belief that nothing exists. This is the *view of nihilism*. It falsely assumes that existence is either inherently existent or it is totally non-existent.

The Buddha found that the only way to achieve any real sense of peace is to find a balanced view that moves beyond these two extremes. When you abandon the view of eternalism, you remove the basis for grasping and therefore you open your mind to all possibilities. When you abandon the view of nihilism, you recognise the capacity for phenomena to arise in all types of manifestations, allowing for infinite creative expression.

Abiding in this state, beyond the two extremes is known as *nirvana*—the ultimate state of supreme peace. It is not something you create, rather, it is the natural, unfabricated state we find when we remove everything that is artificial or obscuring. The way we do that is through directly realising the empty-nature of our selves and thereby remove the ignorance which fuels other afflicted states of mind.

Exercise 11.4—Finding a Middle Way

- *In a relaxed posture, establish a neutral mind through the practice of mindfulness of breathing.*

- *Begin by first identifying the view of eternalism in your life. Identify the types of phenomena you encounter on a daily basis. Walk through different scenarios of your recent past, fleshing out your personal story. The more details you go into, the more solidified your reality becomes. This will manifest in a sense of certainty that these things actually happened and they definitely exist, in and of themselves. This is grasping onto things as eternal.*

- *Now apply the same process for investigating the self (refer to exercise 11.3) to a phenomenon in your life. Choose a friend or family member, or perhaps a possession. Something you confidently feel exists in the way it appears to you.*

- *As you analyse, watch how your confidence shifts. When you can't find any inherently existing person or object, how does this make you feel? When you are successful in establishing that it doesn't exist, rest in that certainty. This is grasping onto things as non-existent.*

- *Now consider when we analyse, what actually disappears? For instance, if we analyse a cup, does the appearance completely vanish, or does our concept of that appearance being a cup vanish? Are we left with absolutely nothing or is there something?*

- *Investigate whether it is possible to have an experience without projecting labels. Are they necessary? Can you experience an appearance without needing to define it? When you do put a label on something, is it necessary to believe that the object is really what you have labelled?*

- *When you analyse you clear away misconceptions. Then you observe how experience arises from this new vantage point. You may find that phenomena start taking on a dream-like quality. Rest your awareness in this feeling.*

Path—The Three Higher Trainings

Based on our understanding of the four seals, a methodology emerges. We can see that as long as we relate to the world through ignorance, everything will be impermanent and uncertain, leading us to experience a wide range of suffering. The root cause of this form of existence is the ignorance which grasps onto phenomena as having an inherent identity. Therefore, by eradicating this ignorance, we are able to abide in a state that is free from suffering. Within this context then, the path is the method for eradicating this root ignorance.

While developing a conceptual understanding of the nature of reality is a step in the right direction, because it is conceptual it is still operating from a gross level of consciousness. In order to achieve a lasting irreversible effect, we need to transcend this conceptual level and experience the reality of emptiness through direct perception. To do this, all Buddhist practices can be summarised by the *Three Higher Trainings*:

1. **Ethical Discipline (shila):** As we have seen, afflictive minds act to distort and unsettle the mind. As long as we are dominated by the three poisons of aversion, attachment and ignorance, we will be unable to

focus our minds sufficiently to actually see subtler levels of existence. Therefore the Buddha taught a wide range of ethical conducts in the form of various levels of vows. Practitioners start by first restraining the actions of their body and speech, which gives them the opportunity needed to focus on their minds. Then through working with their minds they are able to reduce the influence of the afflictions and thereby create the conditions for contemplative practices to be more effective.

2. **Concentration (samadhi):** Emptiness is an example of a hidden phenomenon. It is quite subtle and therefore in order to observe it directly, we need to calm the gross mind completely and focus our attention in a very precise way. This is why meditation practice is so important in Buddhism. Only through developing one's attention through meditation is one able to establish the mind that is actually capable of observing the emptiness of phenomena.

3. **Wisdom (prajña):** Having gathered all of the conditions necessary to actually observe emptiness, practitioners must now familiarise themselves with this phenomenon. Our ignorance is quite pervasive and we are deeply habituated to grasping onto everything that appears to us. Even if we are able to experience a brief moment of emptiness directly, the force of our habit will snap us back into grasping. For this reason, we need to repeatedly rest our mind in emptiness. Each time we do so, we weaken the strength of samsara and we strengthen our capacity to abide in nirvana. Eventually, the destructive patterns of grasping are completely eradicated and we no longer experience afflicted states of mind. Without afflictions, we are finally able to abide in our own nature, free from all suffering.

The first two trainings are often referred to as method or skilfull means. They provide all of the practices that create the conditions for a practitioner to encounter the nature of their mind. They are temporary in nature, merely a means to an end. The actual purpose of practising them is to develop the wisdom of the third training. We can think of them like two wings of a bird.

A bird cannot fly without both wings, likewise a practitioner cannot progress along the path without both method and wisdom. If you were to only practise methods, you may achieve some wonderful temporary results, but you would not experience any deep rooted transformation. Likewise if you only practise wisdom, then you will only be able to penetrate to the level of your current obscurations. This means that the type of wisdom you develop will only be superficial in nature. For this reason, we always need to balance the two as much as possible. When done correctly, method supports wisdom and wisdom supports method, allowing us to go progressively deeper and deeper until we achieve our goal.

Result—The Two Accumulations

Samsara is a way of interpreting reality based on ignorance. The path provides us with a way to cultivate wisdom and thereby remove that ignorance and all of the afflicted states of mind which are derived from it. During this process, the practitioner performs a wide variety of actions which lead to an equally wide variety of results. When we consider the nature of these results we can speak of two main types:

1. **Merit:** Until you are able to directly realise emptiness, your mind will be mixed with grasping and ignorance, therefore any actions you engage in will still generate karmas and therefore they will still condition your existence. But if these actions are motivated by a virtuous intention, they will naturally give rise to happiness rather than suffering. This is crucial in creating the necessary conditions that are most conducive for progressing on the path (such as attaining a precious human rebirth).

2. **Wisdom:** Through the accumulation of merit, we are able to establish a calm disposition, confidence, greater awareness and many other positive states of mind that can then be used to generate increasingly more profound insights. The most profound of which is the direct experience of our sacred truth when we realise emptiness for the first time. Any action which is performed from the perspective of this wisdom will act

as a cause for the cessation of our habitual patterns. These changes will eventually lead to a lasting and stable freedom from all forms of karmic conditioning.

The final result that is produced by these two accumulations will vary depending on the vehicle that is being practised. For the practitioner of the Foundational Vehicle, the result is complete liberation from suffering. For the practitioner of the Great Vehicle, these accumulations produce the omniscient state of complete enlightenment. We will look more closely at these results in their respective chapters.

REVIEW OF KEY POINTS

- Buddha-Dharma is a more accurate term for referring to what is commonly known as "Buddhism". It refers to the collection of teachings that were given by the Buddha.

- The historical Buddha was born and raised as Prince Siddhartha. He renounced his royal life and became the wandering ascetic known as Shakyamuni. Through intensive meditation training, he was able to gain insight into the nature of reality and thereby free himself from the causes of suffering.

- Over the course of his life, the Buddha taught a wide variety of teachings that can be grouped into three progressive themes. In the first turning, he taught mostly about the karmic law of cause and effect. In the second turning, he expounded the teachings on emptiness. While in the third turning he presented the profound characteristics of Buddha-Nature.

- These teachings can be divided into a variety of vehicles which facilitate a particular form of transformation based on the current spiritual development of the practitioner.

- When divided based on when the teachings were propagated we can identify the Foundational Vehicle (Hinayana) and the Great Vehicle (Mahayana).

- When divided based on their approach, we can speak of two: Causal Vehicles that are grounded in the public discourses of the Buddha (sutra); and Resultant Vehicles which were based on the esoteric teachings given to specific disciples in private (tantra).

- Based on which turning of the wheel was emphasised, we can identify three: Hinayana which focuses on the first turning, Mahayana which focuses primarily on the sutra teachings of the second turning, and Vajrayana which focuses primarily on sutra teachings of the third turning and the various esoteric teaching of tantra.

- When analysing vehicles, it is helpful to consider the threefold framework of ground, path and result. The ground represents the view that explains how reality exists. The path identifies the methods that can be used to transform that ground. And the result identifies what can be expected having completed the path.

- The basic ground of all Buddhist practice is known as the Four Seals: all compounded phenomena are impermanent, all conditioned phenomena are unsatisfactory, all phenomena lack true existence and nirvana is total peace beyond extremes.

- The core path used by Buddhist practitioners is based on the Three Higher Trainings: ethical discipline, concentration and wisdom.

- The results of engaging in this path are the Two Accumulations of merit and wisdom. These accumulations will produce different results depending on which vehicle is being practised.

CHAPTER TWELVE

The Foundational Vehicle

The very first teaching the Buddha gave after his enlightenment was on the subject of the Four Noble Truths. He gave this teaching in Deer Park to the five ascetic practitioners who had previously been his companions. It is said that through hearing this teaching, they each achieved the state of an Arhat (one who is worthy), completely freeing themselves from the bonds of cyclic existence. For the remainder of his life, the Buddha gave innumerable teachings that expanded upon the topics presented in this essential teaching.

After the Buddha passed into parinirvana, the elders of the monastic community gathered to compile the teachings, each of them reciting the various sutras they had personally heard from the Buddha. At this time the tradition was transmitted orally, which meant every year or so they would meet to recite the full collection of teachings to ensure they remained authentic.

From the basis of these teachings, various schools of Buddhism arose. The divisions were mainly with regards to how the monastic discipline (vinaya) was being interpreted. The Buddha had proscribed various activities based on what was most beneficial for the monastic community and the supporting laity. Before he passed away, he told his attendant Ananda that some of the vows were fundamental, while others were provisional and could be dropped if the social context changed. Unfortunately, he did not specify which was which and this confusion eventually lead to the introduction of different viewpoints, that resulted in the formation of the different schools.

A few hundred years later, under the patronage of the great Indian King Ashoka, the Buddhist scriptures had grown into what are now known as the *Three Baskets*:

1. **Monastic Discipline (vinaya):** This collection of texts lays out the code of conduct used within Buddhist monastic communities (sangha). While the original disciples of the Buddha wandered the land as spiritual nomads, the vinaya eventually grew to favour a more sedentary style of living with the founding of fixed monastic institutions. As such, this collection includes extensive commentaries that describe different aspects of social behaviour designed to promote greater harmony not only within the monastery but also in relation to the lay community.

2. **Discourses of the Buddha (sutra):** This collection includes more than 10,000 public teachings given by the Buddha during his lifetime, as well as a number of discourses given by his close disciples in the period after his passing. All of these scriptures are grouped based on length or subject matter. They cover a wide range of topics for working with the mind in order to remove suffering.

3. **Higher Teachings (abhidharma):** This collection of commentaries by many of the Buddha's close disciples, forms the foundation of the Buddha's science of the mind. It presents a vast array of treatises that describe in minute detail how physical and mental processes work. As such, this collection is the primary basis upon which the philosophical doctrine of the Buddha is presented.

These three collections of teachings were first committed to writing in the Pali language on the island of Sri Lanka, to the south of India. The tradition followed there was known as Theravada. It is this tradition that spread eastward into parts of Burma, Thailand, Cambodia and Laos.

The Theravada tradition can be characterised by its pragmatic and grounded approach to practice. They place a heavy emphasis on ethical discipline and are known for their extremely austere monastic communities. Renunciation of worldly life is a central theme and practitioners are encouraged to dedicate their time to extended retreats where they can practise meditation.

Figure 12-1: Spread of Theravada Buddhism.

FOUNDATIONAL VEHICLES

Within the general category of the Hinayana, there are two vehicles: the *Vehicle of the Hearer* and the *Vehicle of the Solitary Realiser*. The Theravada tradition is an example of the former. Both of these vehicles are focused on helping the practitioner to achieve personal liberation from samsara. This is done mainly through establishing the realisation of selflessness through the meditative union of shamatha and vipashyana. The following is a summary of these two vehicles:

The Vehicle of the Hearer (shravakayana)

The Shravaka vehicle is also known as the Vehicle of the Hearer, as it involves hearing the Buddha's fundamental teachings on the suffering of samsaric existence and the potential to be liberated from this cycle. Putting into practice the path that the Buddha taught to overcome this experience of suffering, practitioners are motivated by genuine renunciation and disillusionment with worldly pursuits, such as those represented by the *Eight Worldly Dharmas*. Devotion to this path usually involves adopting the simple and contained life of a monk or nun, following in the footsteps of the Buddha's ordained Sangha.

Those on this path take the precepts of the Vinaya and practise the *Noble Eightfold Path*. They adhere to a life of strict discipline with complete focus on such teachings as the *Four Noble Truths* and the *Four Applications of Mindfulness*. This creates the ideal conditions to develop perfect single-pointed concentration (shamatha) and the wisdom necessary to eliminate the afflictions that are the source of suffering. Upon realising selflessness of the individual and overcoming all emotional afflictions, they attain the state of a *Shravaka Arhat*. The most diligent practitioners can attain the state of a Shravaka Arhat in three lifetimes, meaning that the Buddha's Arhat disciples would have been connected to these teachings in previous lives.

This Theravada path is suited to those practitioners who genuinely wish to free themselves from samsaric existence as quickly as possible. For such people the Buddha refused to explore certain questions such as the origin of the universe, as such speculation distracts from the path and fails to address the truth of suffering. For instance, if an arrow lands in your eye, it is best to pull it out straight away rather than ask too many questions about who threw it and how it got there. Instead of getting lost in conceptual elaborations, the Buddha taught his students to cut through to the essential nature using personal experience.

The Vehicle of the Solitary Realiser (pratyekabuddhayana)

This vehicle is known as the Vehicle of the Solitary Realiser because practitioners of this path rely entirely on the habitual propensities that were built up in previous lives. This allows them to develop realisations on a purely instinctual level, without requiring them to listen to the teachings in their current life. Such practitioners only appear during the periods where no teachings of the Buddha exist.

Practitioners on this path begin by scrutinising the conventions of worldly life, deeply investigating the question of suffering and its origins. They develop wisdom using analysis, endowed by the virtues and aspirations cultivated during previous lifetimes. Using methods such as visiting cemeteries to contemplate the nature of death and impermanence, they lead a life of solitude and renunciation. Gradually they discover the *Twelve Links of Dependant Origination* which govern the operation of samsara, recognising the links from ignorance to death and in reverse order from death to ignorance. In this way they realise the sequence of the arising and elimination of samsara, tracing suffering back to its origin in ignorance of the true nature of reality and the false construction of a truly existing self. As a result of exceptional practise they eventually attain the state of a *Pratyeka Arhat* which generally takes one hundred aeons, where an aeon is the period during which life exists between the formation and destruction of a universal system.

Both Shravaka and Pratyeka Arhats have accomplished nirvana, the final fruition according to the Theravada tradition. Worldly attainments such as the temporary abandonment of afflictions can be achieved through shamatha meditation when one accomplishes the mental state of the form and formless absorptions (the jhanas), yet the propensities for afflictions still remain dormant. Shravaka and Pratyeka Arhats go beyond these accomplishments and realise selflessness, whereby all afflictions are completely overcome and the lasting peace of nirvana is then attained. Because a Pratyeka Arhat accumulates so much merit over the course of billions of lives, she is able to realise not only the selflessness of the person, but also a partial realisation of the selflessness of the phenomenal world as well.

We will now examine in detail the fundamental teachings of the Buddha as established by the First Turning of the Wheel of Dharma and presented within the Theravada path.

GROUND—THE FOUR NOBLE TRUTHS

The fundamental teachings of the *Four Noble Truths* (catvāryāryasatyāni in Sanskrit) are also referred to as the *Four Arya Truths*, or the *Four Truths of Arya Beings*. Arya (Sanskrit) can be translated as "noble", "pure" and "not ordinary". The term "arya being" is frequently used in Buddhism to designate a spiritual hero or warrior—a being who has direct understanding of the Four Noble Truths.

Providing the foundation for all practitioners, the Four Noble Truths can be likened to an elephant's footprint, as the entire teachings of Buddhism are encapsulated within them. According to the turning of the First Wheel of Dharma, when the Buddha taught the Four Noble Truths he exclaimed:

> *This is the Noble truth of suffering.*
> *This is the Noble truth of the cause of suffering.*
> *This is the Noble truth of the cessation of suffering.*
> *This is the Noble truth of the path leading to the cessation of suffering.*

Each of these truths can be examined and contemplated in greater detail by dividing them into four specific features, giving us a total of sixteen different aspects. A Shravaka practitioner will meditate upon these sixteen topics in sequence, so as to establish their view through direct experience.

The Truth of Suffering

The First Noble Truth explains the nature of dukkha—the Pali word for suffering and translates into "unsatisfactoriness", "incapable of satisfying", and "stress". Suffering is the main defect of samsara and characterises our experiences within this cyclic existence. It pervades our entire universe without exception and is what we must recognise. We do this through understanding the following four aspects:

Impermanence

Contrary to our mundane perception, all compounded phenomena are impermanent. This doesn't merely refer to obvious impermanent phenomena such as aging and death. Any compounded phenomena, such as the five aggregates which make up the body and mind is naturally impermanent. Requiring no secondary causes, they intrinsically undergo constant change. This subtle level of impermanence is one aspect of suffering (the suffering of change) that Arya beings directly perceive. We should try to develop an intellectual understanding of impermanence and contemplate its deeper meaning until we can also directly perceive it.

Suffering

Nobody wants to suffer, yet because of our ignorance we are immersed in a cycle of suffering and do not know how to escape. An Arya being is able to see the five tainted aggregates as phenomena that are subject to all-pervasive suffering, which is the basis for the suffering of change and pain. As every compounded phenomenon is assembled from causes and conditions, its very nature is impermanent and therefore unreliable. Because of this, it has the characteristic of suffering regardless of how it appears.

As long as our five aggregates remain impure and tainted by negative obscurations, we cannot escape from the suffering of uncertainty. Arya beings directly realise the nature of suffering and its origin and are therefore able to liberate themselves from this suffering. By focusing on this reality and reminding ourselves of the fundamental nature of suffering, we can slowly learn to stop clinging to phenomena and gradually attain liberation from cyclic existence.

Emptiness

All beings in samsara perceive phenomena as truly existing. In reality nothing truly exists, yet we impute existence onto objects, forming concepts and believing them to be real. A truly existing object would have to be a separate entity without being labelled on the basis of its parts. Therefore all phenomena are interdependent and merely imputed to truly exist. Samsaric beings incorrectly perceive phenomena as independent and truly existing and this is the cause of their suffering. The true reality, however, is that everything is empty of existing in any substantial way, which is the Buddhist view of emptiness. This doesn't mean things do not exist, but rather things do not exist as we perceive them to exist. This aspect of suffering is only perceived directly by Arya beings.

Selflessness

Every samsaric being perceives themselves as being the true possessor of five aggregates. In reality however, just as external phenomena have no inherent existence, a possessor or self also does not truly exist. For a self to truly exist it would have to be contained within or independent of the five aggregates: form, feeling, perception, mental formation and consciousness. On examination we find that this is not the case. We cannot find our "self" separate from the aggregates nor in any one of the aggregates, rather our "self" is dependent upon all of them. An Arya has eradicated the acquired habit of self-perception, directly realising selflessness and no longer perceiving the self as existing independently. They do however still have innate self-perception which has been with us since beginningless time, operating without dependence on faulty beliefs or reasoning.

The Truth of the Origin

The Second Noble Truth incorporates karma, addressing the origin of dukkha and the reasons why we suffer. Buddhists believe that the root cause of our dissatisfaction stems from the three poisons (ignorance, attachment and aversion), which are the base for all of our afflictive states of mind. It is these states of mind we must abandon. The four aspects of this truth are:

Origination

As long as there are afflictions, samsara will always arise. This does not happen randomly—it is certain. The origin of all of these afflictions is ignorance and adhering to imputed concepts as though they were real. These create a strong sense of self which forms the basis of karmic propensities. Craving and grasping then leave an imprint which projects to the next samsaric rebirth via the karmic propensities which are stored in the mental continuum. One is therefore born again uncontrollably within the three types of realms: either in the desire realm, form realm or formless realm. This is the aspect of origination which is only realised directly by Arya beings. Focusing on origination allows us to develop a mind of renunciation.

The rebirth of Arya beings is not affected by the projection of these afflictions. Whether or not they have karmic propensities, since their minds are not conditioned by craving and grasping, they will not project a future rebirth in samsara.

Cause

The root causes of samsara are the afflictions of ignorance, craving and aversion, and there is not a single thing that does not arise without involving these causes. Samsaric existence arises as a result of virtuous and non-virtuous actions, but even samsaric virtuous actions are contaminated by these root afflictions. The happiness we experience in samsara therefore is still contaminated. The virtuous actions of Arya beings, however, are not contaminated because they are free from the perception of a truly existing self. This realisation prevents further afflictions from arising.

Condition

The afflictions of craving and grasping are not only the main causes for our rebirth in samsara, they also function as secondary conditions for our experience. This means our afflictions cause the planting of karmic seeds or propensities in our mind stream but they also provide the supporting conditions for those seeds to ripen. For example, if a man steals something, the stealing is the main cause for his going to jail, but the stealing also acts as a secondary condition which causes his family to suffer while he serves his sentence. Similarly, virtues and non-virtues that we engage in now always act as contributing conditions for the ripening of certain karmic propensities, just as fertilizer and rain act as conditions for plants to grow. It is important to know we also have the opportunity to change which propensities ripen by practising Dharma.

Arya beings have abandoned grasping as they realise there is no self with which to grasp. This affliction therefore cannot act as a cause for an uncontrolled cycle of rebirth or as a secondary condition. Fully understanding the role of conditions shows us how we can gradually control all the surrounding conditions in our life, so as not to support the ripening of karmic propensities.

Production

Contaminated virtuous or non-virtuous karma does not necessarily project to just one result. One strong karmic action can result in many experiences and many rebirths within the six realms, all without choice. As we know, karma by its very nature also has the potential to increase.

A small or single action does not always lead to a small or single result and may actually incur large karmic consequences. For example, killing one's parents or breaking tantric commitments can project a person to the hell realms for many aeons. Every natural thing grows or increases with time and other conditions, just like a seed which becomes a shoot, then a stalk and then a tree. In the same way the results of samsaric causes continue to increase. Focusing on production counters the view that things evolve or transform by themselves, as everything depends on many different causes and conditions.

These four aspects of the origin of suffering show how any action or emotion coming from the ego is impure and always leads to suffering, either directly or indirectly. Based on this recognition, one has to understand that the root causes of suffering are mental afflictions, which are not permanent and can be removed with a degree of effort.

The Truth of the Cessation

The cessation of dukkha is the Third Noble Truth and indicates that our suffering can end by transforming our ignorance and our afflictive states of mind. This is what must be accomplished. To understand the nature of cessation the following four aspects are contemplated:

Cessation

Without cessation there is no stable lasting attainment. We need to achieve the cessation of suffering which entails the elimination of the fundamental ignorance that clings to the false idea of a truly existing self. When we finally eradicate this defilement, we achieve the cessation of suffering, and this includes the elimination of all mental afflictions such as attachment and aversion, which can no longer recur. This is the incomparable attainment of nirvana, a state entered into by Arya beings. Having conviction in the truth of cessation gradually reduces our reliance on concepts and imputations and eventually allows us to eliminate all impurities of the mind, confident that complete freedom of cessation is possible.

Peace

Cessation is an eternal state of incomparable, absolute peace. This is the true freedom of nirvana. Ignorance and ego are completely absent, so we are able to dwell in our own primordial true nature, which we all have but are yet to uncover. An Arya being aims to not only reveal this state but to actualise and habituate it. Focusing on the abandonment of discursive thoughts and the three poisons of ignorance, attachment and aversion, brings us to this ultimate peace, completely free from all suffering.

Excellence

The achievement of cessation is excellent and absolutely incomparable because we are parted forever from disturbing emotions. There is nothing superior to be desired or attained other than this true liberation. Focusing on excellence spurs us on with enthusiasm to achieve cessation by eliminating all traces of afflictive mental states and suffering. It also counters the view that nirvana can be reached through shamatha meditation alone. Whilst shamatha is a remarkable achievement, it should not be viewed as the result but as a tool to gaining direct insight into the true nature of reality—the realisation that no "self" exists.

Emergence

Achieving nirvana means we have attained the result of complete renunciation whereby we have totally let go of what binds us to ignorance and are free from both suffering and the causes of suffering. When all worldly concerns have been renounced, including both the positive and negative aspects of samsara, we emerge from its uncontrollable cycle of rebirth, ageing and unavoidable death forever.

When we perceive the ineffectiveness of the worldly concerns such as praise, gain, status and pleasure to bring us truly lasting happiness, renunciation naturally arises. We come to realise that we must understand how to practise the Buddha's path which does not rely on any worldly achievement or material resources. To "emerge" from samsara, experiencing the cessation of suffering and entering the natural peace of nirvana, renunciation is the key factor.

The Truth of the Path

The Fourth Noble Truth informs us that there is a path that if cultivated, will lead to this cessation of dukkha and this is what we must practise. Topics such as the preciousness of human birth, contemplation on death and impermanence, and the value of liberation are all examples of practices found within this path. Any practice within the Buddhist tradition can be connected back to these Four Noble Truths and while some teachings and practices function at a basic level, others are more complex. No matter what form these practices take, since they are all rooted in the same framework, there is no possibility that they can be contradictory. The four aspects of the path are:

Path

Sacred Dharma is the only true way to attain nirvana. Dharma means training our own minds according to the Buddha's teachings which becomes the path to liberate ourselves from ordinary conditioned existence. This is the only way we can discover the total freedom of enlightenment.

Arya beings have discovered this truth, and by following this authentic path with the focused view of selflessness, they continue to deepen their realisation as they journey towards nirvana and liberation. This understanding specifically counters the misconceptions:

1. That there is no path to follow

2. That a solid self or soul exists

3. That someone else can liberate us.

Reasoning

Developing this path through training the mind and cultivating the right attitude with the aim of achieving nirvana, is the aspect of reasoning as the appropriate means. With discriminating awareness and undefeatable logical analysis regarding the truth of suffering and its origins; it is understood that there is no other way or alternative path that leads to this goal. Practising this path requires moral discipline, meditative concentration and compassion united with wisdom. Through this we can achieve both temporary and permanent elimination of suffering and its causes. Focusing on reasoning gives us conviction that the path to nirvana is certainly achievable.

Accomplishment

The most worthwhile accomplishment is the ability to practise the path of genuine Buddha-Dharma. This is the only way to train our own minds and through such training, there is an absolute guarantee that we will achieve our goal of liberation. The most significant element of the path is understanding the need to abandon afflictive obscurations and wrong views, such as those represented by eternalism and nihilism—the belief in an eternal creator or the belief that life is without purpose or meaning. Focusing on the accomplishment of freedom from defilements and correct non-conceptual realisation beyond these two extreme views, helps us realise there is a correct and accurate path to follow. This counters the belief that some other path exists that will lead to true liberation.

Total Freedom

The goal of Buddhist practice is to accomplish total freedom from samsaric existence. To attain this we need to eradicate fundamental ignorance and all of its propensities, preventing afflictions or obscurations from ever recurring. This is total freedom. Understanding this idea opposes the view that we can find freedom within the dualistic mind (with a subject and an object). This aspect of the truth of the path is directly perceived by Arya beings only.

The Sequence of the Four Noble Truths

As we have seen, the Foundational Vehicle takes a very pragmatic approach. The Buddha cuts straight to the essence of the problem, like a skilfull surgeon zoning in on a cancerous tissue. The order in which the Buddha taught these four truths is therefore also significant.

When we look at these four as a set, we can see there are two pairs of causal relationships. There is the origin of suffering which is the cause for the result of suffering. Then there is the path which is the cause for the result of the cessation of suffering. The first set describes samsara, while the second set focuses on nirvana. So why didn't the Buddha teach them according to their logical sequence?

The answer lies in the Buddha's focus on practise. If our intention was to develop a purely intellectual understanding of these four truths, then it may be helpful to look at them in order of cause and effect, however, we are not looking to merely understand the information. We are looking to be free from suffering. The Buddha recognised this and so taught in accordance with the needs of his students.

He began by presenting the Truth of Suffering, because this is the world that we live in—it is our immediate experience. If we do not recognise the dissatisfying nature of this existence, then we will have no motivation to seek a change. He followed this with the Truth of the Origin, because unless we understand the nature of our sickness, we will not recognise the potential for us to change the situation. This is followed by the Truth of the Cessation because we currently cannot even imagine a world that is free from suffering. By introducing us to the nature of nirvana, the Buddha shows us that genuine happiness is possible, giving us a meaningful goal to aim for. Finally, he presents the Truth of the Path, because this is the method for achieving that aim. In this way, the Buddha skilfully guides the practitioner away from samsara and towards nirvana.

Experience	Noble Truth	Relationship	Aspects
Samsara	Suffering	Result	• Impermanence • Suffering • Emptiness • Selflessness
	Origin	Cause	• Origination • Cause • Condition • Production
Nirvana	Cessation	Result	• Cessation • Peace • Excellence • Emergence
	Path	Cause	• Path • Reasoning • Accomplishment • Total Freedom

Table 12-1: The Four Noble Truths.

PATH—THE NOBLE EIGHTFOLD PATH

Having developed a grounded view through the Four Noble Truths, Theravada practitioners then rely on the *Noble Eightfold Path* as their primary method to train their minds. This path provides eight unique aspects to actualise each of the Three Higher Trainings of ethical discipline, concentration and wisdom, ultimately leading to the result of personal liberation.

The emphasis here is placed on practical techniques to help cultivate wisdom and compassion by developing a mind that is more fully aware of its thoughts and actions. It is only through unifying the actions of our body, speech and mind that we can possibly hope to free ourselves from attachment and delusion.

Higher Training	Eightfold Path
Wisdom	1. Right View
	2. Right Intention
Ethical Discipline	3. Right Speech
	4. Right Action
	5. Right Livelihood
Concentration	6. Right Effort
	7. Right Mindfulness
	8. Right Concentration

Table 12-2: *The Noble Eightfold Path in relation to the Three Higher Trainings.*

Traditionally, the Eightfold Path is presented sequentially in order to highlight some of the different relationships that each training has. However, we shouldn't hold too tightly to this sequence as all of these trainings are interdependent in nature. For this reason, they should be practised simultaneously so as to provide adequate support for achieving increasingly deeper and more profound states of mind. It may help to think of them like eight strands of twine that twist together to form a single rope that is strong enough to pull you up. These eight trainings are as follows:

1. Right View

Right view can also be called "right perspective" or "right outlook". It is considered the precursor to the entire path as it provides the guide to all the other aspects, enabling us to understand the starting point and the destination. To have the right view is to see things as they really are, as realised by the Four Noble Truths. Right view can be categorised into:

1. **Conceptual Right View:** A view which describes the intellectual comprehension of aspects such as the law of cause and effect and the impermanent and empty nature of all things. It forms the foundation to attaining experiential right view.

2. **Experiential Right View:** This is a view that has been established through the force of direct perception.

Our view, whether it is expressed or not, governs our attitudes, our choices and our goals and so creates the framework within which we respond to our world. To have the wrong view leads to actions that result in suffering whereas holding the right view promotes actions that result in the freedom from suffering.

2. Right Intention

Right intention is the mental energy controlling our actions and can also be referred to as "right thought" or "right aspiration". It is the second aspect on the path between right view and right speech as our intention forms the crucial link between our cognitive perspective and our active engagement with the world. A correct understanding of right view will assist in the distinction between right and wrong intention, however, having the "right intention" may not always yield what appears to be pleasant outcomes. It is from our thoughts that we develop our aims and ideals and so they become the forerunner to our actions. This leads us to the next factor of right speech.

3. Right Speech

Words are very powerful. They have the ability to make friends and enemies, start wars or create peace. Right speech is therefore the first factor that relates to conduct. Buddha clarified that right speech consists of:

1. Abstaining from false speech, such as telling deliberate lies

2. Abstaining from slanderous or malicious speech

3. Abstaining from harsh words, and

4. Abstaining from idle chatter, such as gossip

There are also three aspects to consider with every action:

1. **Intention:** This relates back to Right Intention. Here we must consider the impact of our words. What is our motivation for speaking to others? Will it be helpful or harmful to them?

2. **Skill:** Along with the ability to speak is our ability to listen, or to choose to remain silent. Knowing which form our speech should take in relation to the context of our situation is the application of the wisdom of Right View.

3. **Result / Response:** The third aspect that needs to be considered is the result. This can be categorised into short-term and long-term results. We need to develop awareness of the consequences of our actions and thereby choose to engage in only those actions that will bring benefit to ourselves or others.

If we can ensure that all three aspects are being influenced by wisdom, then we can have great confidence that our speech is right speech.

4. Right Action

The fourth factor on the path is right action which is concerned with bodily actions that are in harmony with the other aspects of the path. Right action includes actions in accordance with moral principles and virtuous acts. The action itself can be external, for example obvious deeds of the body, or internal, such as spiritual transformation, which is an action of the mind. In essence, right action refers to the precepts of:

1. Not killing or harming other sentient beings

2. Refraining from taking what is not given

3. Abstaining from sexual misconduct

These types of unwholesome actions lead to unsound states of mind and create suffering, leading us away from liberation.

5. Right Livelihood

Right Livelihood means that we should earn a living in a legal and peaceful manner. This training is specifically designed to help us develop greater harmony in our social context so as to provide the necessary conditions for a peaceful and tamed mind. As an extension of right action, it specifies that we should avoid four livelihoods which cause harm to other beings (either directly or indirectly):

1. Dealing in weapons

2. Dealing in living beings (such as prostitution or the slave trade)

3. Dealing in animals for slaughter

4. Dealing in toxicants or poisons (such as drugs and alcohol)

Right Livelihood also refers to avoiding any occupation that violates Right Action and Right Speech.

6. Right Effort

The previous three factors deal with the outer conduct of life whilst the following three are concerned with training the mind. This process begins with Right Effort, which is a prerequisite for all of the other trainings. Without effort, we cannot achieve anything. Since the same type of mental energy feeds both negative states of mind and virtuous ones, we must therefore try to achieve what are known as the *Four Great Endeavours*:

1. Prevent the rise of unwholesome thoughts

2. Abandon unwholesome thoughts once they have arisen

3. Arouse wholesome thoughts

4. Maintain wholesome thoughts that have arisen

We can nourish these four types of activities by developing conviction in their benefits and joy when we successfully engage in them.

7. Right Mindfulness

To put it simply, Right Mindfulness is awareness—the mental ability to clearly see things as they are. It is the ability to watch one's own mind and see where it is going and what it is doing, without getting carried away with intruding thoughts. Our ordinary minds often run after objects of the senses, while the mind of Right Mindfulness provides an anchor for clear perception by allowing us to actively observe and control where our thoughts go. We can do this by training our mind to be mindful of four different fields of experience:

1. Mindfulness of the body

2. Mindfulness of feelings

3. Mindfulness of the states of mind

4. Mindfulness of phenomena

8. Right Concentration

The final aspect of the Noble Eightfold Path is Right Concentration and is defined as wholesome unification or one-pointedness of the mind. The Buddhist method for cultivating concentration is meditation—resting the mind on a single object, without distraction. This practise can then be applied naturally to everyday situations. In time, the mind can become a powerful tool, still and collected; able to transform insight into wisdom. In combination with Right Mindfulness, Right Concentration will eventually lead us to the direct experience of all sixteen aspects of the Four Noble Truths.

RESULT—PERSONAL LIBERATION

As a Theravada practitioner engages with the Eightfold Path, she will pass through a number of major stages of attainment. In total, there are five stages that mark the progression of a sentient being from samsaric existence all the way to the attainment of nirvana. We call these stages the *Five Paths of Attainment*:

1. **The Path of Accumulation:** Theravada practitioners live a very remote and simple lifestyle, avoiding engagement in worldly activities. They are

self-contained and require the very minimum to survive. They practise strict self-discipline according to the teaching of the Three Baskets and are mindful of every action of the body and mind, such as when they are walking, sitting, standing or sleeping (known as the four postures).

To illustrate this, when walking a Theravada monk will be mindful of every instant as the body moves. He will take one very slow step followed by another with awareness of each movement, moment by moment. As the foot leaves the ground and when it is placed in front of the other to take a step, he remains in complete awareness. Theravada practitioners aspire to live with such mindfulness in every action throughout their entire lives. This training is fundamental and while most of us may not be able to maintain such a high degree of awareness, we can certainly benefit from bringing a greater degree of mindfulness into our daily lives. Even if it is simply while we make a cup of tea.

As a result of their flawless conduct, dedicated mindfulness and diligent Dharma practise, the Theravada practitioner gathers vast amounts of merit which is necessary for creating the conditions for progression on the path. For this reason, this stage is known as the *Path of Accumulation.*

2. **The Path of Preparation:** With impeccable ethical behaviour and continual mindfulness as a foundation, the Theravada practitioner develops single-pointed concentration through the practise of meditation. This concentration is the basis for achieving various levels of attainment, including the mind of *Shamatha* and the *Four Form Jhanas.* At some point they begin training in wisdom or insight by focusing on the *Four Applications of Mindfulness* (body, feelings, states of mind and phenomena). In this context, mindfulness of phenomena includes meditating on the five aggregates, the six sense organs, the five hindrances (sense desires, ill will, torpor, restlessness and doubt), the twelve links of dependent origination and, most importantly, the Four Noble Truths.

Since these meditations prepare the practitioner's mind for directly realising the nature of selflessness, this stage is called the *Path of Preparation*. It results in the union of shamatha and vipashyana.

3. **The Path of Insight:** As direct realisation of the sixteen aspects of the Four Noble Truths unfolds, and direct perception of selflessness is attained, the practitioner becomes an Arya being. This marks the entry into the next stage known as the *Path of Insight*.

4. **The Path of Habituation:** The Noble Eightfold Path can now be practised purely, as without a reference to a "self", actions of body, speech and mind are no longer tainted. The insights and realisations experienced previously on the Path of Preparation are now purified completely through the power of the practitioner's realisation of selflessness. This process thoroughly habituates the practitioner to this realisation, therefore this stage is known as the *Path of Habituation*.

5. **The Path of No More Learning:** Once this path is accomplished there is nothing further to attain, thus it is named the *Path of No More Learning*.

The Four Levels of Arya Beings

The Hinayana teachings speak of four different levels of Arya beings which define when certain afflictions are abandoned. Each of these four levels has an Access and Fruition stage—hence there are eight stages in total. These eight stages can be further expanded into twenty categories of practitioner which can then be subdivided even further.

Traditionally about eighty types of Sangha members (four groups of twenty) are studied in a text known as *The Doctrine of Twenty Sangha Members*. This is an extremely complicated text which takes monks a long time to study thoroughly, and therefore we will not elaborate further here. For simplicity we will therefore focus on the following eight stages that map out how a Theravada practitioner progresses along the five paths:

1. **Access Stream-Enterer:** This is a practitioner who has entered into the Path of Accumulation by first attaining a mind that understands the

path to liberation and aims to remove the acquired conceptually-based afflictions associated with the desire, form and formless realms. It continues through to the end of the Path of Preparation.

2. **Fruition Stream-Enterer:** This practitioner has removed all acquired conceptually-based afflictions. They directly realise selflessness for the first time and have thus entered into the Path of Insight. According to the Pali Canon they have eliminated three of the ten fetters. *Fetters* in this context refers to a mental bond that chains sentient beings to samsara. The three fetters that are eliminated at this stage are: the view of a truly existing self either identical with or in relation to the five aggregates (known as identity view), doubt about the Three Jewels and the validity of the Buddhist path, and the belief that external observances such as rituals and ascetic practices can lead to liberation. Generally they have at most seven more births among humans or gods.

3. **Access Once-Returner:** This is a practitioner who has entered into the Path of Habituation. They aim to remove the first six of the nine types of innate afflictions associated with the desire realm.

4. **Fruition Once-Returner:** According to Tibetan texts Fruition Once-Returners have removed six of the nine types of innate mental states of the desire realm. They will attain Arhatship after only one more lifetime, hence they are called "once-returners". According to the Theravada, attachment, aversion and ignorance are weakened but no new fetters are abandoned at this stage.

5. **Access Non-Returner:** This practitioner aims to remove the last three of the nine types of spontaneously arising disturbing emotions associated with sensory desire.

6. **Fruition Non-Returner:** This practitioner has removed the last three of the nine innate afflictions of the desire realm. They are known as a "non-returner" because they will attain Arhatship in this lifetime without ever returning again to a samsaric rebirth. In terms of the fetters, sensual desire and ill will are eliminated at this stage.

7. **Access Arhat:** This practitioner aims to remove the nine types of innate afflictions associated with each of the two higher levels of samsaric existence, the form and formless realms.

8. **Fruition Arhat:** This practitioner has removed all nine types of afflictions associated with the form and formless realms. Having removed all afflictive tendencies based on the self-grasping mind, they reach the goal of either Shravaka or Pratyeka Arhatship. This is also known as the Path of No More Learning. At this stage they have removed the five higher fetters: desire for existence in the form or formless realms, conceit, restlessness and ignorance.

Some Buddhist practitioners choose to practise a path which employs shamatha and the highly concentrated jhana states to focus specifically on subduing certain afflictions, which is known as the worldly path. Having accomplished this they are undisturbed and dwell in peace. Subsequently, to attain the state of an Arya being they direct their minds to the Four Noble Truths which enables them to completely overcome the subtle stains of ignorance.

The worldly path is also practised by non-Buddhist practitioners, who attain shamatha along with various form and formless absorptions. However, this does not lead to the accomplishment of an Arhat. Those who focus on the worldly path are able to eradicate many of the defects of the desire realm and the afflictions subside with the exception of the subtle stains of ignorance. Comparing the mind states of the desire realm with the peaceful mind states of the higher realms, the practitioner arouses disenchantment with existence in the desire realm and strives to achieve higher mental states. This reduces the afflictions to a level where they no longer create a disturbance to the mind. The transcendental path, by contrast, is accompanied by the realisation of the Four Noble Truths.

The following table gives a simplified presentation of the four main stages of the Theravada path along with the fetters or afflictions eliminated at these various stages. It should be noted that the first of the four fruition stages represented in the table begins at the level of the path of insight. At this point, the path of accumulation and the path of preparation have been traversed and transformation from an ordinary being to an Arya being has taken place.

Path	Stage	Fetters	Remaining Births
1. Accumulation 2. Preparation	Access Stream-Enterer	None	Continues to have uncontrolled rebirth in samsara
3. Insight	1. Fruition Stream-Enterer	1. Identity View 2. Doubt 3. Wrong grasp of rules and observances All acquired afflictions	At most seven more births among humans and gods
4. Habituation	2. Once-Returner	Weakens desire, hatred and delusion Six of the nine innate afflictions of desire realm	One more birth in the desire realm
	3. Non-Returner	4. Sensual desire 5. Ill will Final three innate afflictions of desire realm	Spontaneous rebirth in the form realm
5. No More Learning	4. Arhat	6. Desire for existence in form realm 7. Desire for existence in formless realm 8. Conceit 9. Restlessness 10. Ignorance Nine innate afflictions of the form and formless realms	No more conditioned rebirth in samsara.

Table 12-3 Progression through the Four Stages of the Theravada Path.

REVIEW OF KEY POINTS

- The Foundational Vehicle developed out of the public teachings given by the Buddha. They emphasise ethical discipline and the practise of meditation in order to achieve personal liberation.

- The Theravada teachings are compiled in the Pali Canon. This collection is divided into three sections known as the Three Baskets: monastic code of conduct (vinaya), discourses of the Buddha (sutra) and the higher teachings (abhidharma).

- There are two vehicles related to this style of practice: the Vehicle of the Hearer (shravakayana) and the Vehicle of the Solitary Realiser (pratyekabuddhayana).

- The ground of the Foundational Vehicle is the Four Noble Truths: the Truth of Suffering, the Truth of the Origin of Suffering, the Truth of the Cessation of Suffering and the Truth of the Path that Leads to this Cessation.

- The path of this vehicle is the Noble Eightfold Path, which provides eight forms of training that lead a practitioner to achieve personal liberation. These eight are: Right View, Right Intention, Right Speech, Right Action, Right Livelihood, Right Effort, Right Mindfulness and Right Concentration.

- The result of this vehicle is the Five Paths of Attainment: the path of accumulation, the path of preparation, the path of insight, the path of habituation and the path of no more learning.

- Along this path, there are four types of arya beings that can be identified: stream-enterers, once-returners, non-returners and arhats. If each of these is considered from the perspective of aspiring to achieve a state and actually achieving the state, then we can speak of eight stages in total.

The Bodhisattva Maitreya, a spiritual warrior of the Mahayana.

CHAPTER THIRTEEN

The Great Vehicle

When the Buddha taught, he was able to convey his teachings in such a way, that all those who were present, would be able to understand different things based on their own personal capacity. This unique feature of the Buddha's teachings meant that multiple versions based on a single teaching would arise depending on who had listened to it. The Foundational Vehicle presented in the previous chapter was one such interpretation, representing a particular perspective regarding what was taught.

The *Great Vehicle* (Mahayana) is the result of another interpretation which arose from the highly realised beings who also attended the Buddha's teachings. On the top of Vulture's Peak just outside Rajagriha (in the northeast of present day India), the Buddha initiated the Second Turning of the Wheel of Dharma by propounding the *Perfection of Wisdom Sutra*. During this time, the Buddha was surrounded by hundreds of thousands of realised beings who appeared from all the ten directions. Different students heard the same teaching in different ways, leading to eight versions of this sutra, ranging from 300 to 100,000 lines.

At other times the Buddha taught on the subject of Buddha-Nature in places such as Shravasti, Kushinagar and also many non-human planes of existence. These teachings were given to only the most highly realised of beings for they described a level of reality that was simply too profound for ordinary beings to understand.

Many years later after the Buddha had passed into parinirvana, these beings gathered in the south of India to compile the teachings they had received. Led by the great bodhisattvas (spiritual warriors) Maitreya, Manjushri and Vajrapani, they established the *Mahayana Sutras*, which detailed the teachings on how to develop the mind of enlightenment (bodhicitta), the trainings of a bodhisattva and most extensively, the profound teachings on the emptiness of inherent existence.

Based on two subsequent councils, two lineages took shape. The Bodhisattva Manjushri held a council in order to further clarify the teachings and to make the doctrine more concise through a greater emphasis on the subject of emptiness. The lineage which arose from this council was known as the *Lineage of Profound View* and was held by the great Indian master Nagarjuna. It was later expanded by masters such as Chandrakirti and Shantideva.

Meanwhile, the Bodhisattva Maitreya also held a council, choosing to emphasise the teachings of the Third Turning and specifically the subject of Buddha-Nature. This lineage became known as the *Lineage of Vast Activity* and was held primarily by Asanga; it was later expanded by masters such as Vasubandhu and Chandragomin.

The Mahayana tradition that arose on the basis of these two lineages gained great popularity in the north of India. Their teachings were eventually compiled into Sanskrit and spread throughout the land, making their way northward through Kashmir and then eastward into China via the Silk Road. In China, a number of schools arose, each focusing on different portions of the Mahayana sutras. Many of these schools then spread into parts of Korea, Japan and Vietnam.

The Mahayana teachings were characterised by their heavy emphasis on the cultivation of the altruistic desire to achieve enlightenment for the benefit of all sentient beings. This unique motivation known as *bodhicitta*, distinguished it from the Foundational Vehicle where the aim of each practitioner was to achieve their own personal liberation from samsara. On the basis of this more expansive and all encompassing view, Mahayana practitioners actively sought an engaged lifestyle which enabled them to work directly with bringing benefit to others. This feature made the Mahayana considerably more attractive for a growing community of lay practitioners who were searching for alternatives to the renounced life of a Buddhist monk.

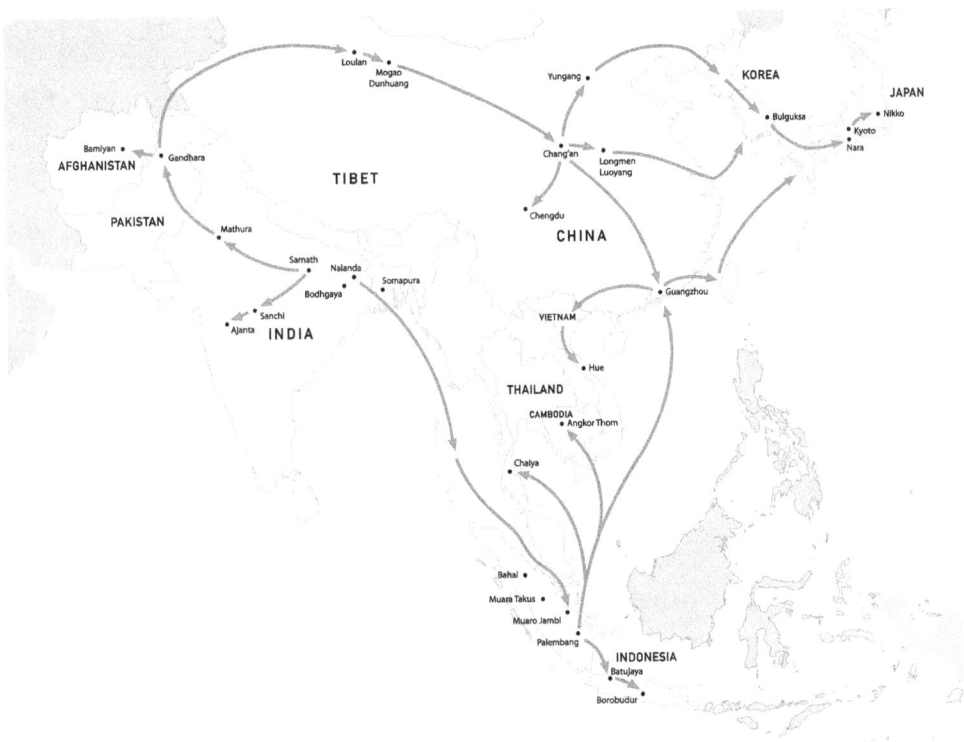

Figure 13-1 Spread of Mahayana Buddhism.

Another key distinction between the Foundational Vehicle and the Great Vehicle is in their different understanding of what it means to become enlightened. For a Theravada practitioner, enlightenment means to achieve a total emancipation from cyclic existence. This is done through clearing away all grasping and thus attaining the state of a Shravaka or Pratyeka Arhat.

For the Mahayana practitioner, this form of liberation is incomplete for it is incapable of removing the very subtle obscurations that produce the appearance of inherent existence. As long as these cognitive obscurations remain, the practitioner will be limited in the benefit they can bring to other beings. The Mahayana practitioner therefore engages in a wide range of skilfull means that allow them to accumulate the vast stores of merit needed to achieve the state of a perfectly enlightened Buddha. As they are driven by the desire to help and bring benefit to others, this level of attainment is the ultimate way to achieve this goal. This state is characterised by four aspects:

1. Complete freedom from the suffering of Samsara (nirvana)

2. The actualisation of a Buddha's *Truth Body* (dharmakaya) and *Form Body* (rupakaya)

3. The actualisation of limitless Buddha qualities

4. Developing the capacity to manifest spontaneously in whatever way is need by sentient beings.

From the Mahayana perspective, after an Arhat dies, their mind will dissolve into emptiness and abide in a state of complete non-grasping, effectively isolating themselves from all forms of suffering. While this is an amazing accomplishment, it fails to do anything whatsoever for those sentient beings who continue to suffer. For this reason, it is believed that in a distant future, even a fully liberated Arhat will need to be roused from their absorption by the Buddhas so that they can once again take rebirth. Only this time, they will do so with the intention of entering the Mahayana path. Because an Arhat is completely free from grasping, they do not experience suffering in the way that a sentient being does. This makes it very difficult for them to arouse the necessary degree of compassion for generating bodhicitta. For this reason, the Buddha taught that it is best to enter into the Mahayana path before achieving liberation.

THE BODHISATTVA VEHICLE (BODHISATTVAYANA)

A bodhisattva is any being who has established in their minds the unwavering resolve to achieve complete enlightenment for the sake of all sentient beings. Such a being is considered a *spiritual warrior* because they have dedicated their lives to this goal and are willing to face whatever challenges and obstacles may arise in order to achieve it. To a bodhisattva, it doesn't matter how long it takes, he will not stop until every single sentient being is freed from suffering.

As mentioned previously, the Mahayana can be understood from the perspective of both the sutras and tantras. In this context, the Bodhisattva Vehicle represents the perspective of the sutras and entry to this path is to first develop the altruistic intention of bodhicitta. It is this mind that shifts the context of everything the practitioner does and makes every action they engage in a contributing cause for the state of enlightenment.

On the basis of this motivation, a bodhisattva practitioner will develop a view that recognises the selflessness not only of their own person, but also of all forms of phenomena. On the basis of this view, they will then engage in what are known as the *Six Perfections* of generosity, ethical discipline, patience, joyful diligence, concentration and wisdom.

Through these practices a bodhisattva cultivates vast oceans of merit. This positive energy is channelled to cut through the self-cherishing mind and to fully realise the true nature of reality. Such a practitioner learns to abide in the wisdom that realises emptiness, while at the same time actively engaging in the illusory world of dependent arisings. This is known as achieving the *union of method and wisdom*. By practising in this way for three countless eons, the bodhisattva is able to completely remove all forms of obscuration and thereby attain the state of a fully enlightened Buddha.

GROUND—THE TWO TRUTHS

The Buddha did not directly teach philosophy in a systematic way. Instead he would expound different principles he knew would bring benefit to the people listening to the teaching. It wasn't until many years later that a more systematic approach was created, when a number of philosophical schools of thought arose out of the rich debate between different Buddhist practitioners.

All of these schools evolved around the Buddha's core teaching on the *Two Truths*. In this teaching the Buddha states that there are two levels in which beings can experience reality: the relative level and the ultimate level. What can be considered "true" will depend on the level in which you are operating. Therefore, some phenomena will be true from a relative perspective, while others are true from an ultimate perspective. In this way we can speak of two types of truth:

1. **Relative Truth:** Everything that makes up this world we currently experience, all of the various phenomena that we encounter, the people and places, our bodies and minds, are all examples of relative truths. It is

a world filled with subjects and objects. There are different people with different perspectives, each interacting with all manner of things. In this reality no two people see exactly the same thing, but instead, each is the centre of their own universe, experiencing the world from a unique and privileged vantage point. When we compare our experiences however, we can see there are similarities. On the basis of these similarities we can agree on certain conventions and on the basis of those conventions we can communicate with each other in order to establish what is true from our perspective.

While a relative truth may be true for one person or group of people, it may not necessarily hold true for another. For instance, consider the differences in our tastes for food. One person may experience a particular food as being delicious, while another may find it completely revolting. Both of these interpretations are equally true from the perspective of the individuals who hold these views. Also consider the ways in which different beings experience the objective world. For instance, the way an ant would experience a puddle of water in their pathway would be completely different from how a human would experience that same object.

This is why relative truths are dependent in nature. They exist only in dependence upon the perspective of an individual. If that individual's view is distorted by the presence of afflicted states of mind, then the relative truths they perceive will also be distorted. This is one of the main reasons why we generate so much suffering in our lives. We grasp onto our relative reality as though it were the only reality, and this leads us to make false assumptions about what we are actually experiencing.

2. **Ultimate Truth:** When we remove all of our misconceptions regarding how reality actually exists, we are left with a mere experience of reality as it is. It is this state of mind that is known as ultimate truth. We can use this term to refer to: the omniscient state of mind that is free from all obscurations; the ultimate nature of our experience that is known as "emptiness"; the wisdom that directly realises that nature; or our Buddha-Nature—the innate potential to achieve enlightenment.

When compared to our ultimate nature, relative truths appear to be temporary and superficial, like a dream. From the perspective of a person who has woken from a dream, everything they believed to be true in that dream was actually false. Likewise, from the perspective of a mind abiding in its own nature of ultimate reality, all of the relative truths we hold to so tightly, are also actually false.

In this way, relative truth is like the ocean and the ultimate truth is like the shore. To survive in the ocean we must learn to swim and, once we have the necessary skills, we can use the ocean (relative truth) to reach the shore (ultimate nature). Through Dharma practice we are using the relative truth in order to discover our ultimate truth. When we consider the Two Truths in relation to the *Four Seals*, we can see that the first two seals are characterised by impermanence and suffering, and therefore they can be identified as describing relative truth. The last two seals refer to the ultimate truth speaking directly of emptiness and enlightenment.

When we have a direct experience of ultimate truth, we see that what currently appears to us as two truths, is in fact merely two aspects of the same reality. Recognising this profound truth through direct experience is to discover the ultimate unity of the two truths.

Buddhist Philosophical Tenets

While all Buddhist Vehicles agree on the premise of the Two Truths, they disagree on which phenomena belong to the category of relative truth and which belong to the category of ultimate truth. When we organise the different views based on the subtlety of their understanding of ultimate truth, we arrive at the following systems:

1. **The Great Exposition School (vaibhashika):** Practitioners who hold this view believe that phenomena like the mind, the various operations of the mind, the material world of objects made up of particles, unconditioned phenomena such as space and the temporal experience of past and future, are all considered to be substantially existent. They believe the coarse objects that arise in relation to the coming together of these

elements are not real. For example, when the sense faculty of an eye encounters an object, it gives rise to a sensory consciousness and all of these aspects are considered ultimate truth. The recognition that what is arising in the mind is an "apple", is relative truth. It is a mere imputation by the mind.

2. **The Proponents of Sutra School (sautrantika):** This school refines the understanding of the Vaibhashika view. They recognise that unconditioned phenomena such as space, the perception of a substantially existing continuum (either physically or mentally), and the perception of past and future moments of time are all mere imputations and therefore should be considered relative truths. Practitioners of this view, hold that the only things which are truly established are minute particles and instantaneous moments of consciousness. Using the previous example, the "faculty", the "consciousness" and the "object" are all relative truths, imputed on the interdependent configuration of physical particles being perceived by a moment of the mind.

3. **The Mind-Only School (chittamatra):** According to this school, everything that appears to the mind is appearing in the mind itself, like the images in a dream. Nothing can therefore be established outside of this sphere of experience. This is to say that since we can only ever experience the physical world as appearances in the mind, then there is no basis to claim the existence of that world as something other than the mind. Therefore, the objective appearances of an eye faculty perceiving an image and the subjective experience of a visual consciousness, are both mere imputations. The ordinary mind that is able to rest in a non-dual awareness of the inseparability of subject and object, is considered to be the ultimate truth.

4. **The Middle Way School (madhyamaka):** This school is considered to hold the most subtle view of all Buddhist schools of thought. Within this school there are two main interpretations based on the two Mahayana lineages that came through Nagarjuna and Asanga. Both agree that the Chittamatra assertion that a non-dual ordinary consciousness is incorrect and that such a consciousness is still grasping onto a subtle

form of subjectivity making it a relative truth. They both agree that all phenomena perceived by the mind are mere imputations, totally empty of any form of inherent existence. Where they disagree is on the nature of the ultimate truth. For one group, the mere absence of inherently existent phenomena are considered to be ultimate truth. For the other, this mere absence represents the nature of only relative truths, it does not represent the nature of ultimate truths. Ultimate truth is the state of non-dual pristine awareness that transcends all conventionalities and is filled with all enlightened qualities. We will be discussing the distinctions between these two interpretations more fully in Book Two of this series.

In summary, every Buddhist system agrees that all conditioned phenomena do not inherently exist but this does not mean that nothing exists. Everything appears (including ourselves) depending on various causes and conditions, through a process of cause and effect in which we participate. It is crucial to always keep this in mind, otherwise regardless of the view we claim to follow, we are in danger of falling into the extreme of nihilism.

Of these four schools, the first two schools represent the views of the Foundational Vehicle while the last two represent the views of the Great Vehicle. As we can see, each school refines the assertions of the schools which precedes it. In this way, a practitioner can work to establish each view in a gradual manner, moving from gross to subtle.

Vehicle	School	Relative Truth	Ultimate Truth
Hinayana	Vaibhashika	gross objects	material particles, mind, space and time
	Sautrantika	gross objects, space and time	partless particles and moments of consciousness
Mahayana	Cittamatra	objective and subjective appearances	non-dual ordinary consciousness
	Madhyamaka	all gross and subtle dualistic appearances	1. mere absence of inherent existence
			2. pristine awareness that is empty of all conventionalities

Table 13-1: Distinctions in how different schools understand the Two Truths.

PATH—THE WAY OF THE BODHISATTVA

The path of the Bodhisattva Vehicle is designed specifically around the removal of the self-cherishing mind. This distorted attitude clings to the self as being the most important, and delegates everything else to being secondary. It is this mind, which maintains the isolated focus of an individual mindstream and therefore it is this mind which acts as an obscuration for achieving the omniscient state of a Buddha.

Bodhicitta

Entry to the Mahayana is through the spontaneous generation of the extraordinary mind of bodhicitta. Fueled by love and compassion, the aspiring bodhisattva develops a genuine aspiration to do whatever it takes to free sentient beings from suffering while recognising that the only realistic way to do this, is through gaining the infinite capacity of a fully enlightened being. Therefore, for the sake of sentient beings, this person develops the resolve to dedicate this life (and however many subsequent lives it takes) to achieving the state of Buddhahood.

In the beginning, this mind must be generated in a contrived way. It is such a vast aspiration that it takes time for it to arise spontaneously. There are many ways to develop this mind, but in Tibet, the most common are:

1. **The Seven Point Cause and Effect Method:** In this method, the practitioner focuses on meditations which help her to establish a loving connection with all sentient beings. This is primarily cultivated through reflecting on the love between a mother and her child, coupled with the fact that all sentient beings have at one time been our mother. Based on this connection, she meditates on the suffering of those sentient beings until her compassion becomes so strong that it motivates her to take action. From this altruistic intent, she establishes the resolve to achieve enlightenment for the sake of her dear mother sentient beings.

2. **Cultivating the Four Immeasurables:** Another technique is through the cultivation of the four universal qualities that provide the natural

conditions for bodhicitta to arise: love, compassion, joy and equanimity. All of these qualities work to dissolve the self-cherishing mind and to focus one's mind on the welfare of others.

3. **The Exchanging Self for Others Method:** This last method can be used to enhance the other two methods. It consists of a series of logical reasonings that demonstrate why it is illogical to cherish one's self over the benefit of others. These contemplations lead the practitioner towards recognising that the self-cherishing mind is extremely harmful and should be abandoned. This opens the door to the cultivation of immeasurable love and compassion.

Through these practises, aspiring bodhisattvas strive to familiarise their minds with this aspiration to such a degree, that eventually it becomes the default motivation for every action they engage in. It is at this point that the practitioner actually becomes a bodhisattva and enters the bodhisattva path.

The Six Perfections

The training of a bodhisattva is divided into a six-fold path that is known as the Six Perfections. This sequence of practices provides a step-by-step path to help develop the qualities that are needed to achieve Buddhahood. These qualities are as follows:

Generosity

The first perfection is an antidote to the mind of attachment, which holds onto things for itself. Through the practice of generosity, the bodhisattva learns to focus on the needs of others and to give whatever they can to bring them benefit. This is done by practicing three types of generosity:

1. **Material Giving:** The bodhisattva recognises that as long as sentient beings are struggling to fulfill their basic worldly needs, they will be unable to engage in spiritual practice. Therefore, the bodhisattva engages in generosity by giving food and material resources to those who need it.

2. **Giving Protection from Fear:** Even if a person has their basic needs met, they may live in a situation that fills them with anxiety or fear. This

is another obstacle for practising Dharma, and therefore the bodhisattva works to bring peace of mind to sentient beings by offering them protection.

3. **Giving Dharma:** Finally, even if a person has the capacity to practise Dharma, if they do not know how to practise, they will not be able to overcome their afflictions. Therefore, the bodhisattva works diligently to provide sentient beings with teachings so they can create the causes for genuine happiness.

Ethical Discipline

The second perfection helps the bodhisattva to build up a greater strength of mind through the practise of ethical discipline. It's focus is to bring awareness into each action so that you can transform any situation into an opportunity to bring benefit to others. This is done in three ways:

1. **Avoiding Negative Actions:** By giving up negative actions, the bodhisattva abandons harming others in both direct and indirect ways.

2. **Generating Positive Actions and Virtue:** Through the cultivation of virtuous qualities, the bodhisattva improves their capacity to bring benefit to sentient beings.

3. **Bringing Benefit to Others:** By focusing on the needs of others, the bodhisattva abandons the self-cherishing mind and is able to make everything they do a cause for sentient beings to be free from suffering.

Patience

Because the path of the bodhisattva is a long and difficult one, the practitioner must develop a great deal of patience in the face of whatever difficulties arise in their experience. Patience from this perspective therefore takes many forms such as discipline and tolerance. No matter what happens, a bodhisattva must never give up. This degree of determination is developed through the following trainings:

1. **Patience of Forgiveness:** The afflictive mind of anger is capable of destroying huge amounts of precious merit in the mind of the bodhisattva. Therefore, she must train to directly counteract this affliction through the practise of forgiveness, which includes patience of people who treat her badly.

2. **Patience as Strength and Courage for the Dharma:** The path is filled with obstacles that a bodhisattva will need to overcome. Through practising patience of hardship, such as cold and hunger, she learns to let go of her attachments to worldly comforts.

3. **Patience to be Fearless before the Profound Truth:** As the bodhisattva progresses on the path, the truth of reality begins to manifest more clearly. This truth can be difficult to accept. This training is specifically designed to overcome the afflicted doubt that prevents a bodhisattva from realising the profundity of her nature.

Joyous Effort

The bodhisattva path is a slow process of perfection that matures the mind over three countless aeons. To maintain this continuity of practise, a bodhisattva must develop an unwavering diligence that joyfully engages in the practise of virtue, no matter the length of time or what is required of them. The training in joyful effort is designed to counteract three forms of laziness through the cultivation of three forms of diligence:

1. **Armour-like Diligence:** This is the antidote for the lack of self-confidence. It is a type of laziness that believes that one is simply not good enough and therefore shouldn't even bother trying.

2. **Diligence of Right Action:** This is the antidote for procrastination. It is the laziness which pushes practise into the future. Through this training, the bodhisattva learns to recognise opportunities for virtue and immediately engages in manifesting that virtue.

3. **Diligence of Perpetual Enthusiasm:** This training is a counterforce for inactivity. It is focused on developing the mind that is constantly striving for enlightenment. This type of diligence allows the bodhisattva to finish whatever he sets out to do.

Concentration

The Bodhisattva Vehicle is a path of engagement. The bodhisattva actively works with everything occurring in her life, transforming those events into opportunities to benefit others. She therefore must be able to accurately assess a situation and recognise potential courses of action. Her capacity to do this depends on the strength and quality of her mind, which must be focused, pliable and free from distractions. This is achieved through developing three forms of concentration:

1. **Concentration practised by ordinary beings:** This is the mind that is absorbed in the experience of bliss, absence of thought and vivid clarity. It is developed through the practise of placement meditation (shamatha). In this state, the afflicted states of mind are dormant, making it a perfect basis upon which to investigate the nature of reality.

2. **Discerning Concentration:** This is the mind that is free from grasping, allowing the bodhisattva to remain in equanimity even when they are actively engaging in analysis of a particular phenomenon. It is developed through the practise of insight meditation (vipashyana).

3. **The Excellent Concentration:** This is the mind that is completely free from all forms of obscurations and is therefore capable of abiding continuously in a state of non-dual engagement with the nature of reality. It is developed through the union of shamatha and vipashyana.

Wisdom

All of the previous perfections provide the conditions for the bodhisattva to develop increasingly subtle forms of wisdom. It is this wisdom that allows the bodhisattva to not only free themselves from suffering, but also to understand the vast array of phenomena and how they can be used to skilfully guide sentient beings to that same enlightened state. This is done through the cultivation of three forms of wisdom:

1. **Wisdom from Hearing:** This is the wisdom generated through the process of listening to or studying the teachings. It produces a certainty

regarding what has been said and how the ideas have been communicated.

2. **Wisdom from Reflection:** This is the wisdom that arises from thinking about and reflecting upon the information that was gathered through study. It produces a clarity of mind that fully understands the meaning of different ideas and how they can be applied to different situations.

3. **Wisdom from Meditation:** This is the wisdom that transforms understanding into experiences. It is this form of wisdom that is able to directly clear away the afflicted mind of ignorance and thereby cut through both the afflictive and cognitive obscurations.

Of these six perfections, the first five are considered to be skilfull means, while the last is considered to be wisdom. When we compare them to the Three Higher Trainings, we can see that the first three are related to ethical discipline, the last two are concentration and wisdom respectively, and the fourth is shared across all three.

Higher Trainings	Perfection	Practices
Ethical Discipline	Generosity	1. Material Giving 2. Giving Protection from Fear 3. Giving Dharma
	Ethical Discipline	1. Avoiding Negative Actions 2. Generating Positive Actions and Virtue 3. Bringing Benefit to Others
	Patience	1. Patience of Forgiveness 2. Patience as Strength and Courage for the Dharma 3. Patience to be Fearless before the Profound Truth
All Three	Joyous Effort	1. Armour-like Diligence 2. Diligence of Right Action 3. Diligence of Perpetual Enthusiasm
Concentration	Concentration	1. Concentration practised by ordinary beings 2. Discerning Concentration 3. The Excellent Concentration
Wisdom	Wisdom	1. Wisdom from Hearing 2. Wisdom from Reflection 3. Wisdom from Meditation

Table 13-2: The Six Perfections.

RESULT—ENLIGHTENMENT

Both Mahayana and Theravada practitioners progress along the five paths of accumulation, preparation, insight, habituation and no more learning. However, because the motivation for engaging in these practices is significantly different in nature, the results these paths produce will also be significantly different. While the Theravada path has the capacity to produce an Arhat, the Mahayana path is capable of producing a fully enlightened Buddha. We will now review the five paths again from the perspective of a bodhisattva practitioner.

1. **Path of Accumulation:** We enter the Path of Accumulation by developing genuine Bodhicitta, and at this point we become a bodhisattva. This path emphasises accumulating oceans of meritorious actions and comprises three sequential levels: small, intermediate and great. Those on the small level practise and master contemplation of the body, feelings, mind and phenomena. Those on the intermediate level practise and achieve perseverance in avoiding unwholesome thoughts or actions, abandoning unwholesome thoughts or actions that have already arisen, developing new wholesome thoughts or actions and maintaining wholesome thoughts or actions that have already been developed. Those on the great level attain unbroken desire and intention to concentrate, unbroken effort while concentrating and unbroken analytical concentration.

   The merit which is created on the Path of Accumulation eventually becomes the cause for a Bodhisattva's ability to emanate in countless worlds and benefit countless beings when he or she becomes a Buddha. This is known as the form body (rupakaya) which includes both the subtle enjoyment body (sambhogakaya) and the gross emanation body (nirmanakaya). At the beginning of this path a Mahayana practitioner first attains true Bodhicitta, becoming a Bodhisattva, yet they still must accumulate vast amounts of merit to strengthen and stabilise the enlightened mind of Bodhicitta. Eventually their mind is completely absorbed in wanting all beings to be fully enlightened and their heart is so developed that they take full responsibility for this.

   Once a Bodhisattva has achieved the great Path of Accumulation, they develop great meditative equipoise along with the ability to visit Buddhas and Bodhisattvas in other realms and listen to their teachings.

2. **Path of Preparation:** During the Path of Preparation, a Bodhisattva is preparing to attain the third level of the five paths of attainment; the Path of Insight, where they directly perceive true reality or emptiness for the first time. The Path of Preparation is further divided into four levels: heat, peak, patience and supreme worldly phenomena.

At the first level the Bodhisattva receives many signs or omens that they will see the ultimate truth, and this is known as heat. This is likened to the heat felt when one draws near to fire. At the second level, known as peak, the Bodhisattva sees signs of their wholesome qualities for the first time. These qualities are the peak of worldly virtues and are known as the five faculties. They are faith, energy, mindfulness, concentration and wisdom.

At the third stage, the Bodhisattva initially gains confidence to overcome the fear of experiencing the emptiness of relative phenomena. This is known as patience. The fourth and final level of the Path of Preparation ensures that the Bodhisattva will experience a direct perception of the emptiness of relative truth at the following stage. This level is thus called supreme worldly phenomenon and is the final ordinary realisation before becoming an Arya being. During this level the five faculties are fully developed and become the five divine powers: faithfulness, energy, mindfulness, concentration and wisdom. This is the stage at which the worldly mind finally ends and the transcendental mind begins.

3. **Path of Insight:** During the Path of Insight the Bodhisattva directly realises emptiness of the relative truth, having eradicated all acquired misconceptions and wrong views regarding the true nature of phenomena which were based on wrong conceptual thinking adhered to during this and former lifetimes. They attain supreme mindfulness, discriminating awareness, energy, joy, tranquillity, concentration and equanimity, known as the seven factors of enlightenment. From this stage until Buddhahood, the Bodhisattva is known as an Arya being. They

gain extraordinary powers and can manifest in hundreds of different places, guiding hundreds of followers during a single instant. Seeing the ultimate truth for the first time, the path of insight is like glimpsing the ocean. Through the Path of Habituation, a vaster and vaster view is cultivated until the entire ocean is seen in all its splendour.

4. **Path of Habituation:** Having removed the acquired conceptual obscurations on the Path of Insight, the Arya Bodhisattva moves onto the Path of Habituation. Here they habituate themselves with the realisation of the emptiness of relative truth, eliminating the innate obscurations to Buddhahood. This process of habituation is essential because our innate obscurations have been with us since beginningless time, operating of their own accord without depending on faulty beliefs or reasoning. During this process the Arya Bodhisattva devotes enormous effort to attaining mastery of the *Ten Perfections*: generosity, discipline, patience, diligence, concentration, wisdom, skilful means, aspiration, strength and supreme awareness.

5. **Path of No More Learning:** At the final moment of this stage they enter into a meditative state called vajra-like meditative stabilisation, in which the subtlest remaining obstacles to Buddhahood are overcome. They arise from this concentration as a Buddha and achieve omniscience. This means that all phenomena of the past, present and future are known directly, at the same time and without effort. This is called the Path of No More Learning, as there is no need to go any further.

The Ten Bodhisattva Bhumis

The Arya Bodhisattva removes the innate afflictive and cognitive obscurations progressively over a series of levels. From the Path of Insight onwards, ten Bodhisattva bhumis or grounds are achieved prior to Buddhahood. Each of these ten has an uninterrupted entrance and liberation stage. At the entrance stage the Bodhisattva's attainment cannot be interrupted by obscurations, which dissolve and are naturally purified as soon as they arise, while during the liberation stage the door to these obscurations is locked and cannot be re-opened. In other words, they have been totally eradicated along with their propensities.

Furthermore, during each of the ten bhumis, one of the ten perfections (or paramitas) is accomplished, meaning one fully develops or perfects certain qualities to the greatest possible extent.

Of the nine Bhumi grounds of the Path of Habituation, the first three are known as the small path, the next three as the intermediate path, and the last three levels are known as the great path. The Path of Habituation generally takes two countless aeons, although there is no fixed time for each individual.

Time is not an issue for an Arya Bodhisattva as regardless of how long they take, they continually experience immense joy from bringing benefit to others. Furthermore, this immensely long period of time is determined from the viewpoint of others, as from the viewpoint of the Bodhisattva's own experience, these levels may be traversed far more quickly.

The ten Bodhisattva bhumis are briefly described below. From the second bhumi onwards, the different stages are attained as certain obscurations are eradicated through progressively deeper levels of meditative absorption. The heaviest obscurations are eradicated first, followed by the finer obscurations. The small, intermediate and great paths are each divided into three levels of realisation—lowest, medium and highest—according to which obscurations are eliminated. There are three types of obscurations—heavy, intermediate and fine—each of which are further divided into three distinct levels. With so many levels within stages, it may seem like an over use of detail, however we should keep in mind that this is an incredibly accomplished and profound path that identifies subtleties of the mind which are difficult for ordinary beings to comprehend.

First Bhumi—Supreme Joy

The first bhumi is known as supreme joy because the Bodhisattva has attained the path of direct insight for the first time and therefore is supremely joyful. In other words, they have directly realised that the self does not exist independently and that everyone and everything are interdependent. With this understanding they overcome the false idea that the five aggregates constitute a truly existing self. At this stage the Bodhisattva attains supernatural powers and can manifest in hundreds of different places at once, with the ability to guide hundreds of followers in a single instant. The Bodhisattva is free from all attachment to phenomena as they are directly seen to be insubstantial and subject to suffering, decay and death.

Perfection of generosity is attained at the first bhumi, meaning the Bodhisattva has the ability to give anything away without regret and with no thought of praise or reward. They would even give away parts of their own body if they were useful to someone else. They do this with great joy, and although they do experience physical pain, no suffering is experienced in their minds. At the higher levels even physical pain is absent for an Arya Bodhisattva as the mind is so strongly habituated to the emptiness of relative truth. Bodhisattvas on the first level are primarily motivated by faith. They train in pure ethical conduct in order to purify their minds of afflictive obscurations and prepare themselves for the meditative absorption of the second bhumi. By this time they have completely eliminated predispositions toward impure ethical conduct, which will not arise again.

Second Bhumi—Stainless

This bhumi is achieved when the lowest level of realisation of the small path removes the heaviest obscuration. During this level the paramita of ethical discipline is completely perfected and the Bodhisattva's self-control becomes so complete that no immoral thoughts arise, even in dreams. Any movements or activities of body, speech and mind are purified of the most subtle defilements. They achieve perfect virtuous actions of body, speech and mind, which include joyfully refraining from any form of killing, stealing, sexual misconduct, lying, divisive talk, harsh speech and senseless chatter and also covetousness, harmful intent and wrong views.

At this stage the Bodhisattva attains supernatural powers which allow them to manifest in thousands of different places at once, with the ability to guide thousands of followers in an instant.

These abilities and powers continue to increase as the Bodhisattva progresses through subsequent bhumis. Because of this, the Bodhisattva's mind becomes purified and abides in equanimity. They also attain the four meditative absorptions of the form realms, which are superior to the attainment of the worldly absorptions; they are more stable, more profound and more useful in developing the subtle mind.

Through the maturation of these qualities their perfection of ethical conduct becomes supreme. These bodhisattvas appear as universal monarchs in order to help living beings, or masters of the four glorious continents and the seven precious objects: the precious wheel, elephant, horse, jewel, queen, minister and general. This kind of wealth naturally belongs to them, helping them in turn to benefit others.

Third Bhumi—Illumination

This bhumi is attained when the second heaviest obscurations are overcome by the middle level of realisation of the small path. It is called Illumination because when it is attained the fire of wisdom burns the objects of dualistic thought. This illumination is by its very nature able to extinguish all dualistic elaborations during meditation. This is the stage when the paramita of patience is fully perfected in a way that far exceeds our ordinary perception of patience.

The Bodhisattva's equanimity becomes so profound at this level that even if someone were to slowly and gradually strip away flesh or bone from their body, the Bodhisattva would not become angry or perturbed. Realising their tormentor is ignorantly unaware of the law of cause and effect and motivated by afflicted thoughts which sow the seeds for future suffering, they would instead feel unbearable compassion for them. Trainees on the third level overcome all tendencies toward anger and never react with hatred (or even annoyance) to any harmful words or actions. Rather, their equanimity remains constant and all sentient beings are viewed with unconditional love and compassion.

Bodhisattvas on this level also cultivate the four formless meditative absorptions, which are superior to the formless absorptions of limitless space, limitless consciousness, nothingness and beyond perception. At this stage the four immeasureables of love, compassion, joy and equanimity are refined, as well as the five clairvoyances: the divine eye (ability to see subtle and distant forms), the divine ear (the ability to hear subtle and distant sounds), miraculous powers (the ability to emanate forms through the power of the mind), knowing others' minds and recollection of previous lives.

Fourth Bhumi—Radiant

The fourth bhumi, Radiant, is achieved with the eradication of the finest level of heavy obscurations by the third level of realisation of the small path. At this time perfect diligence, the fourth paramita, is accomplished and the Bodhisattva then enters the intermediate path. This level is named Radiant because fourth bhumi Bodhisattvas constantly emit the radiance of exalted wisdom. They burn up afflictive and cognitive obscurations with the radiance of their wisdom.

Entering into progressively deeper meditative absorptions and attaining a powerful mental pliancy, they eliminate laziness and increase their ability to practise meditation for extended periods of time. They destroy deeply rooted afflictions and cultivate the thirty-seven practices of awakening, beginning with the four applications of mindfulness. Through training in these thirty-seven practices, Bodhisattvas develop great skill in meditative concentration and cultivate wisdom, weakening the conceptual obscurations which lead to a false understanding of reality.

Fifth Bhumi—Difficult to Overcome

This level is attained with the eradication of the grossest level of intermediate obscurations by meditative realisation of the first level of the intermediate path. It is where the paramita of concentration is perfected and is called "Difficult to Cultivate" because it involves arduous practices that require a great deal of effort to perfect. It is also called Difficult to Overcome because when a Bodhisattva has completed the training of this level, they have profound wisdom and insight that are difficult to surpass or undermine. Cultivating the perfection of meditative stabilisation, they overcome tendencies toward distraction and achieve supreme meditative stabilisation.

Sixth Bhumi—The Approaching

The sixth bhumi is accomplished when the second level of intermediate obscurations is overcome by the second level of realisation of the intermediate path.

Here the paramita of wisdom, the sixth perfection, is developed. The sixth level is called the Approaching because the Bodhisattva becomes habituated to the realisation of dependant arising and signlessness. Signlessness refers to the fact that phenomena seem to possess apparent qualities by way of their own nature, but when examined one realises that all qualities are merely mentally imputed and not a part of the nature of the objects they appear to characterise.

The Bodhisattva manifests meditative wisdom and renounces attachment to either cyclic existence or nirvana. Having overcome all attachments, Bodhisattvas on this level can attain nirvana, but because of the force of the mind of awakening, they decide to remain in the world in order to benefit other sentient beings. They cultivate the perfection of wisdom, through which they perceive all phenomena as lacking inherent existence, similar to dreams, illusions, reflections or magically created objects. All notions of "I" and "other" are transcended, along with concepts such as "existence" and "non-existence". These sixth-level Bodhisattvas abide in contemplation of emptiness with minds that are undisturbed by false ideas.

Seventh Bhumi—Far Gone

At this level the finest level of intermediate obscurations is eradicated by the highest level of realisation of the intermediate path, and the paramita of skilful means is perfected.

The previous six bhumis are known as impure levels because they are still contaminated by innate afflictive and cognitive obscurations, which still require some effort to be eliminated. According to most Mahayana and Vajrayana points of view, all these mental afflictions are eliminated by this stage, leaving only the most subtle obscurations to omniscience. If you put garlic in a container for a period of time and then remove it and wash the container, one can still smell the remnants of garlic for a while. In the same way these subtle obscurations, also known as habitual tendencies, linger on.

Bodhisattvas on this level develop the ability to contemplate uninterruptedly and enter into advanced meditative absorptions for extended periods of time, thus passing beyond the paths of both Shravakas and Pratyeka Arhats. For this reason the seventh bhumi is called Far Gone. On this level they perfect skilful means during meditation practise and also in the post-meditation period and have an exceptional ability to adapt their teachings to meet the individual needs of their audience. They also develop the ability to know the thoughts of others and in every moment are able to practise all the perfections. All thoughts and actions are free from afflictions, and they constantly act spontaneously and effectively for the benefit of others.

Eighth Bhumi—The Immovable

The three remaining bhumis, the eighth through to the tenth, are known as the three pure bhumis, because in these three, only subtle obscurations to omniscience remain, and no gross effort is needed to eliminate these.

The eighth stage is obtained when the heaviest of the fine obscurations to enlightenment are overcome by the first level of realisation of the great path. At this time the paramita of aspiration is fully accomplished. This level is called The Immovable because through non-conceptuality, Bodhisattvas have overcome all afflictions regarding signs, so that everything is perceived nakedly and directly and their minds are completely absorbed in Dharma at all times. There is no possibility that they might waver on the path and they are destined for full Buddhahood, having no inclination to seek personal nirvana. They cultivate the perfection of aspiration, which means they undertake to fulfil various vows, due to which they accumulate the causes for further virtues. Although they resolve to work for the liberation of others and emanate compassion toward all sentient beings in the universe, these Bodhisattvas have completely transcended the tendency to imagine that there are any truly existing beings to liberate.

The understanding of emptiness of these Bodhisattvas is so complete that it overturns all afflicted views, and reality appears in a completely new light. They are compared to people who have awakened from dreams, and all their perceptions are influenced by this new awareness. They attain the meditative state called forbearance regarding non-arisen phenomena, due to which they no longer think in terms of causes or causelessness. They also develop the ability to manifest in various forms in order to teach others; compassion and skilful means are spontaneous and completely uncontrived. There is no need to plan or contemplate how best to benefit others, since these Bodhisattvas skilfully adapt themselves to every situation.

Ninth Bhumi—Good Intelligence

The ninth bhumi is reached when the middle level of fine obscurations is overcome by meditative realisation of the second level of the great path. Here the Bodhisattva accomplishes the paramita of strength or power.

From this point onwards the Bodhisattva moves quickly toward awakening. From the eighth through to the tenth bhumi, huge progress toward Buddhahood is accomplished. On the ninth level they fully understand the three vehicles, the paths of hearers, solitary realisers and Bodhisattvas, and perfect the ability to teach the doctrine. As they attain faultless and complete mastery of the Dharma and have the ability to teach it in all its aspects, this level is called Good Intelligence.

The Bodhisattva acquires the four analytical knowledges of doctrines, meanings, grammar and exposition. As a result they develop eloquence and skill in presenting doctrinal teachings. Their intelligence surpasses that of all humans and gods and they comprehend all names, words, meanings and languages. They can understand any question and have the ability to answer with a single sound, which is understood by each being according to its capacity. They cultivate the perfection of power and with the strength of their meditation and mastery of the four analytical knowledges, they are able to practise the six perfections with unyielding diligence.

Tenth Bhumi—Cloud of Dharma

The tenth stage is attained with the eradication of the finest of the fine obscurations to enlightenment by the highest level of meditative realisation of the great path. The paramita of supreme awareness is thus achieved.

Now tenth level Bodhisattvas need to eliminate the most subtle obscurations to becoming omniscient, at which point they will attain the fully enlightened state of Buddhahood. At this stage they enter into the most powerful meditative absorptions and actualise limitless ability. Cultivating the perfection of exalted wisdom enables them to increase their wisdom and strengthens the other perfections, and as a result they abide continuously in the supreme joy of Dharma.

Tenth bhumi Bodhisattvas spread the doctrine in all directions and each being absorbs what they need in order to grow spiritually. They acquire perfect bodies and their minds are cleansed of the subtlest traces of affliction. They manifest in limitless forms for the benefit of others and transcend the ordinary laws of time and space. In addition, they are able to place entire world systems within a single pore, without diminishing them or increasing the size of the pore. These Bodhisattvas receive empowerment from innumerable Buddhas. This is called great rays of light because the radiance of these Bodhisattvas shines in all directions. This empowerment helps them to eradicate the remaining obscurations to omniscience and gives them added confidence and strength.

At the final moment of this stage, the Bodhisattva enters into a meditative state called the vajra-like meditative stabilisation, in which the subtlest remaining obstacles to Buddhahood are overcome. They arise from this concentration as Buddhas and achieve omniscience. This means that all phenomena of the past, present and future are known directly, at the same time and without effort.

Path	Practice	Ground	Realisation - Obscuration
Accumulation	The 6 perfections are necessarily imperfect. They are called virtues at this time.		
Preparation			
Insight	1. Generosity	1. Supreme Joy	
Habituation	2. Discipline	2. Stainless	Small - Heavy
	3. Patience	3. Illumination	Small - Middling
	4. Diligence	4. Radiant	Small - Fine
	5. Concentration	5. Difficult to Overcome	Intermediate - Heavy
	6. Wisdom	6. The Approaching	Intermediate - Middling
	7. Skilfull Means	7. Far Gone	Intermediae - Fine
	8. Aspiration	8. The Immovable	Great - Heavy
	9. Strength	9. Good Intelligence	Great - Middling
	10. Supreme Awareness	10. Cloud of Dharma	Great - Fine
No More Learning	No practice	Total High	

Table 13-3: Stages of the Bodhisattva Path.

The State of Buddhahood

Through applying one's realisation of emptiness to the perfection of all good qualities, the Bodhisattva unifies the two accumulations of method and wisdom and produces the final result of a fully enlightened Buddha. When an individual achieves such a state, they will manifest two enlightened aspects:

1. **The Truth Body of a Buddha (dharmakaya):** This is the individual experience of the enlightened mind. It is the result of the accumulation of wisdom which completely eradicates every form of ignorance, thereby allowing one's own Buddha-Nature to manifest without limitation. It is a state that is free from all suffering and empty of all afflicted minds.

2. **The Form Bodies of a Buddha (rupakaya):** This is the infinite expression of an enlightened mind from the perspective of sentient beings. It is a direct result of the accumulation of a vast ocean of merits. All good qualities are totally perfected within this mind, spontaneously manifesting in accordance with the needs of sentient beings.

While the Truth Body fulfills the needs of the individual, the Form Bodies fulfill the needs of others. It is this unique quality that defines full and complete enlightenment.

REVIEW OF KEY POINTS

- The Mahayana Vehicle is based on the teachings received by highly realised beings. These teachings focused on the cultivation of the mind of enlightenment (bodhicitta), an active form of social engagement and a profound understanding of the nature of reality (emptiness).

- Within the sutra tradition of the Mahayana, two main lineages were established: Manjushri's Lineage of Profound View and Maitreya's Lineage of Vast Activity.

- The sutra path of the Mahayana is known as the Bodhisattva Vehicle. It provides methods for achieving complete enlightenment over the course of three countless aeons. It is also known as the Perfection Vehicle as it relies on the gradual perfection of various qualities in order to achieve the result of Buddhahood.

- The ground of the Mahayana is distinguished by its emphasis on the Two Truths: relative truth and ultimate truth. Relative truth relates to all dependent phenomena, while ultimate truth is the nature of reality as it is.

- Over time, various schools of thought emerged to define how to understand these two truths: Vaibhashika, Sautrantika, Chittamatra and Madhyamaka. The first two are views based on the First Turning, while the last two are considered views based on the Second and Third Turnings.

- The path of the Bodhisattva Vehicle is divided into two phases: generating bodhicitta as an entry to the path and engaging in the practise of the Six Perfections. The Six Perfections are: generosity, ethical discipline, patience, joyful effort, concentration and wisdom.

- A Mahayana practitioner progresses through the five stages in a similar way to the Theravada practitioner; however, the practices and the specific results experienced are different due to the unique motivation of bodhicitta.

- The progression of an Arya Bodhisattva from the moment they directly realise the empty nature of reality up to full enlightenment is divided into ten stages known as the Ten Bodhisattva Bhumis (or grounds). Each ground represents a progressively subtler level of realisation that clears away increasingly finer layers of obscurations. The first seven grounds are impure in that the bodhisattva is still removing the propensities for afflictive obscurations. The last three are known as pure grounds as they are completely free from afflictive obscurations and are only concerned with the removal of the very subtle cognitive obscurations.

- When a Bodhisattva achieves the state of Buddhahood, they will spontaneously manifest two enlightened aspects: the dharmakaya truth body and an array of rupakaya form bodies.

CHAPTER FOURTEEN

The Vajra Vehicle

During his lifetime, the Buddha reserved his highest and most profound teachings for a very small group of adepts who were capable of grasping their incredibly subtle meaning. With the strength of his own mental absorption, the Buddha was able to manifest his mind in various pure forms known as *deities*. These deities could only be experienced by the most highly realised of beings and it was to these disciples that the Buddha bestowed the esoteric teachings of Tantra. Due to their extreme subtlety, these teachings remained relatively unknown for many centuries after the Buddha passed into parinirvana. They were held as a purely oral tradition, requiring direct transmission from teacher to disciple, which meant knowledge of the tantric teachings remained rare and protected.

When the Mahayana teachings were committed into the Sanskrit language, they became available to a wider audience in ancient India. More and more people began to study these teachings leading to the creation of monastic universities, the most famous of which was the great monastic University of Nalanda. This single institution was successful in drawing all of the great Buddhist minds of its time into a single place, causing an explosion of philosophical debate and refinement of the Buddhist doctrine.

As the Mahayana scholars explored deeply into the meaning of the Buddha's sutra teachings, they were able to achieve amazing levels of realisation. This process ripened their minds to such a degree that they then became suitable vessels for the tantric teachings. Subsequently, many of Nalanda's best scholars left the university in search of the hidden tantric yogis, who could guide them on this varja path.

While some became wandering yogis themselves, others returned to the monastic universities and continued their practise in secret. In this way, many within the Nalanda tradition began to practise a two-fold approach. During the day they would publicly study and practise the sutra teachings and during the night, they would secretly practise in accordance with the tantric teachings.

From Nalanda a number of branch universities developed in the region. One in particular, the tantric college of *Vikramashila*, was instrumental in systematising the vast range of methods embedded within the tantras. During this period, two types of lineages for transmitting the esoteric teachings arose:

1. **Teaching Lineages:** These lineages were largely theoretical in nature, providing details about the various rituals and ceremonies related to different tantric practices, as well as the various theories that underpinned the different systems. They were most often used as a way of preparing potential vajra masters with the skills and understanding necessary to guide others.

2. **Practice Lineages:** These lineages consisted of the pith instructions that described exactly how to practise a given system of tantra. In ancient India these instructions were extremely protected, being given to only a handful of students after they had demonstrated their commitment and devotion to their teacher.

It was from these various lineages that the Vajrayana arose. Bringing together all of the Buddha's teachings (both sutra and tantra), the Vajrayana was by far the most complete and fully integrated presentation of the Buddha-dharma. While some of these teachings made their way east into China and beyond, the vast majority were eventually preserved in the land of snow mountains to the north.

TIBETAN BUDDHISM

The Tibetan plateau had long been home to various nomadic tribes. These tribes were eventually united under the banner of a royal bloodline that was believed to have been descended from gods. As these kings grew in power, so did their ambitions for expansion and under the leadership of the Tibetan King Songtsen Gampo, the Tibetan Empire rapidly dominated the region of Central Asia.

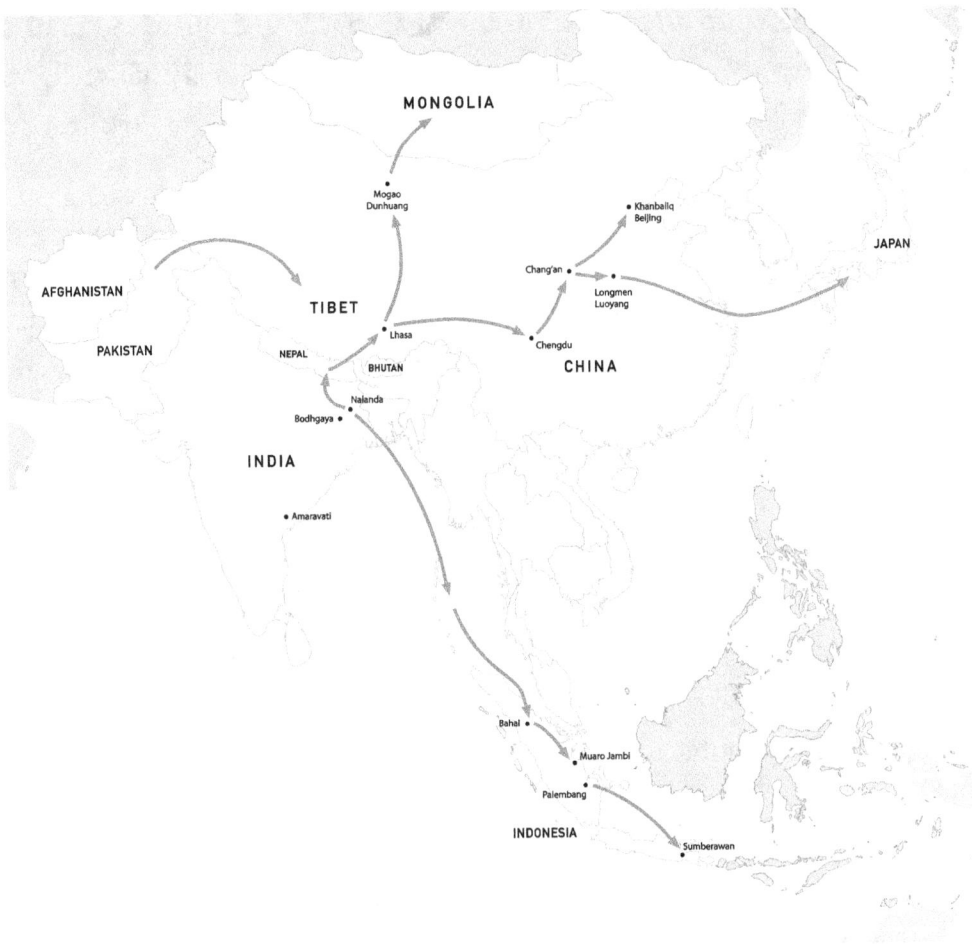

Figure 14-1 Spread of Varjayana Buddhism.

It was during this period of rapid growth that the Tibetans first came into contact with the ancient civilisations of their neighbors. The first culture to have a major influence on the royal courts was to the west in the land of Zhang Zhung (the region now associated with Western Tibet). This land was annexed by Songtsen Gampo and its cultural beliefs were soon recognised as the state religion. This tradition was known as *Yungdrung Bön* and was derived from the teachings of another enlightened being known as Tonpa Shenrab.

In an act of diplomacy, the King agreed to marry the daughters of the Chinese King to the east and the Nepali King to the south. Through the influence of these two princesses, Tibet was introduced to Chinese and Indian Buddhism. Over the coming years, the three traditions of Zhang Zhung, China and India, would each hold different degrees of influence in the royal court, thus shaping a uniquely Tibetan culture.

During the reign of King Trisong Deutsen, Tibet sent an army of translators into India in order to study the Buddhist teachings and translate its texts. The translators made the long and dangerous trip over the Himalayan mountains to monastic centres like Nalanda, where they worked alongside Indian scholars to translate the entire Sanskrit Canon into the Tibetan language.

In addition, the King invited a number of highly realised masters from India to come to Tibet in order to give teachings. Over time, the basis for a Buddhist monastic community was established and the teachings took root in the country. While the foundational teachings of the sutras were given publicly, the esoteric teachings of tantra were given only to the King and a few select members of the royal court.

As Buddhism continued to grow in Tibet, tensions began to develop with the followers of Bön (Bönpos). Under the patronage of a devout Buddhist King, the Bön practitioners experienced increasing restrictions, generating unrest, which eventually lead to the assassination of the King. As power swung in the direction of the Bönpos, Buddhism found itself without royal patronage. Many of the Buddhist institutions were subsequently closed, causing the practitioners to scatter to remote regions of the country and for many decades, Buddhism almost disappeared from the region of Central Tibet.

Eventually though, a new wave of translators arose with the strong intention to revive the Buddhist teachings in Tibet. Taking the responsibility upon themselves, these translators travelled at great personal peril to India, where they studied with the great scholars of Nalanda and Vikramashila. They also practised with many of the highly accomplished yogis of their time, receiving a treasure trove of tantric teachings. They then returned to their homeland and began to propagate the teachings they had received.

In this way, we can identify two main transmissions of Buddhism into Tibet:

1. **The Early Transmission (Nyingma):** The teachings that were introduced from Zhang Zhung and those collected from India through the organised efforts of the Tibetan Kings and their translators.

2. **The Later Transmission (Sarma):** The teachings that were collected by individual translators who travelled to India, that were later propagated on their return to Tibet. Many teachings were also introduced when a number of Indian masters were invited by various Tibetan kingdoms to come and teach in Tibet.

On the basis of these two transmissions, six main spiritual traditions developed in Tibet. Each major tradition is generally distinguished by the distinct philosophical presentation that was established by its founders and the unique tantric practice lineages that it specialises in. Based on the order in which these traditions were founded, they are:

Bön

The Bön tradition can be traced back to the ancient land of Zhang Zhung and the teachings of the enlightened being known as Tonpa Shenrab. Many believe that Tonpa Shenrab was a previous incarnation of Shakyamuni Buddha, making the Bön an earlier form of the Buddhism that was later developed in India.

The Bön teachings contain a vast diversity of methods for temporarily harmonising worldly experience and ultimately for achieving full enlightenment. The tantric practices found within this tradition are centered around developing a view of the *Great Perfection* (Dzogchen) through effortlessly resting the mind in the pristine awareness of its own nature. Much of the form of the rituals found in Tibetan Buddhism are derived from the Bön approach to practice.

Nyingma

The Nyingma tradition arose primarily from the teachings of the great Indian saint Padmasambhava, who is known throughout Tibet as Guru Rinpoche (meaning "precious teacher"). With the help of the Indian pandita Shantarakshita and his main disciple the Tibetan King Trisong Deutsen, Padmasambhava successfully established Vajrayana Buddhism in Tibet.

He was also responsible for preserving the Buddha-dharma when he and his wisdom consort Yeshe Tsogyal, used their miraculous powers to seal away countless teachings in the form of treasure texts. These spiritual time capsules remained hidden within the physical landscape of Tibet and within the non-physical mindstreams of Padmasambhava's closest disciples until such time as the people were ready to receive them. In this way, the Nyingma teachings have continued to evolve over time.

While the Nyingma practices are drawn from a wide range of sutras and tantras, the pinnacle of their path is the *Great Perfection*. Like the Bön, practitioners progress through various stages of practise, purifying their minds of different layers of obscurations. When the practitioner is ready, they are introduced to the pristine nature of their mind through meditation. They then familiarise themselves with this recognition until every single moment is experienced from this enlightened perspective.

Sakya

The Sakya tradition is the first major tradition to have arisen during the period of the *Later Transmission*. It was originally founded by the great Khön Konchok Gyalpo when he lost faith in the authenticity of the Nyingma teachings that had survived after the period of persecution. He chose to actively seek out the various teachers who were disseminating the new translations and became a force for the revitalisation of Buddhism in Central Tibet.

This tradition gets its name from the monastery that was founded by Konchok Gyalpo. Literally it means "grey earth", after the distinctive colour of the ground on the site where the monastery was built. Since that time, the leadership of the Sakya has been maintained within the bloodlines of the Khön family, being passed from father to son or from uncle to nephew.

The unique characteristic of the Sakya tradition is that they are the main lineage holders for the system of practice known as the *Path with the Result* (lamdre). This system based on the *Hevajra Tantra*, originated with the accomplished Indian master Virupa and was brought to Tibet by Drokmi Lotsawa. The teaching lineage became known as the *Lamdre for Assemblies*, and provided the foundational teachings for developing the view in accordance with sutra. The practice lineage was passed down in extreme secrecy and became known as the *Lamdre for Disciples*. It provided the unique practices for actualising the view in accordance with tantra.

Kagyu

During the same period when the Sakya were establishing themselves as a monastic institution, other traditions were taking shape based on the specific teachings being passed on from teacher to disciple. One group of such traditions are collectively known as the Kagyu lineages. Most of these lineages trace their origins back to the Dharma transmitted by the great translator Marpa Chökyi Lodrö. While Marpa had many disciples, his most famous was the Tibetan yogi-saint Milarepa.

It was Milarepa's student Gampopa, who successfully established a monastery combining the sutra teachings he had received from the Kadampas (a lineage originating from the Indian pandit Atisha Dipamkara) and the tantric teachings he received from Milarepa. This new tradition became known as the Dakpo Kagyu and eventually gave rise to four main schools with eight sub-schools.

As a foundation, Kagyu practitioners study the sutra teachings as presented in the *Stages of the Path* (lamrim) system. After completing various preliminary practices, practitioners will generally engage in one of two paths. The *Path of Liberation* is focused on developing the view of Mahamudra in accordance with the sutras, while the Path of *Skillful Means* is focused on developing the view of Mahamudra based on the system of practice known as the *Six Dharmas of Naropa*. Often these two paths will be combined, with the sutra Mahamudra being used as a preliminary to the practice of tantric Mahamudra.

Jonang

During the period of the later transmission, Indian Buddhism had matured significantly with a great many highly realised masters. At this time one of the more popular systems of practice was based on the *Kalachakra Tantra*. This uniquely clear teaching was carried into Tibet by no less than seventeen different lineages holders, who in turn propagated the Tantra heavily in Tibet.

The great yogi Khunphang Thukje Tsondru travelled the land acquiring the transmission of each of these lineages and then practised them all extensively in remote places. He eventually settled into a hermitage that he founded in the Jomonang valley. This hermitage would later be known as Jonang Monastery.

On the basis of his profound realisations of the Kalachakra Path, Thukje Tsondru combined all of the pith instructions he had received into a single unified system of practice. Through practising this system, the omniscient Dolpopa Sherab Gyaltsen achieved an especially clear insight into the pristine mind of Buddha-Nature. He went on to communicate these views in what came to be known as the *Middle Way Philosophy of Other-Emptiness* (Zhentong Madhyamaka). This teaching departed significantly from the accepted philosophical presentations of his contemporaries and was therefore difficult for some of them to accept. Overall though, Dolpopa transformed the way many people thought about ultimate reality, guiding them skilfully towards their own sacred truth.

The Jonang tradition specialises in the highest teachings of the Kalachakra System—the completion stage practices known as the Six Vajra Yogas. These powerful yogic methods provide an extremely efficient way for guiding dedicated practitioners to achieving enlightenment within a single lifetime.

Geluk

The Geluk tradition was founded by the enigmatic Je Tsongkhapa, Lobsang Drakpa. Tsongkhapa studied with a wide variety of teachers from different traditions and was particularly focused on reconciling Tibetan thought with the teachings of the great Indian masters. Based on his extensive research into the works of Nagarjuna, Asanga and many others, Tsongkhapa formulated a very structured and clear presentation of what he felt was the most accurate understanding of the Buddha-dharma.

Tsongkhapa made particular emphasis on the importance of the ordained monastic community and on the use of philosophical debate as a method for sharpening the mind. On the basis of these principles, three great monastic universities arose around his teachings: Ganden, Drepung and Sera. These institutions housed tens of thousands of monks, all engaged in an extraordinarily intense process of study and practise.

The Geluk practices are largely focused on the sutra teachings developed by the Indian pandit Atisha Dipamkara. In many ways, Tsongkhapa identified his own tradition as a continuation of the Kadam tradition that existed in the early stages of the Later Transmission period. As such, the Geluk rely on the *Stages of the Path* (lamrim) and *Mind Training* (lojong) lineages as the foundation for establishing the realisation of renunciation, bodhicitta and emptiness. On this basis, practitioners then engage in whichever system of Tantra they have the most connection with. Most Gelukpas will practise either *Guhyasamaja*, *Yamantaka* or *Chakrasamvara*.

Of these six traditions, the first two belong to the Early Transmission, while the remaining four belong to the Later Transmission. While all six are considered Buddhist, the Bön is unique in that they trace their teachings back to a different founder. Although their origins may be different, when closely examining the result of their practices, it is clear that all of these traditions have the capacity to bring a practitioner to enlightenment.

Origin	Transmission	Tradition	Principal Founder
Zhang Zhung	Early	1. Bön	Tonpa Shenrab
India		2. Nyingma	Padmasambhava
	Later	3. Sakya	Khön Konchok Gyalpo
		4. Kagyu	Gampopa
		5. Jonang	Thukje Tsondru
		6. Geluk	Tsongkhapa

Table 14-1: The Six Spiritual Traditions of Tibet.

THE NINE PROGRESSIVE VEHICLES OF THE NYINGMA TRADITION

If we focus on the five traditions which originated in India, we can see they all use a graduated path to guide practitioners towards their spiritual aims. Each vehicle is considered as only a temporary support to helping the practitioner develop the necessary realisations needed to progress along the path. Once those realisations have been actualised, the focus is then shifted to the next vehicle. In this way, a practitioner moves through all of the Buddha's teachings from the foundations up to the most profound esoteric teachings.

Between the Early (Nyingma) and Later (Sarma) Transmissions, different systems of categorising these vehicles were formed. For the most part, these differences revolved around the different types of tantras that were translated during each period. Since the Nyingma tradition has the most extensive presentation, I will begin with this system and then explore how the Sarma traditions differ.

The Causal Vehicles (Sutrayana)

The Nyingma presentation of the Nine Vehicles is split into three groups of three. The first set are generally known as the *Causal Vehicles*, as their focus is on creating the causes for liberation from samsara or enlightenment. They are also known as the *Sutrayana* because they rely on the teachings presented in the sutras. We have already looked at these vehicles in the previous chapters, so the following is merely a summary:

1. **The Shravaka Vehicle:** This vehicle includes the teachings of the Three Baskets which the Buddha taught openly, leading beings to the state of *Shravaka Arhat* or individual liberation.

2. **The Pratyekabuddha Vehicle:** This is the path of the "solitary realisers" through which beings attain the state of *Pratyeka Arhat* by discovering the view and path on their own. They primarily live during dark aeons when no Buddha has appeared to turn the wheel of Dharma.

3. **The Bodhisattva Vehicle:** This vehicle emphasises the Buddha's profound teachings on emptiness and compassion and leads one gradually to the complete realisation of *Buddhahood* over the course of three countless aeons.

Of these three vehicles, the first two are considered part of the *Foundational Vehicle* (Hinayana) while the third is the entry into the *Great Vehicle* (Mahayana).

The Resultant Vehicles (Tantrayana)

The remaining six vehicles are known as the *Resultant Vehicles* as they focus on working to bring awareness of the resultant state into the present moment. These vehicles are also known as the *Tantrayana* because they rely on the teachings presented in the tantras.

All of these paths take the Bodhisattva Vehicle as their foundation. This means that the practitioner is expected to have already developed the enlightened aspiration of bodhicitta, making all of the following paths part of the Mahayana. In fact, the main reason for engaging in the practice of Tantra is to actualise the state of Buddhahood quickly. Rather than spending billions of lifetimes to achieve one's aim, the different classes of tantra provide skilfull means to achieving the same result in as little as one lifetime, allowing the practitioner to be of greatest benefit to sentient beings as swiftly as possible.

That being said, not everyone is capable of making use of the most advanced techniques right away. Therefore there are a number of preliminary classes of Tantra that allow a practitioner to progress gradually towards the higher practices. Before engaging in any of these practices, one must first receive the necessary empowerments from a qualified vajra master. These empowerments function primarily to ripen the practitioner's karmic propensities. In the Nyingma tradition these tantras are split into two groups:

External Tantras

In these vehicles, the practitioner learns to relate to their own enlightened nature through working with a *meditational deity* (yiddam). The deity is a symbolic manifestation of the union between appearances and emptiness. They are considered external in so far as the practitioner relates to the deity as being different from their ordinary self. As the practitioner progresses through these vehicles, she slowly learns to identify with this pure aspect of reality.

The three vehicles in this set are:

4. **Action Tantra Vehicle (kriyatantrayana):** In Action Tantra, we receive the water and crown initiations and generally visualise the deity in front of us, receiving empowerment from that deity. At the level of relative

truth, this deity is viewed as external and superior to ourselves and there is a clear division between its purity and our own impurity. Action Tantra places great emphasis on external actions such as ritual purification, which are carried out in order to receive blessings from the deity.

5. **Performance Tantra Vehicle (charyatantrayana):** Performance Tantra (also known as Upa-Yoga Tantra) is almost identical to Action Tantra, with the implement and name initiations being bestowed during an empowerment in addition to the water and crown initiations. The deity is still seen as external but is now viewed as a friend, equally pure in appearance to ourselves. This practice allows us to generate ourselves as a deity, though the type of blessings we receive is similar to that received in Action Tantra. While practising either Action or Performance Tantra can give us the ability to expand the length of our life in order to assist with our practice, in most other respects the practice is similar in nature to the sutra vehicle.

6. **Yoga Tantra Vehicle (yogatantrayana):** In Yoga Tantra, in addition to the previous four initiations, we also receive the initiations of vajra, bell, name and commitment, followed by the vajra master empowerment and supporting initiations. The practice involves generating ourselves as an enlightened deity, building a connection with this visualised deity during meditation and then dissolving the visualisation back into emptiness. In this way the wisdom aspect of the deity merges with our own mind like water poured into water. The practice of Yoga Tantra involves meditating on the five symbols of enlightenment, represented by the moon, the sun, the seed syllable, the deity's implements and the entire body or form of the deity. In comparison with the sutra path, this vehicle contains many skilful methods such as the aforementioned five points, and the result of enlightenment can be attained in as few as sixteen lifetimes depending on our ability and intelligence.

While the practice of Action Tantra places heavy emphasis on the concepts of purity and cleanliness, these themes are not so essential in Performance and Yoga Tantra. As the practitioner progresses to higher stages, their focus turns more inward and their practice becomes less concerned with external forms of conduct.

Internal Tantras

Throughout the *External Tantras*, the practitioner is working with the two truths as two objects to be meditated on separately. When meditating on the deity and reciting mantras, one is working with relative truth, while meditating on emptiness after the deity has been dissolved, is working with ultimate truth. As the practitioner moves into the *Internal Tantras*, these two modes of meditation are combined into an inseparable union.

As we will discuss in greater detail below, most of these tantras are practised on the basis of two stages. In the *generation stage*, the practitioner works with a meditational deity in order to transform the way in which they perceive different aspects of their personal experience. Then in the *completion stage*, the practitioner works to establish a very powerful state of meditative absorption which can be used to realise the ultimate nature of reality.

Based on the tantras that were translated during the Early Transmission, the Nyingma tradition identifies three types of tantras that belong to this category:

7. **Mahayoga:** Mahayoga focuses mainly on the generation stage. It begins with meditation on emptiness or ultimate Bodhicitta, where all phenomena are realised as empty in their pure nature, and from this arises the realisation of relative Bodhicitta. The union of relative and ultimate Bodhicitta is expressed as a seed syllable, emanating rays of light which purify the entire environment of samsara. The seed syllable then transforms into the pure appearance of the deity: our body is seen as the form of the deity, the outer environment is seen as the mandala or palace of the deity and all experience is perceived as the retinue or activity of the deity. In addition, all sounds are recognised as mantra and all thoughts as primordial wisdom.

8. **Anuyoga:** Anuyoga focuses on the completion stage, employing practices to control the channels, inner winds and essences of the practitioner's subtle body. Visualisation of the deities is generated instantly and all relative phenomena are seen as the mandala of the male Primordial Buddha Samantabhadra, while in their ultimate nature they are perceived as the mandala of the female Primordial Buddha Samantabhadri. The union of these mandalas is the realisation of the mandala of great bliss, in which all phenomena abide equally.

9. **Atiyoga:** Atiyoga, also known as Dzogchen, is the direct realisation of the empty nature of all things. The nature of mind is directly introduced to the student and familiarity with this view is cultivated in meditation and then integrated into every moment of experience. The Dzogchen tantras are divided into the categories of *Mind* (Semdé), *Space* (Longdé) and *Pith Instructions* (Mengakdé). Of the three, the Pith Instructions are considered superior as they contain the two paths known as "break-through" (trekchö) and "leap-over" (tögal). Trekchö, a form of meditation on pristine awareness, must be accomplished first in order to realise the primordial purity of all phenomena. The practice of Tögal then allows us to "see" the naturally manifesting visions of disks, rays of light, deities and Buddha-fields which arise from within the central channel that joins the heart to the eyes.

Taken together, these nine vehicles provide a wide range of practices suitable for all Buddhist practitioners no matter where they are in their spiritual journey. Individually they each represent a specific approach to practice. The difference between these approaches is often illustrated by way of the analogy of a poisonous plant, where the plant symbolises our emotional afflictions.

The first group of people who discover this poisonous plant recognise its danger and so begin to cut it down. Likewise, the Hinayana practitioner sees emotional afflictions as something to be abandoned and so try to distance themselves from them as much as possible. Their main focus is therefore a path of renunciation.

The second group also realises the plant is dangerous, but recognise that it is not enough to simply cut it down, as its remaining roots will sprout once again. They thus throw hot ash or boiling water over the roots to prevent the plant from ever regrowing. This describes the Mahayana approach, where the realisation of emptiness is used as the antidote to ignorance, the root of all emotional afflictions.

And finally the third group of people see the plant from the perspective of a doctor. They know how to transform the poison of the plant into medicine and so for such a person, there is no need to destroy it. Through wisdom it is possible to know exactly how to use the plant in order to bring benefit. Likewise, in the tantric path, the energy of the afflictions can be used skilfully to cut through the obscurations and thereby fuels the process of realisation.

HIGHEST YOGA TANTRA IN ACCORDANCE WITH THE SARMA TRADITIONS

For the most part, the first six vehicles of the Nyingma Tradition are shared in common with the Sarma Traditions. Where they differ is in the classifications used to describe the most advanced practices. While the Nyingma refer to these systems as the Internal Tantras, the Sarma refer to them as *Highest Yoga Tantra*. The actual tantras that comprise these classes are also different based on the teachings that were collected during each period.

In Highest Yoga Tantra, practising the three lower tantras of Action, Performance and Yoga Tantra is insufficient to actually achieve enlightenment. Eventually, all practitioners will need to practice Highest Yoga Tantra as these are the only systems that actually provide the means for generating the full range of rupakaya form bodies of a Buddha.

All of the systems at this level are self-contained paths unto themselves, providing a single practitioner (with the right propensities) all of the methods needed to achieve enlightenment within a single lifetime. The differences in the systems are therefore based on where they place their emphasis in accordance with the specific needs of the practitioners who follow them. As such, we can identify three categories:

1. **Father Tantras:** These tantras emphasise generation stage practices such as mantra recitation and visualisation. There are three types of father tantras based on the afflictive emotion they work with most: desire, anger or ignorance. Examples of father tantras include *Guhyasamaja* and *Yamantaka*.

2. **Mother Tantras:** These tantras emphasise meditation on the sublime emptiness of the completion stage practices. These paths generally focus on the use of desire as a method for generating a concentrated blissful awareness. Examples of this class include tantras like *Chakrasamvara*, *Vajrayogini*, *Hevajra* and *Chandamaharoshana*.

3. **Non-Dual Tantras:** These tantras place equal emphasis on both the skillful means of the generation stage and the profound wisdom of the completion stage. The focus here is on the union of sublime emptiness and great bliss. The main example of this class is the *Kalachakra Tantra*.

Even within Highest Yoga-tantra, it is possible that some practices are more or less profound than others. It is the purity of the transmission lineage, the pith instructions that lineage carries and the capacity of the practitioner, which ultimately determines how profound a practice can be. Within the Sarma Traditions of Tibetan Buddhism, the Kalachakra Tantra is generally considered the most profound and extensive of all the tantras, having been taught directly by Buddha Shakyamuni.

Source	Vehicle	Nyingma	Sarma
Sutra	Hinayana	Shravakayana	
		Pratyekabuddhayana	
	Mahayana	Bodhisattvayana	
Tantra	Vajrayana	Kriya Tantra	
		Charya Tantra	
		Yoga Tantra	
		Maha Yoga	
		Anu Yoga	Highest Yoga Tantra
		Ati Yoga	

Table 14-2: Classifications of paths according to Tibetan Buddhism.

GROUND—BUDDHA NATURE

As we have seen, the mahayana can be split into two primary approaches: sutra and tantra. In sutra, the emphasis is placed on dispelling the misconception of inherent existence through meditation on emptiness. As this ignorance binds us to cyclic existence, by first realising the emptiness of our own self, we are able to break that cycle. Then by realising the emptiness of all phenomena, we are able to clear away the subtle grasping of inherent existence that prevents us from actualising the omniscient state of buddhahood.

When working with this sort of emptiness, we can say that we are taking a negative approach in that we are negating something that does not exist. In tantra, having already established the relative nature of reality (known as the union of appearances and emptiness), we can now shift our focus towards how things actually do exist. This is done through working with the ultimate nature of reality, what is often referred to as Buddha-Nature.

In Highest Yoga Tantra, Buddha-Nature is also known as the mind of clear-light. It is the most fundamental ground upon which all experience arises. There are generally two aspects that characterise this mind:

1. **Appearance Making (Clarity):** The mind is like space, infinite in potential and completely free from all boundaries. Within this space, anything can arise. It is because the mind is empty of inherent existence that it has the capacity to give rise to all kinds of dependent appearances.

2. **Awareness (Luminosity):** The mind is capable of knowing everything which arises in it. This is not a conceptual knowing, but a direct awareness of whatever is appearing. Like the sun, shining its rays of light, awareness is that which illuminates and shapes what is experienced.

From the interplay of these two aspects of Buddha-Nature, all experiences of samsara and nirvana naturally emerge. Unfortunately, because of our ignorance, we are not able to recognise this nature, and therefore we suffer uncontrollably. We get caught into a single way of seeing the world and on this basis we limit our innate potential. Instead of freedom, we create bondage.

Tantra is called the resultant path because it's primary methodology is focused on helping us to recognise the manifest qualities of this Buddha-Nature within our present experience. From the perspective of Buddha-Nature, we already possess everything we need to manifest enlightenment. There is nothing new that needs to be added or produced. Right now, in this very instant, it is possible to connect with our most sacred truth.

The key to doing this is to first recognise that the ultimate truth of our ground as sentient beings is the same ultimate truth of a fully enlightened buddha. Ultimately, there is no difference whatsoever. We can say that this nature has no beginning and no end. There is nothing that can destroy the mind nor cause it to stop and therefore relatively speaking, it is an eternal continuity. While Buddha-Nature itself has no end, cyclic existence does.

Samsara is merely one way in which Buddha-Nature can manifest. Since Buddha-Nature has the capacity to give rise to anything, it also has the capacity to give rise to ignorance. When ignorance arises, samsara is born and suffering follows. Once the mind is trapped in such a state, it cannot escape until the root of ignorance has been removed.

In this way, we can say that Buddha-Nature is like the sky and the afflicted minds of ignorance, attachment and aversion, are like clouds that adventitiously arise within the space of this sky. While the clouds remain, they prevent us from seeing the sky. And yet, no matter what shape the clouds take or whether they are present for a long or a short time, the sky remains untouched and just as pristine as ever. Likewise, our Buddha-Nature remains primordially pure, free from the stains of our afflictions. It is this fact that makes enlightenment possible.

Another way to think of Buddha-Nature is to imagine it like a wish-fulfilling gem buried deep beneath the ground. Above this precious jewel a poor man lives in a disheveled home, his life is harsh and filled with different forms of suffering. One day a wise man with clairvoyant powers notices the jewel buried in the ground. He recognises that the poor man would greatly benefit from having access to this jewel and so he tells him to dig into the ground beneath his home. The poor man starts to dig through the dirt and stones and upon uncovering a cache of silver, he is overjoyed at his good fortune. But the wise man tells him, "Keep digging! Do not be satisfied with stones that look like silver." And so the poor man continues to dig. Soon he comes to a cache of gold, and again the wise man tells him, "Keep digging! Do not be satisfied with stones that look like gold." Finally, the poor man clears away the final clumps of dirt and is dazzled by the brilliance of the light emanating from the wish-fulfilling gem. In this moment, all of the man's hardships are over.

In the same way, our Buddha-Nature is buried deep within the many layers of our gross and subtle obscurations and through practising the Dharma we are able to dig down through these layers. Along the way we may encounter many different types of concepts. There are those like silver which act as antidotes to our afflicted states of mind, but they are like band-aids that are unable to bring us lasting freedom. Then there are the concepts like gold which help us to recognise the empty nature of our imputed world, but these ideas show us only one aspect of our true nature. Eventually, we must move beyond all of these concepts and rest our awareness in the sublime emptiness that is filled with all possibilities. Only then are we be able to manifest our greatest potential, free from all limitations.

Clearly Distinguishing Ultimate Truth

From this basic premise, we can begin to distinguish a few key concepts that will help us to understand how the tantric path works to bring about enlightenment. These concepts are most clearly presented within the sutras of the Third Turning and the Tantras. For this reason, they represent the most definitive understanding of the Buddha's teachings on ultimate truth.

Two Types of Results

When we say the ground is the same as the result, we need to remember that we are speaking from the perspective of ultimate truth. Ultimately the Buddha-Nature that exists at the time of the ground is the same Buddha-Nature that exists at the time of the result. So in this way they are the same. This does not mean however, that their manifestation is also the same. In general, we can speak of two types of results that can be experienced:

1. **Separative Results:** These are the inherent qualities of our Buddha-Nature that naturally manifest when the afflicted states of mind are removed. We do not have to do anything to create these qualities as they are already present within our ultimate nature. An example of a separative result is the omniscient mind that is capable of knowing all phenomena directly.

2. **Produced Results:** These are the qualities that are generated by conditioning our Buddha-Nature through the practise of Dharma. What we are effectively doing is creating the conditions in which ignorance can no longer arise and therefore preventing the manifestation of samsara. An example of a produced result is the wisdom that realises the emptiness of inherent existence.

Two Types of Lineage

On the basis of our understanding of these two types of results, the question arises whether we all have the capacity to actualise these different qualities? When we look at the potential of different people, we can identify two main lineages (or families) to which we all belong:

1. **Natural Lineage:** All sentient beings, regardless of shape or size, belong to the same family in the sense that we all equally possess the qualities of Buddha-Nature. Everything which arises in the mind is merely a manifest aspect of that nature and therefore we can think of Buddha-Nature as the common thread which binds it all together. The fact that we all have this nature also means we all have the capacity to achieve enlightenment. No matter where we are born, no matter what we have done, no matter what our present situation may be, we all carry this precious jewel inside us. This is our ultimate truth.

2. **Developmental Lineage:** Because we all belong to the natural lineage, then we also belong to the developmental lineage. This is our basic capacity to train the mind through spiritual practice. Through engaging in different types of activities we are able to remove the impure obscurations and thereby reveal the pure qualities of our natural lineage. This is our relative truth. From this perspective, we can identify three stages of practitioner: sentient beings who experience impure appearances based on adventitious obscurations; bodhisattvas who experience a mixture of impure and pure appearances; and buddhas who experience only pure appearances.

Two Types of Emptiness

As we begin to get a clearer sense for how ultimate truth is distinct from relative truth, we come to realise that while both of these modes of experience are empty, they are not empty in the same way. It is this difference in the type of emptiness that establishes how these two truths are capable of giving rise to the full range of appearances.

1. **Emptiness of Self:** This is the form of emptiness that is so heavily emphasised in the Second Turning. It is the recognition that every dependently arisen phenomenon arises within a relative perspective and is therefore empty of its own entity. When such phenomena are analysed, they cannot be found; everything dissolves and the mind is left with a space-like awareness of a mere absence.

2. **Emptiness of Other:** Through familiarisation with the emptiness of self, a meditator is able to cut through all coarse and subtle layers of conceptuality. Eventually, even the very subtle dualistic concepts like the objective reality of a mere absence or the subjective reality of the mind which is aware of that absence, also dissolve. At this point, it is possible to experience one's own Buddha-Nature in a non-dual, non-conceptual way. This experience however is not just a mere absence but is in fact, an experience filled with pure appearances, arising out of the innate luminosity of the mind. This extremely profound level of reality is completely empty of all conventionalities that limit it to being 'this' or 'that'. For this reason, it is known as the *Emptiness of Other* (as in anything other than itself) or as the *Sublime Emptiness that is Filled with all Possibilities*. Whatever you call it, this is none other than the fully established state of Buddha-Nature.

Two Types of Purity

From the above analysis, we can now see that the ultimate ground of Buddha-Nature can be considered pure in two ways:

1. **Natural Primordial Purity:** Since everything that arises in the mind is arising out of our Buddha-Nature, all phenomena are by nature pure. This means that every impure phenomenon we experience as a sentient being, has a corresponding pure phenomenon that is experienced by an enlightened being. For instance, the five elements we experience as the basis of our external world can be experienced purely as the five female-buddhas. While the five aggregates that make up our body-

mind complex, can be experienced purely as the five male-buddhas. Every aspect of impure reality can therefore be potentially transformed by recognising their primordial purity.

2. **Purity of Adventitious Defilements:** Whether a phenomenon is experienced as impure or pure, depends entirely on the presence of ignorance or any of its derivative afflictive states of mind. Therefore, in order to experience the natural purity of phenomena, we must first remove the obscurations. This form of purity is produced through the practice of a spiritual path. It does not occur naturally and takes effort on the part of the individual.

In summary, the Two Truths should be clearly understood as being distinct. They are not two sides of the same coin. While relative truth is dependently arisen and empty of inherent existence, ultimate truth is fully established by the non-dualistic mind that is free from all conventionalities. By mistaking the empty nature of relative truths as the ultimate truth, you effectively negate ultimate truth because self-emptiness is itself a conventionality and therefore it is empty of itself. With no ultimate truth, you are left with only a relative perspective.

PATH—THE TWO STAGES

So how do we avoid this misconception? Ultimately, we must transcend all concepts and experience this reality through direct experience. For this reason, the Vajra Vehicle focuses primarily on contemplative practices and less on intellectual theories and debates. When the mind is free from conceptual thought, then it is capable of knowing reality as it is. Then from this perspective, the innate purity of our experience is capable of manifesting fully without limitations.

Empowerment

The entryway into Vajrayana is through a process of ripening that is known as "empowerment". An empowerment occurs when a Vajra Master creates the necessary conditions for an individual practitioner to gain some direct insight into their absolute nature. This can be done formally through a specific empowerment ceremony, or informally through direct interaction between a guru and his disciple.

Empowerments serve two main purposes. Firstly, they provide the opportunity for a student to enter into a vajra relationship with a qualified vajra master. This relationship is critical for the student to be able to effectively practice tantra. The basis for establishing such a relationship is through the taking of various vows and commitments.

Secondly, the empowerment provides an experiential foundation for the student to work with. During the actual empowerment ceremony, the student may experience some aspect of their Buddha-Nature. This experience is like seeing the first sliver of the moon at the start of a lunar cycle. Then over time, as the student engages in the practices, more and more of that moon will be revealed, until one day, it becomes fully manifest.

In general, all Highest Yoga Tantras use four empowerments to ripen students: the vase, secret, wisdom and word empowerments. Each empowerment reveals a deeper and more profound aspect of Buddha-Nature, thereby providing students with the basis for engaging in different stages of practise.

Generation Stage

During the empowerment process, a practitioner is introduced to a particular representation of the enlightened universe known as a *mandala*. This mandala is a symbolic representation of the innate purity of all phenomena. Each aspect of this mandala is designed to help the practitioner to focus their attention in order to become more aware of that purity. The primary aim of this phase of practice is to substitute our impure perceptions of reality with pure perceptions. While these pure perceptions are still conceptual in nature, they are in accord with the ultimate nature of reality and therefore function as a bridge for bringing us closer to that reality. The main practice of the generation stage is *deity yoga*, which consists of three aspects:

1. **Clear Appearance:** This is the act of establishing a vivid and stable visualisation of the deity in the mind. The practitioner develops this appearance within the context of the wisdom that understands its empty nature. On the basis of this appearance, the practitioner achieves the state of single-pointed concentration known as shamatha.

2. **Recollecting the Purity:** Every aspect of a deity is embedded with a richness of meaning. By familiarising herself with that meaning, the practitioner is able to simultaneously recollect all of these qualities, thereby generating a great deal of merit.

3. **Divine Pride:** This is the act of developing a strong certainty that one's true nature is the deity. Of the three, this is the most important aspect of generation stage practice. For it is this aspect that helps the practitioner shift from identifying with ordinary appearances and instead identifying with pure appearances.

Completion Stage

Once the practitioner has strengthened their pure perception, it is then possible to engage in the completion stage practices. These powerful yogic methods provide various ways of working with the subtle energetic body of the practitioner in order to produce extremely concentrated states of meditative absorption. This very subtle mind can then be used to familiarise the practitioner with his own Buddha-Nature, thereby cutting through the ignorance of both the afflictive and cognitive obscurations. A person of sharp faculties who has accumulated a great deal of merit in previous lives can use these techniques to achieve Buddhahood in a single human lifetime without needing to rely on any other path. The unique methods of the completion stage are focused on manipulating three aspects of the subtle body:

1. **Channels and Chakras:** Throughout our body, there are spaces through which energy can flow. At a gross level we can speak of the nervous system that supports the movement of electrical impulses. At a subtle level we can speak of three main *channels*: the central channel (avadhuti), the left channel (lalana) and the right channel (rasana). These three channels branch out from specific energy centres known as *chakras*. Together, the channels and chakras provide a method for circulating the subtle energy that supports both conceptual and non-conceptual states of mind.

2. **Winds:** Each day, we engage in roughly 21,600 breaths. These breaths carry with them different kinds of energy that help act as supports for different bodily functions and mental states. Normally these winds are moving through the left and right channels which produces the dualistic mind. If these winds are brought into the central channel, then a non-dualistic mind is produced.

3. **Essences:** At a gross level, the movement of wind drives the circulation of various bodily fluids. By controlling how the winds flow, you control the circulation and thereby are able to direct where subtle energy gathers. This subtle energy is capable of producing an extremely blissful and concentrated awareness that can be used to cut through ignorance and thereby break the chains of samsara.

RESULT—BUDDHAHOOD IN A SINGLE LIFETIME

The Vajra Vehicle is also known as the "Lightning Path" because of its vast range of techniques that can be used to very quickly introduce an individual to their enlightened Buddha-Nature. While the tantric practitioner will progress along the same five paths and bhumis as a sutra practitioner, they will do so at a much faster rate. What happens at each stage of this process will depend on the system of tantra that is being practised. In general though, we can consider the following stages based on the Sarma Traditions:

1. **Path of Accumulation:** The path of accumulation has three levels. At the first level we engage in the four contemplations of body, feelings, mind and phenomena, known as the four applications of mindfulness. From a sutra viewpoint the body is seen as disgusting in order to develop detachment and the realisation of selflessness. In tantra, instead of seeing the body as disgusting, we train in viewing our body and the environment as being completely pure. Contemplating the body therefore means familiarising ourselves with the enlightened form of a deity, while all sounds are the deity's mantra and all thoughts and phenomena are the display of its enlightened mind.

At the second level of the path of accumulation we practise the four perseverances which involve giving up non-virtue and cultivating virtue, yet we perform virtuous actions according to the tantric view of the world, and every action becomes an expression of the five wisdoms or activities of the five Buddha-families. We come to see meditation, post-meditation and the dream state as being equal. This is known as the intermediate stage of the path of accumulation. While in the sutra path there is a strong distinction between good and bad, in tantra we train to live in a "pure world" at all times.

On the great level of the path of accumulation, deep concentration brings about fast progress and we achieve refined states of concentration based on aspiration, mind, effort and analysis, known as the four bases for miraculous powers. At this level we achieve a heightened sense of clarity and bliss and may also develop the capacity to accomplish many siddhis or magical powers. Even though we have not yet entered the path of seeing, in tantra we meditate on emptiness by visualising the ultimate truth rather than trying to understand the conventional world in an analytical way, as in the sutra path. This allows us to identify with the qualities of a particular deity and perform actions as if we were that deity.

2. **Path of Preparation:** In the first two stages of the path of preparation we learn to experience peace and bliss by practising the generation and completion stage using five faculties: faith, effort, mindfulness, concentration and wisdom. We continue practising until we attain mastery of the physical body and the subtle movement of mind. At this stage we have not developed a true enlightened form but we are able to manifest ourselves in a subtle form body in accordance with the deity being practised. With such a body, we have the special ability to experience states of mind such as the twenty-four Dakini Realms and we are also able to practise with human and non-human beings to gain three of the four joys, when the winds dissolve into the central channel and enter the crown, throat and heart chakras. At this stage the eighty naturally arising afflictions are removed as the states of mind corresponding to aversion, desire and ignorance dissolve, although their propensities still remain.

We then enter the third stage of the path of preparation, during which we practise the union of consorts (either physical or visualised) with an empty and blissful mind during both the meditation and post-meditation stages. By continuing this practice we may develop five miraculous powers based on the five faculties, such as the ability to see distant objects with extraordinary clarity or clairvoyance. We also experience the first two of the three levels of absorptions known as white appearance, red increase and black attainment. These correspond to the final stages of dissolution at the moment of death and the vanishing of states of mind associated with anger, desire and ignorance.

If you focus on worldly attainments you may potentially develop the five miraculous powers and eight siddhis: the ability to make pills and eye lotion to enhance vision, travelling underground, the magical sword, swift footedness, invisibility, preventing death and healing sickness. You can thus control the five elements and perform other magical feats. However, focusing on worldly accomplishments will delay the attainment of enlightened qualities and thus the attainment of full enlightenment in one lifetime, although you can extend your lifespan through these worldly siddhis.

3. **Path of Insight:** When we practise the final level of the path of preparation we eliminate the eighty naturally arising afflictions and experience two of the three absorptions, white appearance and red increase. When we accomplish the final worldly attainment we enter the path of insight and experience the third absorption, black attainment, which leads directly to the experience of the primordial mind of clear light. In this absorption we master the two stages of practise and experience our sacred truth directly for the first time. We eliminate all propensities for the eighty naturally arising afflictions and receive initiations from emanations of the Buddhas. From this stage on we practise the seven factors of enlightenment with non-dualistic wisdom: enlightened mindfulness, investigation, effort, joy, alert ease, contemplation and equanimity.

4. **Path of Habituation:** Having eliminated the eighty naturally arising afflictions, we practise the union of the generation and completion processes. We always live the right way and uphold the right view, actions and realisations, bringing benefit to everyone we encounter. This path is divided into nine stages which are made up of three levels in each of the three absorptions of appearance, increase and attainment. These stages are similar to the Bodhisattva bhumis, yet in the tantric path there is less difference between the experience during meditation and the post-meditation period, and there are also minor differences in the methods used to eliminate innate obscurations.

5. **Path of No More Learning:** Continually eliminating the innate obscurations and their propensities, as described above, will lead to the state of Vajradhara. This is known as the path of no more learning and is the same as complete enlightenment or Buddhahood. There is now nothing left to be learned.

The Four Kayas of Vajradhara

As the causal approach of the Bodhisattva Vehicle and the resultant approach of the Vajra Vehicle are both part of the Mahayana, both have the capacity to produce the result of Buddhahood. What is different is the degree of subtlety they use to describe this state and the terms they use to do so.

From the perspective of tantra, the ultimate nature of a buddha is referred to as Vajradhara. Therefore in these systems you will often see Buddhahood referred to as the state of Vajradhara. This state is none other than the mind abiding inseparably within a direct realisation of its own Buddha-Nature.

This state can be described in different ways by focusing on different aspects. For instance, when we look at the ultimate and relative aspects of Buddha-Nature we can speak of two bodies: dharmakaya and rupakaya. Then, when we consider the nature of the various rupakaya forms we can speak of three, five or hundreds of different aspects. The main thing to remember though is that all of these are referring back to the primordial ground of Buddha-Nature.

While the relative manifestation of the Buddha mind is infinite, none of these manifestations are anything other than the ultimate truth.

That being said, in the Kalachakra system, four aspects are often emphasised:

1. **Essence Body (svabhavikakaya):** The essential nature of the buddha is the two-fold purity of Buddha-Nature. This is the natural purity of the basic space of reality and the produced purity of being free of adventitious defilements. It is this essence that manifests continually in the aspects of the other bodies.

2. **Wisdom Truth Body (dharmakaya):** This is the aspect of the enlightened mind which abides in a perpetual state of awareness of reality as it is (the essence body). It is completely free from all obscurations, free from the experience of afflictive states of mind and free from the cognitive obscurations that prevent omniscience. As such, the dharmakaya is capable of knowing all phenomena directly and without distortion.

3. **Enjoyment Body (sambhogakaya):** While the Buddha's mind abides in non-dual awareness of reality, he manifests in the minds of others based on their individual propensities. For highly realised bodhisattvas, the Buddha manifests as the sambhogakaya enjoyment body. This extremely subtle form is beyond dualistic grasping and is therefore able to manifest in an infinite number of possibilities.

4. **Emanation Body (nirmanakaya):** For everyone else, the Buddha manifests as what are known as emanation bodies. These forms are like the moon reflecting in an infinite number of pools of water. The shape these forms take is entirely dependent on the minds of the beings that perceive them. The historical Buddha Shakyamuni is an example of a *Supreme Emanation Body*, a particularly pure form that manifested 2,500 years ago for a set of disciples living in ancient India. In Vajrayana practice, the guru is considered to be an especially precious emanation body in that he is the primary method through which the dharma is communicated to sentient beings.

REVIEW OF KEY POINTS

- The Vajrayana represents the culmination of the Buddha's teachings as presented in both the sutras and tantras. It took many centuries before these esoteric teachings were more widely propagated in India. For the most part they remained secret, passed down as oral instructions from guru to disciple.

- The systematisation of these teachings occurred in great monastic universities like Nalanda and Vikramashila. These were the primary sources for the style of Buddhism that was later imported into Tibet.

- Tibetan Buddhism can be divided into two main periods based on the influx of Buddhist teachings into the country. There was the Early (nyingma) Transmission and the Later (sarma) Transmission.

- Based on the teachings collected during these two periods, six spiritual traditions arose in Tibet: Bön, Nyingma, Sakya, Kagyu, Jonang and Geluk.

- These traditions all promote a gradual path structure that integrates the teachings from the Foundational Vehicle and the Great Vehicle. According to the Nyingma tradition, there are three causal vehicles (shravakayana, pratyekabuddhayana, and bodhisattvayana), and six resultant vehicles. Of the resultant vehicles, there are three external tantras (kriyatantra, charyatantra and yogatantra), and three internal tantras (mahayoga, anuyoga and atiyoga).

- The Sarma traditions rely on Highest Yoga Tantra instead of the three internal tantras of the Nyingma. These tantras can be grouped into father, mother and non-dual classes.

- The ground of tantra is based on developing an understanding of the ultimate ground of all phenomena known as Buddha-Nature. This term refers to the capacity of the mind to produce appearances and its capacity to be aware of those appearances.

- There are two types of results that can be identified in relation to Buddha-Nature: separative results and produced results. Separative results are the inherent qualities of the mind, while produced results are the qualities that arise based on conditioning the mind through practise.

- All beings belong to two lineages: the natural lineage represents the fact that we all possess Buddha-Nature, meaning we all have the potential to manifest enlightenment; and the developmental lineage which represents our shared capacity to remove obscurations through training.

- There are two types of emptiness that correspond to the two levels of reality: all relative truths are empty of an inherently existing self (self-empty); while all ultimate truths are empty of relative conventionalities (other-empty).

- The ultimate truth is pure in two ways: the natural primordial purity of Buddha-Nature that is never altered by adventitious obscurations and the purity of when adventitious obscurations are removed through spiritual practice.

- The gateway to Vajrayana practice is through receiving empowerment from a qualified vajra master.

- After receiving empowerment, a tantric practitioner will engage first in the generation stage and then in the completion stage practices.

- Generation stage practice focuses on visualisation practices known as deity yoga which help the practitioner establish pure perception of their experiences. There are three aspects to this practice: clear appearance, recollecting purity and divine pride.

- Completion stage practices work with the subtle energies of the body in order to establish a non-conceptual and non-dualistic state of mind that can be used to abide in one's Buddha-Nature. This subtle body is comprised of channels, winds and essences.

- When a practitioner achieves the path of no more learning she actualises the state of Vajradhara. This state is characterised by four aspects of Buddha-Nature: the essence body (svabhavikakaya), the truth body (dharmakaya), the enjoyment body (sambhogakaya) and the emanation body (nirmanakaya).

Appendices

The Fifty-One Mental Factors

The classification of Fifty-One Mental Factors is derived from the presentation of Asanga in his *Abhidharmasamuccaya*. This text forms one of the key sources of the Mahayana Abhidharma literature, providing detailed information about the Buddhist path in general and a framework for Buddhist psychology in particular.

It should be noted that the following classification is not intended for amassing purely intellectual knowledge. Instead, the descriptions are designed to provide you with enough information to be able to identify each mental state during daily experience. Developing a greater awareness of these states, allows you to skillfully work with your mind in order to reduce the destructive states of mind and to cultivate the constructive ones.

To this end, I recommend you use the following exercise to slowly work through each mental state:

Exercise — Getting to Know Your Mind

- *In a relaxed posture, establish a neutral state of mind through the practice of mindfulness of breathing.*

- *Select a mental factor to investigate. First read through its description so the characteristics of this state are fresh in your mind. Observe your present mind to see if you can experience the mental factor being described. Even if the mental factor is not naturally present, imagine what it would be like if it arose right now.*

- *Once you have a general sense for what the mental factor feels like, spend some time scanning through your memories to identify examples of when this state has arisen before. Work through multiple scenarios to get a sense for the dynamics of this state of mind.*

- *Now consider the intensity of the mental factor. How does it manifest when the mental factor is strong? How does it manifest when it is weak? Identify a few examples to give you a sense for the range of experiences.*

- *Now consider the effect this mental factor has on your mind. Is it something that you would like to strengthen or would you prefer to be without it? Think of a few ways you could work with this factor.*

- *Rest in any insights that may arise.*

FIVE OMNIPRESENT MENTAL FACTORS

1. **Sensation (tshor-ba):** Sensation provides the basis, and is absolutely necessary, for the mind to experience an object with the six senses (including the mental consciousness). When a sense consciousness perceives an object through a sense organ, then a sensation arises. It is not only the gross feeling which everyone recognises but includes the more subtle sensation which pervades every perception. This quality of sensation is inherent in every mental state and comprises all immediate associations with the object whether they are pleasant, unpleasant or neutral, taking place within a nanosecond. The main point to understand is that any type of consciousness that is arising, in every instant of experience, contains an element of sensation. Every living being possesses this type of sensation whether they are an ordinary being or an Arya being.

2. **Discrimination ('du-shes):** Discrimination is when our sense field takes an uncommon characteristic of an object or an outstanding feature of an object and ascribes conventional significance to it. It doesn't label or name the object but discriminates it as one thing rather than another. For example, distinguishing light from dark, or distinguishing a table from the background; no words are required. This is all happening immediately, simultaneously and constantly with everything we are

experiencing. Without distinguishing the mind could not link the object with further mental processes.

3. **Intention (sems-pa):** This is the conscious and spontaneous urge that causes the mind to engage with and experience objects, or a conscious aim that guides action. Without intention, mind could not direct its attention towards an object. All mental activity has intention. Here we are referring to all types of intention including that which arises every split second which may or may not necessarily create karma. This also includes the principal intention which generates all wholesome or unwholesome karma.

4. **Contact (reg-pa):** Contact is how we connect with an object. It occurs with the meeting of three factors: the preceding moment of consciousness (which could be any of the consciousnesses), the object, and the sense faculty with its associated consciousnesses. Without contact, mind could not encounter the object and establish a relationship or feeling with it. It differentiates that an object of cognition is pleasant, unpleasant, or neutral, providing the foundation for experiencing it with a feeling of happiness, unhappiness, or indifference.

5. **Mental Engagement (yid la byed-pa):** Mental engagement is the penetration of consciousness onto an object through paying some level of attention to it. Any type of consciousness, no matter how briefly it arises, is always engaged with a particular object. Attention is present in every split second for all beings, and without it, the mind could not remain fixed on an object experienced by any of the six senses; there would be no stability.

THE FIVE OBJECT-DETERMINING FACTORS

1. **Aspiration ('dun-pa):** Aspiration is concerned with the desire or the intent to achieve or obtain something, whether it is worthwhile or not. Aspiration acts as the basis for effort and produces diligence.

2. **Belief (mos-pa):** Belief is the stable holding of a specific object or subject to be as it is; to have a firm conviction that it is this and not that. Perhaps there is an obvious proof that what is believed is actually true, or there

may be much evidence that it is so, either through direct experience, logical reasoning or scriptural reference. One may also assume or believe "blindly" without any evidence. In each of these cases, the belief arises in direct relationship to the object or subject.

3. **Mindfulness (dran-pa):** Mindfulness can be referred to as a type of "mental glue" which holds an object in focus, keeping it clear in the mind, as if one is conjuring up an image through referring to it in conversation. This can be over a long or short period of time, and the object may include the present moment. Mindfulness is achieved by cultivating awareness of one's thoughts, actions and motivations.

4. **Concentration (ting nge-'dzin):** Concentration means that one focuses the mind single-pointedly in one direction on a single object or a topic of investigation, without any distraction. This is a state of undistracted focus, just like twisting cotton to a fine point in order to thread it through the eye of a needle.

5. **Wisdom (shes-rab):** Wisdom is the antidote to doubt. It is a discriminating awareness that adds a level of decisiveness to distinguishing an object of cognition, knowing the reality of an object regardless of what it is. Comprehending that all of conventional existence is impermanent on a subtle level is an example of wisdom. Real wisdom always leads to peace and tranquillity, as it teaches us that everything is interdependent and naturally gives us insight into what is best for oneself and others. This is very different to some kinds of knowledge which can be harmful and can lead to great suffering, such as knowing how to design weapons. Of course the knowledge itself is not harmful, but it is not grounded in true wisdom.

SIX ROOT MENTAL AFFLICTIONS

1. **Attachment ('dod-chags):** Attachment is when we cling or hold onto an object too dearly, exaggerating its desirable qualities and finding it very difficult to let go, regardless of what it is. Just as oil on our clothes is very difficult to remove, so too is attachment.

2. **Aversion (khong-khro):** Aversion is the perception of an object as being unpleasant, at times exaggerating its undesirable qualities, no matter if it is good or bad. Any living being who has aversion harbours a dislike for a particular object.

3. **Ignorance of Truth (ma-rig-pa):** Ignorance is a lack of understanding the truth of cause and effect and the truth of interdependent existence. Ultimately it means failing to realise our enlightened nature. It is likened to a poor person unknowingly living in a house that sits on top of a goldmine.

4. **Pride (nga-rgyal):** Pride is the distinction between self and others that arises due to the misconception of an inherently existing self, which leads to a lack of respect and overconfidence. This leads to considering oneself to be greater or lesser than another.

5. **Wrong View (lta-ba):** Wrong view is the holding of a fixed and incorrect idea of what is being examined. It includes the extreme views of eternalism and nihilism. Eternalism holds the idea that something exists permanently, such as a creator God, which is the source of everything. Nihilism is the view that denies the existence of subtle phenomena such as a creator or nirvana, and either rejects or fails to investigate the idea of life beyond death. It also lacks an accurate understanding of causes and consequences. From a Buddhist perspective, both of these extreme views lack fully developed logical investigation and therefore can be defeated when subject to rigorous rational reasoning.

6. **Afflicted Doubt (the-tshoms):** Afflicted Doubt is a very negative state. People often think that doubt is not such a serious affliction, however, it is impossible to reach enlightenment with doubt in our minds. To achieve anything, even in our normal lives, we must have confidence that we can accomplish it. If we act with hesitation then our actions will be weak and we will eventually give up. Even performing small actions with misgivings will render them weaker and less stable. The doubt we are talking about here leads us away from wisdom or keeps us in an unhelpful, continuous state of uncertainty; this is different from the type of intelligent doubt which leads us towards wisdom.

TWENTY DERIVATIVE MENTAL AFFLICTIONS

Derived from Aversion

1. **Fury (khro-ba):** This is different from anger or hatred because it is a fleeting reaction to cause immediate harm, but it is not sustained.

2. **Resentment (khon du 'dzin-pa):** Holding a grudge and clinging to an intention to return harm that has been done. Not wanting to forgive.

3. **Hostility ('tshig-pa):** A wish to cause harm, developed from fury or anger.

4. **Harmfulness (rnam-par 'tshe-ba):** A lack of warmth and caring towards oneself and others. It is the wish to cause mischief or harm to other people or oneself and includes taking pleasure in others' suffering. It is the opposite of love and compassion.

Derived from Attachment

5. **Miserliness (ser-sna):** To hold on tightly to one's possessions, not wanting to give them up or share them with others.

6. **Excitement (rgod-pa):** A flightiness of the mind toward a desired object. It is different from distraction as our attention flies from its object to instead recollect or think about something attractive that we have previously experienced.

7. **Self-infatuation (rgyas-pa):** To possess a vain attitude and smugness due to attachment toward something one has, such as one's wealth, youthfulness or children. It is a type of excitement which is distinct from pride and arrogance.

Derived from Aversion and Attachment

8. **Jealousy (phrag-dog):** The inability to bear the success or good fortune of others because of a desire to receive gain and honour for oneself.

Derived from Ignorance

9. **Concealment ('chab-pa):** A wish to conceal any unethical or non-virtuous actions you or anyone with you have committed rather than having true remorse.

10. **Laziness (le-lo):** When the mind does not engage in something constructive or fails to take delight in virtuous deeds due to an attachment to temporary pleasures and frivolous activities such as sleeping. It is the opposite of diligence.

11. **Lethargy (rmugs-pa):** A heaviness of the mind and body making the mind unclear and dull.

12. **Lack of Faith (ma dad-pa):** To lack trust in oneself or in any phenomenon which exists on a subtle level. It also refers to lack of interest in what is true and virtuous or the good qualities of others, which is a support for laziness.

13. **Forgetfulness (brjed ngas-pa):** Causes us to lose our object of focus and not clearly remember virtuous acts. It occurs when one's mindfulness is clouded by disturbing emotions and supports a state of distraction and so is more than "just forgetting".

14. **Heedlessness (bag-med):** A careless, indifferent mind that wishes to act freely in an unrestrained manner without cultivating virtue. The intentional seeking of mental distraction such as daydreaming. This is the opposite of conscientiousness.

Derived from Attachment and Ignorance

15. **Deceit (sgyu):** To deceive others by pretending to possess virtuous qualities you do not have in order to receive gain and honour.

16. **Hypocrisy (gYo):** A deceitful attitude motivated by a desire for gain or honour, that involves finding a way to conceal one's faults, pretending to possess qualities one does not have. It is slightly different from concealment which is the wish to hide something, while hypocrisy involves finding a way to hide it.

Derived from Aversion, Attachment and Ignorance

17. **Lack of Conscience (khrel med-pa):** Not abandoning negative actions even though they may be harmful to others. Failing to be considerate of other people.

18. **Shamelessness (ngo-tsha med-pa):** Failing to avoid committing immoral deeds without caring how these actions reflect on oneself. Having a lack of self respect.

19. **Non-introspection (shes-bzhin ma-yin):** When the mind is not fully aware or alert to the actions of body, speech and mind and does not take steps to prevent improper behaviour.

20. **Distraction (rnam-pa gYeng-ba):** A mental wandering toward an object, causing the inability to stay focused on a virtuous object. This is different from excitement because it is not necessarily toward an attractive object; distraction could be toward any object.

THE ELEVEN VIRTUOUS FACTORS

1. **Faith (dad-pa):** To trust, believe or be devoted to what is true and virtuous. This includes being interested in or admiring such things as hidden phenomena or the wholesome qualities of others. Faith that is generated through merely listening is considered unstable, whereas faith based on wisdom gained through examination and analysis of one's own experience is unshakeable and cannot be lost.

2. **Moral shame (ngo-tsha):** Is a moral self dignity that respects virtuous qualities and so feels shame and remorse when committing immoral deeds. It provides a basis to refrain from negative actions due to caring how our behaviour will reflect upon ourselves.

3. **Fear of Unwholesomeness (khrel-yod-pa):** Is similar to Moral Shame in that it is the sense to refrain from negative actions, but instead, due to a feeling of embarrassment; caring how our behaviour will reflect on

others, especially holy beings and noble practitioners.

4. **Non-attachment (ma chags-pa):** Not having desire towards worldly existence or worldly concerns and being satisfied with sufficient means for survival, without craving more. This prevents one from engaging in negative actions.

5. **Non-hatred (zhe-sdang med-pa):** The absence of desire to cause harm or hold a hostile attitude towards an object or another living being that causes pain. This prevents one from becoming involved in negative actions.

6. **Non-ignorance (gti-mug med-pa):** To have an understanding and awareness of truth rather than being obscured by the afflictions of delusion and doubt. It is a discriminating awareness that is acquired through reading and listening to the Dharma and contemplating and meditating on its meaning.

7. **Diligence (brtson-'grus):** To enthusiastically and joyfully strive to accomplish virtuous actions. Diligence is the antidote to laziness.

8. **Pliancy of Mind (shin-tu sbyangs-pa):** Is a flexibility of the body and mind to remain engaged in virtuous acts as long as one wishes, without interruption from detrimental physical and mental states such as fidgeting or mental wandering.

9. **Conscientiousness (bag yod):** The earnest application of awareness and care regarding what to adopt and what to abandon. This helps one accomplish mental quiescence.

10. **Equanimity (btang-snyoms):** A clear mind, free from the distraction of disturbing emotions. It allows mental activity to remain effortless and undisturbed by flightiness or dullness.

11. **Non-harmfulness (rnam-par-mi-'tshe-ba):** A compassionate attitude of warmth and caring towards others, understanding their suffering and wishing them to be free from it and its causes. Its function is to avoid causing harm to others.

THE FOUR VARIABLE FACTORS

1. **Sleep (gnyid):** Sleep causes the consciousnesses associated with the five sense doors to withdraw inwardly. If the mind contains virtue before the moment it withdraws then sleep will turn towards virtue, while if it contains unwholesomeness then sleep will turn towards non-virtue. This is why it is called changeable. For Dharma practitioners, the sleep and dream state offer valuable and important opportunities to practise, which we discuss extensively in chapter 24.

2. **Regret ('gyod):** This refers to mental displeasure caused by reflecting on a previous action, leading to a change in your mental state and future karmic potential. If you have done something wrong in the past or in a previous life, this imprints negative karma in your mind-stream, however, genuine regret or remorse will purify your mind-stream and prevent the negative consequence from occurring.

3. **Gross Detection (rtog-pa):** This is the general examination of an object, searching for rough or gross ideas and details. It is changeable because one's view can change through further investigation and the investigation itself has the potential to be of a virtuous or non-virtuous nature and so can be very useful in establishing the right view for one's Dharma practice.

4. **Discernment (dpyod-pa):** This is the more precise analysis of an object, to scrutinize and distinguish specific details and meaning. For example, when proofreading a book, gross detection examines whether all the pages are there, whereas discernment detects the spelling mistakes. The greater your discernment, the more effectively you will be able to change your view or perception, leading to correct motivation and action.

Outline of Book One

Glossary

- A -

ABHIDHARMA: One of the three baskets of the Buddha's teachings, emphasising Buddhist psychology and logic. It contains a description of the universe, the different kind of beings, the steps on the path to enlightenment, mistaken views and so on.

ABHIDHARMAKOSHA: A Buddhist classic written by Vasubandhu; the earliest attempt at a systematic representation of Buddhist philosophy, psychology and cosmology.

ABSOLUTE TRUTH: See ULTIMATE TRUTH.

ACQUIRED OBSCURATIONS: Those intellectually acquired states of mind that come about due to adherence to false belief systems or wrong views, which have influenced one over many lifetimes. These obscurations are overcome during the path of seeing. These are distinct from INNATE OBSCURATIONS, which are overcome on the path of habituation.

ACTION MUDRA: A consort in Highest Yoga-TANTRA who assists in generating great bliss so the practitioner can dissolve the inner winds and realise emptiness. See also CONSORT.

AFFLICTIVE OBSCURATIONS: Syn.: emotional obscurations, defilements, mental afflictions, afflictive emotions. Contaminated mental functions, which are obstacles to LIBERATION and are the causes for SUFFERING. They disturb our mental peace and propel us to act harmfully to others (and ourselves). The root afflictions are: IGNORANCE, desire/ATTACHMENT, anger/hatred/aversion, pride, doubt and wrong views. These also include karmic obscurations (those obscurations which are caused by any type of karma which has not been purified, including positive karma). They are distinct from the more subtle COGNITIVE OBSCURATIONS, and are all abandoned when NIRVANA is attained.

AGGREGATE: Mental or physical collection. See FIVE AGGREGATES.

AKSHOBYA (Skt.): Name of a DEITY. One of the FIVE BUDDHA FAMILIES, representing the consciousness AGGREGATE of all Buddhas and the wisdom of all-encompassing space (Dharmadhatu wisdom).

ALAYA (Skt.): The foundation consciousness, where all karma is 'stored'. This has both pure and impure aspects. See EIGHT CONSCIOUSNESSES.

AMITABHA: Name of a DEITY. One of the FIVE BUDDHA FAMILIES, representing the perception AGGREGATE of all Buddhas and their discriminating wisdom.

AMOGHASIDDHI (Skt.): Name of a DEITY. One of the FIVE BUDDHA FAMILIES, representing the formation AGGREGATE of all Buddhas and their all-accomplishing wisdom.

ANALYTICAL MEDITATION: A meditation method whereby one formulates a question (for example 'is the self permanent?') and focuses upon this until some kind of direct understanding is achieved. See also VIPASHYANA.

ANUTTARAYOGA-TANTRA (Skt.): Highest yoga TANTRA. See FOUR TANTRIC CLASSES. Tantric class that contains the method to transform sexual experience into the spiritual path.

ANUYOGA: Second of the three inner yogas and eighth of the nine vehicles (yanas), according to the classification of the Nyingma school. It emphasises the COMPLETION STAGE, especially meditation on the channels, inner winds and subtle essences.

APPLICATION BODHICITTA: A Bodhicitta held by the Bodhisattva vows (as opposed to ASPIRATION Bodhicitta), which includes the practice of the SIX PERFECTIONS.

ARHAT (Skt.): One who has destroyed the enemy of dualistic ego-grasping/clinging, and thus has accomplished LIBERATION from CYCLIC EXISTENCE, also known as foe destroyer. There are three types of Arhats: SRAVAKA, PRATYEKABUDDHA, BUDDHA (or Bodhisattva Arhat).

ARYA (Skt.): Superior, High One. One who has gained direct meditational experience of EMPTINESS, having reached at least the path of insight, one of the FIVE PATHS. See also ARHAT.

ASPIRATION BODHICITTA: Bodhicitta attained by training the mind with practices such as the FOUR IMMEASURABLES and TONGLEN (as distinct from APPLICATION Bodhicitta).

ASURA (Skt.): Being living in the asura or demigod realm of CYCLIC EXISTENCE, within sight of the GODS.

ATISHA: Also known as Dipamkara, a great Indian scholar who arrived in Tibet in 1042 and caused a major purification of the Buddhism present at that time, during which he founded the Kadampa school.

ATIYOGA: The highest of the three inner yogas and last of the nine vehicles (yanas), according to the Nyingma school. It includes the system of practice known as Dzogchen, the Great Perfection.

ATTACHMENT: Inability to separate from a person or thing, and ultimately leading to SUFFERING, usually exaggerating the good qualities of the object. It is one of the biggest mental afflictions, which prevents the achievement of ENLIGHTENMENT.

AVADHUTI (Skt.): see CENTRAL CHANNEL.

AVALOKITESHVARA (Skt.): 1. Name of a specific DEITY, representing the COMPASSION of all BUDDHAS; Chenrezig in Tib. 2. One of the main disciples of SHAKYAMUNI BUDDHA.

- B -

BARDO (Tib.): Intermediate state of existence, or any period of transition. There are SIX BARDOS altogether: the state of waking, dreaming, meditation, dying, Dharmata (the radiance of enlightenment) and becoming (the time between death and rebirth). Commonly, the term BARDO refers simply to the bardo of becoming.

BELL: An implement used in VAJRAYANA practice, symbolising the body and speech of the BUDDHA as well as the feminine aspect of enlightenment, wisdom and empty form. Together with the VAJRA it symbolises the union of wisdom and method, empty form and immutable bliss or feminine and masculine.

BHAGAVAN (Skt.): An epithet of the Buddha. Someone who has overcome the FOUR MARAS, possesses all good qualities of realisation and is beyond SAMSARA and NIRVANA.

BHUMI (Skt.): Stage. Usually referring to one of the ten stages in Bodhisattva-training (Bodhisattva- bhumi) during the path of habituation, one of the FIVE PATHS which follows on from the path of insight. During each stage one of the TEN PERFECTIONS is emphasised.

BODHICITTA (Skt.): The mind of enlightenment, or heart of enlightened mind. For the sake of others, longing to attain complete enlightenment. The mind dedicated to attain Buddha-hood in order to help all SENTIENT BEINGS. 'Relative Bodhicitta' is either APPLICATION or ASPIRATION Bodhicitta. 'Ultimate Bodhicitta' or 'natural reality Bodhicitta' is the WISDOM motivated by relative Bodhicitta which directly realises EMPTINESS.

BODHISATTVA (Skt., Changchup Sempa in Tib.): A warrior of enlightenment, a being who strives for Buddhahood in order to be of utmost benefit to all SENTIENT BEINGS. 1. In general, someone who has taken the Bodhisattva-vows. 2. More specific, a being who has taken that vow and also has attained spontaneous Bodhicitta.

BODHISATTVA VOWS (or Bodhicitta vows): Holy commitments to benefit oneself and others, which lead to enlightenment, giving specific guidelines on how to develop and maintain Bodhicitta. There are eighteen root bodhisattva and forty-six secondary vows.

BODY MANDALA: In the KALACHAKRA TANTRA, the base MANDALA, surrounded by four huge entrance ways, which contains the SPEECH MANDALA and the central MIND MANDALA.

BRAHMA: In Buddhism Brahma is not considered as an an eternal deity (as in the Hindu tradition) but as the ruler of the gods of the FORM REALM.

BUDDHA (Skt.,Sang-gye in Tib.): Enlightened/Awakened/Omniscient One . One who has purified all obscurations and developed all good qualities and the two kinds of omniscience: knowing the ultimate nature and diversity of all phenomena. 'The Buddha' usually refers to SHAKYAMUNI BUDDHA, yet there are really an infinite number of Buddhas who have attained or will attain enlightenment.

BUDDHA-DHARMA (Skt.): 1. BUDDHA's teachings (the Dharma of transmission) 2. The inner REALISATIONS achieved by practising Buddha's teachings (the Dharma of realisation).

BUDDHAHOOD: Complete enlightenment or omniscience, free from the extremes of both samsara and the individual peace of nirvana, also called non-abiding nirvana.

BUDDHA-NATURE (Tathagathagarba in Skt.): Potential of all SENTIENT BEINGS to become a BUDDHA.

BUDDHISM: Religion, philosophy founded by SHAKYAMUNI BUDDHA. All Buddhist schools agree on the FOUR SEALS.

BUDDHIST: Person who has taken REFUGE in the THREE JEWELS and agrees on the philosophy of the FOUR SEALS.

- C -

CENTRAL CHANNEL (Avadhuti Skt, Uma Tib.): Main energy channel in the body, the central axis of the subtle body. It starts at the forehead in the space between the eyebrows, going backwards under the skull and then down to the level of the navel (or lower). Its exact description varies according to the particular practice.

CHAKRA (Skt.): Wheel, circle. A focal centre where secondary (energy) channels branch out from the CENTRAL CHANNEL.

CHANNEL (Nadi in Skt., Tsa in Tib.): subtle vein in which subtle energy or inner wind circulates. The left and right principal channels run from the nostrils to just below the navel, where they join the CENTRAL CHANNEL.

CHENREZIG (Tib.): See AVALOKITESHVARA.

CHITTAMATRA (Skt.): Mind-only-school, a Buddhist philosophical system which holds that only the mind truly exists. See FOUR TENETS.

CLEAR LIGHT MIND: Very subtle mind which, when manifested, perceives everything as clear, empty space. In it the spontaneous, luminous and knowing aspect of this essential nature of mind.

COGNITIVE OBSCURATIONS: These include all concepts of subject, object and action and other more subtle stains or ideas which prevent one from attaining omniscience, or from seeing the ultimate and relative truth at the same time. For example, one might have an idea that the past, present and future truly exist or that suffering exists and nirvana (the end to suffering) exists; however, these are merely ideas, as in truth past, present and future only exist in relation to each other and suffering is only an idea that exists in relation to nirvana. Similarly, the thought that our own suffering is separate from everyone else's suffering is also an idea, and this is overcome by practising the Bodhisattva path. They are distinct from AFFLICTIVE OBSCURATIONS, which are overcome with the attainment of NIRVANA.

COMMITMENT-BEING (Samayasattva Skt.): Visualised BUDDHA or oneself visualised as a BUDDHA. A WISDOM-BEING (Jnanasattva Skt.) is an actual BUDDHA who is invited to unite with the commitment-being.

COMMITMENTS: Promises and pledges taken when engaging in spiritual practices.

COMPASSION: The wish that others may be free from SUFFERING and its causes.

COMPLETION STAGE: Final stage in the practice of Highest Yoga-tantra using methods that cause the inner winds (Prana in Skt. or Lung in Tib.) of the body to enter, abide and dissolve within the CENTRAL CHANNEL and result in BUDDHAHOOD. In the KALACHAKRA practices, this process is described in six stages.

CONVENTIONAL TRUTH: see RELATIVE TRUTH.

CONSORT (Yum in Tib.): Feminine DEITY represented in union with a male deity (yab). She symbolises wisdom inseparable from skilful means, symbolised by the male. They also symbolise the space of emptiness inseparable from awareness, or the bliss of emptiness inseparable from empty form. In the Kalachakra practice there are FOUR CONSORTS, each having a more subtle level of meaning.

CYCLIC EXISTENCE: The cycle of death and rebirth, taking uncontrolled REBIRTH under the influence of afflictive mental states and karmic imprints. The process arises out of IGNORANCE and is characterised by SUFFERING. See THREE REALMS and SIX REALMS.

- D -

DAKA (Skt.): Male equivalent of DAKINI.

DAKINI (Skt.): Female tantric BUDDHA and women who have achieved direct REALISATION of EMPTINESS with the CLEAR LIGHT MIND. Also the feminine principle, associated with wisdom.

DEFEAT OF A VOW: When the FOUR FACTORS LEADING TO DEFEAT are present and a specific amount of time has passed with no feeling of remorse.

DEGENERATE AGE: A period with the FIVE DEGENERATIONS.

DEITY: The symbolic form of a pure being, manifested from BUDDHA's wisdom. Meditational BUDDHA form or wisdom being. Sometimes this term refers to a wealth deity or DHARMA PROTECTOR.

DEMIGOD: See ASURA.

DEPENDENT NATURE: Syn.: other-powered nature. The existence of things in relation to each other, regardless of our concepts and imputations. They are not truly existent because they depend on causes and conditions, the aggregation of parts or the creation of concepts for their existence.

DEPENDENT ORIGINATION: Doctrine concerning the interrelatedness of phenomena. Closely related to EMPTINESS. See TWELVE LINKS OF DEPENDENT ORIGINATION.

DESIRE REALM: One of the THREE REALMS within CYCLIC EXISTENCE, where beings enjoy the five external sense objects (form, sound, smell, touch and taste) and where the SUFFERING of suffering is experienced. It consists of the SIX REALMS (including the desire gods), and is distinct from the FORM and FORMLESS realms of the gods.

DEVADATTA (Skt.): Name of SHAKYAMUNI BUDDHA'S cousin who saw the BUDDHA as full of faults.

DHARMA (Skt.): Doctrine, law, truth. 1. What prevents SUFFERING; usually referring to BUDDHA-DHARMA. 2. Any objects of knowledge. 3. Religion or religious knowledge. 4. REALISATIONS of the path and the consequent cessation of SUFFERING.

DHAMMAPADA (Pali): most popular collection of sayings of the Buddha in the Pali canon.

DHANYAKATAKA: Location in South India where the BUDDHA is said to have taught the KALACHAKRA TANTRA.

DHARMAKAYA (Skt.): Truth Body of a BUDDHA, the pure, omniscient MIND of a BUDDHA, result of the transformation of the ordinary MIND. Also refers to the EMPTINESS aspect of BUDDHAHOOD. See THREE BUDDHA-BODIES.

DHARMAPALA (Skt.): See DHARMA PROTECTOR.

DHARMA PROTECTOR: Guardian of the BUDDHA's teachings, protecting their transmission from becoming diluted or distorted. 1. Worldly protectors: ordinary GODS, spirits etc., bound by a tantric GURU to protect Buddhism and its practitioners. 2. Non-worldly: manifestations of BUDDHAS or Bodhisattvas in wrathful form who protect practitioners.

DHARMADHATU (Skt.): The all-pervading space or ground for all beings as well as the source of all phenomena. All three kayas of enlightenment manifest from this reality as well as all conventional phenomena. The DHARMAKAYA is the enlightened aspect of DHARMADHATU and the source of all enlightened activity.

DHARMODGATA: Bodhisattva from whom Sadaprarudita received the teachings on transcendent wisdom.

DHYANA (Skt.): see JHANA.

DIVINE PRIDE: Non-deluded pride that regards oneself as a DEITY and one's surroundings and enjoyments as those of the DEITY. It is an antidote to ordinary conceptions.

DOLPOPA SHERAB GYALTSEN (Tib.): (1292 – 1361) Highly accomplished master and a founder of the Jonang tradition as is carried on today, who unified the Shentong Sutra and Kalachakra Tantra lineages.

DOWNFALL: A fault due to transgression of a vow (monastic or other).

DROPS: See SUBTLE ESSENCE.

DZOGCHEN (Tib.): Profound practice of the NYINGMA tradition, also known as the Great Perfection.

- E -

EMANATION BODY: See NIRMANAKAYA.

EMOTIONAL OBSCURATIONS: See AFFLICTIVE OBSCURATIONS.

EMPTINESS: Full expression: 'Emptiness of INHERENT EXISTENCE'. The doctrine that all concepts and phenomena lack INHERENT EXISTENCE. See ULTIMATE TRUTH.

EMPTY-FORM BODY: (or Body of Empty Form) Specific for Kalachakra practice, a non-material 'body' which appears in meditation and is developed into the RUPAKAYA or 'form body' of a Buddha. Sometimes compared to the Rainbow Body of other tantra practices, but these are described as being of subtle matter. The Empty Form Body, however, is a production of mind and is non-material.

EMPOWERMENT (Abhisheka in Skt.): Bestowal of permission and a special potential power to practise a specific part of TANTRA, given by a tantric GURU by means of a ritual, usually involving a pledge to uphold specific tantric commitments.

ENERGY CHANNEL: Veins within the body through which the inner wind (Tib. Lung, Skt. PRANA) flows.

ENJOYMENT BODY: See SAMBHOGAKAYA.

ENLIGHTENMENT: Syn.: Buddhahood, full enlightenment/awakening. Highest level of development, having forever eliminated all OBSCURATIONS and karmic IMPRINTS, and having developed all good qualities and WISDOM to their fullest extent. Enlightenment supersedes individual LIBERATION.

EON: 'Great eon': lifetime of the universe (KALPA (Skt.)). 'Small eon': one twentieth of a great eon.

EQUANIMITY: Unbiasedness/impartiality. State of MIND in which one does not distinguish between friend, enemy and stranger, but not a state of dull indifference.

ETERNALISM: The belief in an eternally existing entity, a soul for instance. One of the TWO EXTREMES. See also NIHILISM.

- F -

FEAST OFFERING (ganachakra in Skt., tsok in Tib.): a ritual in which one blesses, offers and consumes food and drink as wisdom nectar.

FIELD OF MERIT (OR FIELD OF REFUGE): The focus, or object of, one's offering, devotion, prayer, prostrations etc., through which one can perform the necessary accumulations of merit and wisdom. It usually applies to a visualised focus of practice such as the refuge deities, the teacher in Guru Yoga, etc. Directing one's actions towards such an embodiment of the Three Jewels gives them a much greater power.

FORM REALM: State of CYCLIC EXISTENCE where no SUFFERING of suffering is experienced. Beings here have renounced the enjoyment of external sense objects but still have ATTACHMENT to internal form (their own subtle body and MIND).

FORMLESS REALM: Highest states of CYCLIC EXISTENCE. Beings here have renounced form and ATTACHMENT to form pleasures, and exist only within their mindstream. Their MIND is still bound by subtle desire and ATTACHMENT to mental states and ego. See THREE REALMS.

- G -

GANDHARVA (Skt.): Smell-eater. Spirit feeding on smells. Also can refer to beings in the intermediate state.

GELUG(PA) (Tib.): Yellow-hats. Biggest school in Tibetan tradition, founded by TSONG-KHAPA. Its main emphasis is on ethics and sound scholarship prior to serious meditation.

GENERATION STAGE: Stage of practice in Highest Yoga TANTRA, wherein one mentally generates oneself as a DEITY, and one's surroundings as the deity's MANDALA. One meditates on forms, sounds and thoughts as having the nature of deities, mantra and wisdom.

GESHE (Tib.): 1. Degree like 'Doctor of Theology', awarded by the principal monastic colleges of the GELUGPA tradition. 2. Title of some masters of the Old KADAM tradition.

GOD (Deva in Skt.): A being in CYCLIC EXISTENCE, temporarily abiding in a heavenly state as a result of virtuous karma (unlike the Christian God).

GOD REALM: DEVA-realm, 'heaven'. State within CYCLIC EXISTENCE. Some god realms are in the DESIRE REALM, others in the FORM and FORMLESS REALMS. See THREE and SIX REALMS.

GOLDEN AGE OF SHAMBHALA: A period of 1,000 or 1,800 years following the 'defeat of the barbarians' by King Rudra Chakrin, in which the DHARMA and the KALACHAKRA TANTRA will flourish.

GROUND: The basis for the Buddhist view and path, divided into the temporary ground (equivalent to the RELATIVE TRUTH) and ultimate ground (equivalent to the ULTIMATE TRUTH).

GURU (Skt., lama in Tib.): Literally one who is heavy of weight in good qualities. Spiritual teacher/friend/mentor.

GURU YOGA (Skt.): Practice of seeing one's GURU as BUDDHA, or merging one's mind with the teacher's mind.

- H -

HABITUAL TENDENCIES: Habitual patterns of thought, speech or actions created by what one has done in past lives; these remain as subtle imprints even after grosser levels of obscurations have ceased, obstructing the realisation of omniscience. They are the most subtle form of OBSCURATIONS TO OMNISCIENCE or COGNITIVE OBSCURATIONS, and are abandoned during the three pure Bodhisattva bhumis.

HEARER: See SRAVAKA.

HELL REALM: A joyless state or realm within CYCLIC EXISTENCE in which intense SUFFERING is experienced. Here one generally experiences the effects of one's actions rather than creating new causes for future suffering. See SIX REALMS.

HINAYANA (Skt.): Fundamental Vehicle (as opposed to MAHAYANA). Buddhist path leading to individual LIBERATION from CYCLIC EXISTENCE (as SRAVAKA or PRATYEK-ABUDDHA), which forms the basis of all the Buddha's teachings.

HUNDRED-SYLLABLE MANTRA: Mantra of Vajrasattva, representing the purity of all Buddhas and the essence of the hundred families, including the forty-two peaceful and fifty-eight wrathful deities.

- I -

IGNORANCE: Unawareness, lack of recognition of our selfless, enlightened nature. 1. Worldly: Not knowing the principles of KARMA. 2. Trans Worldly: Failing to know or realise EMPTINESS.

IMPUTE: To label/name/designate or give meaning to an object.

IMPUTED NATURE: the concepts, names and labels that we impute onto things, such as 'tree', 'house', 'good' or 'bad'. These terms are merely concepts that we use to describe objects and communicate ideas, having no ultimate existence.

INDESTRUCTIBLE ESSENCE: Most subtle essence, located at the heart, formed from the essence of sperm and egg of the parents. It does not melt until death, when it opens and allows the very subtle mind and wind to take rebirth.

INHERENT EXISTENCE: Syn.: true / objective / ultimate / self-powered / self-sufficient / independent / intrinsic / existence. Existence - from the side of the object; - by the way of the object's own character; - from within the basis of designation; - as its own suchness; - as its own reality; - by way of its own entity. INHERENT EXISTENCE is a misconception, a non-existent quality that we project onto persons and phenomena, and does not exist even conventionally. It describes existence which is independent of: causes and conditions, parts, or the MIND IMPUTING it.

INITIATION: see EMPOWERMENT.

INNATE OBSCURATIONS: Those innate faulty states of mind which have been present since beginningless time, in all beings, and which operate without depending on faulty scripture or reasoning. These are distinct from ACQUIRED OBSCURATIONS.

INNER OFFERING: In Highest Yoga-tantra this offering is produced by mentally transforming ten bodily substances into nectar.

INNER WINDS: See LUNG.

INTERMEDIATE STATE: See BARDO.

- J -

JHANA: Advanced form of concentration MEDITATION, after SHAMATHA has been realised. There are four form jhanas and four formless jhanas, which correspond to experiences in meditation equivalent to the mental state of various beings in the GOD REALMS.

JONANG(PA) (Tib.): Tradition of Tibetan Buddhism which combines study of the SHENTONG MADHYAMIKA view with practice of the SIX KALACHAKRA YOGAS, established by Khunphang Thukje Tsondru.

- K -

KADAM(PA) (Tib.): Tradition of Tibetan Buddhism, started by ATISHA. Before Lama TSONGKHAPA known as 'Old Kadam', afterwards known as GELUGPA.

KAGYU (Tib.): School of Tibetan Buddhism, founded by Marpa Chökyi and Khyungpo Nyaljor (11th century). Meditation and philosophy lineage whose special practice is MAHA-MUDRA.

KALACHAKRA (Skt.): Wheel of Time; name of a specific DEITY of the highest YOGA TANTRA class, forming the basis of the main practice of the Jonang tradition, the Six Kalachakra Yogas. This class of tantra was taught by the Buddha and upheld in the Kingdom of Shambhala, before appearing in India and Tibet around the 10th century. Although the deity is commonly depicted as having twenty-four arms, the Jonang tradition uses the two armed form of KALACHAKRA in the GENERATION STAGE, known as Dukor Lhangkye in Tibetan.

KALAGNI (Skt., Dume in Tib.): In the KALACHAKRA system, Kalagni is a 'planet' or heavenly body with spiritual significance, represented by a yellow disc on which KALACHAKRA stands. It is associated with the south node of the moon, solar eclipses and 'the head of the dragon' in Chinese astrology.

KALYANAMITRA (Gewi Shinyen in Tib.): A friend that leads you to the Dharma; someone from an authentic lineage who teaches you the path to enlightenment in order to liberate you. See also GURU.

KALAPA: Capital of the country of SHAMBHALA.

KALKI (Skt.): See KULIKA

KALPA (Skt.): Lifetime of a universe, also known as a great aeon.

KANGYUR (Tib.): Collection of all translated SUTRAS and TANTRAS from Sanskrit into Tibetan. See also: TENGYUR.

KARMA (Skt.): Action. Intentional action, impulse. Also; the IMPRINT which the action leaves on one's mind-stream and the consequences therein. 'The law of karma': the doctrine holding that all experiences are results of IMPRINTS on our mind-stream of previous actions; virtuous actions lead to happiness, NEGATIVE ACTIONS to SUFFERING and unpleasant states.

KAYA (Skt.): Body of a BUDDHA. See also THREE BUDDHA-BODIES.

KRIYAYOGA-TANTRA (Skt.): First of FOUR TANTRIC CLASSES, which emphasises purification and sees the deity as superior to oneself.

KULIKA (Skt., Rigden in Tib.): 'Holder of the Castes' or Shambhala's Knowledge Holder. Titles of the 8th to the 24th Kings of SHAMBHALA.

- L -

LAGHUTANTRA (Skt.): the 'Kalachakra Laghutantra'; this is an abridged form of the original text; the Kalachakra MULATANTRA which is only existent in Shambhala. The Laghutantra was written by SHAMBHALA King MANJUSHRIKIRTI (or Manjushri Yashas). This text fulfills the function of root tantra for us, as the Mulatantra is not available.

LALANA (Skt.,roma in Tib): Left main channel of the subtle body.

LAMA (Tib.): Literally 'one who is above'. Synonym for GURU.

LAM RIM (Tib.): Lamp on the Path. The stages of the Path to ENLIGHTENMENT. Systematic presentation of all BUDDHA's teachings, first presented in this form by ATISHA and presently used mainly in the GELUG school.

LIBERATION (individual liberation): State after removing the AFFLICTIVE OBSCURATIONS and KARMA which cause uncontrolled REBIRTH in CYCLIC EXISTENCE.

LINEAGE: The unbroken line of Buddhist teachers who have realised the teachings (known as lineage holders) through which the DHARMA is transmitted, going back to the time of the BUDDHA. An authentic unbroken lineage is essential in order to preserve the purity of the DHARMA.

LOVE: The wish that beings have happiness and its causes.

LUNG (Tib.): Wind, energy, prana (Skt.). 1. Subtle (life-) wind/energy. In tantra these winds are the vehicle of consciousness, which cause the subtle CLEAR LIGHT MIND to arise when they dissolve in the central channel. 2. Disease, energy disturbance/imbalance in the body. 3. Oral transmission of a DHARMA text.

- M -

MADHYAMIKA (Skt.): Middle-way school. See FOUR TENETS. MAHAMUDRA (Skt.): Great Seal. 1. According to SUTRA: Profound view of EMPTINESS. 2. According to TANTRA: the union of great bliss and EMPTINESS.

MAHAYANA (Skt.): 'Great vehicle' (Maha = great, Yana = vehicle. (as opposed to the HINAYANA). Buddhist path, which leads to Buddhahood, aiming for complete Buddhahood for the sake of all beings. Also called 'Bodhisattva-yana'. It includes SUTRAYANA and TANTRAYANA.

MAITREYA: Loving-One. Name of the next coming BUDDHA, also both teacher and main disciple of SHAKYAMUNI BUDDHA.

MANDALA (Skt.): Centre and circumference, circle or sphere. 1. Symbolic representation of a meditation visualisation, usually in the form of a palace with one or more DEITIES present. 2. Symbolic representation of the universe (see MANDALA OFFERING).

MANDALA OFFERING: Mentally transforming the universe into a PURE REALM and offering it. 'Inner mandala offering': offering one's body, wealth, happiness etc.

MANJUSHRI (Skt.): One of the main disciples of the BUDDHA and one of the EIGHT BODHISATTVAS. Name of DEITY, representing wisdom of all BUDDHAS.

MANJUSHRIKIRTI (Also Manjushri Yashas): The 8th King of SHAMBHALA (first KULIKA- king), who composed the condensed KALACHAKRA TANTRA.

MANTRA (Skt.): 'Tool for thinking'. 1. Prescribed syllables (in Skt.) to protect the mind (from AFFLICTIONS). They express the essence of specific energies. Recitation of mantras is always done with specific visualisations. 2. Often, Mantra is used as a synonym for VAJRA or TANTRA.

MARA (Skt.): Demon. Anything which interrupts the attainment of LIBERATION or ENLIGHTENMENT. See: FOUR MARAS.

MARKS AND SIGNS: The 32 Major Marks and 80 Minor Signs of a BUDDHA - golden skin, webbed fingers & toes etc.

MEDITATION (gom in Tib.): Habituating, familiarising. Habituating ourselves to positive and realistic states of mind, especially the discovery of the enlightened mind. It can be divided into resting meditation (also known as SHAMATHA, tranquillity meditation or calm abiding) and ANALYTICAL MEDITATION.

MERIT: Virtue, positive potential, merit. Imprints on the mind-stream of positive actions, leading to future happiness. The accumulation of merit and wisdom are the two essential aspects of the path to enlightenment.

MIGRATOR: (Or transmigrator) See SENTIENT BEING.

MILAREPA (Tib.): Great Tibetan practitioner (1040-1123), famed for his attainment of Buddhahood in one lifetime and the hardships he endured.

MIND: 'That which is clear and knowing', mind-stream. Non-physical phenomenon which perceives, thinks, recognises, experiences and emotionally reacts to the environment. 1. Mental faculties (Tib.: thugs) 2. Ways of being conscious, conscious phenomena (Tib.: shespa).

MIND MANDALA: In the KALACHAKRA TANTRA, the central, uppermost levels of the Mandala, containing the central Great Bliss Mandala, the Exalted Wisdom Mandala and the surrounding Mind Mandala.

MOUNT MERU: Huge mountain in the centre of the universe according to Tibetan cosmology; frequently used in visualisation practice. MUDRA (Skt.): Seal. 1. Tantric hand gesture, 2. Tantric consort.

MULATANTRA (Skt.): or better: 'Kalachakra Mulatantra'; this is the original KALACHAKRA root tantra. An abridged commentary to this was composed by Shambhala King SUCHANDRA, but both texts are not available outside Shambala. The two basic texts we use are the Lughatantra (which fulfills the function of root tantra) by MANJUSHRIKIRTI, and the commentary the 'VIMALAPRABHA' by Pundarika.

MUNCHUN (Tib.): A thick fabric used to cover the eyes while allowing for eye movements, used as a substitute for a dark room by practitioners engaging in dark room meditation practice.

- N -

NADI (Skt.): See ENERGY CHANNEL.

NAGA (Skt.): Type of spirit living mainly in rivers, oceans or lakes, but can live anywhere. They are generally invisible. Usually depicted with a serpent-like body.

NAGARJUNA (Skt.): Great Indian Buddhist Master who revived the MAHAYANA in the 1st century AD, after its virtual disappearance, by bringing to light the Perfection of Wisdom SUTRAS.

NAMCU (Tib.): Tenfold powerful one: the Kalachakra symbol or 'logo' composed of ten mantra- symbols.

NEGATIVE ACTION: non-virtue, destructive action, black karmic imprint. Action which leaves an imprint on the mind-stream which will lead to SUFFERING in the future.

NIRMANAKAYA (Skt.): Emanation Body of a BUDDHA. The result of transformation of the ordinary body and experience of self. It is the transformation of the SAMBHOGAKAYA into ordinary physical form. A network of grosser forms, emanated from Sambhogakaya, which can sometimes be seen by ordinary persons; the Nirmanakaya is visible to those with pure KARMA, others will just see an ordinary being. BUDDHA SHAKYAMUNI is an example of a supreme Nirmanakaya emanation.

NIRVANA (Skt.): Beyond suffering/sorrow, transcendence of suffering, state beyond the causes for SUFFERING and unsatisfactoriness. State outside CYCLIC EXISTENCE attained by an ARHAT. This is distinct from BUDDHAHOOD, or non-abiding nirvana, which describes a more profound experience of enlightenment.

NGÖNDRO (Tib.): Something which precedes, goes before. Preliminary practice to the practice of TANTRA, generally involving the FOUR CONVICTIONS OF RENUNCIATION and the inner preliminaries of refuge, Bodhicitta, Vajrasattva practice, mandala offering and guru yoga.

NYINGMA (Tib.): Oldest Tibetan Buddhist tradition, founded by PADMASAMBHAVA. Emphasis is on tantric and DZOGCHEN practice.

- O -

OBSCURATIONS: Misconceptions and their resultant afflicted states of mind, including both AFFLICTIVE OBSCURATIONS (or obscurations to nirvana) and more subtle COGNITIVE OBSCURATIONS, also known as obscurations to omniscience. They can also be classified as ACQUIRED or INNATE OBSCURATIONS.

- P -

PADMASAMBHAVA (Guru Rinpoche): Great Indian tantric master, who came to Tibet in 817AD. With his SIDDHIS he dispelled evil forces which obstructed Buddhism in Tibet.

PARAMITA (Skt.): PERFECTION, see SIX and TEN PERFECTIONS.

PARAMITAYANA (Skt.): Perfection vehicle. The MAHAYANA, but excluding the TANTRAYANA. PERFECTION: Going beyond, reaching beyond limitation. (Skt.: paramita). See: SIX and TEN PERFECTIONS.

PRANA (Skt.): See LUNG.

PRATIMOKSHA (Skt.): Vows of individual liberation. Precepts established by SHAKYAMUNI BUDDHA for Buddhist laypersons, monks and nuns.

PRATYEKABUDDHA (Skt.): Solitary Buddha/Realiser. Follower of the HINAYANA tradition who achieves LIBERATION (Not Buddhahood) through their own merit, discovering basic Buddhist teachings like the TWELVE LINKS OF DEPENDENT ORIGINATION.

PRETA (Skt.): Hungry ghost. A being obsessed by greed and ATTACHMENT, living in the preta-realm within the DESIRE REALM, mainly suffering from lack of food, drink and shelter.

PRIMORDIAL NATURE: The ULTIMATE TRUTH of enlightenment beyond all conceptual extremes. According to the Shentong school this truly exists; it is empty of relative truth but is not empty of its own enlightened nature.

PUJA (Skt.): Ceremony/act of worship, offering.

PUNDARIKA: second KULIKA King of SHAMBHALA, best known for his famous commentary on the KALACHAKRA TANTRA called Vimalaprabha (Stainless Light).

PURE PERCEPTION: The main practice in VAJRAYANA, whereby the practitioner trains to perceive all the world and its contents as a pure Buddha-realm, as the display of KAYAS and WISDOMS. This is achieved by visualising oneself as a deity, the outer world as its MANDALA, all sounds as its MANTRA and all thoughts as the deity's enlightened mind.

PURE LAND: Realm outside CYCLIC EXISTENCE where BUDDHAS, BODHISATTVAS and practitioners with sufficient VIRTUE abide. All conditions are conducive for practising DHARMA and attaining ENLIGHTENMENT. 'Pure-Land Buddhism' is a MAHAYANA tradition emphasising methods to be reborn there.

PURIFICATION: Preventing negative KARMA from ripening: this counters the impact of past negative deeds and removes obscurations and obstacles to spiritual realisation. There are many methods of purification but one of the most effective is the VAJRASATTVA practice.

- R -

RAHU (Skt., dachan in Tib.): In the KALACHAKRA system, Rahu is a 'planet' or heavenly body with spiritual significance, represented by a black disc on which KALACHAKRA stands. It is associated with the north node of the moon, lunar eclipses and 'the tail of the dragon' in Chinese astrology.

RANGTONG: Self-emptiness or intrinsic emptiness (as distinct from Shentong).

RASANA (Skt., roma in Tib.): Right main channel of the subtle body.

RATNASAMBHAVA (Skt.): Name of a DEITY. One of the FIVE BUDDHA FAMILIES, representing the feeling AGGREGATE of all Buddhas and their wisdom of equanimity.

REALISATION: A deep and strong understanding / inner knowing (beyond intellectual understanding) that becomes part of us and changes our perception of the world.

REFUGE: Taking refuge means entrusting one's spiritual development to the BUDDHAS, DHARMA and ARYA SANGHA. 'Inner refuge' refers to refuge in our own BUDDHA-NATURE: our own natural WISDOM; this can be understood on various levels.

RELATIVE TRUTH: All-false truth (as opposed to ULTIMATE TRUTH), conventional existence (eg. as it appears to the six senses); the interdependence of phenomena.

RENUNCIATION: Determination to be free or emerge out of the SUFFERING of CYCLIC EXISTENCE, no longer having ATTACHMENT to the pleasures of CYCLIC EXISTENCE which lead to more SUFFERING and AFFLICTIONS.

RIMÉ (Tib.): Ecumenical or non-sectarian movement, lit. without partiality. It is characterised by an attitude of respect for all the teachings and schools of Buddhism.

RINPOCHE (Tib.): Precious one. Referring to a TULKU, or sometimes just a title of respect.

ROOT DOWNFALL: When the FOUR FACTORS LEADING TO LOSS OF A VOW are present and one fails to confess before a session passes (each twenty-four hours being divided into six sessions).

RUDRA CHAKRI (Skt.): Rigden Dragpo (Tib.) (2327 - 2427 CE) 'Wrathful One with the Wheel' the King of SHAMBHALA who is predicted to defeat the 'barbarians' in 2424 in a spiritual war.

RUPAKAYA (Skt.): Form (Rupa) Body (Kaya) of a BUDDHA. Physical manifestation of a BUDDHA. It can be further divided into the SAMBHOGAKAYA and the NIRMANAKAYA.

- S -

SADHANA (Skt.): Tantric method of actualisation of oneself as the Buddha-figure for which one has received EMPOWERMENT; also a TANTRAYANA ritual text which sets out a particular MEDITATION practice.

SAKYA (Tib.): School of Tibetan Buddhism, founded by Khon Könchok Gyelpo (11th century). Their main practice is 'Lamdré' or 'triple vision'. Sakyas ruled in Tibet for over 100 years, before the secular power was handed to the Dalai Lama of the GELUGPA tradition. (13th & 14th century).

SAMADHI (Skt): Meditative stabilisation, concentration. One-pointed involvement in MEDITATION where the meditation object and the practitioner are experienced as inseparable and indistinguishable. As there are many types of Samadhi, the term does not infer anything about the practitioner's REALISATION or accomplishment.

SAMAYA (Skt.): Sacred link or promise between teacher and student, and also between students, in VAJRAYANA. There are many detailed obligations, but the most essential is to consider the teacher's body, speech and mind as pure. See also TANTRIC VOWS.

SAMAYASATTVA (Skt.): See COMMITMENT BEING.

SAMBHOGAKAYA (Skt.): Enjoyment/bliss Body of a BUDDHA which only Bodhisattvas who have achieved the 10th bhumi can perceive, and from which Nirmanakaya forms emanate for the benefit of others. The physical (psychic) form of BUDDHA's WISDOM. The transformation result of speech, communication and inner wind.

SAMSARA (Skt.): See CYCLIC EXISTENCE.

SANGHA (Skt.): Spiritual community. 1. In the broadest sense; whole community of Buddhists: monks, nuns and lay people up to enlightened Bodhisattvas (this is not the original meaning of Sangha). 2. More restricted: monks and nuns. 3. Most specific: ARYA beings.

SELF GENERATION: Practice in TANTRA whereby one imagines oneself to be the DEITY.

SELFLESSNESS: See EMPTINESS.

SENTIENT BEING: (Trans)-migrator. Being that possesses a MIND that is contaminated by AFFLICTIONS or their IMPRINTS, living within CYCLIC EXISTENCE (thus generally excluding plants).

SHAKYAMUNI BUDDHA (Skt.): Name of the historical BUDDHA, living in the 6th century BC.

SHAMATHA (Skt.): Calm abiding, Concentration. 1. MEDITATION method to achieve tranquillity. 2.The resultant tranquil meditative state; the ability to remain single-pointedly on an object with a pliant and blissful MIND. Mental quiescence, stilled and settled state of awareness.

SHAMBHALA (Skt.): Mythical kingdom which is also called the pure land of KALACHAKRA. King SUCHANDRA of Shambhala requested the Buddha to teach this tantra; the Kalachakra teachings are kept and practised there.

SHENTONG (Tib.): Also known as Shentong Madhyamika or Great Middle Way, this is regarded as the highest of all Buddhist philosophical schools. Literally it means 'extrinsic' or 'other' emptiness, as all phenomena are empty of themselves except for Buddha-nature, which is full of enlightened qualities. This is distinct from the Rangtong Madhyamika view of emptiness ('intrinsic' or 'self' emptiness), which holds that the ultimate truth is the negation of the inherent existence of all phenomena, beyond all conceptual extremes.

SRAVAKA (Skt.): Hearer. One who hears, practises and proclaims BUDDHA's teachings. Followers of the THERAVADA tradition, concentrating on RENUNCIATION and pacifying emotions, in order to attain LIBERATION.

SHUNYATA (Skt.): See EMPTINESS.

SIDDHI (Skt.): Supernatural attainment/psychic power defines an ordinary siddhi; enlightened realisation defines a supreme siddhi.

SKANDHA (Skt.): See AGGREGATE.

SOLITARY REALISER: See PRATYEKABUDDHA.

SPEECH MANDALA: In the KALACHAKRA TANTRA, the area of the MANDALA between the central MIND MANDALA and the surrounding BODY MANDALA.

STUPA (Skt.): Buddhist reliquary object. Indian Buddhist Stupas are dome-shaped monuments containing relics of the BUDDHA or his disciples. Tibetan stupas are usually purely symbolic; any size or materials, but of carefully defined shape and proportions representing the BUDDHA's mind.

SUBTLE ESSENCE: (Bindu in Skt., Thiklé in Tib.) The subtle essence of sperm and blood (egg), abiding in the ENERGY CHANNELS or Nadis (Skt.). In the KALACHAKRA TANTRA, these often refer to the four essences (of the states of the waking state, deep sleep, dreaming and absorption of bliss).

SUCHANDRA: King of SHAMBHALA who requested the KALACHAKRA TANTRA from the BUDDHA.

SUFFERING: Any unsatisfactory condition, referring to physical and mental pain, all problematic situations and the unsatisfactoriness that is part of the changing and conditioned nature of cyclic existence. See also THREE TYPES OF SUFFERING and FOUR NOBLE TRUTHS.

SUTRA (Skt.): Discourse/ speech etc. of the BUDDHA, excluding teachings on TANTRA.

SUTRAYANA (Skt.): SUTRA vehicle. Also: 'exoteric or common path'. Name of the HINAYANA and PARAMITAYANA combined, thus excluding the TANTRAYANA (the esoteric path).

SVABHAVIKAKAYA (Skt.): Nature Body of a BUDDHA. The empty nature of the Buddha's omniscient MIND (or wisdom); it refers to all THREE KAYAS taken together.

- T -

TANTRA (Skt.): Continuity, stream. (Continuity or weaving together maintained throughout the practice.) 1. In general referring to the systems of MEDITATION described in the TANTRAYANA texts; practices involving FOUR PURITIES, meditation on ENERGY CHANNELS, CHAKRAS and subtle essences within the body. These esoteric teachings are not found in the SUTRAYANA and require EMPOWERMENT of a tantric GURU. 2. More specific; a scripture describing a TANTRAYANA practice.

TANTRAYANA (Skt.): The tantric vehicle or path; part of the MAHAYANA. See also VAJRAYANA.

TANTRIC SHAMATHA: A special meditation which takes place in a dark room with the eyes wide open; the second unique preliminary for the SIX KALACHAKRA YOGAS according to the JONANG tradition.

TANTRIC VOWS: Holy commitments (SAMAYA in Skt.) in VAJRAYANA to benefit oneself and others, emphasising pure perception of the teacher and one's fellow students. There are many tantric vows, but the core includes twenty-five uncommon directives, pledges to connect with the five (or six) Buddha-families, fourteen root vows and eleven branch vows.

TARA (Skt.): Saviouress; name of a specific female DEITY, representing the enlightened activities of all BUDDHAS.

TARANATHA (Tib.): (1575-1635) Highly accomplished master of the Jonang tradition.

TATHAGATA (Skt.): One Thus Gone; title of a BUDDHA.

TENET: Philosophical view/school. See FOUR TENETS.

TENGYUR (Tib.): Collection of commentaries to BUDDHA's teachings translated from Sanskrit into Tibetan.

THERAVADA (Pali): The tradition of the Elders. Buddhist tradition widespread in Southeast Asia and Sri Lanka. Generally, practices can be said to be HINAYANA.

TIRTHIKA (Skt.): One not following the Middle Way, a non-Buddhist, usually referring to a Hindu.

TONGLEN (Tib.): Giving and receiving. MIND training to overcome selfishness and develop COMPASSION for others; giving one's own happiness and taking others' SUFFERING.

TORMA (Tib.): Ritual offering cake, used in tantric rituals.

TRIPITAKA (Skt.): Three baskets. Three collections of Buddhist scriptures; 1. Vinaya (Skt.): discipline/vows; 2. SUTRA: emphasising concentration/meditation; 3. Abhidharma (Skt.): knowledge/wisdom/phenomenology.

TSOK (Tib.): Tantric (food) offering.

TSONGKHAPA (Tib.): Great Tibetan Scholar (1357-1419), founder of the Tibetan GELUGPA- tradition.

TULKU (Tib.): Recognised reincarnation or emanation of a GURU or enlightened being. There are many different levels of TULKU, with the highest being a supreme emanation such as BUDDHA SHAKYAMUNI (Choki tulku).

TUMMO (Tib., kundalini in Skt.): Psychic heat, inner heat generated in special tantric meditation practices.

TUSHITA (Skt.): Joyous Land. The Bodhisattva PURE REALM of the 1000 BUDDHAS of this AEON. Buddha Shakyamuni was said to have descended from Tushita when he was born in India.

- U -

ULTIMATE TRUTH: (1) the state of Buddhahood (or omniscience); (2) the ultimate nature of reality known as 'emptiness'; (3) the wisdom that directly realises that emptiness; and (4) our Buddha- Nature or potential for enlightenment. Synonyms: EMPTINESS, without INHERENT EXISTENCE, correct view, fundamental true nature, not truly existent, without self-existence, sphere of DHARMA, natural reality, nature of mind, innate mind of clear light, voidness, void of self-existence, sacred truth.

UPASAKA (Skt.): Buddhist lay-person holding EIGHT PRECEPTS.

UPAYOGA (performance tantra): the second of the FOUR TANTRIC CLASSES or vehicles, in which the ultimate truth is represented by a deity equally pure to oneself, who is seen as a friend. USHNISHA (Skt.): The fleshy protrusion on the crown of a BUDDHA's head.

UTPALA (Skt.): Blue lotus flower.

- V -

VAIROCHANA (Skt.): Name of a DEITY. One of the FIVE BUDDHA-FAMILIES, representing the form (or body) AGGREGATE and mirror-like wisdom of all Buddhas.

VAJRA (Skt.): Indestructible/diamond/adamantine. 1. Tibetan ritual sceptre (dorje), symbolising the BUDDHA's mind, the five wisdoms, great bliss and the masculine quality of enlightenment. Together with the BELL it symbolises the union of method and wisdom or immutable bliss and empty form, and masculine and feminine. 2. Anything used in the practice of TANTRA to differentiate it from everyday things. 3. used as synonym for TANTRA or MANTRA.

VAJRADHARA (Skt.): Name of a DEITY, representing the SAMBHOGAKAYA aspect of SHAKYAMUNI BUDDHA. Vajradhara is often regarded as the founder of VAJRAYANA Buddhism.

VAJRAPANI (Skt.): Vajra-Holder. One of the main disciples of the BUDDHA. Name of wrathful DEITY, representing the power of all BUDDHAS.

VAJRA-POSTURE: Cross-legged posture with the feet on the opposite thighs.

VAJRASATTVA (Skt.): Name of a DEITY (Vajra-Being), specifically related to PURIFICATION practices such as recitation of the hundred-syllable mantra.

VAJRAYANA (Skt.): Syn.: Mantra / vajra / secret / uncommon / esoteric vehicle, a MAHAYANA Buddhist path which leads to ENLIGHTENMENT. See also TANTRA. VASE: implement of DEITIES, usually symbolising the first EMPOWERMENT.

VIMALAPRABHA (Skt.): 'Stainless Light', a commentary on the KALACHAKRA TANTRA by PUNDARIKA (second KULIKA King of SHAMBALA). Together with the Laghutantra, it forms the basis of our knowledge of the Kalachakra Tantra.

VINAYA (Skt.): Discipline. Rules governing the conduct of the SANGHA (here usually applying to monks and nuns).

VIPASHYANA (Skt.): Seeing beyond, superior or clear seeing, insight. 1. Meditative technique which identifies and analyses the patterns of the MIND and the world it projects. 2. The resultant WISDOM or perfect knowledge, which thoroughly and clearly discriminates phenomena. See also ANALYTICAL MEDITATION.

VIRTUE: see MERIT.

VISHVAMATA (Skt.): Consort of KALACHAKRA.

VOW: A holy commitment to benefit ourselves and others, divided into three levels: PRATI-MOKSHA, BODHISATTVA and VAJRAYANA vows.

- W -

WISDOM: 1. Prajña (Skt.), sherab (Tib.); discriminating awareness. 2. Jñana (Skt.), yeshe (Tib.); deep awareness, wisdom-knowledge, primordial wisdom.

WISDOM-BEING: See COMMITMENT BEING.

- Y -

YAMA (Skt.): Name of the Lord of (uncontrolled) Death.

YAMANTAKA: YAMA-Opponent. Name of a specific DEITY representing the wrathful form of MANJUSHRI.

YANA (Skt.): Vehicle. Usually; specific path/system of Buddhist practice.

YIDAM (Skt.): Enlightened DEITY or form of a Buddha used in meditation such as KA-LACHAKRA or AVALOKITESHVARA. This forms the basis of one's personal tantric practice.

YOGA (Skt.): Practice, endeavour, application. In the Tibetan system, generally a merely mental tradition, though the six Kalachakra yogas have a very precise system of physical postures and breathing techniques.

YOGA-TANTRA (Skt.): Third of the FOUR TANTRIC CLASSES, which employs self-generation as an enlightened deity.

YOGINI (Skt.): Female practitioner; in the KALACHAKRA TANTRA usually referring to the eighty Yoginis of the Speech Mandala.

YOJANA (Skt.): Distance measure, approximately one mile.

- Z -

ZEN: Japanese variation of the Chinese word 'Chan'. A MAHAYANA Buddhist tradition originating from China as Chan, and further developed in Japan.

NUMBER GLOSSARY

- 2 -

TWO ACCUMULATIONS: Collections of MERIT (virtue/method) and WISDOM.

TWO OBSCURATIONS: AFFLICTIVE OBSCURATIONS and COGNITIVE OBSCURATIONS, or obscurations to nirvana and obscurations to omniscience. See also NINE OBSCURATIONS.

TWO BUDDHA-BODIES: DHARMAKAYA and RUPAKAYA.

TWO CATEGORIES OF PHENOMENA: Permanent and functional.

TWO CAUSES FOR TAKING REFUGE: Fear and faith.

TWO EXTREMES: Views of eternalism and nihilism.

TWO STAGES OF TANTRA: GENERATION STAGE and COMPLETION STAGE.

TWO TRUTHS: RELATIVE TRUTH and ULTIMATE TRUTH.

TWO UNIQUE PRELIMINARIES FOR THE KALACHAKRA TANTRA: Self-generation as the Kalachakra deity; dark room tantric shamatha practice.

- 3 -

THREE ABSORPTIONS (IN TANTRIC PRACTICE): White appearance (nangwa Tib.), red increase (chedpa Tib.) and black attainment (thopa Tib.).

THREE BUDDHA-BODIES: DHARMAKAYA (truth body), SAMBHOGAKAYA (enjoyment body) and NIRMANAKAYA (emanation body).

THREE BASKETS: See: TRIPITAKA.

THREE CATEGORIES OF PHENOMENA: Obvious phenomena, hidden phenomena, very hidden phenomena.

THREE CATEGORIES OF VIRTUE: Natural virtue, associated virtue, mediated virtue.

THREE DEFECTS OF THE POT: An upside-down pot (representing close-mindedness); a pot with holes in it (representing poor recollection); a pot containing poison (representing contamination with preconceived or fixed ideas).

THREE DELUSIONS / POISONS / NEGATIVITIES: IGNORANCE, aversion/anger, ATTACHMENT/desire.

THREE DOORS: Body, speech and MIND.

THREE-FOLD MORALITY: Keeping one's vows, collecting VIRTUE and helping SENTIENT BEINGS.

THREE ISOLATIONS: Isolation of the body, isolation of speech, isolation of mind.

THREE JEWELS: The three objects of REFUGE: BUDDHA, DHARMA and SANGHA. At outer level: SHAKYAMUNI BUDDHA, his teachings and community of ordained persons or spiritual friends. At the inner level: one's own BUDDHA-NATURE, the all-pervading truth and ARYA beings.

THREE KAYAS: see THREE BUDDHA-BODIES.

THREE LEVELS OF BUDDHIST PRACTITIONERS: Initial/basic level: achievement of good REBIRTH, Middle/intermediate level: achievement of individual LIBERATION, and Highest/great scope: achievement of Buddhahood for the sake of all beings.

THREE LEVELS OF REFUGE: THERAVADA refuge, MAHAYANA refuge, VAJRAYANA refuge.

THREE MARKS OF EXISTENCE: Impermanence, suffering, no-self.

THREE NATURES: Imputed nature, dependent nature, primordial nature.

THREE POISONS: ATTACHMENT, aversion and ignorance.

THREE PRACTICES OF ASPIRATION BODHICITTA: Considering other beings as equal to oneself, exchanging oneself for others, considering others as more important than oneself.

THREE PRINCIPLE ASPECTS OF THE PATH: RENUNCIATION, Bodhicitta and WISDOM REALISING EMPTINESS from a text by Lama TSONGKHAPA.

THREE REALMS: DESIRE REALM, FORM REALM and FORMLESS REALM.

THREE TIMES: Past, present and future.

THREE TRAININGS: Training in morality/discipline, concentration and WISDOM/discrimination (the essential trainings of SUTRAYANA).

THREE TURNINGS OF THE WHEEL OF DHARMA: First turning emphasising THERAVADA teachings, second turning emphasising MAHAYANA SUTRA teachings, third turning emphasising BUDDHA-NATURE and VAJRAYANA teachings.

THREE TYPES OF ACTIONS: Actions of the mind, the speech and the body.

THREE TYPES OF FAITH: Spontaneous faith, eager faith, confident faith.

THREE TYPES OF FUNCTIONAL PHENOMENA: Physical matter, mental phenomena and compositional factors.

THREE TYPES OF LAZINESS: Complacency, lack of self-confidence, being habitually busy.

THREE TYPES OF SUFFERING: Suffering of pain, suffering of change and all-pervasive suffering (potential to suffer).

THREE TYPES OF VALID PERCEPTION: Valid perception based on: the five consciousnesses and mind consciousness; logical reasoning; trust in authority.

THREE TYPES OF VOWS: PRATIMOKSHA (individual liberation), BODHISATTVA and TANTRIC vows.

THREE WAYS OF PLEASING A TEACHER: Practising in accordance with what they teach, taking care of their needs and making material offerings.

THREE WAYS OF ATTAINING BODHICITTA: The way of the king, the way of the boatman, the way of the shepherd.

THREE WISDOM TOOLS: Wisdom of hearing, wisdom of contemplation, wisdom of MEDITATION.

THREE YOGAS OF NON-MOVEMENT: Non-movement of body, non-movement of speech, non-movement of mind (elements of the TANTRIC SHAMATHA practice).

- 4 -

FOUR APPLICATIONS OF MINDFULNESS: Mindfulness of body, feelings, mind and phenomena (dharmas).

FOUR AUTHENTICS: Authentic teacher, authentic commentaries, authentic word of the Buddha, authentic experience of the truth.

FOUR BASES FOR MIRACULOUS POWERS: Concentration based on: willingness, mind, effort, analysis.

FOUR BINDING FACTORS: See FOUR FACTORS LEADING TO BREACH OF A VOW.

FOUR BREACHES: (1) breaking a promise, (2) breaking a Vinaya vow, (3) breaking a Bodhisattva Vow, (4) breaking a tantric vow.

FOUR BUDDHA-BODIES: SVABHAVIKAKAYA, DHARMAKAYA, SAMBHOGAKAYA and NIRMANAKAYA.

FOUR CONSORTS: Physical consort (legya Tib.), visualised consort (yegya), the inner tummo fire (damsik gya) and great consort of empty form (shagya chenmo).

FOUR CONTINENTS: East, Purvavideha (Skt.), Noble-body-land; south, Jambudvipa, our human world; west, Avaragodiniya, Cattle Enjoyments; north, Uttarakuru, Unpleasant Voice. These continents appear in the MANDALA OFFERING, and are part of the symbolic representation of the entire universe according to the ABHIDHARMA. The KALACHAKRA description of the universe differs somewhat.

FOUR CONVICTIONS OF RENUNCIATION: Contemplation on: karma, suffering, impermanence and the value of a precious human life.

FOUR DEMONS: See FOUR MARAS.

FOUR DOORS WHICH LEAD TO BREACH OF A VOW: (1) The door of ignorance; (2) the door of disrespect; (3) the door of carelessness; and (4) the door of mental distortion.

FOUR EMPOWERMENTS: Vase empowerment, secret empowerment, wisdom empowerment, sacred word or (fourth) empowerment.

FOUR ENGAGEMENTS (IN MEDITATION PRACTISE): Tightly focused engagement, interrupted engagement, uninterrupted engagement, spontaneous engagement.

FOUR ESSENCES: Essence of deep sleep (essence of mind), essence of dreams, essence of awakening, essence of transcendental bliss (essence of the fourth occasion).

FOUR EXTRAORDINARY ACTIVITIES: see FOUR SUBLIME ACTIONS.

FOUR GREAT STREAMS OF HUMAN SUFFERING: Suffering of: birth, old age, sickness and death.

FOUR FACTORS LEADING TO BREACH OF A VOW: (1) Recognition: a person knowingly contradicts the vow; (2) motivation: they intentionally contradict the vow (with no regret or change of mind); (3) they carry through with the action; (4) this yields a specific result. These factors are generally required to break any vow, although some vows may be breached if only some of them are present.

FOUR FEARLESSNESSES OF A BUDDHA: Fearlessness in the knowledge of all things, fearlessness in the knowledge of cessation, fearlessness to declare that all obscurations have definitely been overcome, fearlessness that the path of renunciation through which all excellent attributes are to be obtained, has been just so realised.

FOUR FORM JHANAS: Four levels of meditative absorption, the fruit of which is to be born in four kinds of realms of the gods of form.

FOUR FORMLESS JHANAS (OR FOUR FORMLESS REALMS): Infinite space, infinite consciousness, nothingness, beyond perception.

FOUR HEAVY NEGATIVITIES: (1) accepting homage from a more advanced practitioner, (2) taking advantage of a genuine practitioner's wealth, (3) preventing devotees from accumulating merit and (4) cheating one's Dharma teacher.

FOUR IMMEASURABLES: Immeasurable LOVE / loving kindness, COMPASSION, EQUANIMITY, and empathetic joy.

FOUR MARAS: The AGGREGATES (the basis for suffering), affliction, death (YAMA) and pleasurable objects (literally the sons of gods - distractions/thoughts of attachment to external objects).

FOUR NOBLE DISCIPLINES: Avoiding responding to (1) anger with anger, (2) physical harm with physical harm, (3) criticism with criticism, (4) verbal arguments with verbal arguments. These disciplines are said to distinguish the real practitioners, as they control the causes of anger and lack of patience. (This is part of the secondary Bodhisattva vows, connected with the perfection of patience).

FOUR NOBLE TRUTHS: Truth of: SUFFERING, the cause of SUFFERING, the cessation of SUFFERING, the EIGHT-FOLD NOBLE PATH.

FOUR OTHER NATURAL HUMAN SUFFERINGS: Suffering of: meeting enemies, separation from loved ones, not getting what you want and getting what you do not want.

FOUR PARADOXES OF ENLIGHTENMENT: (1) Buddha-Nature is primordially pure yet is shrouded by temporary defilements, (2) although the defilements have never been part of the Buddha-Nature, when we practise the path there is seemingly the elimination of defilements, (3) though all the qualities of the Buddha exist within ordinary beings, nevertheless we do not see them, (4) although the Buddha's compassion is infinite, omnipresent and all-pervasive, nevertheless the Buddha doesn't have any intention.

FOUR PERSEVERENCES: Not to cultivate new non-virtue, to give up existing non-virtue, to cultivate virtue, not to allow existing virtue to degenerate.

FOUR POWERS (FOR PURIFICATION): Regret, support, action as an antidote (mantras, prostrations etc.), resolution not to repeat negativities.

FOUR PURITIES (IN TANTRIC PRACTICE): Place (environment is seen as the DEITY'S MANDALA), Body (ordinary body is imagined to be the DEITY'S body), Enjoyments (sense enjoyments are seen as offerings to the DEITY), Action (all one's actions are regarded as the DEITY'S actions).

FOUR RIGHT INTENTIONS: (1) Wanting better conditions during this and future lifetimes, with faith in the Three Jewels, (2) renunciation and the wish for one's own liberation, (3) Bodhicitta, wishing to attain full enlightenment for the sake of others, (4) pure perception, viewing all beings as enlightened while motivated by Bodhicitta on the relative level.

FOUR RIGHT RECOGNITIONS: (1) We are sick; (2) the Buddha and Dharma teachers are like doctors; (3) the Dharma is like the medicine; (4) practising the Dharma is like taking the medicine.

FOUR SEALS: All compounded phenomena are impermanent; anything associated with mental afflictions contains suffering by its nature; the self and all phenomena lack true existence; enlightenment is total peace beyond all extremes.

FOUR STAGES OF THE THERAVADA PATH: Stream-enterer, once-returner, non-returner, Arhat.

FOUR SUBLIME POWERS (IN TANTRIC PRACTICE): pacifying, expanding, controlling and wrathfully subduing/subjugating.

FOUR OR SIX TANTRIC CLASSES: Kriyayoga-tantra (action-tantra), Upayoga-tantra (performance-tantra), Yoga-tantra, Annutarayoga-tantra (Highest Yoga-tantra). In the Nyingma tradition, Highest Yoga-tantra is divided into Mahayoga, Anuyoga and Atiyoga, giving a total of six classes.

FOUR TENETS: Four Buddhist philosophical schools, differing in their view of EMPTINESS: Vaibhashika, Sautrantika, Chittamatra and Madhyamika (which includes both Rangtong and Shentong Madhyamika). 1 and 2 are HINAYANA schools, 3 and 4 are MAHAYANA-schools. The first of these schools posits truly existing partless particles and indivisible moments of time. The later schools have a more profound view, with the Madhyamika tenet holders refuting the true existence of all relative phenomena.

FOUR THOUGHTS THAT TURN THE MIND TOWARDS THE DHARMA: See FOUR CONVICTIONS OF RENUNCIATION.

FOUR VARIABLE MENTAL FACTORS: sleep, regret, gross detection, discernment.

FOUR WAYS OF ATTRACTING BEINGS (STUDENTS): Being generous, speaking in a pleasant manner, teaching in accordance with individuals' needs and acting in accordance with what one teaches.

FOUR WRONG INTENTIONS: to seek profit from the teacher; to receive teachings to further worldly objectives; to base one's relationship with the teacher on self-centred concerns; to receive the teachings for personal gain.

FOUR WRONG WAYS OF REMEMBERING THE TEACHINGS: Remembering the words that appeal to you but forgetting the meaning; remembering the meaning but forgetting the words; memorising the words and meaning but with no understanding; remembering them in the wrong order or with the incorrect meaning.

- 5 -

FIVE AGGREGATES: Form (body), feeling, perception (discrimination, recognition), formation (volition, compositional factors, motivational forces), consciousness (five sense consciousnesses and mental consciousness).

FIVE BUDDHA-FAMILIES: AMITABHA, AKSHOBHYA, RATNASAMBHAVA, VAIROCHANA, AMOGHASIDDHI.

FIVE CHAKRAS: In Buddhism usually the energy centres at the forehead, the crown of the head (centre of great bliss), the throat (enjoyment centre), the heart (centre of Dharma) and four finger widths under the navel (emanation centre). SIX CHAKRAS are used in the KALACHAKRA system.

FIVE COMMON TANTRIC PRELIMINARIES (Inner Preliminaries): Refuge, Bodhicitta, Vajrasattva, mandala offering, guru yoga.

FIVE DEGENERATIONS: Degeneration of: lifespan, time (wars and famines proliferate), beings (becoming harder to help), views (false beliefs spread), and negative emotions.

FIVE ELEMENTS: Earth, water, fire, air and space. These elements have both gross and subtle qualities which determine how the body and mind dissolves at the moment of death.

FIVE FACTORS OF MEDITATIVE CONCENTRATION: Investigation, analysis, mental happiness, bliss and one-pointedness.

FIVE FACULTIES: Spiritual faculty of: faith, effort, mindfulness, concentration and wisdom.

FIVE FAULTS TO MEDITATIVE CONCENTRATION (see also EIGHT ANTIDOTES): laziness, forgetting the instructions, dullness and agitation, under-application of the antidotes, over-application of the antidotes.

FIVE HEINOUS CRIMES (OF IMMEDIATE RETRIBUTION): Killing one's father, mother or an ARHAT; attempt to wound (draw blood from) a BUDDHA, causing division amongst the SANGHA.

FIVE HINDRANCES: Sensual desire, ill will, dullness and drowsiness, restlessness and remorse, doubt.

FIVE MIRACULOUS POWERS: Power of: faith, effort, mindfulness, concentration, and wisdom.

FIVE MUNDANE EXTRASENSORY ABILITIES: divine hearing that hears sounds both near and far, clairvoyance or divine sight that knows the death and rebirth of all beings, memory of past existences, knowledge of the mind of others, supernatural abilities which involve control of the four elements such as flying through space or moving through solid objects.

FIVE OBJECT-DETERMINING FACTORS: Aspiration, belief, mindfulness, concentration, wisdom.

FIVE OMNIPRESENT MENTAL FACTORS: Sensation, discrimination, intention, contact, attention.

FIVE PATHS: Paths of: accumulation, preparation, insight, habituation and no more learning. One becomes an ARYA being having achieved the path of insight. The definitions of these paths differs in the THERAVADA and MAHAYANA.

FIVE PRECEPTS: to avoid – killing, stealing, sexual misconduct, lying with negative intent and intoxicants which cloud the mind.

FIVE ROOT WINDS AND FIVE BRANCH WINDS: Root winds: (1) downward voiding (controlling discharge and retention of waste in the lower orifices, located in genital region), (2) upward-going (controlling swallowing, speaking and other activities of the throat), (3) life-sustaining (maintaining the essence of life, located at the heart), (4) equalising (controlling digestion and the separation of wastes located at the navel) and (5) all-pervading (controlling movement, located through the entire body). Five branch winds: (1) moving (located at the eyes), (2) fully moving (ears), (3) perfectly moving (nose), (4) swiftly moving (tongue), (5) certainly moving (skin surface).

FIVE SCIENCES: grammar, logic, medicine (repairing of things), arts & crafts, philosophy.

FIVE STAGES OF CORRECT MEDITATION: Movement, perceiving, habituation, stabilisation, perfection (according to tantric shamatha instructions).

FIVE SUBLIME TREASURES: the perfect teacher, teaching, place, disciples and time.

FIVE WISDOMS: All-encompassing space or Dharmadhatu, mirror-like, equanimity, discrimination and all-accomplishing wisdom.

- 6 -

SIX BARDOS: The state of waking, dreaming, meditation, dying, Dharmata (the radiance of enlightenment) and becoming (the time between death and rebirth).

SIX CHAKRAS: Usually: forehead, crown, throat, heart, navel, secret (located at the base of the genitals, also known as bliss-guarding centre). Sometimes forehead and crown are considered as one CHAKRA.

SIX ERRORS TO AVOID WHILE LISTENING TO THE TEACHINGS: Pride or close-minded arrogance, lack of faith or a hypercritical attitude, lack of effort and interest, outward distraction, inward tension, and discouragement.

SIX FOUNDATIONS OF DHARMA PRACTICE (OUTER PRELIMINARIES): Contemplations on – karma, suffering, the benefits of liberation, the value of a precious human life, impermanence, finding and following a DHARMA teacher.

SIX EXTRA SENSORY PERCEPTIONS: divine hearing that hears sounds both near and far, clairvoyance or divine sight that knows the death and rebirth of all beings, memory of past existences, knowledge of the mind of others, supernatural abilities such as flying through space or moving through solid objects, knowledge of liberation.

SIX KALACHAKRA YOGAS: The system of Highest Yoga-tantra practice involving the energy channels, inner winds and subtle essences which is the basis for the KALACHAKRA COMPLETION STAGE, as preserved by the JONANG tradition. These six yogas include six specific practices performed in sequence using a dark room at various stages: withdrawal, meditative stabilisation, retention, power of the life force, recollection and meditative absorption.

SIX PERFECTIONS: Generosity, discipline, patience, joyful diligence, concentration and WISDOM.

SIX POWERS (IN MEDITATION PRACTICE): Power of: listening, reflection, mindfulness, vigilance, enthusiastic diligence, complete familiarity.

SIX REALMS OF SAMSARA: HELL, PRETA (hungry ghost), animal, human, ASURA (demigod) and GOD REALM.

SIX ROOT MENTAL AFFLICTIONS: Attachment (clinging), aversion (anger), pride, ignorance of truth, wrong view, doubt.

SIX SENSES: sight, hearing, touch, taste, smell, mental.

SIX-SESSION PRACTICE: Set of daily tantric meditations carried out six times each day intended to keep the daily tantric commitments. The best practitioners will engage in this practice six times per day, yet the most crucial point is to remember these commitments at least six times in every twenty-four hour period. In some traditions the form of this practice is known as the six-session guru yoga.

SIX WAYS OF CLASSIFYING KARMA: (1) Individual and collective karma, (2) karma based on intention, (3) karma based on the magnitude of the result, (4) karma in relation to the moment of death, (5) projecting and completing karma, (6) karma based on the type of result.

SIX YOGAS OF NAROPA: Meditation system of common TANTRA, comprising the heart of the COMPLETION STAGE practice in the KAGYU school of Tibetan Buddhism.

SIX YOGAS OF NIGUMA: Meditation system similar to the SIX YOGAS OF NAROPA.

- 7 -

SEVEN CONTEMPLATIONS OF IMPERMANENCE: Impermanence of the: external world, worldly beings, Arya beings, great rulers. Further examples of impermanence are death and constant recognition of impermanence.

SEVEN FACTORS OF ENLIGHTENMENT: Mindfulness, investigation, discrimination, energy, joy, tranquillity (alert ease), concentration, equanimity.

SEVEN LIMBED PRACTICE: Prostration, offering, confession, rejoicing, requesting the Buddhas to remain and teach DHARMA, dedication.

SEVEN-POINT CAUSE-AND-EFFECT METHOD: A method for cultivating Bodhicitta which involves seven sequential contemplations: (1) Recognising all beings as one's mother, (2) being mindful of their kindness, (3) wishing to repay their kindness, (4) heartfelt love, (5) compassion, (6) resolute intention, (7) faith in the result.

SEVEN-POINT POSTURE OF VAIROCHANA: (1) Legs crossed, (2) hands in the lap (right over left), (3) back straight, (4) elbows and shoulders drawn back slightly away from the body, (5) chin slightly lowered, (6) face relaxed with tongue against upper palate, 7) eyes half open gazing past the tip of the nose.

SEVEN PRECIOUS OBJECTS: Possessions of a Universal Monarch (symbolising the SEVEN FACTORS OF ENLIGHTENMENT): Precious:- Wheel (mindfulness), Elephant (WISDOM), Horse (Energy, LUNG), Jewel (Joy), Queen (tranquillity), Minister (concentration) and General (equanimity).

SEVEN VAJRA POINTS (ASPECTS OF ENLIGHTENMENT): BUDDHA, DHARMA, SANGHA, BUDDHA-NATURE (the element), qualities, activities.

- 8 -

EIGHT ANTIDOTES IN MEDITATION PRACTICE: aspiration, faith, diligence, pliancy, mindfulness, vigilance, applying the remedy, equanimity.

EIGHT AUSPICIOUS SYMBOLS: umbrella, golden fish, treasure vase, lotus, conch, (long-life)-knot, banner of victory, Dharma wheel.

EIGHT BODHISATTVAS: (Close entourage of SHAKYAMUNI BUDDHA) MANJUSHRI, VAJRAPANI, AVALOKITESHVARA, Kshitigarbha, Sarvanivaranaviskambini, Akashagarbha, MAITREYA, Samantabhadra.

EIGHT CONSCIOUSNESSES: Principal consciousness of: eye, ear, nose, tongue, body, mind, deluded mind and foundation consciousness.

EIGHT-FOLD NOBLE PATH: Right, view, right intention, right speech, right action, right livelihood, right effort, right mindfulness and right concentration.

EIGHT FREEDOMS AND TEN ADVANTAGES: Eight Freedoms: freedom from being born: (1) as a hell- being, (2) as a preta, (3) as an animal, (4) as a long-living god, (5) as a person who lacks interest in spiritual or ethical values, (6) in a spiritually remote location, (7) with sensory or cognitive impairment or (8) in a dark aeon where a Buddha has not come. Ten Advantages: (1) human birth, (2) born in a spiritually central place, (3) faculties intact, (4) no conflicting lifestyle, (5) having faith in the Dharma, (6) the Buddha has come, (7) he has taught the Dharma, (8) the Dharma still exists today, (9) the Dharma is considered precious, (10) one has been accepted by a spiritual teacher.

EIGHT INTRUSIVE CIRCUMSTANCES AND EIGHT UNSUITABLE MENTAL CHARACTERISTICS: Eight intrusive circumstances: (1) strong mental afflictions, (2) limited intellect, (3) following a false spiritual friend, (4) laziness and complacency, (5) being overwhelmed by heavy negative karma, (6) enslavement to worldly pursuits or unbreakable commitments, (7) practising out of fear or wanting to escape, (8) being motivated by worldly concerns. Eight unsuitable mental characteristics: (1) being held captive by worldly commitments, (2) lack of humility, (3) lack of true understanding or determination to be free, (4) lack of faith in the teacher or teachings, (5) taking pleasure in non-virtue, (6) apathy towards Dharma practice, (7) breaking PRATIMOKSHA or BODHISATTVA vows, (8) breaking TANTRIC vows.

EIGHT MAHAYANA PRECEPTS: Vows for not: (1) killing, (2) stealing, (3) sexual activity, (4) lying, (5) intoxicants, (6) more than one meal in twenty-four hours., (7) sitting on high, expensive seats or beds, (8) wearing ornaments, dancing & playing music with ATTACHMENT. These vows can be taken for various time spans.

EIGHT OFFERING GODDESSES: Goddess of Beauty, Garlands, Song, Dance, Flowers, Incense, Lamps and Perfume.

EIGHT PERVERSE ACTS: See EIGHT WRONG MODES OF CONDUCT.

EIGHT PRECEPTS: to abstain from: (1) causing harm and taking life, (2) taking what is not freely given, (3) sexual misconduct, (4) intentionally lying or using hurtful words, (5) intoxicants which cloud the mind, (6) eating at the wrong time (the correct time is once, after sunrise and before noon), (7) singing, dancing or wearing ornaments, (8) sleeping in a high or luxurious place or overindulging in sleep.

EIGHT QUALITIES OF ENLIGHTENMENT: Three qualities which benefit the enlightened one himself (uncompounded, spontaneously realised, self-aware), three qualities which benefit others (great wisdom, compassion and power to benefit), the quality to benefit oneself, the quality to benefit others.

EIGHT SIDDHIS: the ability to make pills and eye lotion to enhance vision, travelling underground, the magical sword, swift footedness, invisibility, preventing death and healing sickness.

EIGHT VERSES OF MIND TRAINING: Short essential text of the Kadampa master Langri Thangpa, emphasising the practice of TONGLEN.

EIGHT WORLDLY DHARMAS: Desire for: fame, worldly pleasure, material gain and praise. Feeling unhappy when: losing fame, worldly pleasure, material gain and when hearing harsh or unpleasant criticism towards ourselves.

EIGHT PRINCIPAL TYPES OF CONSCIOUSNESS: see EIGHT CONSCIOUSNESSES.

EIGHT TANTRIC BRANCH VOWS: See Book Three (also mentions three additional tantric branch vows).

EIGHT UNSUITABLE MENTAL CHARACTERISTICS: See EIGHT INTRUSIVE CIRCUMSTANCES AND EIGHT UNSUITABLE MENTAL CHARACTERISTICS.

EIGHT WRONG MODES OF CONDUCT (EIGHT PERVERSE ACTS): (1) Criticising good, (2) praising evil, (3) interrupting the accumulation of merit of a virtuous person, (4) disturbing the minds of those who have devotion, (5) giving up one's spiritual teacher, (6) giving up commitments to one's deity, (7) giving up one's vajra brothers and sisters, (8) desecrating a mandala or disobeying rules while on retreat.

- 9 -

NINE CHARNEL GROUND CONTEMPLATIONS: (1) a corpse one, two or three days dead, bloated, livid and oozing matter, (2) a corpse being devoured by crows, hawks, vultures, dogs, jackals or worms, (3) a skeleton with flesh and blood held together by sinews, (4) a fleshless skeleton with blood held together by sinews, (5) a skeleton without flesh and blood held together by sinews, (6) disconnected bones scattered in all directions, (7) bones bleached white, the colour of shells, (8) bones heaped up, (9) bones more than a year old, rotted and crumbled to dust.

NINE STAGES OF MEDITATION: Placing the mind, continuous placement, patched placement, close placement, disciplining the mind, pacifying, fully pacifying, one-pointedness, equanimity.

NINE OBSCURATIONS: Seven AFFLICTIVE OBSCURATIONS (1-3. three poisons in their latent state, 4. six secondary afflictions arising from the the three poisons, 5. the instinctive level of ignorance, 6. abandonments on the Theravada path of seeing, 7. abandonments on the Theravada path of meditation) and two COGNITIVE OBSCURATIONS (1. abandonments of the seven impure Bodhisattva levels, 2. abandonments of the three pure Bodhisattva levels, or habitual tendencies).

NINE YANAS: The progressive vehicles of the Buddhist path according to the Nyingma tradition of Tibetan Buddhism. They include: Shravakayana, Pratyekabuddhayana, Mahayana, Kriyayoga, Upayoga, Yoga-tantra, Mahayoga, Anuyoga and Atiyoga.

- 10 -

TEN ADVANTAGES (OF A PRECIOUS HUMAN BIRTH): See EIGHT FREEDOMS AND TEN ADVANTAGES.

TEN DIRECTIONS: The eight cardinal points as well as up and down.

TEN BHUMIS (STAGES): stages on the path to Buddhahood after one has accomplished the path of insight. These are (in order beginning with the first bhumi): supreme joy, stainless, illumination, radiant, difficult to overcome, the approaching, far gone, the immovable, good intelligence, cloud of Dharma. The 'eleventh bhumi' is Buddhahood.

TEN FETTERS: identity view, doubt, wrong grasp of rules and observances, sensual desire, ill will, desire for existence in the form or formless realms, conceit, restlessness, ignorance.

TEN NON-VIRTUES: three of body: killing, stealing, improper sexual conduct; four of speech: lying, divisive words, harsh words, worthless chatter; three of mind: covetousness, ill-will, incorrect view.

TEN POWERS OF A BUDDHA: (1) Knowing what is worthwhile or advisable and what is worthless or inadvisable; (2) knowing the ripening of all actions (karma); (3) knowing the varying abilities and potential of all beings; (4) knowing the temperaments of all beings ; (5) knowing the wishes and aspirations of all beings; (6) knowing the paths reaching the entire range of samsara and nirvana; (7) knowing meditative stability and so on, and when it is afflicted and without pollution; (8) recollecting previous existences; (9) knowing the transference of consciousness at birth and death through divine sight; (10) knowing that all afflictions have ceased and ultimate peace has been attained.

TEN RECOLLECTIONS: the Buddha, Dharma, Sangha, virtue, generosity, deities, mindfulness of death, mindfulness of the body, mindfulness of breathing, recollection of peace.

TEN SIGNS (in Kalachakra completion stage practice): These ten signs are: smoke, mirage, clouds, fireflies, sunlight, moonlight, blazing gemstones, eclipse, starlight, rays of light.

TEN VIRTUES: three of body: saving others' lives, practising generosity, developing moral discipline and encouraging others to do the same; four of speech: speaking the truth, reconciling disputes, talking sweetly and calmly, speaking meaningfully (such as praying or teaching); three of mind: having few desires, having goodwill towards others and holding correct views.

TEN PERFECTIONS: SIX PERFECTIONS plus: skilful means, aspiration, power and exalted wisdom.

- 11 -

ELEVEN VIRTUOUS MENTAL FACTORS: Faith, moral shame, fear of unwholesomeness, non-attachment, non-anger, non-ignorance, diligence, pliancy of mind, conscientiousness, equanimity, non-harmfulness.

ELEVEN WAYS OF HELPING BEINGS: Helping those who are SUFFERING; are ignorant of KARMA; have previously helped you; are in danger; full of grief; poor; homeless; already on the true path; or on a wrong path; helping skilfully and helping by using any SIDDHIS you possess.

- 12 -

TWELVE ACTS OF A BUDDHA: Dwelling in Tushita, descent and entry into the womb, taking birth, proficiency in the arts, enjoyment of sensual pleasures, renouncing the world, practising asceticism, reaching the point of enlightenment, vanquishing demonic forces, attaining perfect enlightenment, turning the Wheel of Dharma and passing into final nirvana.

TWELVE LINKS OF DEPENDENT ORIGINATION: Ignorance, karmic formation, consciousness, name and form, the six sense doors, contact, feeling, craving, grasping, becoming, (re-)birth, ageing & death.

-13-

THIRTEEN ORNAMENTS OF A SAMBHOGAKAYA BUDDHA: Five silken garments: (1) headband, (2) upper garment, (3) long scarf, (4) belt, (5) lower garment. Eight jewelled ornaments: (1) crown, (2) earrings, (3) short necklace, (4) armlets on each arm, (5) two long necklaces, one longer than the other, (6) a bracelet on each wrist, (7) ring on each hand, (8) anklet on each foot.

- 16 -

SIXTEEN ASPECTS OF THE FOUR NOBLE TRUTHS: impermanence, suffering, emptiness, selflessness, origination, cause, condition, effect, cessation, peace, excellence, renunciation, path, reasoning, accomplishment, total freedom.

SIXTEEN MINDFULNESS BREATHS: Awareness of the: long breath, short breath, whole body, calming the body, feelings, calming the feelings, joy, happiness, mind, gladdening the mind, concentrating the mind, liberating the mind, impermanence, fading away (suffering), liberation, letting go.

- 18 -

EIGHTEEN ROOT BODHISATTVA VOWS: Six vows for rulers and administrators (first four counted twice), eight vows for ordinary people. Sometimes the four root vows of Asanga's tradition are also included. See Book Two for details of specific vows.

- 20 -

TWENTY DERIVATIVE MENTAL AFFLICTIONS: fury, resentment, concealment, hostility, jealousy, miserliness, deceit, hypocrisy, self-infatuation, harmfulness, lack of conscience, shamelessness, lethargy, excitement, lack of faith, laziness, heedlessness, forgetfulness, non-introspection, distraction.

- 25 -

TWENTY-FIVE UNCOMMON DIRECTIVES: Five actions to abandon; five actions to avoid; five forbidden killings; five to respect; five groups not to disrespect; five non-attachments.

- 31 -

THIRTY-ONE UNATTRACTIVE FEATURES OF THE HUMAN BODY: head-hairs, body-hairs, nails, teeth, skin, flesh, sinews, bones, bone-marrow, kidneys, heart, liver, diaphragm, spleen, lungs, intestines, mesentery, stomach, faeces, bile, phlegm, pus, blood, sweat, fat, tears, grease, spittle, snot, oil of the joints, urine.

- 32 -

THIRTY-TWO MAJOR MARKS OF A BUDDHA: (1) Soles of feet even and marked with wheels, (2) feet broad and ankles not visible, (3) long fingers and toes, (4) digits entwined with a delicate web, (5) skin soft and flesh youthful, (6) body with seven elevated and rounded parts (palms, soles, shoulders and neck), (7) calves like an antelope, (8) genitals hidden as are an elephant's, (9) torso like that of a lion, (10) hollow between clavicles well filled, (11) curve of his shoulders perfect and beautiful, (12) hands and arms rounded, soft and even, (13) arms long, (14) body surrounded by an aureole of light, (15) neck like a conch, unblemished in hue, (16) cheeks like those of a lion, (17) forty teeth equal in number in upper and lower jaw (twenty in each), (18) teeth supremely pure and beautifully set, (19) teeth immaculate, of similar length and aligned in even rows, (20) eyeteeth supremely white and sharp, (21) tongue long, speech unlimited and meaning inconceivable, (22) supreme sense of taste, (23) speech amiable like the melody of Brahma, (24) eyes pure like blue utpala lotuses, (25) eyelashes dense and shining like those of an ox, (26) stainless white urna hair embellishing his face, (27) an ushnisha (crown protuberance) crowning the centre of his head, (28) skin pure and delicate, (29) skin golden coloured, (30) hairs on his bodies fine and soft, each curling from a single pore right and upwards to his crown, (31) hair immaculate resembling in colour a deep-blue gem, (32) well-proportioned physical stature like a nyagrodha tree and body firm and unbreakable with the strength of Narayana. There are also eighty minor marks of a Buddha such as the quality of his fingernails and so forth.

- 37 -

THIRTY-SEVEN PRACTICES OF A BODHISATTVA: Sequential set of practices which embrace all aspects of the BODHISATTVA's path to enlightenment (known also as the thirty-seven wings of enlightenment, these practices also apply to the THERAVADA path). They include: the FOUR APPLICATIONS OF MINDFULNESS, FOUR PERSEVERANCES, FOUR BASES FOR MIRACULOUS POWER, FIVE FACULTIES, FIVE MIRACULOUS POWERS, SEVEN FACTORS OF ENLIGHTENMENT and the EIGHTFOLD NOBLE PATH.

- 40 -

FORTY MEDITATION OBJECTS (ACCORDING TO THE THERAVADA): Ten kasinas (objects representing the elements, colours, light and space), ten kinds of foulness (stages of decay of human remains), TEN RECOLLECTIONS, FOUR IMMEASURABLES, FOUR FORMLESS JHANAS, one perception (the repulsiveness of food and nourishment), one defining (the four elements).

- 46 -

FORTY-SIX BODHISATTVA BRANCH VOWS: 1-6: perfection of generosity; 7-16: perfection of discipline; 17-20: perfection of patience; 21-23: perfection of joyful diligence; 24- 26: perfection of concentration; 27-34: perfection of wisdom; 35-46: morality of accomplishing the good of others.

- 50 -

FIFTY VERSES OF GURU DEVOTION: Important text by Ashvagosha which describes the proper attitude towards one's tantric master.

- 51 -

FIFTY-ONE DERIVATIVE MENTAL FACTORS: FIVE OMNIPRESENT MENTAL FACTORS, FIVE OBJECT-DETERMINING FACTORS, SIX ROOT MENTAL AFFLICTIONS, TWENTY DERIVATIVE MENTAL AFFLICTIONS, ELEVEN VIRTUOUS MENTAL FACTORS, FOUR VARIABLE MENTAL FACTORS.

- 80 -

EIGHTY NATURALLY ARISING AFFLICTIONS (according to TANTRA): Thirty-three afflictions arising from aversion, forty afflictions arising from attachment, seven afflictions arising from ignorance. (These disappear as the inner winds dissolve, corresponding to the THREE ABSORPTIONS of white appearance, red increase and black attainment).

About the Author

Khentrul Rinpoché Jamphel Lodrö is the founder and spiritual director of Dzokden. Rinpoche is the author of many books including Unveiling Your Sacred Truth, The Great Middle Way: Clarifying the Jonang View of Other-Emptiness, A Happier Life, and The Hidden Treasure of the Profound Path.

Rinpoche spent the first 20 years of his life herding yak and chanting mantras on the plateaus of Tibet. Inspired by the bodhisattvas, he left his family to study in a variety of monasteries under the guidance of over twenty-five masters in all the Tibetan Buddhist traditions. Due to his non-sectarian approach, he earned himself the title of Rimé (unbiased) Master and was identified as the reincarnation of the famous Kalachakra Master Ngawang Chözin Gyatso. While at the core of his teachings is the recognition that there is great value in the diversity of all spiritual traditions found in this world; he focuses on the Jonang-Shambhala tradition. Kalachakra (wheel of time) teachings handed down from the Kalki Kings of Shambhala, contain profound methods to harmonize our external environment with the inner world of body and mind. This tantra is connected directly to the Karma of our earth to bring about the Golden age of Peace and Harmony (Dzokden). Khentrul Rinpoche has made it his life mission to spread these precious teachings in as many languages as possible globally so that we can truly transform our world, one person at a time from their inside out.

Rinpoche's Vision

Dzokden was founded with the express purpose of supporting Khentrul Rinpoche in realising his vision for greater peace and harmony in this world. As our community continues to grow and develop, more and more people are getting involved with this extraordinary effort.

To give you a sense of the scope of Rinpoche's vision, we can speak of eight goals that reflect Rinpoche's short and long term priorities:

IMMEDIATE GOALS

Ultimately speaking, lasting, genuine happiness is only possible through profound personal transformation. Now more than ever, we need methods to develop our wisdom and actualise our greatest potential. It is for this reason that Rinpoche places such a heavy priority on the preservation of the Jonang Kalachakra Lineage. There are four ways in which Rinpoche proposes to do this:

1. **Create opportunities to connect with an authentic and complete Kalachakra lineage in close collaboration with dedicated meditators in remote Tibet.** Our goal is to create all of the supports for practicing Kalachakra in accordance with the authentic lineage masters who have upheld this tradition for thousands of years. We do this by commissioning statues and paintings, writing books and giving teachings around the world. We place particular emphasis on ensuring the authenticity of our materials, drawing on the profound experience of highly realised meditators who are dedicating their lives to these practices.

2. **Establish international retreat centres for the study and practice of Kalachakra.** In order to integrate the teachings into our minds, it is crucial to have the opportunity to engage in periods of intensive practice. Therefore, we are working to create the necessary infrastructure that will support and nurture the members of our community to

engage in both short and long-term retreat. This includes the purchase of land and the construction of everything that is needed to conduct group and solitary retreats. Our long-term aim is to develop a network of such centres around the world, forming a global community that supports a wide variety of practitioners.

3. **Translate and publish the unique and rare texts of Kalachakra masters.** The Kalachakra System has been the subject of countless texts over the course of Tibet's long history. So far, only a small fraction of these texts have been translated and made accessible in the West. While the theoretical texts are important, we aim to focus particularly on the pith instructions that will guide dedicated practitioners to a deeper experience of these profound teachings.

4. **Develop the tools and programs for a structured learning experience.** With pockets of students distributed throughout the world, we believe it is important to make the most of modern technologies to facilitate the process of learning for our students. Our aim is to develop a robust online educational platform that allows our international community to access quality study programs that are intuitive, structured and engaging.

LONG-TERM GOALS

While we each work towards achieving ultimate peace and harmony in our own minds, we must not lose sight of the fact that we exist within the context of a world filled with a great diversity of individuals. These individuals give rise to a wide variety of beliefs and practices that in turn shape how we relate and interact with each other. In this interdependent reality, it is vital to find viable strategies for promoting greater tolerance and respect. To this end, Rinpoche proposes four specific areas of activity:

1. **Promote the development of a Rimé Philosophy through dialogue with other traditions.** With the desire to be constructive members of a pluralistic society, we need to learn ways of reconciling our differences. To this end, we aim to help people develop the positive qualities that promote an attitude of mutual respect, openness to new ideas and an

inquisitive desire to overcome our ignorance.

2. **Develop highly realised role models by offering financial support to dedicated practitioners.** In order to ensure the authenticity of our spiritual traditions, it is imperative that there are people who actualise the highest of realisations. Therefore, we aim to create a financial scholarship program which facilitates genuine practitioners who wish to dedicate their lives to spiritual development, regardless of their system of practice. By helping people actualise the teachings, they become positive role models for those around them, inspiring and guiding the generations to come.

3. **Actualise the great potential of female practitioners by developing specialised training programs.** The Tibetan culture has a long history of cultivating highly realised masters through the intensive training of those who are recognised to have great potential. Unfortunately, all too often the search for potential was focused only on male candidates. Rinpoche believes that it is increasingly important to have strong, highly realised, female role models who can help to bring greater balance into our world. For this reason, we are working to develop a unique training program for providing women with the opportunity to actualise their spiritual potential. It is our aim to design a specialised curriculum as well as the financial infrastructure to fully support all aspects of their education.

4. **Promote greater flexibility of mind and a broader understanding of reality through modern educational programs.** In a world that is rapidly evolving, we need to rethink the types of skills that we are teaching our children. The rigid structures of the past are often ill equipped to prepare students for the challenges that they will face during their lives. Therefore, we aim to develop a variety of educational programs that can help children to become more flexible and more capable of adapting to their context. An important part of these programs is the development of greater awareness of the role that our mind plays in our day-to-day experiences. We also aim to bring reforms into the monastic education system that would help make them more relevant for this modern world.

HOW CAN YOU OFFER YOUR SUPPORT?

The above will not be possible without your support and participation. A vision of this magnitude requires a great deal of merit and generosity from many benefactors over many years. If you would like to offer your support, please do not hesitate to contact us.

Dzokden
3436 Divisadero Street
San Francisco, California 94123
United States of America
www.dzokden.org